The League That Lasted

To Dad,
my candidate for the Father's Hall of Fame,
who talked and taught me baseball

The League That Lasted

1876 and the Founding of the National
League of Professional Base Ball Clubs

NEIL W. MACDONALD

McFarland & Company, Inc., Publishers
Jefferson, North Carolina, and London

LIBRARY OF CONGRESS CATALOGUING-IN-PUBLICATION DATA

Macdonald, Neil W., 1936–
 The league that lasted : 1876 and the founding of the National League of Professional Base Ball Clubs / Neil W. Macdonald.
   p.   cm.
 Includes bibliographical references and index.

 ISBN-13: 978-0-7864-1755-1
 softcover : 50# alkaline paper ∞

 1. National League of Professional Baseball Clubs—History—19th century.   I. Title.
 GV875.A3N366   2004
 796.357'64'0973—dc22   2004005503

British Library cataloguing data are available

©2004 Neil W. Macdonald. All rights reserved

No part of this book may be reproduced or transmitted in any form or by any means, electronic or mechanical, including photocopying or recording, or by any information storage and retrieval system, without permission in writing from the publisher.

Cover photograph: Louisville Grays, 1876. Special Collections: Photographic Archives, University of Louisville

Manufactured in the United States of America

McFarland & Company, Inc., Publishers
  Box 611, Jefferson, North Carolina 28640
  www.mcfarlandpub.com

Contents

	Preface	vii
1	Darkness Upon the Face of Baseball	1
2	The Signing of "The Four"	12
3	Creation	21
4	Western Wooing	33
5	All Quiet on the Eastern Front	43
6	A Day Reserved for Groundhogs	52
7	Press Reaction	59
8	The Dickens with Great Expectations	71
9	Picked Nines and the Pick of Nines	83
10	The First Game	92
11	May Days	103
12	Baseball Bustin' Out All Over	116
13	Happy Birthday America	126
14	31 Innings, 2 or 3 Days, 1 Game	133
15	Striving to Be Second	140
16	No No	143
17	Dog Days	153
18	The Runs of August	162
19	Summertime and the Livin' Ain't Easy	175
20	Days Dwindling Down	185
21	Westward No! The Mutes and A's	191

22	The Many Misters of October	201
23	Hail Hulbert!	212
	Epilogue: Extra Innings	219
	Chapter Notes	223
	Bibliography	245
	Index	251

Preface

The story of the formation of the National League of Professional Base Ball Clubs, like the myth of baseball's origins, has at least two versions—both apocryphal and both widely believed. The most prevalent, and the older of the two, depicts the league founders as a group of highly principled and very wise men who saved the morally decadent game of baseball and worked such a change on its operations and personnel that the game became a popular model of godliness and goodliness. The second and revisionist version of the story describes a league founded by unprincipled robber barons who eventually enslaved players under the infamous reserve clause and squeezed every cent they could from not only the players, but the spectators and even each other while baseball, the purest of games, was played in conditions befitting a gulag.[1]

The truth, of course, is somewhere in between. The league formed in 1876 was not the salvation of baseball, falling far short of expectations in its inaugural year. It was founded by neither altruistic nor evil men.

How much each of the major figures contributed to the league's founding is in dispute. The general consensus is that Chicago White Stockings president William Ambrose Hulbert was the prime mover; that his immediate helper was Albert Spalding; that Hulbert received considerable advice from Boston manager Harry Wright; and that Chicago newsman Lewis Meacham helped indoctrinate the public by publishing Hulbert's point of view concerning the direction the league would take.[2]

The contrary argument is that Spalding, not Hulbert, was the principal power in organizing the National League, working out the constitution, strategy and tactics that led to the league's establishment with Hulbert as his helper.[3] Since the two men worked together it is difficult to ascertain which ideas were exclusively Hulbert's, Spalding's or any of a number of others'. Many people, no doubt, contributed to its formation.

At present, the weight of historical evidence favors Hulbert as the prime mover in establishing the league. A final settlement of the argument awaits another book. Until then, it is perhaps most sensible to follow the example of Isaac Newton, who admitted to Robert Hooke, in a letter of February 5, 1675 or 1676, that if he had seen further than Hooke or Rene Descartes, it was "by standing on the shoulders of giants."[4] Success in forming the National League may have been spearheaded by Hulbert, but he was definitely not alone in his efforts.

I was struck, while researching how the National League struggled through its early years, by the underlying reality that it survived not so much because of anything Hulbert or his friends did, but because of the game itself. Hulbert and company did start professional baseball on a long, slow evolution toward respectability and permanence, but the key constant throughout all its turmoils, despite incidents of scathing scandal, abject stupidity and such, was that the game itself was appealing enough for fathers to continue playing catch with sons, for both small and big boys to gather in vacant lots and open fields to play pickup games and for spectators to continue to come out to the ballpark. Without that appeal, baseball would have gone the way of the dodo.

I am indebted to the patient people at the Blaine and Bellingham public libraries who helped track down microfilm, magazines and material from sources far and near. I especially thank Duane McDonald and the personnel of the Chicago Historical Society who helped me through the stacks of material in their collection of William Hulbert's papers. I am particularly indebted to my writer son Scot, whose knowledge of writing and publishing and whose help and encouragement were surpassed only by his scalpel-sharp mind. His insights were invaluable.

Finally, a word about the many shortcomings of this interim report on the National League's earliest days. In examining the historical material, I became quickly acquainted with the incredible number of inconsistencies in the newspaper coverage, books, and personal papers that dealt with the relevant events. In things as simple as reporting game scores and dates, conflicting accounts from newspaper to newspaper were common. Many stories were grossly inaccurate. Speculation was often reported as fact and fact as speculation. Both newspaper material and Hulbert's personal papers were difficult to decipher at times, primarily due to the quality of paper and ink used in that era. Some remained a mystery even after careful examination with special high power lenses. My research assistant and wife, Lea, and I used only material that we agreed was unambiguous in readability. Although we took care that inferences, interpretations and attributions were logically and psychologically supportable, no one is infallible. Lea's help was invaluable. Any errors are my responsibility.

1

Darkness Upon the Face of Baseball

The National League of Professional Base Ball Clubs did not emerge from any idyllic Garden of Eden. Nor was its creator, William Ambrose Hulbert, the brightest or the best or the purest of heart. Hulbert was as flawed a fellow and as contradictory a character as any human being then or now. He was 6' 2" in an age when a 5' 10" man could call himself "tall,"[1] a mass of 215 pounds at a time when a 160-pound man was above average weight.[2] He was wagon-wide at the shoulders, his massive head supported by a well-muscled neck and topped by a fine crop of hair. His huge body commanded twice the space of any ordinary person. He seemed a stony boulder of a man, an enormous muscular presence whose very appearance ordered attention and respect from any nearby mortal. His awesome physique was augmented by an intellect of superior quality. He was as mentally sharp as he was physically imposing.[3] He would become baseball's guiding hand in 1876, his gray eminence influencing all decisions in the coming years.[4]

In the spring of 1875, however, he was far from being baseball's all-powerful agent of change. He was a successful businessman, a prominent member of the Board of Trade and the Studs Terkel of 1870s Chicago boosters.[5] Hulbert had a reputation for being both energetic and honest.[6] As an executive board member of the cellar-bound Chicago White Stockings Base Ball Club,[7] his team was the equivalent of an "easy out" in the National Association of Professional Base-Ball Players, a ramshackle organization that was formed in March 1871.[8] The Chicago White Stockings would finish sixth in the league, having lost more games than they had won.[9] There were probably as many malingerers, crooks, drunks and associated riffraff on Hulbert's team as on any other in the association.[10]

Born in a small town in Otsego County, New York, not far from the yet to be famous Cooperstown, Hulbert had been raised in Chicago, the

Jefferson Street Grounds, home of the Philadelphia Athletic, was the site of the National League's first ever game on April 22, 1876. This illustration is difficult to date, but some experts believe it depicts the N.L.'s first game. Others argue that the Athletic pennant waving down the right field line suggests this game occurred in 1872, since the Athletic won the National Association pennant in 1871. If this is the National League's first game, the pitcher is Boston's Joe Borden; the catcher, Tim McGinley; and the umpire (the man kneeling to the side of the catcher), William McLean. (Transcendental Graphics)

city he came to love. He was repeatedly quoted as saying, "I'd rather be a lamp post in Chicago than a millionaire elsewhere."[11] After attending Beloit College in Wisconsin, he had dabbled in commodities from coal to grain and groceries. Coal put his ledgers in the black and gave him the prosperity to pursue his interests in the brokerage business and baseball.[12] But, being a man of business efficiency and of moral consequence, Hulbert was a total misfit in the financially and ethically bankrupt National Association.[13] Such men as Hulbert seem to chafe at society's grosser ethical imbalances. They want to eradicate all evil and bring righteousness to the earth.[14] Problem is, they often aren't too ethical in the way they try to bring about such changes.

The triad of booze, betting and baseball made up the National Association in the spring of 1875. America's first major professional league had,

1—Darkness Upon the Face of Baseball

by its fifth year, become completely corrupt, cursed by rampant hippodroming, revolving and drinking. Hippodroming involved throwing a game for money.[15] Revolving described the practice of jumping from one team to another.[16] The third vice, drinking, was an alcohol-only enterprise.[17]

Although he dearly wanted a league based on both sound business and moral principles, Hulbert, a born fighter, industrious worker and shrewd businessman, did not seem to have been overly zealous[18] (except perhaps for his love of Chicago) while pursuing his goals. He was never charged with religious bigotry or fanaticism. He was not a moral reformer. Yet he was steadfast in demanding clean management and protecting the integrity of baseball against dishonesty.[19] Hulbert was both pragmatic and idealistic. These seemingly opposing modes of thought would collide, mix and meld together in a crucible of mental conflict in the coming year and it would be Hulbert's ability or inability to resolve this incongruity that would make or break baseball.[20]

Hulbert's management style would be considered normal business practice to the cynical, but atrocious to the holier-than-Hulbert faction since his strategy was to profess intending only conduct of the highest principle while being "willing to unscrupulously disregard all proprieties for self-serving ends."[21] With baseball in the throes of National Association mediocrity, saving it with large doses of hypocrisy could, perhaps, be expected.[22] Professional baseball, in the form of the National League, "survived due to stern, uncompromising management and solid foundation that was laid down by Hulbert and the rest of the men who established the league."[23] The more empirical, of course, could argue that the National League survived "due in no small part to the extensive scheduling of exhibition games with excluded teams ... where grudge matches filled with a special tension" reigned.[24]

In 1875 anyone above the intellect of an idiot could see that the national pastime was half a spike's length from going into past time. The *New York Times* described the typical baseball player as a "worthless, dissipated gladiator; not much above the professional pugilist in morality and respectability [who spent his off-seasons] in those quiet retreats connected with bars, and rat pits."[25] If baseball's public persona didn't change, it could quite easily become *persona non grata.*

Not only were the majority of National Association teams well over the verge of bankruptcy in 1875,[26] but any semblance of competitiveness was gone. The Boston Red Stockings won their first 26 games before losing. They would come within 1/1,000th of a percentage point of winning 90 percent of their games by season's end. The two teams closest to them would finish 15 and 18.5 games back. Six of the 13 teams that started the season didn't finish. Fewer and fewer people came to the games. As autumn approached, top amateur teams were pulling in more people than the pros. The drawing power of the Mutuals, Philadelphias and Chicago was virtually nil. Cranks (1870s slang for fans) weren't even going to risk the price of admission on the outside chance they'd see an honest game. The labyrinth of baseball's problems needing to be solved in 1875 to save baseball (to use a 1920s turn of phrase) was easy to recognize, basically a multi-mix of mismanagement and corruption. How to rectify these problems was anything but simple.

The eastern interests ran the game.[27] Only four of the 13 teams that started the 1875 season were western clubs and two of them had dropped out long before summer saw September.[28] If Hulbert was going to do anything, he'd have to anticipate what the easterners were going to do and move before they could act against Chicago's interests. Albert Spalding would later recall Hulbert saying, "I have a scheme. Let us anticipate the eastern cusses and organize a new association before the March annual meeting...."[29] It would be a matter of changing the present association structure before those who would oppose such a move could act.[30] A certain amount of secrecy would also be needed. Malice before thought could poison any process aimed at rearranging the National Association.

One of Hulbert's great strengths was his astuteness in determining which members of the press were truly in agreement with his ideas and in knowing which were trustworthy.[31] Without the aid of the fourth estate Hulbert's efforts would have been considerably more difficult. Hulbert's friend Lewis Meacham, a sportswriter for the *Chicago Tribune*, was privy to Hulbert's ideas, shared his concerns and faithfully conveyed Hulbert's ideas to the public when Hulbert wanted them conveyed.

In a sense, Hulbert's job would be a battle against tolerance as much as a fight against corruption, which often crept in when tolerance walked on the arm of avarice. The more the association executive let this or that indiscretion go, the quicker the delinquency became criminality. And the more delinquency and criminality, the more lenient the executive seemed to become. Since players held key positions in the N.A.'s councils, "there was little disposition to act; and even if the players submitted proposals for reforms, the association lacked the executive machinery to enforce them, for member clubs valued their independence and only by making them accept authority from the top could a reform program stand a chance."[32] Boston, the Association's on-field powerhouse, exerted little influence despite its position of potential power. The club was led by Harry Wright, one of the nicest guys in the game.[33] Harry was often incapable of thinking ill of others, which may have made him an easy mark for the machinations of men like George Concannon of the Philadelphias, who shared the City of Brotherly Love with the Athletic[34] and the short-lived Centennials, who made it to late May 1875 before dropping out of the association with a 2–12 win-loss record and disappearing from major league baseball. The Philadelphias, sometimes called the White Stockings, sometimes the Pearls, had the distinction of having in their three years of existence at least eight players of dubious character — George Bechtel, Bill Craver, Jim Devlin, Cherokee Fisher, Mike McGeary, John Radcliffe, Fred Treacey and George Zettlein.[35] These eight men weren't out, of the National Association that is, for any appreciable time as they bounced from team to team despite reputations for being either dissension-spreading growlers (masters of on-field bickering), fixers or drinkers.[36] The notorious eight and a few questionable others continued to play and plague the N.A.

While Wright was the best and Concannon the worst of association operatives, most were like William Cammeyer, then president of the New York Mutuals. He had been associated with the club since 1867, when they moved their home grounds from Elysian Fields in Hoboken, New Jersey, to his Union Grounds in Brooklyn.[37] The Mutes, although situated in Brooklyn, represented the city whose name they carried to cranks across the country. The history of the Mutuals was a chronicle of corruption, a team reportedly being in league with gamblers as far back as 1868. They showed "a propensity for losing to inferior foes under unusual circumstances"[38] during their five years of N.A. play. Cammy's path was always a journey of convenience; his was a "pretend to hear no evil, pretend to see no evil, have to tell no evil" philosophy. Time and again he chose whichever way suggested the least hassle even if it meant less profit. Cammy evidently wished, above all, to avoid unpleasantries.

Boston's Al Spalding, the association's premier pitcher of the previous five years, would write that baseball in several cities, especially in New York and Philadelphia, was largely under the domination of the gambling element. He didn't mean the officials were gamblers but they were of the opinion that professional baseball, like horse racing, must tolerate betting in order to attract spectators in sufficient numbers.[39] Cammeyer was, no doubt, one of these officials. He had perfected the art of appeasement and accommodation.

There would always be the odd person who couldn't see a player in the throes of hippodroming, no matter how blatant; most N.A. executives, like Cammy, saw it but refused to do anything about it. With the managements of league-leading Boston and population-dominating New York shrinking from exercising the authority needed to censure the culprits, owners, managers and players were free to do whatever they pleased. It was a case of what has come to be called Burke's law: "The only thing necessary for the triumph of evil is for good men to do nothing" (the pithy truth of the axiom is not lessened by the little known fact that scholars have never found the quote in any of Edmund Burke's writings).[40]

The job of judgment, jury and perhaps Jehovah fell to Hulbert. The Chicagoan's approach would be a combination of iron fist in a velvet glove and velvet fist in an iron glove. Discussing future strategy, Hulbert would write to St. Louis baseball executive Charles Fowle, "We have got to use molasses for the present."[41] The bittersweet would come later. Hulbert appears to have been a Vince Lombardi in a different sport and a different age. His style, as historian Thomas Melville succinctly notes, was "confrontational, uncompromising and uninhibited ... indicative of [his being] known for an 'overbearing' and relentlessly 'bull dozer' attitude in all his personal dealings.... [Hulbert's] personality that comes through his correspondence is hard-charging, calculating and relentless."[42]

Hulbert's desire to assemble the best team in baseball would have a positive, long-lasting side effect if he was able to build a club capable of both dominating the opposition and, so fitting for a baseball club, collecting a conglobation of cash.[43] If Hulbert's White Stockings were the top team in wins and gate receipts in 1876, other club officials would be more likely to buy his argument that an honest and competitive league was the best guarantee of continual financial success.

A key question was how many fixers and fixees could be tolerated in the association. To be baseball's best league, the loop would need the best players, but some of the best on the field were of the worst character. Dick Higham, a .300-plus career hitter, was a not-so-shining example of what scout Mike Gonzales would most likely have called, "Good hit, no honesty."[44] The problem was that when a talented player was caught betting or boozing, little happened, but if a mediocre player was found gambling or drinking, he'd be quickly dismissed or asked to resign. No good player was ever bounced.[45] Hulbert would have to sup with a few devils for some time to come. But there were degrees of goodness and badness, just as there were degrees of competence. A group of players might all be fellows of the shade, but some would be lesser Satans on the scale of sin. Some would be dishonest, but criminal conformists more than unbridled felons. These borderline lawbreakers represented the plethora of players who found it easier to profit dishonestly than honestly in the non-professionally run professional National Association. These players didn't play straight because their colleagues didn't play straight. In a properly policed league peopled by owners who would pay an honest day's enumeration, they would, in all likelihood, stay honest.

But there was a more serious species of serpent in baseball's Eden. These were the felonious fellows who suffered from a case of chronic evil. Compared to the borderline lawbreakers, who wouldn't even consider a dishonest practice if they were profiting by honest means, these creatures were perpetual perpetrators who almost always followed the path of illegality. It seemed to be a matter of principle with them. The job facing Hulbert would be to establish mechanisms that would remove the perpetual perps as instantly as possible and oust the criminal conformist a bit more gradually.

A game between Chicago and the New York Mutuals must have been an afternoon of agony for Hulbert. His 1875 Chicago team had Higham and Zettlein, the dubious duo of Philadelphia White Stocking infamy, both with reputations for questionable play. The *Louisville Courier-Journal*, noting that Zettlein was "always a stiff betting man,"[46] once described Zettlein's openly conducted betting during a game in Chicago in the summer of 1875.[47] The *New York Clipper* reported that in one game both Philadelphia and Chicago were trying to throw the game to the other team.[48] The only reason Hulbert's Chicago team was not called the Black Stockings was that no sportswriter had yet thought of the name. The Mutes were known for shady play in even the brightest sunshine.[49] And to add to concerns about hippodroming, there was always the possibility that two-fifths of the players had become acquainted with a fifth of bourbon or, at least, a half dozen beers, by the time they stepped on the field.[50]

Baseball was not a primary source of revenue for Mutes owner William Henry Cammeyer, whose family was a major player in the leather business.[51] Cammy was not a truly hard man in an age when some human beings seemed forged as cold as steel and as rugged as wrought iron. The 1870s was the era of the entrepreneur. Although not the stature of a Morgan, Carnegie, Gould or Rockefeller, Cammy was very much the enterprising capitalist in his own field, which quite literally was a field. In the early 1860s, when the nation was convulsing with civil conflict, Cammeyer had a fence built around the site of an old skating club at Lee Avenue and Rutledge Street in Brooklyn. He added a stepped series of benches, which at first looked like an awfully wide stairway to nowhere. The nearest thing to a *grand*stand was a long wooden shed, supplied with benches for the ladies.[52] Cammeyer, in a sense, invented the ballpark and it was called Union Grounds.[53] But Cammy's enclosure was not the first field to be encircled by a rickety wooden fence. An enclosed cricket field in Philadelphia had occasionally been used for baseball games before Union Grounds was enclosed.[54]

Union Grounds is sometimes confused with Capitoline Grounds, a park built in 1864 by Reuben S. Decker and Hamilton A. Weed. Both Union

Grounds and Capitoline Grounds were on Marcy Avenue in Brooklyn. Both opened in May in the early 1860s— Union Grounds on May 15, 1862, Capitoline on May 5, 1864. Capitoline Grounds has sometimes incorrectly been called Union and Capitoline Grounds. Union Grounds was in Williamsburg, just across the East River from Manhattan. Capitoline Grounds was in Brownsville.[55]

All National Association clubs played on enclosed fields. The sole purpose of the fencing was to regulate admission by keeping the nonpaying out. Fences were not walls to drive baseballs over.[56] And Cammy's field continued to be a skating rink when winter was cold enough to permit snow and ice.

Baseball began to boom in the 1850s when people actually started flocking to see other people play what was, at first, called the New York game.[57] For years, local games had been played on open fields, parks and vacant lots, and only the wealthy played. No one got paid to play and no one paid to see others play. It was a gentleman's sport, upper-class leisure supported by the idea that the only good ballplayer was a rich ballplayer.[58] Such a code kept the "unsavory" out, allowing a refined approach to athletic pursuit. As far as Cammeyer was concerned, the minds that concocted the code were avoiding the inevitable. Cammeyer didn't invent professionalism. He was simply the first to recognize and capitalize on what many people felt was a normal and natural social motion. The gentleman's desire to win led to sudden improvements of this or that team by the addition to the club's roster of an honorary gentleman here, there, and eventually, pretty well everywhere. Before the Civil War, most ballplayers were gentlemen who filled in their leisure time playing. Professionalization brought in the social classes below them.[59]

At first, Cammeyer rented his Union Grounds to Brooklyn's better amateur clubs and, after a period of free admissions to increase interest, charged the cranks a modest entry fee to watch the clubs play. It ranged from 10 to 25 cents as baseball's popularity grew enormously between 1865 and 1870.[60] Things had gone well and the more proficient the amateurs became, the more the cranks came. The enclosed field meant control. It led to the spectator paying far more than an admittance fee as Cammy put souvenirs, score cards and refreshments on sale. The possibilities seemed almost endless.

By 1870, the leading spectator sports in America were harness racing and baseball.[61] The notorious Boss Tweed controlled the Mutual Baseball Club of New York, an amateur outfit originally organized by firemen in a New York fire company, who were dependent on Tweed for patronage and favors. Tweed easily made the Mutuals, who were not a quality team, a franchise holder when the National Association of Professional Base-Ball Players was formed in 1871. By the time Tweed went to jail later that year after being convicted of illegal political practices, Cammeyer was well established with the Mutuals.[62]

With Tweed in jail, Cammeyer couldn't prevent the Atlantics, the New York–Brooklyn area's most celebrated and powerful amateur club in the 1860s,[63] from paying the ten dollar entrance fee and joining the National Association in 1872.[64] The Atlantics, also playing in Brooklyn, led the Mutes at the gate as Cammeyer suffered the summer of his discontent. But wily William found a way to take care of the Atlantics. He nominated that fine gentleman and star playing captain of the Atlantics, Robert Ferguson, for the presidency of the National Association. Ferguson's surprise at Cammeyer's nominating him was probably as colossal as his swelling self-pride at being nominated. It was a well-considered move on Cammeyer's part. As association president, Ferguson,[65] already known for his belligerence,[66] might have made life unbearable and business unprofitable for Cammeyer; but, as the wily one suspected, the fiery Ferguson was no Machiavelli. Ferguson's feistiness soon had him so involved in the internecine politics of the poorly organized National Association that he was unable to pay attention to building the competitive strength of the Atlantics. They steadily deteriorated as Ferguson fussed, fiddled and fumed with association matters. Ferguson's folly was Cammeyer's triumph.[67] The Atlantics, drowning in an ocean of red ink, eventually collapsed.[68]

By 1875, Cammeyer represented a potential problem to the success of any revised major league. The blatantly crooked managers and owners were much less of a threat. Their corrupting influence could easily be recognized by other owners, but Cammy's kind of contamination was much subtler. Since Concannon's White Stockings club was not the dominant team in Philadelphia, he could be circumvented by simply favoring the more dominant Athletic with a franchise in any reorganization of the league. The Mutuals, however, were the only New York area team of any consequence. Cammeyer, therefore, controlled the team representing the nation's biggest city; actually it was two cities since the Mutuals played in Brooklyn, a separate political entity from New York. If the Mutuals players' criminality could be contained, many of the game's prevailing evils would not prevail; but could the wishy-washy Cammy be persuaded to exercise such a role? Hulbert simply did not know.

Just as it does today, the media would have its part to play in reporting, commenting on (both pro and con) and even propagandizing the sporting events of the day. The 1870s media was print, and print was primarily the newspaper. America's premier baseball writer by 1875 was Henry

Chadwick, who has sometimes been called the "Father of Baseball."[69] Chad founded the *Chronicle* in the 1867, a weekly paper that primarily covered baseball. He edited an annual baseball guidebook that claimed a circulation of 65,000 in the mid–1860s. Chadwick was, in a way, one of the "inventors" of baseball. Chadwick's "continuous presence on the rules committee ... significantly influenced [the game's] evolution ... his development of the box score, tabular standings ... annual baseball guide ... most of the common statistics"[70] established the game's historical essence. A reporter for many of the major New York metropolitan papers and editor of various baseball guides, Chadwick was the most influential reporter in the game.[71] But Chadwick was 52 in 1876 and represented "a generation that had known an America without corporations and monopolies."[72] His opposition to monopoly was not an alignment with trade unionists, but an expression of middle class ideals of open competition in athletics and markets and it was the consensus viewpoint, damnation of the "plutocrat" and "monopolist" being in favor with workers, craftsmen, storekeepers, professionals, and politicians.[73] It would be this aspect of Chadwick's idealism that would clash with Hulbert's realism.

Hulbert's chief co-conspirator in transforming the National Association into the National League would be Boston's Albert Goodwill Spalding. His cooperation would be complete since the epitome of Spalding's being was that "he never met an opportunity to make money out of baseball that he didn't like."[74] The game's leading pitcher in 1875, he would become one of baseball's greatest entrepreneurs and he would have no qualms about using his influence to promote his business when he became a baseball executive. He would go on to publish the *Official League Book*, and *Spalding's Official Base-Ball Guide*, which would help sell his sporting equipment. He would break up the Player's Brotherhood, the first players' strike, in 1890 and would help create and promote the asinine Doubleday myth concerning the origins of baseball.[75]

Another man essential to changing the course of baseball's destiny in the mid–1870s was nice guy Harry Wright, the most influential personage in the game at the time.[76] Wright, who managed the Cincinnati Red Stockings, the first professional team ever, to a 56–1 won-loss record in 1869, and who would earn the title "Father of Professional Baseball,"[77] was the 1870s Mr. Clean. He once reversed an umpire's decision in favor of his team and ruled his own man out. Wright had integrity. He neither drank nor swore and seldom raised his voice.[78] He could, however, be very persuasive.[79] In 1875, he was on his way to guiding the Boston Red Stockings, primarily an extension of the 1868–69 Cincinnati team,[80] to their fourth straight National Association pennant. Excelling in organization and instruction, Wright was the first manager to use coach's signals and became so proficient at heckling opponents that the N.L. considered a rule in 1877 that would ban managers from sitting on the bench so that they could get rid of him.[81] He was a pioneer in the development of baseball strategy, his teams executing the hit and run, hitting behind the runner, giving up an out for a run and other such "modern" techniques.[82] He was also a shrewd businessman, driving a hard bargain when negotiating his team's share of the gate receipts.[83] He was "tough-minded about practical realities ... he wanted a basic admission price of fifty cents, arguing that if a team was well trained, serious, sober, and honest to the man, it was worth the price."[84] After all, the public paid 75 cents to $1.50 to go to the theatre and more people preferred baseball to theatricals. He argued that a "good game is worth 50cts, a poor one is dear at 25cts."[85] Wright's encyclopedic knowledge of the rules was also important to Hulbert.[86]

Hulbert's first step towards restructuring the N.A. would be to turn Chicago into a team of bull-strong, cat-quick athletes. To this end he would speak to Spalding, gain his cooperation and then ally himself with executives like Boston's Harry Wright, bargain with owners like Cammeyer and circumvent criminals like Concannon. His overall aims had to go unreported until the right time. Influence would be a matter of masking *realpolitik* with a bodyguard of good intentions.

2

The Signing of "The Four"

Hulbert and Meacham met frequently as the spring of '75 uncoiled toward summer. The motivations of each man went beyond friendship. Hulbert needed to filter his ideas before he acted on them. Although some had to be kept secret, some had to be publicized. Hulbert needed to know how owners, players and the public reacted to his ideas. Meacham kept secret what Hulbert wanted confidential and kept before the public what Hulbert wanted in print. It was a reporter's normal reaction to a steady stream of story material.[1]

Having identified the need to turn his lowly White Stockings into a highly rated ball club, Hulbert was thinking about ways to bring about the transformation. It didn't take much of a mind to realize that Cincinnati's success of 1869–70,[2] and Boston's during the last few years, had been based on what some people would call a dubious form of recruitment, basically persuading the available premier talent away from rival teams. In building the first pro team in 1869, Cincinnati manager Harry Wright had scoured the nationside, convincing the best ballplayers to come and play for pay.[3] Later, in 1871 when he moved to Boston, Wright had simply "raided" Cincinnati and any other club unfortunate enough to have a coveted player.[4] There was, of course, no rule against such freewheeling free enterprise at the time of Wright's "transgressions." The ultimate capitalist, Hulbert was comfortable doing what any captain of industry would do, hiring a top-flight staff by picking the best from this or that competitor. In baseball, it was called raiding and considered bad. In other enterprises, it was considered clever and called good business.

Hulbert was ready to act when Chicago and league-leading Boston met in Chicago in April '75. He was seeking the best and Boston, without doubt, had the best. Al Spalding, a 6' 1", 170-pound sinew of sheer athletic excellence, was Boston's and baseball's premier pitcher. In an era when teams carried one regular and one change pitcher, Spalding had hurled Boston to three straight pennants. If wins had been credited to pitchers in the 1870s, Spalding would have accumulated 150 between 1871 and 1874. On his way to a 57–5 win-loss record for 1875, he was the key. Sign him and others would come. Hulbert calculated that Chicago should be able to get Spalding if the man were offered enough money, the captain's job and, perhaps, some other little thing or other.[5]

But appointing Spalding captain and therefore field manager for '76 might not be particularly politic. It would mean retiring Jimmy Wood, whose situation was made in misfortune. A leg injury during the '73 season while playing for the Philadelphias led to an abscess, which led to medical malpractice. Doctors treating Wood's leg managed to break it. The break led to complications, the most complicated being the amputation of Wood's leg.[6] Unable to play, Wood managed Chicago for '74 and '75. Wooden of leg but not of personality, Jimmy had become one of the best-known captains (a job approximating today's manager) of the N.A. era in the early '70s.[7] If Spalding were to join the Socks (Sox was not a part of 1876's sports writing lexicon), Wood would need to find other employment. Not a great prospect for a 31-year-old, one-legged ex-athlete, who had learned few skills other than fielding ground balls with his bare hands and hitting a rapidly moving baseball with a round stick.[8] To persuade Spalding to leave Boston, Hulbert wasn't above giving Wood the axe. After all, no one managed a team forever. Hulbert would see if any of his business associates had an opening. The White Socks would later urge that Wood be made a National League umpire for the 1877 season.[9]

The 1875 season wasn't half over before Hulbert had put his proposition to Spalding, assuring the Boston ace $4,000 a year, the captaincy and a chance to work with him on revamping the N.A. He only had to change his socks from red to white in 1876.[10] Hulbert suggested, "You've no business playing in Boston; you're a Western boy."[11] The latter appeal probably had little effect influencing Spalding. The fact he was going to play a part in building a powerful organization possibly did.[12] The highly ambitious Spalding may have had to hold back a smirk when Hulbert said his oft-quoted, "I don't know how you feel about it, but I'd rather be a lamp post in Chicago than a millionaire elsewhere."[13]

Spalding was a complex person, a man with a multifaceted personality.[14] A friend of his described him as pontifical, persuasive, personable, a man with "the manner of a Church of England bishop."[15] Spalding was accustomed to the good life. Friends often spoke of his preference for the pedantic. Even his mother had complained that he had an irritating habit of eating the inside of a slice of bread while hiding the crust under the edge of his plate. This culinary peculiarity seemed to symbolize his arrogant antagonism to the hard, crusty parts of life.[16] Even more than Hulbert,

Spalding was confidence incorporated. He probably had no doubt about his deserving three times more money than any other mortal player and of his being capable of managing Chicago, but his arrogance was tempered with a firm touch of reality. The foot-of-the-rainbow quality of Hulbert's offer was no doubt enhanced by Spalding's ideas being much akin to Hulbert's in the first place. Spalding, for example, wanted gambling and alcohol barred from ballparks as much as Hulbert.[17] When Spalding agreed to come west, baseball changed.

Hulbert's sights and Spalding's insights instantly centered on three of Spalding's teammates — catcher James "Deacon" White, outfielder Cal McVey and infielder Ross Barnes — as prospects to join Spalding in Chicago. They were an awesome threesome. Backstop White, whose meek, self-effacing countenance made him resemble a clerk rather than a catcher,[18] had hit .343 over the past four years with the Cleveland Forest Citys and Boston Red Stockings. He was without peer, working without mask and glove behind the plate,[19] a fearless

Despite his meek, clerical countenance and nickname, James (Deacon) White, one of the Big Four who jumped from Boston to Chicago, was a tiger behind the plate. Without mask, mitt or other protective equipment, White caught up-close to the batter, frequently getting hit in unprotected body parts. He led the National League in RBIs with 60 in 66 games in 1876. A 40-year-old White is shown in an 1889 Pittsburgh Allegheny uniform, a team he played for in his next-to-final major league season. (Transcendental Graphics)

ferocity of a man whose play totally belied the timidity of his appearance. Nemec has called him "the N.A.'s first great star."[20] McVey, the Iowa-born outfielder, looked and played as if he were made of the ingredients of nails. He was a recreational boxer who some believed could have succeeded as a professional prize fighter; a baseball phenom at 16, invited to play for a local university team; the only teen-ager on Harry Wright's original professional Cincinnati Red Stockings in 1869 and versatility itself, able to play every position on the field.[21] He had batted .366 over the past four years with the Lord Baltimores and Boston. His bat guaranteed him fourth or fifth spot in any lineup. Barnes was the quintessential leadoff hitter. Lipman Pike, the veteran St. Louis outfielder who once raced and beat a trotter in a sprint, might still be faster, but Pike didn't seem the wizard with the wood that Barnes was.[22] The 5' 8" Barnes had hit .382 over the previous four years and, most importantly, had crossed home plate 346 times from 1871 through 1874, scoring an average of 1.84 runs per game. Such productivity ran beyond phenomenal even in the 1870s. Pike had hit .313 from '71 to '75. Barnes led N.A. second basemen in fielding in 1871, '72 and '75. He "was really the star"[23] of all second basemen. Spink noted that Barnes "was a magnificent fielder and thrower and a royal batsman and base runner."[24]

Hulbert, with the help of Meacham, continued to commit to newspaper the multitude of ideas he had on improving baseball (except, of course, making any mention of his desire to radically revamp the National Association). Hulbert's thinking had already progressed to the realization that he'd have to turn the N.A. into an entirely new kind of baseball association. The National Association was a lost cause. Hulbert concluded that any attempt at reform could become bogged down in endless verbal imbroglios with those who benefited one way or another from business as usual. Free speech, when allowed to become a Tower of Babel, stifled common sense. To cover costs, pay good salaries, and maybe realize a "modest" dividend, the schedule of games would have to be limited to the better teams.[25]

If Hulbert couldn't get the players he wanted under contract for 1876, the whole venture of revamping baseball would be academic. If he failed, he would be back to being a full-time businessman and the National Association would take baseball into the rat pits.

While Hulbert was conspiring to fill his White Stockings with stars, William Cammeyer, owner of Union Grounds in Brooklyn and president of the "always suspect Mutuals,"[26] was suffering through a lucre-less season. A chaos of contradictions, Cammy was a deceptively difficult man to understand. He had inherited his father's leather business, the Cammeyer Shoe Company, and was one of the leading leather merchants in the country; but he was also an entrepreneur in his own right.[27] He had invested considerable capital in 1862 when he enclosed Union Grounds. He had graded its diamond, built stands, constructed a clubhouse and then persuaded people to pay to watch other people playing baseball, but he didn't make a great deal of money from his grounds or his team.[28] The team had little chance of finishing the 1875 season in the black. His grim, thin mouth, tilting slightly from left to right while terminating at each end in a slight downward turn, was perhaps most symbolic of the man. It formed a flattened "m," an "m"[29] that could stand for miser, money, mine or for manager, Mutuals, magnificent. This grimness of face may have mirrored the Mutes' monetary situation, which perpetually had a malignant quality to it. Yet Cammeyer did not give up on his Mutuals and concentrate his energies on his shoe business. There was something about his being associated with baseball that outweighed increasing his overall earnings. He did, however, operate his team as if every dollar was minted by the All Mighty. His role in the months to come would be relatively easy to predict but as difficult as usual to explain.[30] One thing that was easy to expect was his not making money with the team in 1875[31] and his Mutuals not completing 1875 season.[32] The ugliness of 1875 might make Cammeyer pliable to change.

Henry Chadwick was a different matter. The nation's foremost baseball writer, now principally with the *New York Clipper*, Chadwick was as old as the National Pastime itself.[33] He was the nation's first reporter to receive regular play for covering sports and was already a legend. He had popularized baseball, modified most of its rules, designed the box score, and invented much of its vocabulary. Assists, passed balls, fungoes, grounders, pop-ups, and double plays were all his making. He once even promoted the idea of games going 10 rather than 9 innings.[34] He took every game seriously and wrote with the dedication of a war correspondent.[35] Being as much in love with numbers as he was with words, Chadwick usually accompanied his stories with a wealth of statistical data. Unfortunately, fifty-something Chadwick[36] was becoming alienated from many of the younger sports journalists.[37] Although affectionately still called "Chad" by many of his colleagues and still a formidable presence in the sport, English-born Henry was going the way of most pioneers. His ideas had become more and more conservative and old-fashioned. He opposed a recently proposed idea that statistics on strikeouts be kept. Henry saw strikeouts as a sign of poor batting rather than of good pitching.[38] He believed that "it is to excellence in fielding that we are to look for the beauty of base ball."[39]

2—The Signing of "The Four" 17

Hulbert would soon be in direct conflict with the veteran reporter from New York. Whether unwittingly, or perhaps witlessly, opposition to Hulbert would be fomented by people like Henry Chadwick, their good intentions, if followed, threatening chaos. Chadwick had opposed extensive expansion of the National Association in the past, but now he wanted everyone to have a say, every team applying to be admitted to a giant size association, every idea and opinion, the brilliant and the banal, the relevant and the irrelevant, to be treated equally.[40] Chadwick's belief in fair play caused him to overlook the thoughtlock formed by a cacophony of competing voices.[41] Chadwick simply didn't seem to understand that all ideas are not equal. As far as Hulbert was concerned, Chad was becoming a liability.

Spalding signed a secret contract to play for Chicago in '76 shortly after talking to Barnes, McVey, White and a couple of other teammates.[42] Assured the captaincy, the manager's job, the highest pay in the league, even freedom of action in managing, Spalding was now certain his Boston buddies would be joining him in Chicago. One of the most important incentives to Spalding probably involved the offer's recognition of his intellectual, not physical, prowess, and its involving power. Hulbert was willing to give the bright, young Spalding a chance to use his brain, the part of his body he probably valued the most and the only part baseball hadn't allowed him to show off to perfection. Spalding was considered the smartest player in the sport, but that would be nothing compared to the praise and power awaiting the game's savior. Working with Hulbert, Spalding could take on the greatest mental challenge facing the game — reorganizing baseball, revising the association's old constitution, rewriting the rules, developing a corruption-free league.[43] Spalding would come to Chicago in the fall, stay with Hulbert and work reviving baseball.[44]

He also had a deeply personal reason for agreeing to come to Chicago. The money, the captaincy, the almost certain possibility his teammates would also sign with Chicago and the chance to be in on a total revamping of baseball were all powerfully appealing to Spalding,[45] but the clincher may have been something Spalding had been observing since the season's start. In Hartford, it had been the actions of Tommy Bond, the Dark Blues' young pitcher. In New York, it was the veteran hurler Bobby Mathews.[46] A new pitch was appearing and disappearing before the batter's eyes with increasing frequency.[47] It was called a "curve" and Bond threw it with the velocity of vehemence.[48] It was bad enough when 20-year-olds like Bond came into the association with air-heating fastballs. Spalding, who no longer had baseball's fastest fastball, accepted that youth should triumph in contests of strength and speed, but when they came with a pitch that suddenly fell off the edge of the earth just as it reached the plate ... well, that was another matter. Trick pitches were supposedly the dominion of the veteran hurler, not the infant of face and arm. It was even worse when a fellow veteran like Bob Mathews was also able to throw this supposed optical illusion that threatened to turn a horde of hitters into civilians.[49] Worst of all was Spalding's realization that no matter how hard he practiced, he couldn't throw the cursed curve.[50] Although he was not yet 30 and still supposedly trim, Spalding also realized he was accumulating flab at body center and losing agility in both arms and legs.[51] He probably saw Hulbert's generous offer as a chance to conclude his on-field career gracefully. His last full season as a hurler would be 1876.[52]

Hulbert assured Barnes, McVey and White that the potential defectors had nothing to worry about as far as the National Association was concerned, telling them, "Don't worry about any problems if you come with us. There won't be any. I'll take control of the game away from the Easterners."[53] The N.A. wouldn't expel them since, Hulbert argued, "in the eyes of the public you players are bigger than the Association."[54] When Hulbert said he'd still pay their salaries if the totally unexpected occurred and they were expelled and that he'd put this promise in writing, the trio agreed to pull up white rather than red stockings.[55] The two other Boston players approached by Hulbert and cajoled by Spalding resisted revolving.[56] Three for five was a great batting average any day in baseball.

The Big Four continued to play like angels (demons presumably being bad players), helping Boston overwhelm the opposition, including Chicago, for the rest of the year.[57] Such action was the best advertising for honesty and Hulbert's campaign for change. There would be considerable talk in the following weeks of expelling the free-floating four, but with every club being guilty at one time or other of having raided a fellow league member and no one willing to act against anyone else, nothing happened. Talk was inexpensive. Legal action could amount to considerable costs that National Association members could ill afford to spend. The Civil War having ended less than 10 years before, the Big Four were reviled as "seceders" in the press. The standard sour grape sarcasm soon appeared. The Boston press and small boys predicted that "Your White Stockings will get soiled"[58] in Chicago. Other than these paper-borne pellets, and the occasional lung-launched lashing by a crank, little happened. The National Association executive roared in silence. There were, of course, the usual errors. "The *Chicago Times* heard that Chicago, at last, was to have a second-to-none baseball team, but it heard the wrong names; it said Harry and George Wright were coming to Chicago."[59]

2—The Signing of "The Four"

Hulbert knew the eastern teams could move against him, kick his club out, re-sign any stars he had carefully gathered and put him out of business. He counted on being able to get his ideas operational before the divided, decadent and hopelessly mismanaged National Association "officials" would ever get their act together and do anything destructive to his and Chicago's interests.

Buoyed by his successful signing of the Big Four, Hulbert strove to finish his raiding as quickly as possible. With the two other Boston players he and Spalding had sought adamant about staying in New England, Hulbert and Spalding realized they had to go fishing in other waters. Even with the Big Four, a '76 pennant for the White Stockings would only be a near certainty. One or more good import players for insurance against slumps and injuries would be welcome. Spalding noted that Boston wouldn't be a serious contender without any sign of "The Four," but the Philadelphia Athletic, now presumably a shoo-in for second place, could be.[60] If the Athletic's, for example, came up with one good rookie or if one Chicagoan slumped or got hurt or if one or two A's got hot and had a best-of-career season, then Hulbert's hopes could be dashed. And Hartford was no melange of muffins, either. Hulbert or Spalding decided to go after the A's Adrian Anson (he would not acquire the nickname "Cap" for years to come).[61] Although he was slow of foot and defensively less than ept (some would say inept, but they would be of a more literate age), the big Athletic infielder could cinch things for Chicago. He could hit.[62] A strict disciplinarian who considered "manliness" all-essential in the male make-up, Anson would also be a moral asset: rumor had it that the big fellow didn't smoke, didn't drink and although it was, perhaps, a bit hard to believe, was reputed to live according to a personal code of rigid honesty and unyielding pride.[63] How important Anson's reputed sterling character was to Hulbert or Spalding is questionable. He was known to use vile language on the field and had a history of having running battles with umpires, opponents and fans.[64] Probably most important was the fact that landing Anson, who had hit .352, .381, .353 and .367 in the previous four years in the National Association, would make Chicago stronger and the Athletic weaker. This enticing idea must have stimulated the pleasure centers in both men's brains. To sign a morally upright player was worth half a dozen lusty, drunken oafs and if he could hit like Anson evidently could, such a player would be worth his weight in troy ounces.[65]

It would only be years later that the press would reveal Anson's pathological hatred of blacks. Anson displayed a history of anti-black activity. He referred to a black mascot who accompanied an American team on a world tour in 1874 as a "no account nigger." In 1883, he refused to take the field in an exhibition game when Moses Fleetwood Walker, a black, was catching for the opposition. Anson only backed down when a forfeiture was threatened. In 1887 when John Montgomery Ward tried to sign George Stovey, a black, Anson went into a tirade. Many baseball historians believe Anson set the precedent that kept blacks out of Major League baseball for 60 years.[66]

It, of course, was no certainty that Anson could be induced to come to Chicago. It would not be easy. In case he couldn't be induced Chi-ward and, still liking the idea of plucking a player from the Athletic roster, Hulbert and Spalding picked A's infielder Ezra Sutton as a back-up target.[67] Sutton was already rated one of the best third basemen in the game.[68]

On the assumption that two could bring more influence to bear than one, especially if one of the two knew the people to be persuaded as well as Spalding knew Anson and Sutton, the pair took advantage of Boston having a three-day break in its schedule and met in Philadelphia to proposition Anson and Sutton.[69]

Both Hulbert and Spalding were probably surprised that Anson almost instantly agreed to play for $2,000, only $200 more than the Athletic would have paid him for the upcoming season.[70] The lesser-desired Sutton, on the other hand, said he'd think it over. If he decided to come to Chicago, all the better; but he wasn't essential.[71] With Anson in the bag or on it (he played third and first base), Hulbert and Spalding could turn their attentions to getting their innovative ideas out of mind and imagination and into reality. Whether Hulbert or Spalding worried over the permanence of Anson's commitment is unknown. He seemed to have accepted Hulbert's offer of too little too quickly. It would be a decade or two before a Viennese physician would even start to tackle such mental machinations. As it was 1875, Sigmund Freud was only 19 and unavailable for comment.

3

Creation

The National Association season of 1875 ended with little fanfare. Harry Wright's team finished 15 games ahead of the second-place Philadelphia Athletic.[1] The pennant flew over Boston's South End Grounds. The gamblers gravitated indoors to their winter wagering sports and the cranks waited for the more individual, participatory sports on snow and ice — skating, sledding and such. Soccer, cricket, lacrosse and baseball were tried on frozen surfaces in the 1870s,[2] but didn't catch on since spectator sport in winter was limited. Indoor walking races, complete with drinking and gambling, were popular. Prize fights could pop up indoors or outdoors. Boxing flourished in the second half of the 19th century. Football was more than a first down away from drawing a crowd. Basketball was two decades away from even entering Dr. Naismith's mind and hockey meant chasing a disc, ball or puck across windswept, icily aired expanses of frozen water, which few people were given to watching.[3]

Al Spalding came to Chicago to work on framing the constitution, by-laws and playing rules for an entirely new league. In the halcyon hours of the midwestern autumn with the central continental weather as splendid as it could ever be, Hulbert, the middle-aged doyen of dollars, and Spalding, the ambitious younger seeker of success, became compatibility's model. Hulbert, a father figure of clear counsel and rugged honesty, was, to many, the self-reliant money-made man of business, stern and unapproachable. This may have been the working Hulbert. Adrian Anson described Hulbert as "good-hearted, convivial when business hours were over."[4] Hulbert could be as sociable as any extrovert in the right company and at the proper time.[5] Spalding was evidently the correct company, and the autumn of '75, was the ideal time.

Meacham would often drop by since Hulbert fed the *Tribune* sportswriter many a story. Not only was Meacham Hulbert's public voice, he also was a convenient buffer to any criticism of Hulbert's proposals.[6] The key to the happy lexicon of "Hulbert-to-Spalding-to-Meacham" combination centered around Hulbert and Spalding. The fact the latter's quality of brain equaled his excellence of pitching arm allowed Spalding to see through the bluff and bluster of the exterior Hulbert and see the solid substance of the ideas that were within. Hulbert was obviously shrewd enough to see through the caricature of arrogance and conceit that the Reverend Father Spalding exuded and recognize that A.G. was a young man with a good mind and an almost demonical desire to do well in everything he did.[7] This and Spalding's keeping a lid on the more arrogant and autocratic aspects of his personality while dealing with Hulbert would have kept their interactions on a productive plane.

In forming and reforming their proposals, Hulbert and Spalding had the National Association as a template and did not have to re-plate from scratch. The N.A.'s major errors probably could be circumvented. Paramount among the N.A.'s major failings was its lack of competitiveness. The two or three clubs with the wealthier backers had bought up all the best players, rendering the remaining teams impotent.[8] Boston had been the most dominant, winning four of the five N.A. pennants. The Philadelphia Athletic had won the other pennant and been runner-up three of the five years. The least competitive clubs were usually the cooperative ones, where each player received a share of the gate receipts.[9] Since this stipend was a minuscule amount, the players on the poorer paying teams were more likely to supplement their cash flow with side money through gambling connections. Both Hulbert and Spalding felt that stock company ball was not only good for the players themselves, but pointed to National Association figures to prove it. Players on stock company teams averaged $1,200 a year. Players on cooperative teams averaged $300.[10] Although it couldn't be accomplished overnight, it seemed logical to replace cooperative teams with corporate ones. For the moment, however, they'd probably have to go with a cooperatively structured team or two to get the locales needed for a viable league. But the profitless, small town franchises had to be eliminated.[11]

The cooperative-corporate argument was only part of a debate already sifting its way through the public presses. The poor-of-purse cooperative clubs, whose players sought side money through gambling,[12] claimed that hoarding, the concentration of quality players on a few teams, was baseball's key problem.[13] The rich-of-purse corporate clubs, who took the competing out of competition, rejected the idea that the problem was their hoarding of the best players, counter-claiming that gambling was the primary problem.[14] The press found gambling of more interest to readers than hoarding. The issue of cleaning up the crookedness, therefore, became more prominent than the problem of competitive imbalance.

The corporative-cooperative conflict touched closely on the issue most fundamental to Hulbert, the Board of Trade member, entrepreneur and Republican,[15] and Spalding, the competitive athlete, soon-to-be sporting goods manufacturer and later-to-be GOP aspirant to the U.S. Senate.[16] Since both were biased to the right in all things business, social and political, their views on the proper organizational structure and division of labor for baseball were no surprise. Hulbert and Spalding preferred the corporate structure of the midwestern teams since they were stock companies, but were not enthusiastic about the organizational makeup of the eastern teams since they were membership (as in co-op) clubs.[17]

The basic struggle was, as Spalding would say, "the irrepressible conflict between Labor and Capital asserting itself under a new guise."[18] For years, players had been responsible for financial affairs, scheduling and a dozen other administrative things[19] that Hulbert firmly believed most players (with the occasional exception, like Spalding) were ill-equipped to handle. Spalding agreed. If anyone wanted proof, they need only consider the dismal five-year record of the player-run National Association. A player became a successful ballplayer because he was good at baseball, just as a successful businessman was successful because he was good at business. You might find the occasional good businessman among the players, but you wouldn't find enough of them to run a league any more than you could field a competent big-league baseball team if you recruited from a pool of businessmen. Hulbert and Spalding felt a player-run league was an invitation to chaos. Bob Ferguson, who while still playing third base for the Atlantics had became association president in '72 due, in part, to Cammeyer's conniving, was a case in point.[20] It had been nothing but downhill dollars for the association after Ferguson's ascendancy to the presidency. Hulbert and Spalding decided the players should do what they did best. Play ball. They would be the salaried part; the businessman would be the executive component. The new league would be an association of clubs, not players.

Hulbert insisted that the new league not play on Sunday and not sell beer or hard liquor in its parks whatever day it was.[21] If their new league was to be the vanguard of Victorian virtue, then there could be no beer (or alcohol of any kind) and no Sunday games.[22] This moral orientation naturally meant no swearing or excessive drinking by the players either. Hulbert wished to cater to the best class of customer. Both the real hoi polloi and the not-so-real McCoy hoi polloi would be willing to pay 50 cents per game and the riffraff would be discouraged from attending and thereby prevented from polluting the league's parks.[23]

Hulbert also advocated actively seeking female patrons.[24] Many men (and women) in the 1870s firmly believed women were a civilizing force in the social fabric. The more ladies at a game, the less cussing, spitting, boozing, fighting and gambling. The view was aided by the feminine anti-alcohol crusade of the mid–70s, which was especially nonviolent. The violence associated with anti-saloon activity was a decade and many peaceful anti-alcohol parades away. Since females who came to ball games were usually of the cultured class (the less well-to-do female would be busy working her fingers to the sinews in a slum workshop), it was little wonder that Hulbert and Spalding considered femininity an ally in building baseball respectability.[25]

What the founding of the league actually accomplished also gives a glimpse into the minds that molded it. First, it established a legally connected web of baseball clubs operating on business principles which enabled the club owners to claim the largest percentage of the profits. Second, by excluding the players from the business side of baseball, the new league ensured that "they would get a much smaller percentage of the gate receipts."[26] The mix of Hulbert's and Spalding's Christian morality and shrewd entrepreneurial practicality appears to have been tilted towards the practical. Although much of the moral side of Hulbert's pleading could be considered more a pose of convenience than an indication of hardened attitudes, later actions by Hulbert suggest he definitely believed establishing a morally solid circuit was essential. Hulbert, in 1877, for example, expelled four players from the National League for throwing games. Jim Devlin, a personal friend of Hulbert's, was one of the expelled players. When a financially and psychologically devastated Devlin later pleaded with Hulbert for reinstatement into the N.L., Hulbert handed him a $50 bill, saying, "That's what I think of you for old friendship; but damn you, Devlin, you are dishonest; you have sold a game; I never want to look upon your face again."[27]

Regardless of Hulbert's motives, there was always the reality that baseball had to make some accommodation to the blue laws. This was regrettable since Sunday baseball attendance exceeded attendance on all other days by three to five times.[28] Since people equated observing the Sabbath and sobriety with goodness, a league associated with such godliness should eventually be a profit maker. The argument was that a squeaky clean league could make it worthwhile for players to be honest. The league's association with piety should lead to an increase in attendance and, hence, revenues. The latter should cause players' salaries (and owners' returns) to increase. Well-paid players wouldn't need to cheat. Putting such faith in capitalistic Christianity was debatable, but with corruption driving cranks away in droves, banning baseball on Sunday was a propaganda ploy of necessity as much as an article of faith. Realistically, the state of baseball in 1875 demanded such action.

The league's proposed position of moral integrity dictated that the players observe certain proprieties. There would be restrictions on drinking, profanity, rowdiness and such. Each club must hire enough police to keep order in the stands and on the field.[29]

Hulbert and Spalding drafted a constitution based on financial practicalities. The two framers agreed that no team would be admitted from any city within five miles of any club already in the league. This was simply an awkward way of prescribing one club per city.[30] The directors would have exclusive and absolute charge of all league affairs. This codified their sought after power structure. They were assembling a league government of the owners, by the owners and for the owners. Deciding which owners of which teams to have in their league was not as difficult as it might appear. They would essentially go with teams already functioning in the National Association.

The sheer volume of teams wanting in the N.A. could be a problem. The National Association started the '75 season with 13 teams. Of these, three disbanded—the Philadelphia Centennials, Keokuk Westerns and Brooklyn Atlantics—and three—the Atlantics, St. Louis Reds and the New Havens—refused to play any away games.[31] Several cities had more than one entrant. There were three teams in Philadelphia (Athletic, White Stockings and Centennials), two in St. Louis (Brown Stockings and Red Stockings) and a couple in the New York–Brooklyn area (Mutuals and Atlantics). At least one team in each of those multiple-team cities went broke. Half the teams in the association didn't complete anywhere near their schedule of games.[32] With these facts before them, Hulbert and Spalding concluded that one team per city would be most sensible. They also concluded that every team in their league must complete its schedule of games. These solutions had to be sold to a selected number of team owners. Hulbert and Spalding not only had to figure out whom to select, but how to convince this select few to join their venture on Hulbert-Spalding terms. All this had to be accomplished even before beginning to worry about selling their revamped association to the public.

They knew that between 15 and 17 teams, besides Chicago, wanted to play National Association baseball in 1876. There was the Americus club of Philadelphia, Athletic (also of Philadelphia), Boston Red Stockings, Brooklyn Atlantics, Buffalo, Burlington, Cincinnati, Cleveland, Hartford, Louisville Grays, New Haven, New York Mutuals (who actually played in Brooklyn), another New York club as yet without a name, the Philadelphias, St. Louis Brown Stockings, St. Louis Reds and Washington.

They began their search for suitable candidates by focusing on possible western entrants. Their push for brewless baseball wouldn't be easy to swallow in cities like St. Louis or Cincinnati, but the need for respectability demanded a dry league. St. Louis, with a population of at least 330,000,[33] was a must for the west even though Catholic groups in St. Louis encouraged Sunday baseball.[34] The Browns were the only St. Louis team worth considering since the Red Stockings had won 4, lost 14 and collapsed in '75. The St. Louis Brown Stockings looked promising. Their owners, John B.C. Lucas and Charlie Fowle, could be expected to cooperate. John B.C. Lucas was born into wealth. His father, James H. Lucas, was one of the founders of the Missouri Pacific Railway and a banker in St. Louis.[35] Fowle would be one of several western baseball executives who would contribute to the development of a new league.[36] Fowle contributed sufficiently enough for the *St. Louis Republican* to later claim the whole plan concerning the development was his.[37] The Reds were crossed off and the Browns were penciled in for St. Louis on Hulbert's wish list.

Cincinnati, the birthplace of professional baseball, seemed the only other western city of sufficient size to warrant a franchise. The National Association had teams like the Keokuk Westerns (1871) and the Fort Wayne Kekiongas (1875). Neither center had enough people to support Sunday social games, let alone professional contests. Keokuk and Fort Wayne had paid their $10 entry fee and, thus, had gotten in. Hulbert and Spalding were determined that the admission fee into their league would be high enough to discourage such superfluous entrants. They set their league's admission at $100, no small sum in 1876, to keep the half-baked and quarter-brained dreamers and schemers out.[38]

Cincinnati was added to St. Louis and Louisville as candidates to join Chicago in the western half of their league. No other western city seemed populated or wealthy enough to be included. Hulbert and Spalding knew they had to keep their league competitive. Lack of competition had eroded association attendance in '75. Even pennant-winning Boston had experienced problems at the gate.[39] By winning every single home game and almost every away game, Boston made the outcome of their games too predictable. Boston's attendance dropped off in the latter half of the season. It was worse for the other teams. Six teams failing to complete their scheduled allotment of games and four failing to win even 20 percent of their games wasn't a formula for attracting people into a ballpark. Baseball sold competition first, winning second.

Inviting Louisville into the league appeared more of a gamble than including St. Louis or Cincinnati. Louisville, never having had a team in the National Association, made the Ohio River port appear to be a long shot to succeed in the National League. But one of the team's owners was Walter N. Haldeman, the man who had consolidated two Louisville newspapers—the *Journal* and the *Democrat*—with his own *Courier* to form the *Courier-Journal* in 1868. The influential editor Henry Watterson, who became a part-owner of the *Courier-Journal* with Haldeman after the merger, had, by the mid–1870s, become the voice of the New South advocating the reconciliation of North and South.[40] The Civil War had brought baseball to the South, which had a climate that definitely favored the game. Louisville, situated 90 miles southwest of Cincinnati, had the advantage of being a western city that would be perceived as a southern city by the Eastern owners. With the *Courier-Journal* on its side, the Louisville Grays would not want for publicity and, if Haldeman and fellow co-owner Charles Chase[41] could cobble together a reasonably competitive team, the club would probably not want for patrons either.

Walter N. Haldeman, part-owner of both the Louisville Grays and the *Louisville Courier-Journal*, was a key figure in the formation of the National League. Louisville had the virtue of being a western city that was perceived as a southern city, allowing the four eastern–four western team design of the fledgling league. The Grays, who hadn't been a member of the National Association, were the first Louisville team to play major league baseball. (The Filson Historical Society, Louisville, Ky.)

If St. Louis, Cincinnati, Louisville and Chicago formed the western part of the league, the Atlantic seaboard cities would have to be limited to four or five to keep regional interests reasonably balanced. Hulbert and Spalding had decided that any more than eight or nine teams would be a disaster. Choosing which eastern clubs to include was even more important than choosing the right western clubs. There were, of course, more potential entrants in the east. A number of clubs bounded in and out of the National Association in the '70s—Washington was represented in 1871,

1872, 1873 (by two teams) and in 1875; Baltimore, in '71, '72, '73 and '74. The National League would be little different. Eight new teams— Buffalo, '79, '80; Cleveland, '79, '80; Providence, '78, '79; Troy, '79, '80; Indianapolis, '78; Milwaukee, '78; Syracuse, '79; and Worcester, '80 — would appear in the N.L. between 1878 and 1880 alone. Detroit would have an N.L. team in '81 and '82 and Pittsburgh would enter in '82.

Some of the teams wanting in were from areas that were more town than city, others were anathema incarnate, and still others were candidates of class and competence. That the Boston Red Stockings should be wooed and won caused no brain strain. Neither president N.T. Appolonio nor secretary Harry Wright would decline membership simply because the Red Stockings had been the victims of Hulbert's recently concluded four-player raid. Boston had built their association domination on a multi-player raid of their own on the original 1869 Cincinnati club. Hulbert wouldn't even have to point out that Appolonio and Wright couldn't call their recruiting activities "honest recruitment" while labeling his very similar activities "raiding."[42] Hulbert's passion for probity was in sync with Harry Wright's outlook on the game. Baseball's icon of uprighteousness was forever advocating honesty, his ideas paralleling Hulbert's cerebral processes thought by thought.[43] Wright agreed with Hulbert's idea of keeping small towns and the financially fragile out of the league and his idea of establishing a firm schedule of games.[44] Persuading Boston to come aboard would also be aided by pitcher Spalding and manager Wright having been student and mentor.[45] The pair had been together at Boston since 1871. Boston topped the Hulbert-Spalding wish list. Hulbert might be "rough and unhewn [with] little of the urbane sophistication and liveliness of intellect characteristic of such eastern baseball figures as ... Appolonio,"[46] but he expected to get along with the Boston sophisticate.

Hartford, although population poor, was easily placed on the "to be designated now and not later" list. The Dark Blues, who won 54 of 82 in '75 to finish second in wins and who were third in winning percentage, seemed a viable choice. The public would always go with a winner. Morgan Gardner Bulkeley was the Connecticut club's president. He was also a Civil War veteran, a member of the Aetna Insurance Company's board of directors and an organizer of the U.S. Bank of Hartford.[47] Such impeccable credentials could be public relations gold. The only problem with including Hartford was Hulbert's desire to exclude the New Haven Elm Citys club. That team, which lost 40 of the 47 games they did play, had been unable to complete the '75 season. They concentrated primarily on playing at home, where they received two-thirds of the gate. Problem was, New Haven's opponents got the short end of such a policy. Chicago had received $240.86 for their share of a three-game 1875 series in New Haven. Since each game cost a visiting club about $400, the White Stockings lost about $1,000 on the series. The New Haven payment hardly covered the horsecar fares and hotel bills for the trip. This inability to attract an adequate quantity of paying patrons could be linked to the city's insufficient population, which could form the basis for their exclusion.[48]

Hulbert and Spalding consequently decided that no team should be admitted from a city having less than 75,000 inhabitants.[49] "To insure quality control two negative votes of League members prevented a new club from receiving a franchise," one account noted.[50] Such a rule would keep New Haven out but allow in Hartford. The latter's inclusion was not only justified by its having completed the season, but also its ability to provide a competitive team with the potential to put people in its ballpark despite the city's small population.

The roster-rich Philadelphia Athletic, 53–20 and third in '75 on wins (second on winning percentage), seemed another good possibility. The Philadelphia Centennials were not even a factor. After winning two of 14 games as professionals in '75, this hapless team folded. The Philadelphia White Stockings, playing under the alias Pearls, had been the Athletic's real rivals, going 37–31 in '75. There was a farcical episode at the end of August 1875 involving the team's third baseman Mike McGeary accusing pitcher George Zettlein and left fielder Fred Treacey of fixing a game against Hartford. Zettlein and Treacey returned fire, casting doubt on McGeary's honesty in said game. In short, the trio were casting fellow Pearls as swine. The pots and the kettles continued to call each other black as accusation piled upon accusation. This not being an isolated incident, the Pearls, along with Hulbert's Chicago nine and the always mendacious Mutuals, were 1875's usual suspects, each vying for the perverse honor of being selected the team that was as crooked as the original concept of sin. Although his respect for the Athletic club wasn't much better than it was for the Pearls, Hulbert included the A's on his to-be-approached list. Before the 1876 season ended, Hulbert would express his long-held attitude towards the A's in a letter to Charles Fowle of St. Louis: "I for one should be glad to bid adieu to the Athletics. From my first experience they have always been a double dealing set of *bastards*."[51] He might not have any brotherly love for any Philadelphia team, but he did have the pragmatic realization that it would be difficult to run a league without one of the nation's biggest cities in its fold.

Hulbert also realized that players with the Pearls, Centennials and other excluded clubs could be expected to revolve toward teams who joined the new league. Experienced players were hard to come by. Unsavory citizens, especially those who could hit, field and throw (a word to be taken in all its meanings), never had any trouble finding employment. Dick Higham, whom Hulbert asked partway through the 1875 season to find employment elsewhere, was instantaneously picked up by the Mutuals, a team "ever on the qui vive for unsavory characters."[52]

There were some things that could be done. Owners could be persuaded to crack down on the gamblers who roamed the playing fields prior to game time.[53] It would cost a few pennies for policing, but it would be worth it if these undesirables could be kept away from the players. Policing, visible policing, would have the benefit of showing the cranks that the league meant business.[54] The league would have to have a rule that if a troublemaking player was dismissed, no other club could negotiate with him, let alone hire him. It was another way of saying the league would have a blacklist. The key was to persuade club owners that crookedness simply was not good business.[55] Placing the basis of the Philadelphias' exclusion on a dollar-and-sense basis, they could bring the very same compelling motive to bear that they would use for keeping New Haven out. Like New Haven, the Philadelphias simply didn't make money for the clubs they played against. Chicago had only received $58 a game in contests against Concannon's club. It was even less than Chicago realized from New Haven or Hartford.[56] Using money as an argument was about as businesslike, convincing and effective as anyone could get.

Ever the realists, Hulbert and Spalding decided it would be risky not to include the New York Mutuals, the unruly bad boys of baseball. By 1875, only three teams had played in all five National Association seasons since the league was founded 1871—the Boston Red Stockings, the Philadelphia Athletic, and the New York Mutuals. Chicago, for example, had missed '72 and '73. Baseball's roots were also cleat deep in New York–Brooklyn soil and the area's cranks were faithful and plentiful.[57] Two greater Manhattan area teams had started the National Association's '75 season, the Brooklyn Atlantics, a once great team that had dominated the age of amateurism in the '60s,[58] and the Mutuals. The Atlantics had collapsed after winning but two games in 44 tries and were not capable of a rebirth. The Mutuals simply had a lock on any future pro games in Gotham. This created a chaos of problems for Hulbert and Spalding.

Promoting a league supposedly basing its future on honesty while including a team as reputably corrupt as Cammeyer's Mutuals would be a hard sell. Hulbert and Spalding may have worried that, without the Mutuals, the New York–Brooklyn area would be wide open for the Philadelphias or any other outlaw outfit to link up with Cammeyer in Brooklyn to form the basis of a revitalized National Association. A reborn N.A. could bumble

3—Creation 31

along, picking up the Allegheny club in Pittsburgh, the Wolverines in Detroit and maybe even teams from Washington and Baltimore. Such an association would get a few good players and Hulbert's league would get a few and neither one would survive. Players might even be able to get clubs in the two leagues into a bidding war for their services, thereby sending salaries upward and profits downward. Like it or not, Hulbert and Spalding put the Mutuals on their short list.

Ironically, the paramount importance of having a New York or Philadelphia team in a major sports league in the 1870s and early 1880s may be more of a present day belief than any that existed in Hulbert's time. The National League would operate for six years—1877 through 1882—without a team in Philadelphia and for five years—1878 through 1882—without a New York–Brooklyn representative. The Quakers would bring Philadelphia back into the National League in 1884 and the Gothams would return New York to the fold in 1883. A rival major league—the American Association—would have the Philadelphia Athletic as a charter member in 1882 and the New York Metropolitans would enter the AA in 1883.

There were a few positives about the Mutes. Although they were one of the most notorious teams in the National Association for fixing games, they always had a loyal following of cranks. Only the devil or God knew why, but the Mutes put people in Cammeyer's Union Grounds stands.[59] The horsecars going along Flushing, Division and Greenpoint to the ballpark were always packed on game day. Half of the Williamsburg district seemed to be a Cammeyer collective.[60] The cranks didn't always come out in overwhelming numbers, but there was always a core who attended the games regardless of how blatantly the Mutes consorted with gamblers, collected bribes, consumed alcohol or competed unsuccessfully. The cunning, the naive, the crooked and the honest all cascaded into the confines of Cammeyer's ball castle. They were a mix of mankind, humankind and the unkind. Perhaps the New York–Brooklyn area was simply so big that sufficient representatives of each category of humanity and inhumanity would always come to a Mutuals game.

With the Mutes two shades past the line between crookedness and honesty, only the naive could expect them to change their ways even if they wanted to. The Chicago pair would simply have to keep expounding honesty, integrity and high morality and hope their rhetoric could compensate for (cover up) the fact the biggest city in the circuit was fielding one of the most criminally infiltrated teams in or outside of tarnation (let alone New York). The Mutuals also represented another problem. They were a cooperative, not a corporative, club.[61] But compared to the criminal complexion of the Mutes, their being a collective combine was of little significance.

On October 24, 1875, Meacham, on Hulbert's instigation, outlined in the *Chicago Tribune* the main changes needed to improve the National Association. Meacham did not mention his source's name or his source's desire to totally transform the N.A. into an entity of quite a different character.[62] The ideas were merely put forth as the musings of a reporter filling space in the autumn after the end of the baseball season. It would not be long before other reporters commented on their ideas. Still other reporters would talk to owners, players, interested and disinterested parties and more grist would grind into the mill. The telegraphic internet quickly provided an opinion polling, 1875-style.

Although Hulbert and Spalding had worked from sunrise to star shine in a month-long mental marathon to produce the proposed constitution, they did not, as yet, want any credit for its conception. All they wanted at the moment was for matters to be discussed to death as time accumulated a bit more of what we call the past. The new league's constitution now in draft form, Hulbert turned to the strategy for putting it into effect. He left the crafting of changes in the game's rules to consultations with Boston's Harry Wright and the player Spalding, who, for the moment, left for Boston and a November marriage to Josie Keith of Brockton, Massachusetts.[63]

For Hulbert, there would be many problems, many things to smooth over and many contradictions to live with in the name of expediency, but he was ready to live up to the promise he had given Spalding and the other seceders when he signed them, telling them not to worry and saying, "I'll take control of the game away from the Easterners."[64]

4

Western Wooing

The *Tribune's* lengthy article of October 24, 1875,[1] on baseball's needs that carried no byline but was known by all on Sunday to have been written by Lewis Meacham received far more praise than criticism.[2] There was, of course, no mention of any new league being formed — just suggestions for improving the National Association. These ideas, if not the article itself, were picked up by other papers and it wasn't long before every owner was aware of Hulbert's proposals to revise the association.

His thoughts distributed, his partnership with Spalding sealed in sweat and a league constitution roughed out, Hulbert turned to wooing the western owners whose teams he wanted. The last two months of 1875 became a time of considerable letter writing, occasional telegram exchanges and a spot of train travel. Charles Fowle, owner of the St. Louis National Association Browns, became a staunch supporter of Hulbert's ideas. Although Chicago and St. Louis formed the western frontier of the National Association and represented a natural rivalry, they had many shared interests. There was, however, the question whether St. Louis cranks could be persuaded to accept the idea of beer-less ball and ball-less Sundays. If St. Louis bought the no-beer, no–Sabbath baseball argument, then Cincinnati, the other city lederhosen deep in German immigrants who saw beer as daily bread, would probably go along. Friend Fowle, as Hulbert addressed him in letters, accepted the majority of Hulbert's proposals and agreed to a secret meeting with Chicago, Louisville and Cincinnati representatives sometime in December to consolidate western opinion on reform and strategy on handling the east.[3]

With St. Louis firmly behind him,[4] Hulbert moved to bring Louisville and Cincinnati into his fold. His techniques would be familiar to a 21st Century marketing executive. A November 8, 1875, letter to Charles Chase of Louisville was typical of the Hulbertian approach. It revealed Hulbert's gift for winning friends (like Fowle) and influencing people (like Chase). He proposed having Spalding travel to Louisville via Cincinnati for the express purpose of an interview with Cincinnati executive John Joyce, noting that "Spalding and Joyce are old acquaintances and I think we can best accomplish our purpose this way."[5]

Hulbert incorporated Chase into the conspiracy by using "we can best accomplish"[6] rather than "I can best accomplish." Now Chase would feel a part in any action relating to reforming the old association. Hulbert could have gone and talked to Joyce, but he sent Spalding because Spalding was more likely to get the job done. This was Hulbert the team player, not Hulbert the dictator. Hulbert the persuader went on, using a technique that propagandists would later call "bandwagon"[7] writing: "I can safely say the St. Louis people are ready to join us."[8] Then he would mix in a bit of pure information with a final "we're on the side of right" reference, another tool of later-day propaganda, writing: "My idea is to hold at Louisville about Dec. 1st ... a conference of two delegates from each of the four Western clubs. The purpose of the meeting to give the governing & playing rules a thorough overhauling ... and ... take measures for protecting ourselves from the ... present National Assn. Our object is a laudable one."[9]

This was vintage Hulbert, the natural marketing man. His mix of going succinctly to the point about one thing or other, then adding the idea of the reader joining a praiseworthy enterprise *et al.* was common in his letters that fall. Interestingly, Hulbert argued in this early November letter for "at most eight clubs"[10] being in the league and wrote that "one from a city and one only is our motto."[11]

By November's end a blizzard of paper had passed between Hulbert and Fowle in St. Louis, Chase in Louisville and Joyce in Cincinnati. The rush was necessitated by the fear that the eastern owners might move and destroy Hulbert's chances of creating an informal alliance of western owners with their own version of friendly persuasion. Referring to Louisville and Cincinnati joining Chicago and St. Louis in an informal agreement, Hulbert expressed this fear in a letter to Friend Fowle in St. Louis: "I want to have the nuptials [before] our new friends are seduced — or — flattered by attentions from others."[12]

A December 7, 1875, letter from Spalding to Charles Chase revealed the enormous progress made in November. It also contained a continuing appeal for secrecy. Concerning Hulbert and himself, Spalding wrote, "I found [Mr. Joyce] ready and anxious to join us.... We think it advisable to keep this matter *entirely* quiet for the present at least, and don't care to see too much about it in [the press]. It might tend to defeat or rather to make our plans more difficult to carry out."[13]

Spalding's concern with absolute secrecy was not shared by Hulbert, who was willing, at least, to trust the western papers. This was readily apparent in a letter of December 8, 1875, that Hulbert most likely sent to Fowle. (The name of the letter's recipient is indecipherable, but the mention of the Chicago, Louisville and Cincinnati papers, coupled with the comment about a paper in each of the four cities, strongly suggests it was sent to one of Hulbert's St. Louis "Friends" since St. Louis was the only other city Hulbert was wooing in the west.) Hulbert wrote: "I have in <u>general</u> terms [told] the owners of the [Chicago] Tribune [about] the proposed conference. The paper is loyal to the west ... and as I am sure they would keep faith with us, I see no great objection to giving papers friendly to us an inside view. I am sure we can trust Meacham and the Tribune — The [Louisville] Cour[ier] Journal — and Enquirer of Cinte [Hulbert's abbreviation for Cincinnati] are practically represented anyway...."[14]

Hulbert went on to recommend that Fowle bring a newsman along if he liked. His letter suggested that having a leading paper interested in their cause in each of the four western cities would be a positive. It is perhaps significant that Hulbert mentioned a paper sympathic to his cause could be found in Chicago, Louisville and Cincinnati and that he listed no St. Louis newspaper.

Hulbert then demonstrated his way of involving "his Dear friends" in decision-making and, interestingly, his detached businesslike attitude to Meacham, writing, "Of the propriety of this however, you shall be judge ... for the decision cannot be traced to <u>you</u> or <u>your club</u>. I am in no way committed to Meacham."[15]

Hulbert's emphasis on secrecy was always relative. On first approaching each western owner, Hulbert kept his designs for a separate league in deep cover. Once he had exchanged letters or met with each western owner, he evidently made a decision whether the approached owner was likely to be with him or not. His decision for each was evidently "with me." Once he made this decision, Hulbert only emphasized the need to keep the idea of forming a new league from eastern ears.

Hulbert's confidence in having a confidential connection with St. Louis Browns owner Charles Fowle and his friend Campbell Orrick Bishop was apparent in a letter Hulbert sent to Bishop on December 4, 1875. Bishop, a former player and a lawyer, had, at Hulbert's request, put the National League constitution in legal form.[16] If he had been unreliable, he could have leaked all Hulbert's aspirations to the eastern owners with ease. Hulbert wrote "Friend Bishop" that he agreed "that the best, in fact the only, [way] to bring about better organization, is for the leading respectable clubs, to ... form a <u>New</u> Association.... We should <u>knit</u> the Western clubs together ... <u>form close connections with each other and with Louisville & Cincinnati!</u>"[17]

Now writing in terms of a separate league, Hulbert revealed the strongest lure for the appropriate eastern clubs to join his new enterprise, "The one club to [a] city ... will prove the strong point—for all cities cursed with two clubs [we] get Boston, Hartford, Mutuals & Athletics to agree to <u>that</u>, and the rest is easy...."[18]

Hulbert even expressed a growing optimism about William Cammeyer, the Mutuals man, writing that "Cammeyer would go <u>with</u> us, if he thought we were pretty sure to succeed."[19]

Perhaps one of the most powerful psychological forces that helped Hulbert unite the western owners was the overwhelming emotional effect of their being brought in on a secret, of being trusted to keep it and of being part of a great endeavor. The chance to make money, to make a great deal was in itself a powerful incentive, but to be part of a secret enterprise could have been even more powerful.

Winning over owners and executives was not Hulbert's only problem. Like the politician who has to deal with spurious suggestions from the opposition, Hulbert was plagued with handling a number of inane ideas floated in the nation's press. One such inanity was the continual advocating of a 15-team league with each club playing the other six times. Hulbert noted in his early December letter to Fowle that "should we consent to this we all burst—all go to the bottom together."[20] It essentially meant playing a plethora of poor teams before few fans. Hulbert's rebuttal was to "get up an argument irresistible."[21] Hulbert's motto for this method of dealing with advocates of positions anathema to him was his "molasses now—vinegar later on"[22] philosophy.

The person whose ideas were most resented, most distrusted and most disturbing as far as Hulbert was concerned was Henry Chadwick. Hulbert would write of his and Spalding's feelings concerning America's first sportswriter in one of his many autumn 1875 letters: "We don't like Chadwick ... we don't expect to prevent his saying anything it suits him to say. We <u>do</u> mean to strip him of the <u>Official</u> character he has assumed.... Personally, I so dislike Mr. Chadwick.... To a great extent it is more his manner ... to which I object.... There is a want of <u>fairness</u> running through everything he writes.... We <u>must</u> throw this man off."[23]

Besides the endless recommendations floated by Chadwick, there was a seemingly endless agitation by New Haven to stay in the majors. Of all the eastern clubs in the National Association, New Haven was the *enfant terrible* as far as Hulbert was concerned. He wrote in a letter of November 16, 1875, to Charles Chase that the including of Hartford and excluding of New Haven would be a thorny piece of controversy. He noted that the small clubs were getting anxious about their chances of remaining in the association and explained having received a serious letter from the New Havens. It asked Hulbert to aid them by demonstrating from Chicago's books that New Haven paid Chicago as much for games as Hartford did. "It's true they do that," Hulbert admitted, "but when away from home they don't begin to draw as the Hartfords do."[24]

New Haven's and Chadwick's griping were minor matters compared to the distraction of the real threat to the linchpin of his whole strategy to remodel the National Association and build a pennant-producing baseball team. It surfaced in a letter from G.W. Thompson of the Athletic in early October 30. Noting that he was writing Hulbert at the request of Mr. Anson, Thompson explained that Anson did not want to leave Philadelphia and would like to be released from his promise to play for Chicago in 1876. Thompson then noted that "Mr. Hines [Paul Hines, a Chicago outfielder who was supposedly going to Philadelphia] had told him that he did not want to come to Philadelphia." All this was windup, Thompson's pitch then followed as he wrote, "Would it not be as well for all of us to let them stay as they are? We do not, and supposed you do not, want men who are unwilling to play!"[25]

Thompson's solution to the situation might seem simple and logical to an outsider, but to a baseball insider it was not. Anson was a player of Ruthian stature. He would play in the National League for 22 years, bat .329, fall five hits short of 3,000 and be elected to the Hall of Fame. Hines would play 16 years, bat .301 and collect 1,881 hits in the National League. None of this was known in 1875, but anyone the least knowledgeable about baseball at the time who compared the pair

Chicago and Philadelphia vied for the services of Adrian (Cap) Anson prior to the 1876 season. Anson, a future Hall-of-Famer, was reluctant to come to Chicago, where he would win fame as an awesome hitter and notoriety as an outspoken racist. (Transcendental Graphics)

with an objective eye or two would conclude that Hines was a very good player and Anson a very great player. Anson had played five years in the National Association and hit .329. Hines had played four years and hit .302. Both Thompson and Hulbert were at least knowledgeable, but neither could be expected to look at the situation with one objective eye, let alone two. Thompson was making a bid to keep Anson, the best prospect, and was offering Hines as sop. Most interestingly, he ended his letter with a ploy of practical and psychological significance: "P.S. I see some very sensible remarks in your 'Tribune' of 24th regarding next season's club, which I hope are the views of your management. There ought also be some decided action, to prevent pool selling [a form of wagering], which is fast ruining the game; we have had a very unsuccessful season, and attribute it mainly to this cause."[26]

Thompson was telling Hulbert that he liked the ideas Hulbert was pushing through the *Tribune* and did not want to alienate himself or his club from any alliance with Hulbert or his club. Thompson knew the *Tribune* spoke for Hulbert and Hulbert knew Thompson knew it. That P.S. may have encouraged Hulbert to try and keep both Anson and Hines and the friendship of Thompson and the Athletic. He'd only have to play the game of power politics properly.

Hulbert began his power play for Anson with a reply to Thompson on November 5, arguing, "Our main incentive (independent of Anson's being an excellent player and an upright man) for seeking to engage Anson was—the fact of his being a Western man."[27] Hulbert explained that he desired to collect "a distinctively western nine"[28] and followed this with a touch of reconciliation, writing, "I agree with you when you say the pool box is ruining the game. We will gladly join you in any effort you may devise to break it up."[29] Hulbert consistently mixed considerable molasses with his vinegar as the ploy by ploy of their correspondence acted itself out.

Beside not wanting his contractual coup reversed, Hulbert probably feared the possibility of Anson teaming with the hard-hitting Levi Meyerle in Philadelphia. If both had a good year, the Athletic might have too much power at the plate. Hulbert turned down an offer by Anson to pay the White Stockings $1,000 to be released from his contract and asked Anson to honor his word. Hulbert argued that it was a case of a contract being a contract and a man's word being his bond. Hulbert may have targeted Anson's primary weakness, his conscience, with his appeal to Anson's honor. The struggle ended shortly after Hulbert's demand. Anson would play for the White Stockings in 1876. Anson must have considered himself a man of honor. This view would be severely questioned in later decades as Anson's virulent hatred of blacks manifested itself.[30]

4—Western Wooing

Baseball historians William McMahon and Robert Tiemann note that "in the value system of his time [Anson] was regarded as a man of integrity.... [He] epitomized the WASP values of the late nineteenth century, which, unfortunately, included a belief in white supremacy.... In his autobiography Anson repeatedly refers to the team mascot as a 'little coon,' treating him as sub-human."[31] They summarized Anson's character and career as player and manager, noting that he was "strict to the point of rigidity ... decried his players' drinking and smoking [and was] a sanctimonious prig."[32]

Ezra Sutton decided to stay in Philadelphia and play for the Athletic.[33] Hulbert didn't challenge Sutton's decision to stay in Philadelphia; his acquisition would only have been an extra piece of insurance.

Hulbert culminated his carefully arranged courtship of the western owners by holding a secret meeting with St. Louis' Charles Fowle and Campbell Orrick Bishop, Cincinnati's Josiah (Si) Keck and Louisville's Walter Haldeman and Charles Chase on December 17 in Louisville. Hulbert's purpose is shown in a letter he wrote to Fowle before the meeting: "You and I can carry the day for everything we want. Then, firmly established with four powerful clubs welded together, we can easily influence such of the remainder that we desire to join us."[34] Hulbert "took shrewd advantage of western resentment of eastern domination to win support for his plan."[35]

The meeting this late autumn day was to make certain all four western clubs would be completely united when they met with the four eastern owners Hulbert hoped to keep in a much revised association.[36] Hulbert wanted to set this crucial meeting of east and west for late January or early February in New York, if possible four or five weeks before the National Association would hold its regular convention in New Haven on March 1.[37] Various members of the National Association executive were already talking publicly of instituting a pile of reforms.[38] To take a phrase from one of the cruelest sports of the time, Hulbert wished to beat them to the punch.

With Fowle and Keck already in total accord with Hulbert, the Louisville meeting went well. The western representatives had little to no difficulty adopting Hulbert's constitutional and conspiratorial conspectus (a term used several times to mean Hulbert's ideas and general point of view).[39] Acceptance of Hulbert's proposals probably wasn't so much that the St. Louis, Cincinnati and Louisville owners avidly desired a policy of no beer and no Sunday baseball as it was their realization that they either accept Hulbert's proposed new league or stay in an unchanged National Association. The latter was simply too unpleasant and unprofitable an alternative to consider.

The western owners' acceptance of Hulbert's manifesto was aided by their awareness of the depressing economic realities of the National Association. It was little wonder that the western bosses were willing to follow a man who proposed a rule that, barring rain and acts of God, every team must complete every game on its schedule.[40] The incompetence of the National Association executive, having run a league in which each team decided which games it would play and which games it would not play, was acknowledged.[41] Hulbert's logical plan, based on realistic business principles, was also accepted. There was no difficulty in choosing sense over nonsense.[42]

It appeared that acceptance of the idea of presenting a Simon Pure league to the public led the owners to examine anything that might detract from such an image — crowd control, keeping riffraff out of and away from the ballpark and such.[43] It became an iron-hard requirement that each club hire sufficient police to maintain adequate order within and around the confines of the club's playing grounds.[44] The western owners agreed to back literally every Hulbert proposal advanced for the new league.[45] There would be an entrance fee of $100, no paltry $10, to insure that dreamers and schemers could not get in with an utterly inadequate team. No club would be admitted from a city having fewer than 75,000 inhabitants, except by unanimous vote.[46] A cascade of unspoken thoughts probably accompanied discussion of this exclusionary clause. Hulbert may have silently sighed that this should take care of New Haven once and for all.[47] Haldeman and Chase may have been pleased that this kept a Memphis club from creeping in and replacing their Louisville club as representatives of "The South." Adding the concept of territorial exclusiveness (an idea relatively new to 19th Century athletic enterprise) that "no club would be admitted from any city within five miles of any club in the association" was a clincher. Each owner and executive, all followers of free enterprise felt it was best to be free of any rival enterprise invading their city.[48] All agreed such an exclusionary clause would eliminate the nuisance applicants from places with nine players and 9,000 inhabitants. Any chance the St. Louis Reds would be a threat to the Browns, or that the Covington Stars (just across the river from Cincinnati) would compete for a place in the sunshine with the Red Stockings was dissolved. It would have been a rare owner who would have rejected Hulbert's proposal that the league directors would have exclusive and absolute charge of all league affairs. The westerners saw Hulbert and his agenda as the guide to their respective team's popularity and prosperity par excellence.

A number of details were agreed upon. Umpires would be paid a nominal wage[49] and would be chosen by the home team from a list of five submitted before game time by the visiting side.[50] Acceptance of this proposal was probably based on the fact that modestly paid umpires would keep league and team costs down.[51] The submitting of several names for an umpire by the visitors coupled with the acceptance of one of them by the home team insuring a reasonable shot at fairness was probably of lesser concern. Hulbert's attempt for purity was purchased with economic caveats.

The western owners' symphony-style harmony suggested Hulbert's chances of making the new league a reality were getting better every day. They would go east with drafts of a constitution, by-laws and playing rules and would present a united front to the eastern owners.[52] This should prevent the old National Association guard from ruining everything.[53] The western teams' trust in Hulbert was exemplified by the owners deputizing he and Fowle as their proxy holders to the upcoming eastern confrontation. It would be eventually set for February 2, 1876.[54]

If hope springs eternal from the human breast, its converse — despair — could still leap forward forever from the human brain. Hulbert had the western votes in his pocket, but if all the eastern clubs opposed him his side would be overwhelmed. Six of them finished the past season, albeit on foundations of varying fiscal frailty.[55] He still had pause to worry. He'd have to make absolutely certain that only the four chosen eastern clubs (the Mutuals, Bostons, Athletics and Hartfords) came to the meeting.[56] All others must be outflanked somehow. It was a maneuver that might not be as easy as it seemed. So this time, Spalding was chosen to write Charles Chase of the Louisville Baseball Club that misdirection and secrecy would be the key.[57] Hulbert's solidifying the west behind him didn't raise any eyebrows in the east. This was primarily because the essential contents of the December 17 meeting were kept secret by the western owners. Neither Meacham nor Louisville owner Haldeman, who was also the editor of the *Louisville Courier-Journal*,[58] felt any pangs of reportorial conscience over not publishing their real understanding of all that was going on. Haldeman, like Meacham, was after all, a member of that great fraternity, the press, which truly believed in freedom, particularly its own freedom to pick and chose what it should publish.

As Christmas neared, the press seemed occupied with the upcoming festivities common to this Yule-side time. Tidings of good will dominated. There was a story about Boston's financial good fortunes. The team had made $3,261.07 in 1875. That should make them happy. Pleased people were always more open to persuasion.[59] Josiah Keck, already one of Cincinnati's major meat packers, was now officially the city's baseball club's president.[60] It had been a foregone conclusion when Hulbert had dealt with

Keck earlier in the month. He should be able to field a solid club. Cincinnati spawned the first professional team that was so good they didn't lose a game for a year and a half.[61] Hulbert probably hoped Keck wouldn't be quite that successful this coming year. He would not, however, want Cincinnati, or any other club, to be noncompetitive.

All was still quiet on the eastern front by December 24, 1875, the night before Christmas. A new newspaper, the *Daily News*, had been launched in Chicago.[62] It would provide Hulbert with another publicity outlet. The *Tribune* could always be counted on, as could the *Times*, a real rag specializing in the media's three S's: scandals, sex and sports.[63] If Hulbert's proposed league was ever to survive, it would need all the publicity it could get.

5

All Quiet on the Eastern Front

By January 1876, the possibility still existed that an eastern clique in the National Association could unite behind a competent leader and effectively oppose Hulbert, put him out of business and re-sign his carefully gathered stars.[1] Unsubstantiated rumors and substantiated reports had circulated around the league since the close of the 1875 season that the seceders would be expelled from the National Association.[2] More threatening, however, was the reality that although a few compromises might not derail Hulbert's plans, a few too many might be sufficient to weaken the foundation that a new league would need to attain even a modicum of success. With this possibility of death by a thousand cuts hanging overhead, Hulbert continued to move with dispatch after the western owners formed a solid wall of support behind him. He quickly contacted by post and by person, when possible, the representatives of the four eastern clubs he desired to keep in his league: the Boston Red Stockings, Hartford Dark Blues, Philadelphia Athletic and New York Mutuals.

The Boston Red Stockings presented the least of his problems. As far as Boston president N.T. Appolonio and manager Harry Wright were concerned, the seceder issue had itself seceded. Appolonio and Wright had agreed to play an exhibition game on October 22, 1875, between their Red and Hulbert's White Stockings with the Big Four playing for Chicago before a crowd of Boston cranks. Chicago won, 14–0. One of the largest crowds of the season turned out and cheered the Big Four and both the Red and White Socks from first pitch to final out.[3] Wright and Appolonio were on board. Hulbert appreciated Boston being a stock company, but disliked its ownership being divided between at least 11 owners.[4] This meant the Beantown club had as many owners as it had ballplayers. More importantly, it meant that responsibility for club decisions was more diffuse than with a sole owner team. Such situations sometimes led to a certain lack of involvement by the team's executives as compared to the white-hot intensity of the man who had everything he owned on the line. But this was a compromise Hulbert could accommodate without reservation. Amiable relations between the Chicagoan and the Boston duo boded well for acceptance of his proposal. The amity may also have stemmed from most Bostonians, including Appolonio and Wright, still basking in winning yet another pennant and expecting their Red Stockings to repeat in '76. Such expectations made a certain amount of sense. Harry Wright's Red Socks had dominated the National Association, winning their fourth straight championship in 1875. The Boston faithful, perhaps even its management, might not have expected the loss of four players to cripple a team that had a previous season record of 71–8. The righteous Wright would be a positive presence in any organization and was, therefore, a prize recruit for Hulbert's cause.

The principled, honest-to-a-fault Wright possessed a personality that seemed to prevent him from thinking ill of anyone.[5] He did, however, deeply resent the disparaging accusations often penned by New York–Brooklyn sports scribe Henry Chadwick, who frequently depicted the National Association as being riddled with corruption. To Harry Wrighteous such accusations were slander. Wright felt baseball would be better served if Chadwick wrote of "suspicious play" and "crooked players" much less frequently. Wright felt continual writing on this theme caused the public to get the impression that all games were dishonest.[6] Although Wright's loyalty was sadly misplaced concerning many of the association's assorted crooks, his endorsement of Hulbert's league would be an asset of great public relations value and a counterweight to much of Chadwick's sniping, albeit truthful. Considered by his colleagues as the association's moral pillar, Wright had the potential of being an entire colonnade of morality for any new league.[7] Hulbert's emphasis on purifying the National Association sat well with Wright, who even opposed Sunday baseball on religious grounds.[8] Wright had been urging reforms and since they were not occurring, there was an excellent possibility that he'd throw his whole-cardiac support behind Hulbert and friends. The similarities in belief between Wright and Hulbert practically guaranteed that Boston would be in. It also guaranteed that Wright would become part of the process. As the weeks passed, Hulbert consulted more and more with Harry and got numerous "ideas for changing the structure of baseball" from Wright.[9]

Hartford, coveted for different reasons, was, perhaps, most important for its ability to field a competitive club and for the prestige its aristocratic, socially significant chief executive Morgan Bulkeley brought to a sport needing the Social Register's seal of approval. The son of the founder of Aetna Insurance, a man of prominence and prestige,[10] Bulkeley was the prince among the Philistines. It was of minor significance that he had once asserted that baseball was merely a pastime for him and that he did not devote his full energies to the game.[11] Reasonable ideas based on sound economics should appeal to this Hartford business baron. He should be adequately impressed by Hulbert's dollar and sense solutions to baseball's problems, the dollar part meaning a balanced ledger financially, the sense meaning ideas firmly based in the three R's of business: reality, rationality and apparent righteousness.

Philadelphia presented a serious set of problems. It had the Philadelphias, one of the more dishonest outfits, and its corruption incarnate creatures like George Concannon,[12] but it also had the Athletic—the team's name on the club's letterhead was singular and the newspapers rarely went with the plural—who were Hulbert's compromise candidate for his new league since Philadelphia's other teams had to be excluded. Hulbert, however, had to mend fences with the A's executive. A host of things could derail relations between the Athletic management and Hulbert. The Anson business was, of course, the most recent.

Chicago and the Philadelphia Athletic had been bickering and battling for years. Some said the Chi-Phi feud went back at least to 1871 when Ned Cuthbert signed with Chicago and then successfully jumped to the A's. It continued in 1873 when Levi Meyerle, secretly linked by ink to a Chicago contract, tried to renege. Open warfare flared in 1875 with the Davy Force affair. The Athletic perceived the Force fiasco to be another instance of "Chicago's relentlessly underhanded attempts to sign away its best players, in this case by backdating a contract."[13] The matter turned thermonuclear when the contract "upheld by the National Association's outgoing judiciary committee, was overturned by the Association's newly elected committee ... that was controlled by Philadelphia baseball officers, among them the A's highly detested president, Charles Spering."[14] Hulbert would confide to Campbell Bishop of St. Louis that he wouldn't admit the A's into his league until the A's ousted Spering, which the A's would do at the end of 1875. This didn't change "Chicago's belief (also shared by Harry Wright) that the Athletic were the most uncooperative and unsportsmanlike club in professional baseball."[15] In wooing the A's for membership in his new league, Hulbert was not demonstrating his open-mindedness nor his hypocrisy so much as his ability to accept certain unavoidable unpleasant realities in getting what he wanted. He accepted the necessity of wooing the hated Athletic because he wanted a team in Philadelphia. They were simply the best of a very bad lot.

A's president Thomas Smith and secretary Al H. Wright were "still smarting under the loss of Anson to Chicago."[16] If their "smarting" represented too extreme an emotional upset, then dealing with Smith and

Wright could become akin to a confrontation with Smith and Wesson. The Athletic's head honchos could feel that losing Force had prompted Hulbert to sign Anson, his motivation being more spite than sense, or that his stubborn refusal to let Anson go even when Anson offered to pay Chicago $1,000 to release him from his contract[17] was nothing more than vindictiveness. Such thoughts would turn the most sanguine of citizens to the psychopathic. Hulbert could only hope the Athletic ownership believed what he told them just after the decision, that he truly felt no animosity toward them. This was not true, of course, but lying and deceit has never been much of a negative in business or baseball. Most likely, the Athletic's bosses correctly attributed Hulbert with deep feelings of negativity toward them. But dislike for Hulbert could be eclipsed by his offering exclusive rights to big league ball in Philadelphia. Having territorial rights to the city of Philadelphia would leave the field to themselves.[18] Their competition with Philadelphia's White Stockings, the Centennials, and even the Kleinz club for crank cash would be gone. Prosperity should be guaranteed. Hulbert's transgressions might not be forgiven, but they could be forgotten.

This was the dawn of business-based spectator sport. The reality of this was most significant in the major cities like Chicago, Philadelphia and New York. In the 1860s and '70s, men like Will Cammeyer and Harry Wright had already shown the possibilities of converting baseball into a paying entertainment business, Cammeyer with his invention of the ballpark and Wright with his guidance of the first professional baseball team ever — the 1869 Cincinnati Red Stockings— to national prominence.[19] Even the often idealistic sportswriter, the *New York Clipper's* Henry Chadwick, had admitted as early as 1868 that "professional baseball" was a business.[20] Baseball had changed from an after work pastime for clerks to play to an after work pastime for clerks to watch. People had now begun to buy their entertainment, just as they were buying everything else from vegetables, which they use to grow, to ready-made clothes, which they used to make. Where they used to play games on the village green, they now paid to watch someone else play.[21] Like many social changes, this transformation had developed smoothly, unobtrusively, almost unnoticed. This change was actually just another silent revolution where people would wake up long after the upheaval was over and realize the past was no more. Professional baseball was now for the elite player and the middle and upper class spectator, the people who had enough time, energy and wherewithal to afford a ticket. The amateur baseball of the 1850s was now only a memory. Those who played baseball on a casual basis played at picnics and were watched only by their fellow players and the ants.

Baseball, as a spectator or participant sport, had never been for the poor even in the 1850s, '60s and '70s. Poor people worked. This included young boys, who (someone said) only had time to glance up and watch the rich playing.[22] It has been estimated that 100,000 children toiled in metro New York factories and 15,000 more drifted from one factory to another at this time.[23] This mirrored the entire country. From 1865 to 1900, unskilled laborers earned $1.00 to $2.00 per day, working 10 to 12 hours per day and six full days per week.[24] Since National League games would be on weekdays and Saturdays only, they would be excluded from the eyes of laborers and people of similar income and circumstance. Whoever (Spalding was one) had the audacity to call the game "the great fountainhead of democracy" was either the purest of propagandists or the most feckless of fools.[25] Baseball was now as autocratic as King John and as capitalistic as Adam Smith.

At the same time, baseball was not an upper-class endeavor either. The wealthy, and mainly the *nouveau riche* wealthy at that, did invest their fortunes and time in sports-oriented enterprises, but these were the activities dear to the hearts of the rich such as polo and yachting.[26] Baseball was for entrepreneurs who were reasonably rich and unreasonably optimistic. They were often the athletes themselves, and organized and promoted clubs. Baseball team ownership was not an investment for the prudent of purse. The demography of the mid–1870s crank now differed distinctly from the crowds that patronized pre–Civil War baseball. Before the war they were distinctly on the lower edges of the upper class or upper edges of the middle. Now the cranks were more likely factory hands and office clerks and, ethnically, Irish and German Americans were replacing the predominately English American crowds of the 1850s.[27] The 1870s crank was most likely a man of more than modest means, ticket costs being roughly 20 percent of a worker's daily pay.[28]

The big cities — like Chicago, Philadelphia and New York — were collection centers for factory workers, office clerks and such persons. Baseball had kept step with the march of industrialization and urbanization. This made the most crucial communications, whether conversation, letter or telegram, those between Hulbert and William Cammeyer. The future of baseball appeared to be in the big cities and New York was the biggest of American cities. Without New York, Hulbert's league might not get off the ground. Cammeyer's career as owner-manager of the Mutuals revealed a man of intellect who was clever and quite capable of finding a creative solution to a problem when needed.[29] But he was also a man of flexible character, always opportunistic and quite capable of turning a blinking if not a blind eye when required.[30] Cammy's Mutuals had a history of being suspect; his Union Grounds was a hotbed of gamblers.[31] His New York Mutuals were exclusively a Brooklyn enterprise, but this didn't detract from the team looking like an arrangement to mint money. It was not, however, and never had been. The latest non-cash calamity had been in '75 when Cammy's Mutuals had to compete with the Atlantics, who finished dead last and dropped out of the National Association, but still managed to affect Cammy's team negatively at the gate.[32] The Mutuals had not even been able to come west to complete their final road games in the dying days of the National Association.[33] It was public knowledge that Cammeyer had to bail the Mutuals out at the end of the year with several thousand dollars from his own pocket.[34] That was a crisis of a catastrophic kind for the Mutuals, causing Cammeyer considerable pain. If he made money in a new league, however, he wouldn't be forced to tolerate the hippodroming practiced by some of his players who saw throwing the odd game as the only way to bring their season's earnings in line with the pay packets of players on more successful teams. Including the Mutuals and the Athletic in his plans may not have been Hulbert's idea of an ideal business practice, but business didn't operate in an ideal world. Needing the Mutes and A's, Hulbert would have to hide his distaste with doses of diplomacy, deception and duplicity.

Owner-manager of the morally suspect New York Mutuals, William Cammeyer is one of baseball's most controversial figures. His tolerance of shady play and his inability to make the Mutuals a money-making machine were negatives. His pride in owning the Mutuals and the ballpark they played in and his love of baseball were positives. He was welcomed into the new league with considerable reluctance. (National Baseball Hall of Fame Library, Cooperstown, N.Y.)

Hulbert's attempt to form a new league probably was not perceived by anyone as anything more than another attempt to get a viable baseball association going. The National Association of Base-Ball Players had first met in '57 and had became a permanent body in 1858. Its founders had drafted a constitution and a set of by-laws, but it had been a loosely knit organization and had failed to stabilize its rules, schedules and club membership. It was followed in 1871 by the National Association of Professional Base-ball Players, which was now appearing to go the way of all flesh. Prior to the National Association's formation, it had not been uncommon for games to dissolve into riots. With drunkenness rampant, betting extensive and ethnic rivalries common, disputes had often flared into conflagrations of fists, curses, gouges, bites, blows and kicks. The Troy Haymakers, run by ex-champion prizefighter and machine politician John Morrissey, and Boss Tweed's New York Mutuals engaged in epic wars in the late 1860s more worthy of analysis by Karl von Clausewitz than Henry Chadwick. Grass tainted with blood and ballplayers with bruises, scratches and bone breaks would be vividly described.[35] Lucas and Smith have argued that this constant bickering arose as baseball was played more and more by the masses, who lacked the British upper class notions of sportsmanship and fair play that characterized the 1840s and 50s.[36] Tyrrell noted that until the late 1850s, baseball matches were models of decorum, but during the next 15 years, riots were not uncommon.

It had also been an era of colorful characters, of men like Fred Waterman, a third-sacker with the original Red Stockings, who seemed to survive on less sleep and more booze than any player who ever drew on spikes. More than one crank must have quibbed, "Waterman! What a misnomer!"[37] The National Association had followed and probably tempered the violence somewhat, but the N.A. had been equally well stocked with men like the misnamed Waterman. The game's first great pitcher, Asa Brainard, whose name inspired the idea of designating a team's top pitcher "Asa" (later "Ace"), enjoyed his evenings with booze and blondes and often avoided meeting his contractual obligations to show up and play.[38] The National Association's inability to cope with gambling, revolving and hippodroming coupled with its gradual decline in competitiveness reduced its crowd appeal. As sins of commission, like throwing a game, were more and more frequently followed by sins of omission, as in doing nothing about such shenanigans, cranks abandoned the game in larger and larger numbers. The press's freedom to note that "unless crooked players were expelled, they were not really being punished"[39] was matched by the association's freedom to ignore anything the press said.

Expulsion of wrongdoers would be a given for any new alliance proposed by Hulbert. As would league control of scheduling. No longer would scheduling be left to the teams.[40] Hulbert's league would construct "a seventy-game schedule for each club, and [deal] severely with an old problem that had long plagued professional baseball: the reluctance of losing teams to finish their schedules at the end of the season."[41] Teams must play, weather permitting, every game on their schedule in the coming season. Ducking a trip late in the season was a case of economic myopia. Hulbert's ban on gambling, the selling of beer at the ballpark and Sunday games, even rules such as one that limited the privilege of disputing an umpire's decision to the team captains, were based on the basic principle that rules are not made to be broken, they are made to be kept. The player-controlled N.A. had produced inflated salaries, revolving, gambling, scandals, competitive imbalance, unfinished schedules and a profitless enterprise.[42] Hulbert was convinced it was because of its slipshod approach to running a league. The N.A. was a league where "even winners ... could lose money, as [Boston] did in 1872."[43]

His limiting his league to eight teams had historic validity of a sort provided by the National Association seasons of 1874 and '75. Seven teams finished the '74 season. "The year ... had proven that an eight club organization was most desirable as all clubs weathered September and Baltimore only dropped out about two weeks before the close of the season."[44] All seven re-entered the N.A. for the 1875 season, which started with 13 teams and ended with seven. Eight seemed about right. As early as November 8, 1875, Hulbert had argued in a letter to Charles Chase of Louisville for a balanced league. If there were to be four clubs in the west, then there should be four clubs in the east.[45]

Nothing would be definite until eight signatures had committed their clubs to the constitution that presently reposed in unsigned silence in Hulbert's desk. Even then there would be a mass of misunderstandings to iron out. Despite the conversations, communications and cablegrams, Hulbert's message must have been misinterpreted now and then. To begin with, some eastern executives might still question Hulbert's depth of commitment to the idea that each club finish out its schedule. The National Association had winked at the Mutuals' failure to make its final western swing in '75. These people may have thought Hulbert was winking and blinking at reform while twinkling at financial success. They and others may have felt Hulbert's sanctimonious posturing about goodness and such was the same old drivel, since public displays of sanctimony were often necessary in things human. And one owner or other probably felt that Hulbert might clamp down on so-and-so's team, but not on his. The bottom line was that most owners probably didn't care what changes were instituted as long as they brought profits.

The press was informed of the upcoming Wednesday, February 2, meeting of the National Association's Grand Council. The notice implied that nothing of importance was on the agenda. Reading the lines (or between them) suggested that it would be just discussions over the drawing up of reform proposals, minor changes in the rules for the financial organization of professional clubs and a few adjustments to the playing rules. In a sense, this was the truth. In another sense, it was not. The stated objectives were a skillfully designed stratagem that buried the truth beneath paragraphs of puffery.[46]

The invitations went out to the teams Hulbert wanted in his league on January 23,[47] leaving little time for the invited easterners to put together any unified front and less time for those not invited to find out the meeting's true purpose or even the fact they had been excluded. Chadwick received the invitation about a week before the meeting and after reading the notice, decided not to attend. He would later condemn the media releases about the meeting as part of a Hulbertian conspiracy. He didn't put Hulbert's name to it at first and only used the all-encompassing "they" in his stories, claiming "they" had a grand design that, if known ahead of time, would have caused such an outcry that a number of delegates would have been frightened away. His decision not to attend the meeting would have a profound effect on the next century of American baseball.[48]

6

A Day Reserved for Groundhogs

The meeting of the National Association's Grand Council that would become the founding meeting of the National Baseball League was held Wednesday, February 2, at New York's elegant new Grand Central Hotel.[1] It was a gigantic step up from Collier's Rooms in New York where the National Association of Professional Base-Ball Players had been founded five years earlier on March 17, 1871.[2] The difference in elegance of location reflected Hulbert's drive to make baseball not just respectable but crown close to royalty on the American sports scene.

The weather outside featured cold, ice-oriented wind that tore along New York streets, scattering falling snow into a chaos of swirling, twirling whiteness.[3] Simply put, it was a blizzard. Only the brick, stone and wood of the buildings kept it from turning the city into a typical prairie panorama of drifting snow. The snow would bank up against a wall, only to be swept away by the twisting, relentless wind. It seemed as cold as the arctic tundra. Weather watchers recorded air movements of 70 miles per hour.[4] It was a paradoxical setting for the founding of America's longest-running professional summer sports league.

Each of the eight teams was represented by one or more delegates. The Athletic management had deputized G.W. Thompson[5] and Al Reach, an executive[6] who would garner a contract to print the league's official publications if all went his way.[7] Hartford had their owner, the bulky Morgan G. Bulkeley, in attendance. Boston sent N.T. Appolonio, the Hub club's chief executive,[8] and Harry Wright, who would present the upcoming year's playing rules and regulations.[9] New York had William Cammeyer, the boss of the Mutuals. These were the eastern delegates. Nicholas Young, a resident of Washington, was the only other easterner there.[10] He attended as the present secretary-treasurer of the National Association.[11]

Mingling among the eastern men were the two western delegates,

Charles Fowle of the St. Louis Browns and William Hulbert of the Chicago White Stockings.¹² The pair carried proxies from Cincinnati's Si Keck, Louisville's Walter Haldeman, and St. Louis' John Lucas in their pockets.¹³ The western reps were few in number but a multitude in resolution. The man who could have wreaked havoc with Hulbert's machinations, Henry Chadwick, did not attend. In all probability, the absence of Chadwick changed baseball history. If anyone could have derailed the Hulbert express, it was Chadwick.¹⁴

The meeting began with Hartford's Morgan Bulkeley as chairman. He quickly turned the floor over to Hulbert. As chairman of the Western Committee, Hulbert outlined the rationale behind the carefully crafted new constitution and by-laws he and his friends had devised. Fowle read out the 13-point formal draft of the proposed new league's constitution after Hulbert spoke.

Many stories would circulate concerning what happened in the Grand Central Hotel meeting room that cold February day.

Chicago president William Hulbert was the prime mover in founding the National League. Conflicting accounts report he did or didn't lock his fellow owners in the room when he was addressing them at the league's founding meeting. Hulbert described his approach to negotiating with owners, players and sportswriters as a matter of "molasses now, vinegar later." (Transcendental Graphics)

No one but those in attendance would ever know for certain. A collage of conflicting accounts has emerged over the years. The general consensus is that Hulbert locked the main door to the room, pocketed the key, walked to a podium,¹⁵ took out his watch and promised to talk for no more than 60 minutes.¹⁶ There is debate whether Hulbert locked the door to keep intruders out or his audience in. Since the locked door effectively accomplished both, the question is moot. Hulbert started by appointing Harry Wright as secretary for the meeting.¹⁷ In his hour-long speech, Hulbert outlined his blueprint for the destiny of baseball. The concepts were simple: a baseball league run as a business, a league based on morality (no betting, no drinking, no Sunday ball), and so forth.[18] The owners knew much of it from correspondence and previous mini-meetings with Hulbert.[19] Their minds inoculated to the ideas, their brains vaccinated against opposing arguments, the group accepted all that Hulbert advocated.[20] And, of course, there was flattery. Hulbert told them the new league would be run by businessmen, specialists, experts and they were the businessmen, specialists and experts. The players would do what they did best — play ball — and would be the salaried participants.[21] The owners were told their power would be absolute. The job of baseball club executives was to form leagues, secure grounds, erect grandstands, lease or own the appropriate property, make schedules, fix firm game dates, pay salaries, assess fines, discipline players, make contracts with players and vendors;[22] in short, they would control every economic aspect of the sport. Executives would relieve the players of all responsibility for any of the legitimate functions of management[23] and would only require that the players perform at their best on the field.[24]

It was a heady wine that narcotized the critical faculties, an elixir that fed the vanity, an opiate that complimented imagination and intelligence and made all who listened pleasant of personality, pliable of position and absolutely certain of their own superior creativity and cognitive abilities. Despite their overwhelming overestimation of their capabilities, these men still had good business sense. They were astute enough to realize the logic of Hulbert's arguments. They knew he was correct when he argued that although a great deal of money could be realized in the short run by playing on Sunday, not playing on the Sabbath bought considerable credit in the morality market and, perhaps, even more money in the long run. A lot of folks would give grudging and, even more, ungrudging support to a businessman who demonstrated he considered the word of God as being more important than the word of his club's accountant. They agreed that such a stance would be a powerful propaganda force in a game needing the appearance of morality as much as it needed money to survive.

At least two variations of how the National Baseball League's constitution came to be signed would appear in the press. The most consistent to emerge was that after hearing Hulbert's speech, those present had little to nothing to say and simply filed up and signed the manuscript.[25] Neither Hulbert nor any other member who attended ever disputed this scenario. The other version appeared in print from time to time arguing that the principals involved fought over the principles presented.[26] This diametrically different depiction emphasized the conflict between the forces who wished to retain the old association and those who desired an entirely new league. But it appears there was little drama. The National Association, like T.S. Eliot's world, went out with a whimper, not a bang. The meeting evidently progressed with little conflict or confrontation — not much discussing or cussing.[27]

Harry Wright presented the league's playing rules, revised somewhat from those of the National Association.[28] A foul fly would now be in play only if caught in the air,[29] ending the practice of a player charging over to a foul ball, then pulling up short and picking it off on a lazy bounce for an out. Now it would be an all-or-none rush to catch the ball.[30] A base runner could now return to his base on a foul grounder without any risk of being put out.[31] This encouraged more running. Now a runner on first, for instance, could charge for second on a grounder down the third base line and not worry about it going foul and having to scramble all the way back to first to keep from being thrown out. The runner could just keep charging for second until the umpire indicated "fair" or "foul" ball.[32] It was a good rule and so was the first. Great games do not spring full-blown in all their intricacies. Rules, like living things, evolve, as do apples, apricots and associations. The men at the meeting probably hoped that the rule changes would lead to better attendance. Images from past seasons of rows and rows of empty benches at a third to half of all 1875 games haunted the meeting.[33]

The oddest of the proposed rule changes seemed more a mutation than a worthwhile alteration in the body baseball. It involved the third strike. Essentially, it said that a batter with two strikes on him *may* let a good ball pass, but he is to be warned "good ball" by the umpire.[34] It was a curious accommodation. Why not just have four strikes? The rule should have raised a tidal wave of protest, questioning, speculation and counter-speculation, but it did not.[35] Perhaps it passed because the hour was late, the stomachs present were empty and growling, and the heads aching. Whatever the reason, the rule passed quickly. Of course, there was also the very good possibility that any rule good or bad presented by Saint Harry was a little like the Israelites agreeing to follow the edicts Moses brought down from the mountain. Wright was perceived to be integrity incarnate.[36] The most vehement of reprimands he was reputed to have ever handed out was when he reminded his team after a loss that they "needed a little more ginger."[37] He had been a fair to average baseball player in his day. His friends of winter recalled, without a hint of mockery in their voice, that Harry was a very, very fine figure skater.[38] The rough-and-tumble men of baseball in the 1870s deeply respected Harry Wright.[39]

Most of the various rules and regulations accepted were expected and respected. A standard admission charge of 50 cents passed without a murmur of heart or tongue.[40] It was in line with prices charged for other forms of entertainment.[41] More important decisions, such as expulsion of the New Haven club and the Philadelphia White Stockings from the National Association, were achieved by circumvention. The Hulbert-nominated teams that were technically still in the N.A.—the Boston Red Stockings, Chicago White Stockings, Hartford Dark Blues, Philadelphia Athletic, New York Mutuals and St. Louis Brown Stockings—formally withdrew from the National Association. Then these six sides plus the Cincinnati Red Stockings and Louisville Grays formed the National Association of Professional Base Ball Clubs with each team being voted on for inclusion.[42] The National Association's transformation to the National League was more of a metamorphosis than a birth.

In another clause, no club would be admitted that carried one or more persons of color on its roster.[43] Without debate, reflection or a flinch of conscience, the Grand Assembly of Delegates agreed to a color ban.[44] Supposedly determined to base their new league on a firm moral foundation, the delegates had no intention of risking its future on the admission of blacks. From their 19th century point-of-view, such an action was unthinkable.

Constitution signed, rules and regulations set, the task of electing officers to officiate over the new league came to the fore. Like all that happened during this historic meeting, several versions exist concerning the nomination and election of Morgan Bulkeley as the National League's first president.[45] The stately Bulkeley, 39-year-old president of the Hartford Dark Blues, the portrait of quiet elegance, was an obvious choice.[46] Always dressed immaculately, Bulkeley cut a figure of conservative calm. His sweeping steer-horn moustache, erect soldier-straight posture and serious, stoic countenance made him, on appearance alone, the ideal candidate for almost any presidency.[47]

One grandiose version of the election pictured Hulbert opening a campaign to get Bulkeley elected, delivering an eloquent speech, outlining the qualities needed in a league president and explaining how Bulkeley was so concisely endowed with these qualities. This grandiloquent story noted that Hulbert didn't emphasize that Bulkeley was from the east and that all his good qualities wouldn't be worth six bits if Bulkeley were a westerner.[48] Another story based Bulkeley's ascendancy to less ostentatious oratory, arguing that Bulkeley had simply been nominated by Hulbert. A few words of praise from the big Chicagoan, the nomination seconded by Charles Fowle with even fewer words (I second the motion), and when no one else's name was forwarded, Bulkeley was elected by acclamation.[49] A third variant depicted the club owners as wanting Hulbert as head, but Hulbert wanting Bulkeley to assume the presidency. Hulbert "figured the

Bulkeley name, prominent in banking and politics would lend a touch of respectability to the game."[50] Yet another variation argued that the names of the clubs had been written on identical cards, the first name drawn being named president and a member of the league's board of governors, the next four names drawn gaining places as members of the board. This version argued that Hartford, Bulkeley's club, had been drawn first, giving the stately easterner the post by a mere turn of fate.[51] If this is true, there was an equal chance that anyone, including the Mutuals' William Cammeyer, could have headed the league. It is unlikely that Hulbert and friends would have allowed even a 7-to-1 chance of Cammeyer becoming president.

The National League board of directors, whether chosen or elected, included president Bulkeley of Hartford and directors Appolonio of Boston, Fowle of St. Louis, Cammeyer of the Mutuals and Chase of Louisville. Hulbert, the league's founder, would have no official place in the league's executive structure.[52]

Nick Young would be "re-hired" as league secretary (and treasurer) in the next few days. He had held an identical post in the old National Association.[53] He was competent enough to be relied on to handle the league's correspondence, honest enough to be trusted with the league's meager operating funds, and diplomatic enough to handle routine interactions with players and owners. Young was the ultimate survivor who had paid his dues. He had assembled and managed several National Association teams, umpired games, served on numerous committees and eventually worked for Hulbert's Chicago White Stockings. This latter association—combined with a history of pushing the organization of playing schedules as early as 1871, "raiding" rival teams to assemble his latest team, speaking out against gambling influences and such—reflected a Young mind attuned to resonate on Hulbertian frequencies.[54] He would be described to the press as "a gentleman of intelligence, honesty and good repute" who was "versed in baseball but not connected with the press or a member of any pro club."[55] As secretary, Young was also responsible for writing more than the occasional press release.[56] This last skill blended well with Young's having an attitudinal history so reflective of Hulbert's viewpoint.

Probably of most interest to the average crank was that each team in 1876 would play five home and five away games against every other league team over a season that would run from April 22 to October 21.[57] That allowed for a three-game-per-week schedule with plenty of time to make up rainouts and to schedule extra games against non-league teams.

There was no mention of the founding meeting in the papers of February 2 or 3. The *New York Times* of February 3 covered the New York Yacht

Club elections and a pit dog fight.[58] The *Louisville Courier-Journal* reported that the practice uniforms for the Louisville Grays had been ordered and plans were being made for a mid–February trip to New Orleans.[59] The sports news in Meacham's *Chicago Tribune* focused on the turf and pedestrianism. A pair of female walkers were continuing a contest at the armory of the second regiment in Chicago.[60]

Perhaps it meant nothing, perhaps it was an omen, but the tail of the storm that raged through New York this historic day trailed its windswept wildness through Philadelphia, taking the Jefferson Street grandstand where the A's played to the ground as it passed.[61] Windstorm or snowstorm, the National League of Professional Base Ball Clubs was a reality, but it had only begun.[62] The test of the game was going to be in the playing. It was, as Churchill would have said, the end of the beginning.

7

Press Reaction

Within less than 24 hours of the formation of the National League of Professional Base Ball Clubs, the National Centennial Athletic Association of New York was formed to promote pro and amateur track athletics. The New York Yacht Club held its annual elections and an international rifle match was set up between the U.S., England and Scotland.[1] Five days later, the National Trotting Association's annual convention opened.[2] Organized sport was coming of age in America.

On February 4, 1876, the *Chicago Tribune* covered cock-fighting, female pedestrians, prize skating and the turf. It also informed the Chicago public of the founding of the National League of Professional Base Ball Clubs. On reading the *Chicago Tribune* that day, Hulbert and Spalding must have smiled with the deepest of pleasure, savoring each word as if it were a cream-centered chocolate bonbon. Success, the ultimate elixir! They must have read and re-read the first few lines just for the heaven of it:

> BASE-BALL.
> A NEW ERA.
> Special Dispatch to The *Chicago Tribune.*
> NEW YORK, Feb. 3.— The most important measure ever adopted by the professional baseball clubs of this country has been considered and approved by a council of representatives of the eight principal clubs of the country....[3]

The *Tribune* went on to treat the National League's constitution as if it were a new Declaration of Independence. In a way, it was.

Press reaction to the league was abundant and mixed; even some newspapers from cities granted National League franchises were critical.[4] The *Hartford Times* accused the league of tossing out 20 players, the greater number of whom were honest, by excluding New Haven and Concannon's Philadelphias.[5] League defenders could argue that the better players would be hired within weeks by the new National League teams. Six weeks later, the *Philadelphia Item* would note that, despite the National League's barring the Philadelphia White Stockings, the N.L. teams had engaged almost all the players on Concannon's 1875 team by mid–March.[6] The *St. Louis Globe-Democrat* was as frank as any, arguing Concannon and his club were out because of a repugnant reputation and New Haven was out because it had not proven itself a bona fide organization since it failed to make a scheduled western trip in 1875.[7] The *Globe-Democrat* noted that the Philadelphias were also barred because the city was already represented by the Athletic while the Mutuals were admitted because adequate gate receipts in New York could come from that club only. The *Globe-Democrat* even named the Mutual players, the three H's from Hades who were considered dark of deed, Nate Hicks, Dick Higham and John Hatfield.[8] Libel suits involving ballplayers were neither likely nor expected to be expensive.

Hulbert's explanation that the National League had rejected Concannon's Philadelphias due to the team's abundance of "crooked players" seemed to be supported by the press. But a good number of papers felt the Philadelphias' exclusion and the Mutuals' inclusion composed a picture of hypocrisy.[9] Starting a new association based on honesty, integrity and high morality with the largest city in the proposed circuit fielding a team with the questionable character of the Mutuals wasn't the most plausible position to defend. The fact that the Philadelphias never had a chance to be heard in their own defense also irked the sensibilities of a few editors.[10]

The *Philadelphia Times* had nothing but high praise for the new league. Baseball, the *Times* said, would no longer be left at the level of the dog or cockpits. The *Times* felt the game would not only be elevated by its rejection of the dark side of 19th Century sport, but would bring back lady spectators who would, in turn, provide baseball with their restraining influences, further elevating the status of the sport.[11]

As expected, the *New Haven Register* was negative.[12] The New Haven team being rejected because the city incorporated fewer than 75,000 people while Hartford, which also had fewer than 75,000 people within its boundaries, was a contradiction bound to generate controversy.[13] After pointing out this inconsistency, the *Register* noted that New Haven was a genuine stock company and not, as evidently erroneously labeled at the meeting, a cooperative nine.[14] The *New Haven Union* insisted that New Haven did everything to comply with being in the league.[15] Another New Haven paper, the *Palladium*, thought New Haven a sound club and thought that the team would apply to enter if the new National League really did exist.[16] The latter part of the sentence must have enraged Hulbert and company. Did the *Palladium* think the league was a figment of propaganda?

The *St. Louis Globe-Democrat* argued that the Mutuals were obviously only included for the team's gate receipts and said, "This club has been accused of more crooked playing than any other."[17] The *New Haven Register* noted the National League directors argued they were only open to stock-company organizations, but had admitted the Mutuals, who had been a player-run cooperative ever since a money-strapped Cammeyer had been forced to let the players share in the team's meager profits.[18] The *Register* accused the National League's officials of not acting in good faith.[19]

In general, however, far more papers were in favor of the new league than were against it. The press was basically for the National League because the fourth estate supported any organization that would clean up the gambling, drinking and associated corruption which was contaminating baseball and turning it into America's irrational pastime.

The leader of the reportorial minority who opposed Hulbert's creation was, as Hulbert had predicted, Henry Chadwick.[20] Part of the reason for his anti–N.L. stance was personal. He was hurt and angry, deeply resenting being snubbed by the league's founders.[21] Hulbert and Spalding had only talked to him about minor changes to the old National Association and hadn't involved him in any of their discussions about the new league.[22] The premier sportswriter in America, the originator of the box score, writer of dozens of rules and regulations and leading promoter of the game,[23] was livid. He had devoted his life to the improvement of the game, always striving for the best with favor to none.[24] The "Old Veteran"[25] of the game was simply overwhelmed by his being left out. Usually a gentle person of precise manners, Chadwick, for a number of weeks, at least, wrote with an acidity that belied his customary courtesy. His pen was dipped in the venom of self-righteous indignation. His vehemence was fueled most assuredly by the fact that, in his heart or more exactly his rational mind, he was not certain whether the new league was a clear improvement over the National Association or not.[26] His writing betrayed as much. He wrote of the crooked play in the old National Association, particularly so prevalent in Philadelphia and Brooklyn, then semi-excused these transgressors by noting the larceny was not exclusive to these two cities.[27]

Chadwick's logic was neither Newtonian nor Copernican. It was Chadwickian, sometimes brain poor, sometimes very insightful.[28] Chadwick had read the dulled-down notice sent to him announcing the upcoming February 2 meeting in the exact way Hulbert had wanted him to read it. The notice, of course, had portrayed the meeting as being another useless get-together only concerned with trivia.[29] The latent message was that reporters need not attend. Chadwick got the message, but did not realize it masked ideas of deeper intent.

In his first writings on the meeting, Chadwick seemed to have considerable opinion and considerably less fact.[30] He was still writing enthusiastically about the National Association in the *Clipper*'s February 19 edition.[31] His Chadwickian wanderings of mind did not just appear in his comments after the league's formation. The main thrust of his pronouncements on February 5, written before he knew the National League had been formed, seemed to be that Chicago was to be the first truly western club in the N.A. since it was staffed with western-born men. But a few paragraphs later he would suggest that Chicago was as eastern as elegance. Still later, Chicago was proclaimed a western club again.[32] The whole process of reading Chadwick's copy that day must have left many readers with a headache.

On February 12, 1876, the *Clipper*, the bible of baseball, the foremost sporting paper in America, finally published its first story directly focused on the National League. It, of course, was written by Chadwick. Almost every paper in the country concerned with baseball news had already covered the meeting. The *Clipper*, a

Henry Chadwick, who popularized baseball and codified the game's rules in the 1850s and '60s, was America's premier sportswriter of the 19th Century. Shunned and stunned by National League founder William Hulbert, who kept him from sharing in the development of the league, Chadwick bitterly criticized the way the N.L. was founded, but soon came around to supporting it. (Transcendental Graphics)

weekly, appeared on February 5 and February 12. The first mention of the new league appeared in the *Chicago Tribune* on February 3. The February 2 meeting and inauguration of the National League caught the *Clipper* at press. The February 12 *Clipper* called the league's formation a startling coup d'etat, criticized the founding as being entrusted to inexperienced men, suggested the meeting could not be called a convention and asked why the founders couldn't have openly discussed all at a general convention of the National Association.[33]

Chadwick's criticism of the National League detailed inconsistency after inconsistency. The league claimed to strive for purity of player, but did not prohibit the re-engagement of any suspect National Association player. The Philadelphias had been turfed out for questionable play while the equally questionable Mutuals were allowed in. The stock company New Havens were out of this so-called conference of capitalists while the cooperative Mutuals were in. No city of less than 75,000 was to be let in, so little New Haven was excluded, but little Hartford was in.[34] Probably motivated by the wishful thinking of the utterly upset, Chadwick's writing was peppered with pessimistic interpretations of crank acceptance of the National League. This onslaught lasted for a number of weeks. On February 19, Chadwick wrote that many cranks were aroused against the duplicity of the National League.[35] By March 26, Chadwick concluded that "the unjust actions of the Chicago and St. Louis clubs has awakened quite a sympathy for the New Havens, who have a strong pro team now, in the East."[36] The veteran sports scribe appeared to believe that both the National Association and National League would operate over the coming summer in a cauldron of discontent.[37]

Chadwick's campaign continued. He wrote that the National League "had an eye to the profits, and not to the interests of baseball."[38] If he was still reading Chadwickian columns, Hulbert would have agreed with what he probably considered a half-truth. To Hulbert, the league had its sights on both profits and the interests of the game. Chadwick's dire predictions for the future suggested that some men would be ousted soon "who think themselves snugly ensconced in quarters for the season."[39] He argued that the only purpose of a secret meeting could be that "there was some secret object in view which it was not considered desirable to have made public."[40] He accused the National League of not advancing its true reasons for its actions. Keeping the crooked, cooperative Mutuals in the league wasn't being explained to anyone's satisfaction.

The west responded to Chadwick's challenges. The Hulbert-loyal Meacham was probably the harshest of these reactionaries. His malice and contempt went naked when he called Chadwick "the Old Man of the Sea," a dead weight on the neck of the game.[41] He suggested that any argument over the league being an eastern or western idea was a crock of rot whiskey and a waste of time. This particular scarlet herring had the eastern press arguing the new league had been an eastern and not a western idea and the western press insisting the league's inception was a western idea.[42] Neutrals in the argument could only conclude that these editors held the idiotic belief that ideas had origins of a geographic and not a mental nature.[43]

Chadwick's comments came close to the childish in the April 22 issue of the *Clipper*, suggesting that if the western clubs didn't come east first, the eastern clubs would break away and would do quite well on their own. A kind of wishful, spiteful thinking had replaced reason in Chadwick's *Clipper* columns.[44]

The formal printing of the National League constitution and rules did not roll off the press until almost mid–March, the contract having been let to Reach and Johnson of Philadelphia. Baseball, if nothing else, believed in family; that is, keeping any chance of profit within familial confines.[45]

There was much in the National League constitution to attract critical or complimentary comment depending on the reader's viewpoint. It took a two-thirds vote of the member clubs to expel a fellow club for a number of neatly defined reasons.[46] Two-thirds made political sense, destroying any chance of league domination by a block of eastern or western clubs. To get a two-thirds majority, an eastern block of four clubs would need two western clubs to vote its way. The same need for two eastern clubs, of course, was true for a western block of four. Five of eight clubs didn't give you 66 percent, but equaled 62.5 percent, a subtle mathematical nicety that was a stroke of genius. Any club facing removal from the league would not, of course, vote itself out. Hulbert's 66 percent really meant a club facing removal needed more than one friendly other club to stay alive. It was a reality which the league would teeter its tottering structure on by December 1876, when two teams would face exclusion[47] and, because of this rule, could not stay in merely by voting for each other to remain in the league.

The management-labor structure that gave absolute power to a single club owner over a dozen of his ballplayers[48] was of a questionable nature. If ever asked, it would be a close call if the N.L. was within its legal rights to ban the Philadelphias while admitting the rival Athletic or excluding New Haven while including Hartford. The United States Constitution, of course, said what the Supreme Court said. And, most importantly, the Supreme Court only spoke after an argument had been brought and paid its way through the lower courts with the appeal process making each step upward less and less appealing. By then, the Philadelphias and New Haven would be broke five times over and the National League's teams (if the league still existed) would be fighting for the 1895 pennant. With such a reality courtside, the National League executive curtly and conveniently, and in all practical correctness, blithely ignored the possibility that their doings might be unconstitutional and went about their business as usual.[49] It was the American way.

The players were hired hands, having no elected representatives, no voice in the conduct of league affairs and no justice through a court of their peers. The name change said it all. The National League of Professional Base Ball Clubs had replaced the National Association of Baseball Players.[50] While readers were digesting the intricacies of the league's rules and regulations, its most ardent booster, Al Spalding, was trumpeting the league as another triumph of capitalism.[51] He and his brother, J. Walter Spalding, were also in the process of opening their Chicago baseball emporium at 118 Randolph Street.[52]

Many of the threats Hulbert had anticipated against the formation of the National League never materialized. No one, not even George Concannon, led any significant insurrection against Hulbert or his new league. Concannon tried a few stratagems. He voiced his opinions at a February 10 meeting of the Philadelphia club, arguing that the purity the Philadelphias tried to introduce was nullified by the clubs who looked the other way when dishonest acts occurred on their teams. These very clubs were now members of the so-called National League. Some of these clubs even re-engaged players who had been discharged by his Philadelphia team. He charged the League's officials with selfish and mercenary motives. In general, Concannon painted himself and his team as honest, upright, forthright and honorable. History judged him differently.[53] Cammeyer and the eastern owners came into the fold like lambs, not lions. A minority within the press, particularly the New Haven papers and Chadwick's *New York Clipper*, printed the bluster of the beaten. As the days passed, Chadwick remained the leading critic of the new league.

As often occurs in bitter rivalries, the antagonists were more alike than anyone would have thought. Both were ethically oriented, wanting a clean, criminally free league. Essentially, they agreed in principle, but nothing else. Chadwick wrote, "For the past year or two we have been calling the attention of professional club-managers to ... put a stop to ... fraudulent play in the form of "hippodroming" ... "selling" or "throwing" of games for betting purposes, practiced by knavish members of the club-teams, and countenanced by still worse club officials."[54]

Although the majority of the press praised Hulbert concerning the new league's reforms, many papers criticized the methods used. Chadwick charged Hulbert with using a star-chamber method of getting his way.[55] The critical elements in the press considered Hulbert's machinations to be of a dictatorial quality, which they were.[56] Even the local *Chicago Union* was critical, calling the league nothing more than a monopoly, which it was.

Hulbert despised Chadwick, whose continuing carping about corruption was the biggest threat to the National League's survival.[57] Corruption itself was not the main threat. The constant hinting of day after day of foul doings was. Talk about crookedness, both real and imagined, had killed the National Association and was the basis of Hulbert's founding of the National League.[58] The National Association could have survived its actual criminality. Chadwick simply did not seem to understand this simple reality. Hulbert's hatred for Chadwick lasted until the Chicagoan's dying day in 1882.

The *Chicago Tribune* continued to be the league's leading proponent and gave themselves (through Meacham's articles) a certain amount of credit for its existence. The *Tribune* praised the league's creators for "planning, engineering and carrying out the most important reform in the history of the game."[59]

February was cold time in Chicago. The city's citizenry stayed close to hearth and fire, reading the paper, writing letters, snoozing, boozing and such. One short little item appeared in the *Tribune* on February 23. A team of 20 men representing Northwestern University had played a football game against a Chicago (evidently non-university) team of 15 the previous afternoon at Evanston. The ground had been frozen solid. Neither goal posts nor line-stakes could be put in. The Chicago 15 had won 3–0 scoring something called a touchdown, or perhaps it was three touchdowns. The story wasn't entirely clear. The teams evidently pounded heads in scrimmage after scrimmage.[60] Odd game, football. Sounded more like body ball. Hulbert and his fellow baseball execs, busy with National League baseball, probably paid scant attention. Many may never have seen a game of football. Hulbert might be one who had, since the Chicago Foot-ball Club played its home games on the White Stockings' ball grounds.[61] More importantly, the long winter shadow cast by these occasional football games was of no significance to Hulbert and his peers. They saw no omen in the slowly increasing popularity of this new game. Baseball's magnates had more immediate threats to consider.

News concerning the activities of the expelled teams slowly trickled into print. It had little to do with any deliberate wall of silence being erected by the remaining National Association teams, but more to do with the slow speed at which the bypassed clubs reacted. Concannon's Philadelphias were thought to be planning a mass migration to Baltimore, where they would apply to enter the new league. It was a possible way of circumventing the one city, one club rule.[62] Time revealed it was a figment of frustrated, wishful thinking with little relation to reality. One rumor suggested the idea may have been a sportswriter's creative craving for filling space. It was difficult to believe the self-serving gaggle of questionable characters left in charge of the National Association would ever do much of anything as a group. The 1870s shady player was an individualist. Organized skullduggery needed time and sophistication to mature.

In a desperate attempt to attain a position in the National League, the New Haven club secretary came to Chicago in mid–February to argue his case. He came to see Hulbert. Everyone evidently knew that the power behind the new league was in Chicago, not Hartford. The New Haven emissary made a complete western tour, stopping in St. Louis, Louisville and Cincinnati to talk to the western executives only after first having spoken with Hulbert. The meetings were cordial; the results, unproductive. Hulbert listened to the New Haven representative, but declined to offer an opinion one way or other. Meacham echoed western opinion on New Haven's plight by noting that the poor fellow might as well have stayed home. Meacham reported that Hartford, Boston and the Athletic were in favor of admitting New Haven.[63] He didn't mention Hulbert's fierce antagonism to New Haven,[64] nor did he describe Hulbert as not being a man to forget or forgive, especially if not forgetting and not forgiving made monetary sense.[65]

New Haven withdrew from the National Association on February 26. The *Chicago Tribune* reported the club's reason for withdrawing as unclear, but speculation ran wild.[66] New Haven was throwing itself on the mercy of the National League's owners as well as dissociating the club from Concannon and the guileful and guilty Philadelphias.

The sports columns of the February press weren't all praise for or condemnation of the National League. The sporting press even had space and time for accusations aimed its way. A rebuttal by one of the N.A.'s most infamous characters, Dick Higham, of all charges against him appeared in a number of papers in late February.[67] Since there always seemed to be charges being discharged against deceptive Dick, readers probably wondered why Higham the Hornswaggler chose this present moment to issue a rebuttal to charges the press had been cascading his way for years. Higham gave the reasons for his behavior, all honorable according to him. Higham noted that, while he was with the Chicago White Stockings in 1875, he failed to win the love of the Chicago reporters. He argued that the press convinced the public that he was responsible for all games the club lost. Higham asked Hulbert to be released. Hulbert gave him an honorable discharge. The *Tribune* quoted Higham admitting that in addition to the release, Hulbert gave Higham $500, "which amount was not my due, nor would it have been until the close of the season."[68] Hopefully, the *Tribune* noted, "It is … within the reach of possibility that Tricky Dick will end his intimacy with professional thieves and become a reputable man."[69]

In a move that fringed the futile, the New Havens applied to join the National League soon after their withdrawal from the N.A. The National League's rules allowed a single 'nay' from any of its member clubs to deny entrance to any team applying.[70] The two-thirds rule concerning kicking a team out of the league did not apply since New Haven was never in the N.L. Speculators on New Haven's chances charted the voting with differing degrees of clarity, but most agreed. Hartford, because of its geographic proximity, was expected to vote "aye." The Athletic management openly admitted to being favorable to New Havens' admittance. Five clubs—Boston, Louisville, St. Louis, Cincinnati and the Mutuals—did not reveal their positions publicly. Cynics might speculate that Boston, with Harry the self–Wrighteous on its pay ledgers, would vote "aye," especially since brother Sam Wright was with the New Havens. Everybody knew blood was thicker than nays. It was unlikely, however, that the New Haven club would get in. The club directors of Louisville cast the eighth and final vote after the bizarre voting process proceeded by an interchange of wires from league secretary to each city (please vote nay or aye to the following…).[71] New Haven was excluded.

There seemed to be some confusion as to how many nays were cast New Haven's way. At first, a Louisville club official was said to have disclosed that it was the eastern clubs that blacklisted New Haven, not the western clubs. Various western clubs were accused of the dark deed by eastern executives.[72] But as time passed, the press dropped the "s." The excluders became excluder and speculation as to New Haven's excluder continued for weeks, the last recorded rumor surfacing as late as opening day, April 22. The unconfirmed accusation was that Cincinnati and not St. Louis, a nominee by many speculators for weeks, voted against New Haven's admittance.[73] Amazingly, Chicago, despite Hulbert's open anti–New Haven stance, didn't seem to be on the suspect list. The New Haven executive accepted the inevitable before March gave way to April, courteously releasing second-sacker Ed Somerville so that he could play for Louisville, and accepting their exclusion from the National League.[74]

New Haven's short time in the sun, a 7–40 record in 1875 in the National Association, was forever over.

The five-year-old National Association met on March 1 as scheduled.[75] But the existence of the four-week-old National League was already overshadowing the aged N.A., which seemed an anachronism in the eyes of almost all baseball onlookers. New Haven didn't even bother to apply for a place in the National Association, having publicly distanced themselves from the N.A. even before the National League rejected their bid for inclusion.[76] The N.A. officials made a constitutional amendment requiring every club official to swear before he took office that he would not countenance the throwing of a game.[77] Most cranks probably felt the laddies did protest too much. Over the next few weeks, Chadwick would write about both the National Association and the National League operating in 1876 and an overall United States championship involving teams from a host of leagues.[78] State and inter-state games (the best of New York playing the best of Ohio) were included.[79] It made for mildly interesting fiction as Chadwick's assault against the N.L. became a zephyr in a coffee mug.

Chadwick's column in the *Clipper* carried a comprehensive account of the National Association convention. The Philadelphias' president, George Concannon, hoped to salvage his franchise and the association. Chadwick didn't say it, but the teams that attended weren't going to strike any fear in the corporate heart of the National League. There were four from Philadelphia, the Philadelphias, Centennials, Kleinz and Atlantics. The other teams included the Quickstep of Wilmington, Delaware; Camdens of New Jersey; Actives of Reading, Pennsylvania; Niahannock of Newcastle; Baltimore, the St. Louis Red Sox and some team calling themselves the New Haven Stars.[80] The association had a considerable collection of teams from tiny towns. The four Philadelphia teams would split the gate into quarters, making them no better off than the village nines, competing against the N.L.'s Athletic for crank cash. Besides a lack of potential ticket purchasers, the N.A. had an even more serious lack of potential big-league class players. Even the majority of the Philadelphias had already signed with National League teams: Mike McGeary, St. Louis; Levi Meyerle, Athletic; Cherokee Fisher, Cincinnati; Charley Snyder, Louisville; Bob Addy, Chicago; Bill Craver, Mutuals; Tim Murnan and Joe Borden, Boston. George Zettlein was listed incorrectly by the *New York Clipper* as signing with the Athletic.[81] That left Concannon's Philadelphias with a smattering of no-name players with aging arms and larcenous hearts. The other teams were even worse off.

Associations and leagues die just like Gibbons said nations die — when their followers cease believing in them. The National Association had no believers, true or untrue. It was kaput to the Germans in Chicago and

Cincinnati, gone and good riddance as far as the Irish in New York and Boston were concerned, and dead as a doornail in a multitude of languages in various cities around the league.[82] The National Association's status tottered, teetered and toppled.

Chadwick continued to castigate the National League, but his wrath continued to wane, and his means of assault was changing. He now wrote about the dissatisfaction of eastern clubs with the scheduling of playing days with the west. The pen of the *Clipper* was focusing on more and more minor problems. His wishful thinking, "Now if the East clubs pull out...."[83] was declining. He still thought it foolish for clubs to offer special individual rewards to players, not because he opposed rewarding merit or professionalism but because individual awards encouraged players not to play for their side, but to play solely for themselves. It echoed an earlier age of amateurism when "playing for fun" overshadowed any professional concept of a "dash for cash."[84] His scolding players for changing teams for something so vulgar as money sounded of another age. It was unlikely that Chadwick considered himself contaminated even though he had, during his career, moved from one paper to another to accept a higher salary for writing about baseball.

Like the National Association, the National League's exclusion of blacks met with little opposition.[85] The democratic *Brooklyn Eagle*, one of several papers Chadwick wrote for, supported exclusion.[86] Chadwick's main place of employment, the *Clipper*, however, had been opposed to the New York State Association's ruling in 1870 "that if any of the clubs admitted were found to be composed of gentlemen of color, their association membership would be voided."[87] The *Clipper* of the time advised black clubs to organize "a National Association of their own."[88] The *New York Times*, leaning to Republican ways and no doubt remembering Lincoln, condemned the N.L.'s ostracism of blacks. *Wilkes' Spirit of the Times*, independent of politics, noted that only in America did color bar a person from playing. George Wilkes, considered a rebel by most news people, argued that it was "not a lessening of dignity nor in the least disparaging" for white men to compete with black men.[89]

John W. Jackson, a black, using the name "Bud" Fowler, played for New Castle, Pennsylvania, in 1872. His teammates were all white. He appears to have been the first black to play on a white team.[90] Aristides won the first Kentucky Derby in 1875 with Oliver Lewis in the irons, but Lewis and many other black jockeys were commonplace aboard horses. For some reason, the aristocratic rich owners tolerated their "dark" riders, probably because their black jockeys were considered on the same track as their black servants. The sins of the nation were being visited on the sports of the society.

8

The Dickens with Great Expectations

Spring training of one sort or other had been a part of the preseason baseball scene since Tom Foley took Chicago south to New Orleans before the 1870 season. That was the year Cincinnati's slick second sacker Charlie Sweasy refused to report until he received a $200 raise to $1,000 per annum. He shocked management, but got the money. He also shocked the 1870 census takers, being the first human being to describe himself as a professional baseball player.[1]

Springtime of '76 saw all eight National League teams exercising and training in March and April, and Adrian Anson playing the part of holdout.[2] There was no horde of players in each camp competing for every playing position. In 1876, most of the choosing had been done long before spring workouts. Spring training was just what it said—training that took place in the spring. It was a hardening of muscles and hands, a sharpening of reflexes, a conditioning of body and mind. Many players trained on their own until the team gathered for group workouts in March.[3]

The requirements for baseball success in 1876 were fundamentally the same as they are today. Outfielders had to be fast, quick off the mark, able to judge the trajectory of baseballs travelling by air, and capable of covering copious quantities of ground to their left or right, front or back in a very limited amount of time. Since most parks had fences situated 400 to 500 feet from home plate, outfielders also had to have the ability to throw for distance. Like today, outfielders constantly shifted to play various batsmen, moved in on ground balls and were required to get the ball back into the infield quickly.[4] Boston's South End Grounds was an 1870s version of a later-day New York Polo Grounds. Architecturally a rectangle, it was "like a bowling alley. It had only one field: center."[5] The first enclosed ballpark—Cammeyer's Union Grounds—had a seating area shaped like a horseshoe with benches on three sides to accommodate 1,500 people. The outfield fences were more than 500 feet from home plate.[6] The best outfield for fields of such dimensions would be a trio of center fielders—DiMaggio, Mays and Mantle, perhaps.

First basemen had to be superb fielders. This was barehanded baseball and the human species hadn't evolved with a web between thumb and forefinger to take infield grounders with one-handed ease. The shortstop was usually the quickest and most agile; the second baseman, similar, but usually not endowed with the strongest of arms; and the third baseman, the most courageous and the infielder with the most powerful arm.[7] The idea that shortstops had to be even quicker of release than the other infielders and have an arm able to throw "strikes" of air-blistering speed from deep short to first appears to have been a more modern tactical concept. Third basemen also had to be willing "body barriers" to outfield-seeking shots that sped from bat to third in a blink of bat time, hence the need to be "plucky." It was believed the pitcher should be the "smartest" man on the field—a requirement now reserved for catchers. Considerable emphasis was placed on the pitcher being a good fielder. The teams of 1876 were primarily one-man pitching propositions. Advice concerning the use of a "change" pitcher, someone to hurl the occasional game, was to keep the faster of two pitchers in reserve since it was better to follow slow with fast, than fast with slow. Pitchers had to have the accuracy to place the ball in high or low areas specifically asked for by the batter and the particular skill to slip the ball through the requested space with speed and finesse so that the batsman couldn't make good contact. Pitchers also had to be able to throw baseballs that gyrated in twists and disappeared into wisps, to have the power to send a baseball through a board fence and the endurance to do this from start to finish, game after game.[8]

Catchers, without mask, shin guards, chest protector, mitt or cup, had to be two steps away from athletic perfection and one step away from insanity.[9] Baseball was a hard game in 1876. Barefaced catchers, catching up close with runners on base, often stood a few feet behind foul tick–producing bats. Their job, as now, was the toughest in baseball.[10] Catchers, as well as second basemen, shortstops and third sackers, also had to be quick of foot, as coordinated as cats and fearless in the face of sliding foes with septic spikes. Flesh could be sliced open instantly by rust-stained spikes with blood poisoning following with microbial malevolence and malignancy.[11] Fortunately, the standard way for a runner to avoid being tagged was to run around the waiting infielder, bend and touch the base from the rear.[12] Sliding might be a rarity, but it did occur, as did collisions. An occasional runner stretching a sure single into a doubtful double or trying to score that all-important run might occasionally hit the dirt like a chilled cast iron or crucible steel plow, leaving a furrow of ruffled dirt for future seeding behind him and ripping into any piece of player blocking his way with hard steel-edged spikes. A bare hand clutching a grass-smeared baseball intent on getting an out would occasionally venture into this zone of contention. A nanosecond later the runner was either out or safe, an infielder's or catcher's hand or leg was either whole or wounded, a runner's face was either scathed or unscathed. This was where skill and bravery combined to keep a man on the team and, if talent and bravado parted company, to remove him. Farmers planted, fields sprouted, managers sorted, teams cavorted and lovers did what lovers always do. These were the rituals of spring.

Handicapping teams was another ritual of spring. It was a primary passion of sportswriters. The *Louisville Courier-Journal* outlined the comparative strengths of the National League's teams as well as any newspaper in the league. Many a crank summarized these essentials in telegraphic memory. Athletic: Only two new men. Almost green at pitcher and catcher. A strong team at the plate. Hartford: Experienced at working together. Will be formidable. Likely to do very well at first, then fade. St. Louis: One of the strongest teams. A force to be reckoned with. No real weaknesses, but talent not expected to harmonize together. Chicago: Rebuilt. Should win pennant. With the exception of third base, a splendid and perfect team.[13] The *Courier-Journal* had Fred Andrus or Adrian Anson slated for third.[14] Mutuals: Far stronger than they were last year. Mathews, Hicks and Start were an exceptional combination. If they were supported as well as they should be (meaning if the remaining Mutes played up to their capacity), the Mutuals would prove hard to beat. Louisville: Too many weaknesses. A couple of players lacking "self-command" (a euphemism for an inability to avoid pre-game alcoholic encouragement). Cincinnati: A dark horse. Not likely to win many games. Boston: Still formidable, but not as good as in '75. "In summing up," the *Courier-Journal* writer said, "we prefer Chicago, Hartford and St. Louis, in the order named."[15] It probably meant, judging from the author's comments on the other five teams, that he believed it would be Boston, fourth; Cincinnati, last; with Louisville, the Athletic and Mutuals muddling along in some indeterminable order in the fifth, sixth and seven spots.[16]

Across the eastern and midwestern countryside, the eight league teams practiced outside on sun-touched afternoons, inside when it rained. As compared with seasons that were to follow, the skill difference between the worst and the best player in the 1870s was considerable.[17] In 1875, the 13-team National Association had been the epitome of the extreme — the composite batting average of the six worst teams was .194, while the combined average of the seven best teams was .266, a difference of 72 percentage points. Simple shrinkage from 13 N.A. teams to the eight National League teams in 1876 probably contributed significantly to the difference of 37 percentage points—a .283 composite average for the top four N.L. teams and a .246 composite average for the bottom four. By 1900, the top four averaged .285, the bottom four, .274—a difference of 11 percentage points. By 1961, the last year of an eight-team National League, the margin had closed to .263 for the top four and .260 for the bottom four. The extreme difference in the 1870s meant a manager had to ensure that his lesser players improved enough to eliminate any glaring deficiency and that his better players stayed motivated to play up to their most skillful capacity.

At Boston, the team that had dominated the literally defunct National Association and that would have been called the defending champions if the N.A. hadn't been headed for the great graveyard of associations, worked under the solemn stare of Saint Wright. Harry was faced with the problem of finding replacements for the four players his team had lost to Chicago: Ross Barnes, 2b, .379 N.A. batting average; Deacon White, c, .347; Cal McVey, of/c, .362, and Al Spalding, p, 207 wins in 263 decisions, the best hurler in the N.A. It was not going to be easy. Harry's Red Stockings were set at third and short with Harry "Silk Stocking" Schafer, .270, and Wright's incomparable brother George Wright, .353. The Boston outfield of Jim O'Rourke, .317, Jack Manning, .282, and Andy Leonard, .321, didn't give Harry much to worry about either, except he'd have to use Leonard at second when young John Morrill, his rookie pivot sacker, was catching. That meant he'd have to work 18-year-old newcomer Lew Brown into the catching spot. Tim Murnane, .263, would be adequate at first. That left pitching. The answer was Joseph "The Phenomenal" Borden, 2–4 in '75. One of Borden's two wins was a game in which the opposition failed to get a hit. Borden was not a Spalding. He had speed, which was essential, but as Chadwick would write: What is pace without strategy? Chad also argued James (Deacon) White would be sadly missed, no matter how good a catcher Tim McGinley was, but Barnes' absence would be less felt because of Leonard's being able to play second base. Chad admitted it was unlikely that Boston would repeat as pennant winners.[18] He was wrong about who would assume Boston's catching duties in '76. McGinley would play nine games for the Hub nine, hitting .150 before disappearing into obscurity as a civilian. Murnane (or Murnan) would move from first to catch 69 games for Boston and bat a respectable .282.

Rumor was that George Wright wasn't going to dominate pitchers like he used to because he had trouble hitting the curve.[19] Pitchers used to fool batsmen by changing speed and location. Now the curve was arcing its way into baseball prominence. George, and all others considered deficient in hitting the ball as it twisted through locations not conducive to consistent hitting, would face a meandering stream of curves all year long. The press did like the way George played so deep at shortstop. They recognized that this allowed him to back up third and second, something no one else in the association could do in '75. The kinder critics in the Boston press, however, argued that George was the ultimate shortstop, possessing range and speed, often tossing the ball behind his back to a waiting second baseman, and being quite capable of making one-handed catches with flair and panache.[20] Sportswriters couldn't avoid mentioning Georgie's elegant looks, either. His long blond curls coupled with a trim moustache, aquiline nose and flashing eyes made him a lad for the ladies.[21] The handsome, dashing and body beautiful infielder was probably sport's original Gorgeous George. His face, complete with endearing smile and topped with wavy hair, adorned the cover of many leading magazines. George simply was the greatest.[22] He was also a businessman. Like Spalding leaving Boston for Chicago in 1876 to open and manage a sporting goods emporium, George left Boston for Providence in 1879 to manage the Grays and open a sporting goods outlet with Henry Ditson.[23]

Outfielder Jim O'Rourke was another Boston star quality player. Ironically, when James Henry O'Rourke first came to Boston several seasons previous, objections were instantly made to his Hibernian handle. The Boston management wanted him to change his name to Rourke. Jim refused.[24] The incident was mostly forgotten by 1876. The simple reality was that to many Americans, the Irish were distinctly lower class. Despite his elegant speech (he would eventually be called The Orator) and his Hall of Fame potential, O'Rourke was still a Celt and Celts were somewhere between a serf and a swearword.[25]

At the other end of the talent spectrum from George Wright and Jim O'Rourke was William Parks, a former outfielder-pitcher for the National Association's Washington Nationals and Concannon's Philadelphia White Stockings. Wright had engaged Parks as Boston's 12th man.[26] Parks didn't have a prominent pedigree, having hit in the low .120s while posting a 3–9 pitching record in 1875. George Wright and Jim O'Rourke could keep Boston close to the top but Harry's Red Hose would win or lose the pennant on the arm of Joe Borden and on the ability of Andy Leonard, John Morrill and Lew Brown to play outfield, second base and catcher, respectively.

Hartford's Dark Blues were a definite pennant contender. To begin with, the Dark Blues had two quality pitchers or feeders (as some cranks called the man under-arming the ball in from the pitcher's point).[27] The elder half of the Dark Blues pitching staff was Candy Cummings, a future

Hall of Famer who stood 5' 9" and whose I.Q. in all probability exceeded his weight of 120 pounds. His sugar-coated nickname was an 1870s term of admiration, being a popular expression for "the best."[28] Bond was quicker, but Candy, in 1876, was truly dandy. The frail Cummings, whose health hovered between poor and pitiful,[29] was King of the Curveball Chuckers, his pitch having no burn, but all turn.[30] The younger half of the Hartford hurling duo was Thomas Bond, a fiery 20-year-old Irishman who already had two years of big-time experience. He had worked 55 games in '74 for the Brooklyn Atlantics and 39 tilts for the '75 Hartford nine. Bond was expected to challenge Cummings for the starting pitcher's position. Behind the plate were the weak-hitting lefthander Bill Harbidge and the veteran 30-year-old Doug Allison (.274 in five N.A. seasons). With two pitchers and two catchers, Hartford had more depth than most clubs. There was a general theory that each pitcher required his own catcher, a man used to fielding the peculiarities of his particular pitches. This theorem for success was seen in Chicago's Al Spalding and Jim White, St. Louis' Grin Bradley and Tom Miller and the Mutuals' Bob Mathews and Nate Hicks. A club had to have a comparable combination of pitcher and catcher or cease to be a contender.[31]

The rest of the Hartford team was similar to the side that finished third in '75, except for the ethically questionable Dick Higham, picked up from Hulbert's White Stockings. With Everett Mills (.281 in five N.A. years) at first, John "Black Jack" Burdock (.265 in four N.A. years) at second and Tom Carey (.283, five N.A. seasons) at short, only third base was suspect. But since the suspect was .243-hitting

Depicted on an Old Judge Cigarettes baseball card, Jim O'Rourke, a future Hall-of-Famer, got the first hit ever in the National League. It was the first of 2,304 hits O'Rourke recorded in a 19-year National League career. (Transcendental Graphics)

manager Ferguson, little was expected to change at the hot corner. Tom York (.267, five N.A. seasons) and Jack Remsen (.247, four N.A. seasons) would most likely be joined in the outfield by newcomer Higham (.288, five N.A. seasons). Judging from Hartford's batting averages, those who saw them as contenders were placing great faith in the team's double batteries: Cummings-Allison and Bond-Harbidge.

The Mutuals, Cammeyer's clan, was the usual amalgam of average players. Pitcher Bobby Mathews had accumulated the worst earned run (2.33 per game) and base hit (11.39 per game) averages in the National Association in '75. With about 150 different players putting in official appearances at the plate, the team's batsmen in the hits-per-game rankings came 8th (Bill Craver), 15th (Jim Hallinan), 34th (Bill Boyd), 43rd (Joe Start), 59th (Nate Hicks), 90th (Ed Booth), 108th (Al Nichols) and 110th (Bobby Mathews). Not reassuring when Chicago had woodsmen ranking 1st (Ross Barnes), 3rd (Jim White), 4th (Cal McVey), 10th (Adrian Anson), 11th (Al Spalding) and 16th (Paul Hines). Even less reassuring when Boston, the perennial winners of the whip pennant, despite player losses, still had hitters ranking 2nd (George Wright), 5th (Andy Leonard) and 13th (Jim O'Rourke) in hits per game.[32] Statistics in the 1870s were not always reliable. The National Association counted on each club to keep a statistical record for its games and to submit them to league headquarters.[33] The owner was motivated to produce good stats for the press and poor ones for negotiations with players. The latter, of course, was hearsay. Besides this, a statistic based on hits per game was not as accurate as hits per time at bat. Worst yet, walks were counted as hits by some scorekeepers and not by others.

Not all the teams' 1876 rosters were finalized. Managers of the weaker teams were still recruiting, looking for a semi-pro or amateur player who'd come cheap, but play rich. This was an era when players advertised for tryouts, often giving an established player's name as a reference to their abilities. Potential players by postal service![34]

Henry Chadwick's prose concerning the Mutuals bubbled with optimism and hyperbole. He admitted in early February that the Mutuals needed a couple of players.[35] Later, in early April, he cautioned his readers that when he wrote highly of the Mutes, he spoke of them, "be it understood, simply in regard to what they are *capable* of doing."[36] With this caveat in mind, Chadwick picked the Mutes to finish at least second.[37] It was great publicity, sold a serious sum of tickets and endeared Chadwick to Cammeyer, who knew that most of what Henry wrote was sometimes unrelated to reality, but neither sportswriters nor baseball owners were in the business of selling reality. Chad could be excused for boosting his hometown team, but to commit to print that the Mutuals were a candidate for at least second place was little more than grist for the gullible. Chadwick argued that if the team was on the "Boston plan" that year, no team would be entitled to win a game from them except, of course, by way of the uncertainties incident to any baseball game. The "Boston plan" was Harry Wright's method of training and managing.[38] Wright had successfully demonstrated its validity by winning four straight association pennants for Boston. It involved what Chadwick called "scientific" play. Wright guaranteed his players were in the best physical condition through rigorous training, got them to work together through constant practice, and, most importantly, applied his regime with a reasonable mix of authority, charm and versatility.[39] If Cammeyer could keep to Wright's formula, everything should turn out right for the Mutes. It was a big IF.

Chadwick's rundown on the Mutuals was best read between the lines. Hicks was a remarkable catcher, peculiar in his style of play, a firebrand with too great a tendency to talk and growl (Chadwickian for "lose his temper"). If Hicks could adopt Deacon White's mildness of manner and complacency of composure, he could share the Chicago catcher's top-seed ranking.[40] The operative word was "could." Chadwick's fantasizing aside, people were what they were. Mathews was an adequate pitcher, but Chadwick described him as having "no superior in effectiveness of delivery."[41] Chicago's ace, Al Spalding, was likely to disagree, as would six or seven other pitchers. It was Chadwick's firm belief that Mathews was as good as he described if Mathews would only take care of himself and go into every game bent on doing his best. Most times, however, Mathews' pitching was something less. Chadwick sometimes wrote of such matters in an oblique way that only hinted at reality. Thus, Jim Hallinan, another suspect, was hard to beat at shortstop as long as he was true to himself, whereas big Joe Start, not a suspect, was a great first-base player, a model of honesty. To draw a conclusion about any player, an astute reader only had to consider which players would be great if they tried—and ask, wasn't a professional supposed to try? The reader need only ask why Chadwick set aside certain players (such as Joe Start) as models of decorum and why certain other players (Hallinan or Mathews) were not so described. Other sportswriters, even the least vitriolic, cast many a Mute as a criminal in a baseball suit.[42] Chadwick was most non-critical when he described the unsavory-of-character Bill Craver[43] as one of the most earnest and effective infielders in the league and a good change catcher. He was blind when he referred to Al Nichols as a promising youngster who had the potential to become a second Charley Smith.[44] The latter played 14 games for the Mutes in 1871, batting .236. Al Nichols would play 57 games for the Mutes in 1876, hitting

.179 and six games for Louisville in 1877, batting .211. Why Smith was a model for comparison was beyond all comprehension, except Chadwick's. Chad also stated that Ed Booth, Jim Shanley and Bill Boyd provided the team with a more than adequate defensive outfield. He may have been correct about the defensive side of a Booth-Shanley-Boyd outfield, but Shanley only played two N.L. games in 1876 and Boyd never played any.

Chad truly wished that the Mutuals were a Simon-pure outfit. What his mind wanted, his mind could well imagine. It was only when he wrote of Joe Start, a truly magnificent and honest player, that his accounts of the Mutuals came across as true. But this was probably only an accident. One suspects he would have called Start a superstar even if he had been a .216-hitting fallen angel. The paper Mutuals were truly a team of Chadwick's mythic imagination. An outsider could only imagine how good or bad they were until he saw them in action for himself. Reading about them in the *Clipper* only revealed a team of Chad's considerable creativity.[45] He noted that the Mutuals were second to none in batting strength, continuing to qualify his remarks with the revealing "we speak of them, be it understood, simply in regard to what they *are capable* of doing."[46]

Long, lean Lon Knight was the nominated arm of the A's for '76. He had worked only 13 games, going 6–5 in the old National Association for the Athletic. Knight's inexperience was balanced by a quad of quality batsmen in George Hall, Dave Eggler, Ezra Sutton and Levi Meyerle. Each was a plus-.300 hitter. The rest of the team was a mixed bag. The Athletic boasted the second shortest and probably the second lightest player in the league in Davy Force, the 5' 4" Tom Thumb of shortstops. Only St. Louis' Dickey Pearce had failed to grow higher than Force, the top of Pearce's pate being a mere 5' 3½" above the bottom of his spikes. Pearce was considerably wider than Force, outweighing Davy 161 to 130. The A's also carried one of the three tallest players in the National League on its roster with Meyerle matching Nate Hicks of the Mutuals and Everett Mills of Hartford in height at 6' 1". The oldest Athletic, West Fisler,[47] a 35-year-old outfielder and middle infielder, was one of the more ancient athletes in the league. Chicago's Bob Addy, at 38, and St. Louis' Dickey Pearce, at 40, were the only older regulars. Like any team, Philadelphia had its optimistic on-lookers who gave the Athletic an "A" for much of what its players did, while others waffled concerning the team's prospects, perhaps following the old adage that if you can't say anything nice, don't say anything precise.

Cincinnati was led by hard-hitting Charlie Gould, their manager and regular first-sacker. His gangly physique allowed him to cover a copious section of ground radiating halfway to second base from his first base position. In an age of defensive baseball, Gould, who sprouted a magnificent goatee, was a tremendous asset.[48] Unfortunately for Cincinnati, he was mostly surrounded by has beens, never would be's and a few who had not quite yet reached their potential. Charles Wesley Jones, who had two nicknames—Long Charley and Baby—and whose real name was Benjamin Wesley Rippay,[49] was the exception. He was destined to be one of baseball's first genuine sluggers.

Although Cincy had put together the first all-pro, all-successful baseball team in '69, it was one of two new entries in big league baseball. Neither Cincy nor down-river rival Louisville had ever fielded a team in the National Association. As a result, both were new to major league ball and both were question marks. Cincinnati was a collection of castoffs from defunct N.A. clubs: men like Bobby Clack, an outfielder with a .139 lifetime batting average, ex-nobody of the Brooklyn Atlantics, so unwanted no team had picked him up when the Atlantics' tide ebbed; Charlie Sweasy, with a .188 lifetime batsman's average over five years of play at second base in the National Association, late of the St. Louis Reds; Sam Field, who was .179 with the wood during eight games with the Philadelphia Centennials and the Washington Nationals; and journeyman pitcher Cherokee Fisher, late of Concannon's Philadelphias and author of a 51–64 win-loss record in five N.A. seasons. Cincinnati's future looked bleak.

Several hours down river, the giants of the west, the Louisville Grays, were also working out. Like Cincy, Lou'ville was composed mostly of players from defunct teams. Their roster (association averages in parentheses) included shortstop Chuck Fulmer (.257) and catcher Pop Snyder (.228) formerly of the Philadelphias; third baseman and shortstop Joe Gerhardt (.227) late of the Mutuals; second sacker Ed Somerville (.211) from the Philadelphia Centennials and New Havens; and outfielder Johnny Ryan (.168) from New Haven. Only catcher Scott Hastings (.295) and Jim Devlin (.275) from Chicago had lifetime N.A. batting averages predictive of future success. Devlin was, perhaps, the key. Louisville manager John Chapman had penciled in Devlin as his premier pitcher for '76. It was a choice based on necessity (there really wasn't anyone else) and observations of present springtime capabilities (Devlin's 6–16 one-year N.A. average with Chicago wasn't worth a predictive penny). Chapman could only hope the pitcher he saw in Devlin these past few afternoons was correct. Otherwise, it was going to be a long season in Louisville.

The St. Louis Brown Stockings had gone 39–29 for fourth place in the National Association in 1875, their first year in the majors. Many sporting souls considered St. Louis, not Hartford, to be the team to challenge Chicago. The boys in brown trim had experience in an outfielder like Edgar Cuthbert, who was gutsy and creative. The record books remembered

Eddie, or Ned as he was sometimes called, as the first man ever to steal a base in organized baseball of any kind. Of course, that was in 1865, more than a decade ago, but Cuthbert gave their outfield a veteran's steadiness.[50] Lip Pike was unfettered speed, lightning on the loose in center field.[51] He owned a .321 five-year N.A. batting average. The Browns' other outfielder, Joe Blong, at least had experience in right, playing 16 games in the N.A., but hitting .143.

The St. Loo infield was experienced, boasting a .309 hitter (five years, N.A.) in little (5' 7", 138 lbs.) jack-of-all-positions Mike McGeary, a solid defensive duo at short and second in converted first-sacker Denny Mack (.240, four N.A. seasons) and keystoner Joe Battin (.267, four N.A. seasons), a team leader in weak-hitting manager Herm Dehlman (.213, four N.A. seasons) at first, and a utility infielder in veteran shortstop Dickey Pearce (.254, five N.A. seasons). Dehlman's dilemma might only be choosing which one of his infielders to sit out. Backstopping wasn't considered a St. Louis problem with John Clapp, a .284 woodsman (four years, N.A.) back of the bat. As far as pitching went, Dehlman placed his team's pennant potential on the arm of George Washington "Grin" Bradley, who had broken into big-league ball in '75 with the Browns, winning 33 and losing 26.

The fortunes of Hulbert's handpicked Chicago White Stockings depended first and foremost on the right arm of player-manager Albert Spalding. A serious injury to any one of a multitude of muscles in Al's arm anatomy could mean disaster. Chadwick noted that the confident (some would say overconfident) White Hose did not appear to have a seasoned backup or change pitcher if anything befell Spalding.[52] More importantly, since it wasn't just Spalding's coraco-brachialis, biceps, brachialis anticus, triceps, subanconeus, pronator radii teres, flexor carpi radialis ad latin named muscles almost ad infinitum et nauseam,[53] but all of Spalding (arm, body, brain, etc.) that accounted for the pitches he threw, Hulbert's Pale Hose was putting its money on Spalding staying a healthy specimen for the entire season. But, of course, all the other clubs except Hartford were also betting on the staying power of a single starting pitcher. Chicago did have a potential change pitcher in outfielder-catcher-first baseman Cal McVey, who had a 1–0 National Association record with Boston in 1875 and who would go 5–2 in 1876 for the White Stockings and end his major-league pitching career with a 10–12 record.

Spalding was admittedly a prize pitcher. In a world of right-handers, Albert had left all others behind, but he was aging in an era and in a game totally groomed for young men.[54] Spalding was plagued with a once omnipotent right arm that couldn't conquer the intricacies of making a baseball curve.[55] This probably bothered Spalding's super-sized ego something serious, but the team was looking like the best in the business. The Big Four from Boston gave Chicago an awesome aura that threatened to addle its opposition into defeat. Besides Spalding, Barnes, McVey and White, Chicago was stocked with a number of players only a little less talented. Paul Hines was a splendid outfielder. No one knew it in the spring of '76, but some perhaps could have predicted that Hines would play 20 years of big-time ball, four with the N.A., would hit .301 and would, in 1878, actually be the N.L.'s first triple crown winner. It was a feat that drew absolutely no attention from anyone in 1876.

Anson was not yet in camp. The big bat from Philadelphia was rumored to be making arrangements to open a racket court in the City of Brotherly Love and, some said, was not going to play ball at all that season.[56] Others said Hulbert was in the "brokerage business" and the business he was brokering concerned how quickly Anson was going to get off his duff and come to Chicago.

With or without Anson, the White Socks' interior defense was considered first class: the trio of McVey at first, Barnes at second and John Peters at short was probably better than most four men infields. Peters was a very active, agile shortstop with about as much range as Texas and Oklahoma combined.[57] The outfield of John Glenn in left, Hines in center and Bob Addy in right was solid.

Only Chadwick's *Clipper*, that alien assortment of gray type run off in faraway New York, had anything critical to say of what other papers were calling Spalding's superb specimens. Chadwick didn't even emphasize the contribution that catcher Deacon White, the best in the league, would bring to the White Stockings. He did, however, clearly note that "the team as a whole is the best the club have ever presented."[58] Chad was also an advocate of the "Anson won't come" cabal.[59]

Chadwick's viewpoint, of course, was a minority opinion. Chicago was expected to win it all in '76. The proof, of course, would be in the hitting, pitching, fielding and playing. Pennants were won with spikes on ground, not ink on newsprint.

9

Picked Nines and the Pick of Nines

Over 2,000 baseball clubs had been active in 1875 and it was expected on the best of statistical authority, namely Henry Chadwick, who kept copious records, that there would be between 2,600 and 2,700 teams in the field in 1876.[1] It was an era when pro teams filled in three or four off days playing college and even amateur teams. This resulted in a constant scramble to choose from an army of adversaries on mutually suitable playing dates. With pro schedules never cast in granite even at season's start, a team's preseason string of games was a makeshift disasterpiece of mismatches. Last second scheduling was common. N.L. teams played picked nines, semi-amateur and amateur teams in their home city after working out indoors and outdoors for a few weeks in early spring. The informality of it all led to more rumors of games than games.

These games were, in general, sad affairs, mostly due to the disparity of team skills. In covering pro vs. picked nine games in spring 1876, the *Clipper* reported the pros over the picked nines 95 percent of the time.[2] A weak Cincinnati team beat Picked Nines 40–0, 46–2, 54–3 and 48–4 during their first few weeks of pre-season play. Sometimes the professionals helped the amateurs with a player or players. In one spring 1876 tilt, which the Athletic lost 8–7, A's pitcher Lon Knight hurled for the Picked People. In a Hartford 16–2 win over Trinity College, the Dark Blues' catcher Bill Harbidge played second and pitcher Candy Cummings pitched for Trinity College. Although most players, owners and cranks probably saw these tilts as mere meaningless exhibitions and little else, sportswriters reported these questionable contests as if they were of considerable importance.

Cammeyer had scheduled his New York Mutuals to commence outside practice the week of March 18, weather permitting. But on March 18, Cammy's Union Grounds were unplayable as a result of weather not permitting. A week previously the Grounds had mimicked a pond; now they resembled a lake. To dispel the Mutuals' unsavory reputation, Cammeyer had decided to switch the team name from New York to Brooklyn Mutuals[3] and to change their team colors from blue to red. He told the press his red-trimmed Brooklyn club would be a totally different team: new name, outfits and outlook. They could be called the Brooklyn Red Stockings, the Brooklyn Reds or the Brooklyns.[4] All this cosmetic silliness fooled very few. As far as research can ascertain, the press never did put Brooklyn prior to Mutuals in its headlines or stories. Cammy's choice of crimson for his club's stockings only confirmed that herrings were sometimes red.

His multi-monikered Mutes were slated to practice every afternoon at 3 P.M. against a series of thrown-together teams selected at the playing ground each day. But heavy rains inundated the playing facility. The field was completely hydrated, some wags noting tidal conditions in effect on its Atlantic-like surface. The Mutes remained barn-bound, incarcerated and cursing while working out in a dusty gymnasium.

The rain gave Cammeyer other worries. With deluges like this, no wonder his and other wooden stands rotted so fast. After being soaked to the cellulose with rain, a park's wet boards would be kiln dried under a hot sun guaranteed to warp the worst of wood (the grade used in ballparks) into a wavy, wobbly sea of decaying planking. The irony was that Cammeyer's, and all the other "well-watered" spring parks, were instant flash-fire zones come summer. Since ballparks took precious capital to build, there wasn't an owner who didn't cut corners here, there and everywhere. Each used the cheapest of lumber, spread the thinnest layer of cut-rate paint on bleachers and grandstands and usually neglected to provide adequate drainage for their playing fields. It was saying something that cash-conscious Cammeyer's field of flood was considered one of the most extensively and expensively drained.[5] If this was the best, how dry could the rest ever be?

The first eight days of April came and went, giving new meaning to the term "April Showers." There wasn't a practice field usable in the entire metropolitan New York–Brooklyn area.[6] Some people were doubtful the rain would ever stop. Others feared the endless torrential rains would sweep Manhattan Island into Lower New York Bay and the Atlantic Ocean. A slough of games was washed out, but Manhattan Island didn't appreciably move any closer to the Atlantic. The only news during this diluvian phase of weather came from Florida where Harry Wright, who was rumored to have been ailing, was evidently boating and regaining his health.[7]

The weather, turning a bit drier in the Chicago area, allowed Hulbert's hirelings to practice on their grounds near the university on Cottage

Grove Avenue and 35th Street. The full team was now out, including Anson, who ended his short holdout by appearing on April 5.[8] Fred Andrus was the most insecure of the Chicago players. Signed to a trial contract for three months, Fred was working and worrying his way through each training session with an abnormal mixture of moxie and anxiety.[9] It was the gauntlet, the trial, the moment of truth, the big exam, the final judgment that all rookies had to go through. If Andrus' skills were sufficient to conquer his nerves, he'd be a regular someday. If not, he would not make it. There was no way it could be made easier. The player either demonstrated he had the natural talent, aptitude to learn and internal drive to be a big-leaguer or he did not. Whether he was a nice guy, a man of high morals or a good friend did not matter. What mattered was whether he could field, throw and hit. Very little else entered into the decision of whether a man stayed or left. Sentimental managers finished last. The general public might doubt Darwin, baseball people did not.

Louisville, its southern instincts aroused, set up to play a three-game series with Memphis in the Tennessee town in early April. The Grays won the opener 15–5 on April 5 with the battery of Jim Devlin and Pop Snyder working well together. Lou'ville manager John Chapman umpired the game and was found a satisfactory arbitrator by both teams. Louisville scored three earned runs and Memphis none. Both teams committed errors galore. It was typical early season base bobble. But the second game of the series was cancelled when snow, that icy stuff of cold Northern nonsense, came down in Canadian size clumps in disparate and despairing parts of the United States, Tennessee being one of them. The stuff, perhaps confusing Memphis for Montreal, fell on the southern city to the depth of 10 inches. Louisville was able to play on April 10, topping Memphis 31–5 to complete the new league's southern exposure.

It was during this preseason spate of inclement weather that the *Cincinnati Enquirer* erroneously reported Harry Wright's death.[10] This led to a flood of conflicting rumors concerning the health of Mr. Wright. The ever alert *Louisville Courier-Journal* reported on April 29 that the "news of Harry Wright's death, which occurred Thursday at Boston, will be received with unfeigned regret by his many acquaintances."[11] The story added that Harry, after seeking relief in southern climes, had returned to Boston to die of consumption. Next day, the *Courier-Journal* reported that their story of Wright's demise had been a hoax.[12] The *Chicago Tribune* had predicted very early in April that Wright, much benefited by his Florida trip, would be in good shape for the season opener.[13] The *Trib* had waxed poetic re Wright as early as April 9, noting, "Harry Wright still continues to die one day and recover the next. Let him alone and he'll come home, wagging his bat behind him." The *Cincinnati Enquirer* admitted on May 6 that their report of Harry's death was erroneous.[14]

The Athletic got out on their own grounds on April 5, only to be edged 8–7 by a Picked Nine. One positive note for the A's was that Lon, their Knight with the hopefully shining arm, pitched for the opposition and beat the regulars. Out west, the St. Louis Browns beat a Field Nine 13–4 at their Grand Avenue Park in a benefit game for an ailing *St. Louis Republican* sports reporter. A few days later the Athletic got their exhibition record even at 1–1, besting a Reserved Nine (another name for Picked Nine) 10–7. About the time the A's were splitting with teams of the instantly assembled kind, Cammeyer's Mutuals bested a Field Nine 11–5 in a sod-soaked exhibition at Capitoline Grounds on April 8. Reporter John Rankin of the Press Club pitched for the losers. Hartford finally got going, opening with a 12–2 win on April 11 over a Picked-at-the-last-moment Nine while the Mutuals managed to get in another game and a 36–0 win over a Selected Nine.

Spring games were in abundance by the 13th. Boston beat a Picked Nine 11–3 at Boston; Hartford, with young Tommy Bond pitching for the opposition, bested a Chosen Nine 8–1 at home in 11 innings and Old Sol finally flattered the New York area with his radiant presence as the Mutuals got 33 hits in defeating the Arlingtons 33–8. Cincinnati's Reds crossed the river to play the Covington Stars at Star Grounds. Extra streetcars were put on the Covington line to carry crank commuters over the Ohio to watch the game.[15] The two teams didn't disappoint, Cincy edging the Stars 7–4 in the second real fight of the year for Charlie Gould's boys. The closeness of the game should have, perhaps, raised a few eyebrows in Cincinnati. Gould, often called "Bushel Basket" because of his ability to collect baseballs at

Announcements of the supposed death of beloved Boston manager Harry Wright in early April 1876 brought on a flood of public grief and conflicting editorial reports. Like Mark Twain, Wright had "died" before his time. (Transcendental Graphics)

ease at first base, for example, appeared to be in the twilight of his career. It probably had not been sentiment that led Si Keck to hire the veteran first baseman as player-manager.[16] Those who knew Keck well were more likely to believe it was the modest price tag an aging, declining player who was inexperienced at managing could demand. Keck ran a meat packing firm in Cincinnati and was rumored to treat his players on a par with the pigs he purchased for slaughtering. This sentiment extended to player-managers as well.[17] The excitement over the Covington game was good news, however. A large clutch of cranks had even gathered around Hawley's store in Cincinnati to read the inning-by-inning scores that were telegraphed from across the river and posted in the store window. With enthusiasm like that, optimists asked, "How could the league not succeed?"[18]

The Cincy transportation authorities scheduled extra trains to the ballpark starting opening day—Tuesday, April 25—when the Reds were slated to begin their National League season against the year-old St. Louis Brown Stockings. Railed vehicles would leave Plum Street Depot for the ballpark at 2, 2:30 and 3:30 the day of each game.[19] The 3:30 departure, however, seemed superfluous since games started at 3 P.M.

The Cincinnati playing grounds were being readied for the summer assault of cleats, bounding baseballs, scorching heat, soaking rain and such. The space between the diamond and the stands on the first and third base sides was filled, tilled, tamped and leveled to the smoothness of a billiard table. The outfield was so thoroughly rolled and leveled that it was as smooth as a dance floor. The well-drained grounds only needed 10 hours of old Sol to be ready for business.[20]

Things were considerably different in Louisville. On the night of April 13, a windstorm sent gale gusts upwards of 80 mph through the city. This overagitated air whisked a forest of trees, a debacle of debris and the roof of the Louisville grandstand away with it. Some timbers were wind-borne for 300 feet.[21] With the anticipated inauguration of the Louisville baseball club into the active ranks of the National League of Professional Base Ball Clubs a couple of weeks away, the wind damage set off a sequence of enterprises guaranteed to stimulate the lagging local economy and place that all-envied stamp "progress" on the city's collective image. Construction workers swarmed over the wind-damaged Louisville stands carrying timbers and struts, beams and counter-beams, joists and cross-joists, spikes and nails, in short, all the paraphernalia of modern 19th Century construction. The new gable roof would soon be in place and would prevail over wind and storm.[22]

While the woodworkers completed the roof, a hard-muscled, bare-backed band of navvies were completing the final section of the Fourth Street Railway's extension to the new Louisville grounds. The rail owners planned to have 75 cars coursing along the steel rails bringing cranks to and from the game.[23] The Fourth Street Railway's extension was not unique in the baseball business. It seemed that as soon as the sod was stirred for a new ball ground anywhere in America, an elevated mole of packed earth and crushed rock, wooden ties and steel rails would instantly begin to creep park-ward. It was much like a spider coming forth upon detecting a fly stirring in the extremities of its web. The street railway and the ballpark, often under the same ownership, were integral financial necessities of 19th Century baseball.

Besides the re-roofing and the rail extending, a third activity brought even more workers into the Fourth Street area. W.A. L'Hommedieu, the affable local manager of the Western Union Telegraph Company, had arranged to have a telegraphic office built on the grounds of the Louisville Base-Ball Club. His workmen were now busy completing construction of a branch line of wires that would, by Tuesday, April 25, connect the ball grounds with the company's downtown office and from there with the rest of the league. The game would be telegraphed inning by inning directly from the site of excitement to baseball headquarters around the league.[24]

This was progress. This was baseball. Advertisements already proclaimed the upcoming contest. Reserved seats in the grandstand would go on sale at 9 A.M. Thursday. Any gentleman escorting a lady to the game was advised to engage a pair of seats at once and avoid the rush. The admission fee was 50 cents with 25 cents extra for the privilege of reserving the seat (no extra charge, of course, for the ladies). Tickets were available at No. 2 Tyler Block, home of the Louisville Base-Ball Club, Warren and Merrill's establishment on 74 Fourth Street and at the cigar stand in the Louisville Hotel.[25] The work on the Louisville grounds would be completed by Saturday, April 22, when the Pros would play a Picked Nine of amateurs in a joint 3 P.M. practice.[26]

The mid–April editions of the newspapers around the league reported that William Boyd, a Mutuals ballplayer of dubious moral distinction, had been expelled from the league by Cammeyer for violation of contract. It was in keeping with the new league's pious posturing. Jim Holdsworth had been signed to take his place.[27] The Mutes were getting in a little game practice. Cammeyer's Union Grounds were still as wet as water. But spring training, the appetizer for the coming entrée, rolled along.

New Haven might not be welcome in the league, but exhibition encounters were still kosher.[28] Boston defeated New Haven 4–1 on Friday, April 14, before nearly 4,000 cranks and stayed around to win 11-3 on Saturday,

9—Picked Nines and the Pick of Nines

April 15. Fleeing from the wet-as-water Union Grounds, the Mutuals scored 13 times in the first inning and went on to beat the Young Frontiers 32–5 in seven innings at Capitoline Grounds. The ultra-amateur Young Frontiers had unfortunately decided to use an elastic rubber ball instead of the usual all-yarn dead ball, the result being that the Mutes got 30 hits. Chadwick concluded, quite correctly, that when amateurs played pros, the only hope for a close contest depended on using the deadest of deceased baseballs. He also concluded, incorrectly once again, that the Mutuals were one of the strongest teams in the country.[29] Wags probably wondered, which country? Sweden, Scotland, Switzerland or some other national baseball power was most likely suggested.

Cranks continued to come out to games in both drays and droves. Their curiosity was peaking and the price for exhibitions was only 25 cents. It was time to talk baseball, see who was who, anticipate, point out the new first baseman or the veteran shortstop. Most of all, it was the time of eternal hope and the time to savor the slightest of new variations in what was already the grand old game. This was the time an occasional player might wear a pair of gloves, but such a cowardly concession was unlikely. Ever since St. Louis outfielder and first baseman Charlie Waitt was ridiculed from hand to foot, pillar to post and all around the league for wearing such atrociously unmanly things, players were quite reluctant to put on gloves.[30] Those who did wore only flesh colored affairs with finger ends snipped off. These were difficult to discern from a distance. They had no webbing or lacing and were simply work gloves of one sort or other modified (and disguised) as best suited the ballplayer. No rule prohibited their use. Doug Allison, while catching for the 1869 Cincinnati club, was believed to be the first player to ever wear a baseball glove or gloves. His hands had been bruised, battered and broken from catching chain lightnin' in a ball flung his way by one of baseball's earliest greats, Asa Brainard. Doug simply cut the fingers off ordinary winter dress gloves and wore them for protection, but his adventure in common sense did not catch on.[31]

Besides squinting in bright sunlight to pick out and then to ridicule the occasional glove-clad player, falcon-eyed cranks might spot George Wright inserting his tooth-covering mouth protector.[32] A few cranks in the crowd, familiar with the college scene, would look for a National League catcher to wear the crude contraption developed by Yale's Fred Thayer. It was little more than an elongated oval donut-shaped pad with a maze of heavy wires crisscrossing the front to form a web-like face protector.[33] Cranks would go, wanting a view of this unmanly mask that only college boys and cowards would wear.

The usual cascade of preseason injuries, ills and ails mounted sorely.

Spring training (players getting in better shape) meant spring braining (so-and-so carried off after being struck in the head by a ball) and spring straining (son of so-and-so suffering from a groin pull). A trio of Cincinnati players were still playing injured. Pitcher Cherokee Fisher was hobbling on a sprained ankle. Charlie Gould was lame in the hips and Dave Pearson (or Pierson) was nursing a sore finger.[34] Chicago outfielder John Glenn had been laid up since the second week of April. Oscar Bielaski was ailing.[35] Injury was common from team to team. Boston catcher John Morrill suffered the typical backstop injury — a foul in the face — and was moved from catching to playing outfield as preseason wound its wounded way down.[36] An unnamed Louisville player was described by the *Courier-Journal* as dreaming that he, on putting out the last man on a long running fly, had tumbled over a bench and broken two of his ribs. Louisville players even injured themselves in their dreams. This dream, however, had a happy ending. Louisville won, 1–0.[37]

The New Haven papers, their reporters still smarting from the local club not being admitted into the league, accused Hartford of causing New Haven's ouster. This was particularly galling to Bulkeley. Unbeknown to New Haven supporters and the American public, Bulkeley had been an avid New Haven supporter at the February 2 meeting.[38] Bulks was probably beginning to wonder if being the league's first president was going to be a potent pain in the posterior.

Hartford was reported as securing the services of a player named Shandley. Bulkeley, however, had never heard of the man.[39] Then a young James Shandley surfaced in New York trying to find a slot in the Mutuals outfield.[40] He had been a fine fielder, strong batsman and an excellent all-around player with the semi-pro New York Flyaways.[41] Now he was setting his cleats on a more formidable field. Fine, strong and excellent as a half-pro could translate into blatantly inferior as a pro. Each step up, the competition in general got faster of foot, quicker of reflex, stronger of body, and more experienced of mind. There were only eight National League clubs, each carrying no more than 12 or 13 men at any given time on their roster for 1876. This meant room at the league's self-proclaimed top for 96 to 104 men in a nation of about 45 million, about half of whom were men — odds about 1 in 225,000. *Spalding's Guide 1876* listed 84 players for that year,[42] mainly regulars, which would make it odds of about 1 in 268,000. Shandley would play two games in his major league career, getting one hit in eight trips in 1876 for the Mutuals.

Chicago defeated a Picked Nine 37–6 on April 20 at 23rd Street Grounds, a.k.a. State Street Grounds and Association Park. In a bizarre Abbott and Costello attempt to identify who was on first, the Chicago players wore an assortment of colored caps: Spalding, blue; White, red;

McVey, black and blue; Barnes, black and yellow; Peters, black and red; Anson, black and white; Hines, white; Bielaski, white and red; Addy, white and brown. The experiment was a flop. Cranks found the flurries of colors akin to those worn by racehorses and commented critically on the similarities. Color-coding by cap died in a deluge of derogatory remarks.[43]

The Chicago grounds were in fairly good condition, except perhaps for being a bit beyond moist. The ball, for instance, failed to bounce on a number of landings, preferring to sploosh into the surface of the earth like some down-rocketing meteorite in a lantern show. A new fence crossed the east side of the outfield. It, and the rest of the walled and wooded place, had been covered by a coat or two of new paint.[44]

While Chicago was showcasing its colored cap scheme and painted lady of a stadium, the Louisville National League entry prevailed over the Louisville Amateurs 4–3 in 10 innings on April 20. The unpaid pickup team was augmented by the pro presence of John Chapman, Will Hague and Art Allison in an improvised lineup. Lou'ville's John Carbine drew the praise of the impressed as he made pickup after pickup of a series of errant balls thrown to him at first base.[45] The tall, powerfully built newcomer from the Keokuk Westerns was being given the optimists' overview by the on-viewing cranks as they contemplated a future of Lou'ville victories culminating in a pennant. It was a familiar phenomenon. If baseball's spring came, could anticipations of greatness be far behind? The hometown crank from Lou'ville to St. Loo always perceived his home team as the league's best in the spring. Reality came with the yellowing leaves of September. Carbine was a wonder of April, but with the potential of being anything from an unemployed civilian to an average player come October.[46]

The White Stockings defeated the Franklins 28–3 a couple of days later. In the usual vain attempt to make things interesting, the Franklins were allowed five outs an inning. This rule variation gave the Franklins 45 outs and Chicago more precious fielding practice. Jimmy Wood umped, hopping around on his wooden leg, sometimes getting the new rules totally and irretrievably wrong.[47]

The National League of Professional Base Ball Clubs' season was set to start in late April. The scheduling of precise dates was left to the teams involved, but schedules were no longer the calendars of chaos that had plagued the National Association.[48] Hartford's first National League game was set for April 27 against the Mutuals in Brooklyn.[49] Chicago and Louisville were scheduled to start Tuesday, April 25, in Louisville, and Cincinnati and St. Louis were slated to play the same day in Cincy.[50] The Athletic and Boston were scheduled to start April 22 in Philadelphia.[51] It was "Play Ball!" time for the National League of Professional Base Ball Clubs.

10

The First Game

It was raining across most of the eastern United States on Saturday, April 22, 1876. Yet "somewhere the sun was shining" and that somewhere was Philadelphia. An aura of sunlight filtered through an icy-gray cover of cloud. Had it been February, people would have thought it cold and chilly; but it being April, many thought it mild and favorable. It rained all morning, but a copious quantity of optimistic cranks headed for 29th and Jefferson. Hundreds more from the neighboring villages and towns were joined by throngs of merchants, clerks and city fellows, a few with wives or lady friends, a few more with young sons, some even with their entire family. The grounds at 29th Street and Jefferson Avenue became a congestion of more than 3,000 cranks.

The Jefferson Street grounds were similar to most ballparks of the time. Used by the Athletic since 1871, this wooded wonder featured at least one oddity. This was the exceedingly short fences down each foul line. The distance to deepest center field was 500 feet, standard for 1870s ballparks. The distances down the lines were not most secret, top secret or even hush-hush. They were simply of little significance to the baseball mind of 1876. Fences were for keeping people out and were not considered barriers to blast baseballs over.[1] Out-of-the-park home runs were almost as rare as a rooster's dentures. The ratio of home runs to at-bats was 1 to 503 in 1876; 1 to 172 in 1901; 1 to 96 in 1926; 1 to 42 in 1951; and 1 to 59 in 1976.[2]

There was one other oddity to the Jefferson Street grounds. A swimming pool was situated immediately behind the right field fence. In summer it caused sounds of splashing water, childish squeals of glee and such to drift temptingly over the fence to many a sweat-smeared, heat-hurting right fielder standing in dirt-stained uniform beneath a blazing sun.[3] The fact no player was ever known to vacate his post on the heat-hardened summer turf for a nice refreshing plunge suggested either the professional ballplayer's steadfast dedication to duty or, more likely, his desperate need for steady pay.

10—The First Game

The Athletic management had spent pre-spring renovating the Jefferson Street grounds. The transformation was more than spectacular. This was, after all, the Gilded Age when architectural elegance curlicued itself into ostentation beyond anything sensible or beautiful. The "Grand Duchess," as grandstands were often called, was a picture of profuse ornate opulence. About the only things functional were the hard plank seats and the rearward sloping roof. The rest was for show. The palatial pavilion had one other function. It kept the gambling riffraff from coming into close contact with the middle and upper classes. This was Hulbertian-led baseball fighting for moral purity in 1876. Lady spectators, along with Sunday closings and beerless breath, were now part of a formidable moralistic thrust.[4]

In keeping with the overly ornate architecture, the ladies came covered in a canopy of calico, crinoline and designer knows what. The most amazing "what" being the bustle, a sort of imitation behind plumed out

Special seating was provided for ladies in the 1870s. Owners believed that attendance by the "fair sex" would reduce rowdy male behavior and counter the perception that baseball was only a step above the prize ring. One owner threatened to remove any male spectator boorish enough to smoke in the presence of a lady. This depiction appeared in *Harper's Weekly* in the 1880s and is, in all likelihood, more idyllic than reality. (Transcendental Graphics)

behind their behinds, which, aided by a gore skirt[5] that was exceptionally tight at the tummy and incredibly wide at the knees, made them appear more like mobile mannequins than active human beings. They were almost all accompanied by a male in dowdy drab-colored attire. The entire effect made the ladies appear to glide rather than walk, while the dark-clothed males seemed like stick figures, fit only for a part in the background. When the ladies sat, it was bolt upright, their assorted plumage set just so. With their false hair, flaring ruffles and laces, brocade and such, they suggested crowded lines of haughty, regal birds of various feathers. The net effect of this flock of muslin, cotton, calico, poplin and cashmere was to have the stands appear like a giant aviary, the ladies chatting and chirping, the males quiet, unruffled and dour.[6] The league's policy of admitting ladies into their grounds free was paying off.[7] The fairer sex were bringing decorum, dignity and, most importantly, their dutiful paying male accompaniment to the proceedings. One can easily imagine the scene. While the ladies chirped and male companions spoke softly in the special sections reserved for the elegant, the other parts of the place emitted a babble of buzz much like the hum of social insectica. What was this new league going to be like? Would it be an improvement on the National Association? Or would it be more of the same?

This Boston-Athletic game had the added condiment of pitting the defending champions against last year's second-place finishers.[8] The champion Boston Red Stockings, weakened by the loss of four top players to the White Stockings of Chicago, still presented a formidable squad and a big question mark: Everyone asked everyone else whether the Bostons still had enough to repeat, or, at least, to come close to repeating. The Athletic was one of those on-the-edge outfits. After winning the 1871 National Association flag, the A's had come second in '72, fourth in '73, third in '74 and second in '75. The question was how close would they come this year.

Like baseball buffs on opening day at any place at any time, the Philadelphia faithful were buoyed beyond reasonable expectancies concerning their team's prospects. The A's may have lost .325–hitting Adrian Anson to the Chicago, but they had been awarded Davy Force over Chicago's complaints, and Force was "one of the game's finest middle infielders"[9] and a .311 hitter. They had Ezra Sutton, a .327-hitter over five National Association seasons and a player Hulbert had wanted and gone wanting. The A's also had Levi Meyerle, a .353-hitter during those same five N.A. years, the hard-hitting George Hall, and Dave Eggler, star center fielder, .300-plus hitter and recipient, in 1875, of "it is said, the highest salary ever paid to an outfielder."[10] With these stout fellows, the A's were, to their backers, a pennant contender.

10—The First Game

Less enthusiastic Philadelphians probably pointed out that Boston might have lost their "Big Four" to Chicago, but they were still formidable with players like George Wright, Jim O'Rourke, Tommy Beals, Tim Murnan, Harry Schafer and John Manning.[11] More than one crank must have talked of Wright, league runner-up in batting in 1875, his athleticism being mentioned in an aura of awe. This was a fellow who once got a force-out at second by kicking a ball over to the second baseman when a line drive had sent him sprawling backwards on the grass.[12] Such mental machinations about Boston, however, didn't keep the A's from being slight favorites with the Athletic faithful.[13]

The first piece of news to spin across the crowd-ways was that O'Rourke, Boston's holdout left fielder, had decided to play, steady pay being preferential to perpetual unemployment.[14] Probably few had doubted he wouldn't be in the line-up come opening day. The son of a poor farmer, O'Rourke was a mass of muscular athleticism, one of the finest minds in baseball and a batsman of the first magnitude.[15]

Wright chose rookie Bill Parks to play an arid-etched left field this day. The dry ground should augment Parks' speed. It would be the only National League game Parks would ever play.[16] The rest of Boston's line-up was solid and fairly well set except, perhaps, for pitcher and catcher. Young Tim McGinley, however, should do adequately behind the plate. He was, as a southerner in the crowd was heard to say, "a right good catcher."[17] Pitching was something else again. Saint Harry had a number of possible pitchers to choose from, a luxury in an age when clubs only carried a regular and a change pitcher. Perhaps the premier pair were Jack Manning, destined this day to play right field,[18] and Joe Borden, who pitched under the names of Joe Jos, Josephs and, occasionally, Borden. Joe B was Wright's choice for the opening day's work. Borden, Boston's hope to fill the gap left by the departed Al Spalding, delivered a very swift fastball and a side-sliding curve that swept down and away from right-sided batsmen. Both were delivered from a comparatively low position. His control was tolerable.[19] Young Joe had only to live up to Wright's high expectations and all would be well with Boston and Borden. Perhaps to convince themselves that Borden was good enough to replace the best pitcher in the game, the Boston directors had handed him a no-cut, three-year contract at $2,000 a year.[20] The press had added their seal of journalistic approval, calling Borden "Josephus the Phenomenal."[21] He had thrown the first ever professional no-hitter on July 28, 1875, in a game against Chicago. At times he looked as fast as fury and as impressive as elegance itself. But some observers wondered if Borden was as good as advertised. Time, in which a whole parcel of ball games could be crammed, would tell.

Athletic manager Al Wright countered with Alonzo "Lon" Knight, the promising youngster. Knight had, of course, appeared only 13 times in professional anger. That was during the previous season when he won five, lost six and had two no decisions for the Athletics, who were 53–20 overall and 47–15 without Knight. Such a comparison wouldn't inspire much faith in Knight's future had he been 43 or 33, but he was 23, as young as April itself.

The day's umpire, chosen by the visitors, was William McLean, part-time prizefighter, boxing instructor, and hard-nosed presider over difficult decisions. Players and managers might argue with little Billy, but none would push their disagreement beyond the verbal. Everyone in the league had heard about the time Adrian Anson, the six-foot, 200-plus pound mound of muscle now playing for Chicago,[22] had tangled with McLean. The arrogant Anson entered his brawl with little Billy confident, believing he had little to learn about fighting. He left void of confidence, knowing he had much to learn about fisticuffs.[23]

It was now 3:40 P.M., April 22, 1876. Umpire McLean screamed, "Play ball." Tall, lean Lon Knight faced Boston's leadoff batter George Wright. No one had yet coined the appellative "Super Star" so Wright was merely the best shortstop in baseball. He had hit .409, .336, .378, .345 and .337 over the past five years in the National Association. Any negatives he ever displayed in his play were buried in the corpse of time while the positives clung like glue to this first god of the game. The ladies in the crowd, caring less about George's past, present or future on-field triumphs, saw an awesome athlete, a curly haired, strikingly handsome Apollo,[24] who caused their hearts to skip beats and their minds to contemplate things romantic.

Wright indicated that he wanted the ball up.[25] Knight stared in at catcher Bill Coon or Coons.[26] The A's catcher crouched a few feet behind batsman Wright, ready to retrieve the ball on a bounce or charge out from behind the plate after any attempt by Wright to reach first on a fair-foul hit. Unlike today, a ball landing in fair territory and bounding over a foul line was a playable ball. A swift-shoed batsman like Chicago's Ross Barnes would practice for hours, perfecting the art of fair-foul hitting.[27] Against the quick George Wright, A's first baseman West Fisler and third basemen Ezra Sutton might position themselves in foul territory at times while the rest of the Athletic defense played Wright straight away. But the crowd's eye was on the man in the six-foot pitcher's box. Knight brought his right arm back, then drove it forward with a mighty swish that sent the ball sizzling, whizzling in toward batsman and catcher. The National League of Professional Base Ball Clubs was born!

Wright culminated his at-bat by grounding out short-to-first[28] or Force-to-Fisler, the former getting the first assist and the latter getting the first National League putout. After Andy Leonard went out, O'Rourke singled to left. The hit, the first in National League history, probably meant little to O'Rourke since the following Boston batter went out leaving him stranded. The first hit in the new league. So what? This was the third big-time league in a decade: the defunct National Association of Amateur Base-ball Players having proceeded the equally moribund National Association of Professional Base-Ball Players into obscurity. Who knew how long this new league would last? The country was still in the trough of an economic depression and, although no one knew it yet, the Big Bad Bear would hold sway for two or three more years.[29] The life expectancy of a professional baseball league was numbered in half-decades during the best of economic times.

Boston now took the field in their ritualistic manner pioneered by manager Harry Wright. The starting nine marched smartly to first base then broke into a starburst as each player ran to his defensive position.[30] Even the most partisan Philadelphians must have grudgingly conceded this was an exhibition of class and discipline.

Fisler singled and big Levi Meyerle doubled for the Athletic after two A's were out, but the Boston defense prevailed and the first inning ended with neither team scoring a run. Boston got Tim McGinley abroad in the second when Sutton came up with a bouncer at third only to hurl the ball well beyond the grasp of West Fisler's outstretched hands.[31] McGinley, not yet slowed by years of catching, streaked around second, his left and right legs competing with each other to see which would reach third first on Sutton's error.[32] Jack Manning was next up. Hitting seventh in the Boston batting order, Manning was considered neither the most nor the least menacing of batsmen. He would eventually play eight seasons in the National League and one in the American Association. His batting average would hover in what latter day sportswriters would call mediocrity (.257). But sportswriters don't make a living striking at a quickly passing round ball with a thin round bat. This April afternoon Manning's career lay before him. How he would do was still in that mystery of mysteries—the future. Manning crouched slightly at the plate, about to make history and never know it. His ascent into historic reality started as he lofted a long fly into the Athletic outfield.

The ball soared in a sky-arcing rainbow to come down in the hands of the waiting Philadelphia outfielder, but driven so deep that it allowed McGinley to tag up at third and score. Manning's long distance shot turned into a sacrifice fly to give him the first RBI in National League history. But

RBIs were not recorded in 1876 or for many years thereafter.[33] Manning returned to the Boston bench happy over his team having scored, most likely a wee bit unhappy over having flied out and totally unaware of his sometime-to-be place in baseball history. McGinley probably didn't think much of his scoring the first ever National League run[34] either. His young mind was on the game and a 1–0 lead was of little significance against a high-scoring team like the A's. But hits by Coon and slugger George Hall let the Athletic tie it up in the A's half of the second.[35] It stood 1–1 after two innings.

Trouble came in the top of the third for the Athletic. Gravity caught up with an Andy Leonard pop-up into short right and brought it earthward between converging first sacker West Fisler and right fielder Bill Fouser. At the last second Fisler declined to try for it,[36] probably believing Fouser, who was approaching the ball face-on, would have the best chance of catching the down-spinning sphere. It was baseball by the book, but Fouser's fingers proved incapable of corralling the plunging ball.[37] It was scored an error.

Boston had a Red Stocking on first. O'Rourke now stood at the plate, the afternoon sun tinting his white flannels with an ever so yellowish hue, his stocky stump-like frame silhouetted against the sky. His left foot forward, toe pointed almost directly at the pitcher du jour, O'Rourke waited, his bat held with hands four or five inches apart. It was the classic grip of the day. He held the bat barrel tilted back at a 45-degree angle toward the Athletic catcher, elbows in, his stance cast in shadow upon the grass and dirt.[38] It was a stance alien in decades to come, today only a shadow in the past, but a stance totally functional for its day. With a pitcher only 45 feet away able to propel the five and a bit ounce ball[39] at high speed, the game demanded the shortest and quickest of bat strokes. It was not an era for the long, graceful swing of a Joe DiMaggio.

Basically, baseball is not precise scientific law (if a batter hits a ball travelling at X feet per second at point Y, the ball will go to point Z). The absolute core of the game is the exact opposite. The game's appeal is actually dependent on the chaotic reality of life's equation — the slings and arrows of outrageous fortune, so to speak. It was not certain that Knight could throw the ball where he wanted or that O'Rourke, in turn, could hit it where he wanted. The initiative began with Knight as he whipped the ball toward his aiming point and, in so doing, passed the initiative to O'Rourke. A mass of calculations mentally timing the changing location of the oncoming baseball whisked through O'Rourke's cortex. Then came a sudden activation of his body, legs and arms that swept the bat around to contact the bat's barrel with the oncoming ball.

In seeming light-speed swiftness, a sizzling shot left O'Rourke's bat and went whistling into the outfield, coming down beyond center fielder Dave Eggler.[40] A double! Boston had runners on second and third with Tim Murnan coming to bat.[41] A flood tide of apprehensive anxiety surged through the Philadelphia multitude. Here was the biggest man on the Boston team at bat with two mates aboard; a crouched, coiled mountain cat of a man, his eyes fixed on Knight, ready to pounce.

The vicarious heart of baseball continued to beat from crank to crank. The fun was partly in the waiting, in the what-might-be, in the impending disaster that really held no real consequence for all but the betting crank and, of course, the ballplayers. Knight pitched. Murnan swung, turning Knight's offering into a single. Two Bostons scored[42] and for a few moments there was a lot less joy in Philadelphia. Boston was now in ascendancy.

The score stayed 3–1 for Boston till the top of the fifth. By then, the more philosophical Philadelphians in the crowd were probably commenting on how lovely it was to be at the ballpark on such a nice day even if an afternoon wind was bringing cooling weather. They became even more philosophic after George Wright and Andy Leonard's hitting and base running led to Boston's fourth run. Boston was scoring while the Athletic was going down one-two-three, one-two-three. A certain silence must have settled in ever enlarging pockets of people around the grandstand as the Athletic continued to go down in order.

As the afternoon shaded into the early edge of evening, the Athletic backers were now hoping that Joe Borden would tire so that his offerings would be less puzzling for Athletic batsmen, who seemed unable to consistently get good wood on anything Borden threw. They could hit him, occasionally. Meyerle proved that in the first inning, but scattered hits are not the wood-struck entities that baseball runs are spun from; baseball demands a sequencing of safe hits for victory.

Then came the Athletic half of the sixth and more than a wisp of wish fulfillment for the Philadelphia faithful. Fisler singled, Meyerle walked, Sutton went out, Coons hit and Hall hit. When the inning was over, the Athletic had tied the score. The cranks came closer together, coalescing run by run again into a crowd, the focus coming back to the game as three thousand separate thought patterns converged into a similar set. The game was again the common cause of emotion and thought. It stayed that way through the seventh and eighth as Knight and Borden blanked the opposition. A heart-stopper came in the seventh when the A's Eggler made a fantastic running catch of a hard shot by McGinley in the left-center field gap, whirled and threw a bolt of lightning to catcher Coons at the plate.[43]

Ball and base runner O'Rourke converged on Coons nanoseconds apart. Dust and fury stormed skyward as runner and catcher collided. The sound of awe rose from the crowd. Coons spun dizzily and came up clutching the ball as umpire Bill McLean screamed "Out!"[44] The crowd had hushed to hear his verdict (umpires did not yet use arm signals to indicated their decisions).[45] Cheers greeted his decision. Those who didn't hear McLean, and they were in the majority, turned the sound into a roar, knowing what those instant cheers meant. A double play!

The game also provided a glimpse of gore (always an exciting cardiac stimulant). A nine to nine and one-quarter inch, five ounce baseball moved at eye blink speed when foul tipped, the bat imparting further speed and skin-slicing spin to the incoming ball. A foul tip sizzling and swizzling tore into the unprotected eye of Boston's young catcher, Tim McGinley, in the seventh inning.[46] Then, as now, the human eye is a soft center of see-ability imbedded in fat in an area called the orbit. It is surrounded by a thin membranous sac, the capsule of Tenon, which, according to *Gray's Anatomy*, isolates the eye, allowing free movement.[47] There was no *Gray's Anatomy* to consult in 1876, but there was McGinley's eye to insult and it was the primary point of contact for the foul tip. The horrid sound of a hard ball sinking into flesh and striking skull at eye's orbit sent a shiver of nausea through the crowd. A nasty moment for the sensitive! A nastier night of pain-filled moments for McGinley, who completed the game[48] despite a blazing headache and a reddening, yellowing mass of bruised flesh rapidly closing his throbbing, injured eye. Young McGinley was putting on baseball's multi-color badge of courage.

The Athletic defense changed in the eighth. Sutton, the Athletic third baseman, took his rheumatic arm into right field. Fouser came in from right to play second and second sacker Meyerle rotated around to third. Shortstop Force held his breath and stayed where he was.[49]

The game went into the ninth still knotted at 4–4. How dramatic! How stirring! Again, anticipation went wild! The tension immediately went taut when big Tim Murnan led off the Boston ninth with a base hit. The winning run was on. Harry Schafer, a .250ish hitter, followed and singled to tighten the cranks' collective anxiety into an even more aggravated angst. Murnan stopped at second.[50] Two on. None out. Knight bore down and got the eye-aching, half-blind, half-sighted McGinley for the first out. The knot slackened a bit. But Murnan stole third.[51] Still the Athletic might get out of it. John Manning[52] preceded the rookie Bill Parks. John was hot at the plate. Parks' batsmanship was of unknown quality. As any pitcher would in such circumstances, Knight worked carefully on Manning, trying to make each throw as tempting as Delilah and as inaccessible as Isis.

But Manning, a .285 hitter in 1875, was patient, waited on his preferred pitch, then uncoiled. A sizzling sphere of white blurred past second-sacker Fouser for a base hit. It brought Murnan and the off-and-running Schafer home.[53] Boston 6, Athletic 4.[54] One out. Runner on base. Disaster for Philadelphia! Parks was now up. Could Knight stem the hemorrhage, put out the fire, turn back the tide? Cliché crashed past cliché in the assembled multitude of minds. Parks terminated the tension with one ill-executed swing as he sent a ball into the Athletic infield. Shortstop Force grabbed the ball, flipped it to Fouser who relayed it to Fisler for an inning-ending double play.[55] Force to Fouser to Fisler! Magnificent! Some cranks, remembering that the Athletic were still down 6–4, muttered if only this had occurred one play earlier. "What if…?" "What if…?" "What if…?" So beat the throbbing heart of baseball.

Boston mind: bottom of the ninth, two runs up. Philadelphia mind: bottom of the ninth, two runs down. There was a last-ditch possibility for a rally. Knight raised the hopes of the multitude, leading off with a long ball to left field which sent Bill Parks scurrying toward the far, far away fence that stood those unknown feet away. Parks, his legs moving his body across the grass with a swiftness born of desperation, did not get to the ball until it had struck near the top of the outfield fence. It boomed off the boards and came directly back to the on-rushing Parks who pulled it in, turned and threw in the general direction of second base, Wright recovering it on one bounce. This held Knight to a double.[56] There was no use in gambling for third when your team was two runs down and you represented the first of the two.

Davy Force, short shortstop for the A's, was now at bat. Force stood 5' 4" (some said only if measured by a boastful fisherman's rule) and weighed a mere 130 pounds (but only when fully fed and with considerable coinage in his pockets). His .326 lifetime National Association average suggested, however, he was a force to be contended with.

Force's diminutive frame gave little room for Josephs to work any magic. While Josephs was worrying about Force, Knight stole third, putting the Athletic's possible fifth run 90 feet from reality.[57] Force lofted the next pitch into left field. Knight tagged up at third. Parks, who had been shaky afield all day, ran under the ball. Maybe he'd muff it. Maybe … No! Parks juggled the ball, but hung on. Knight streaked for home. Parks' throw was late and off line.[58]

Eggler was now up. One run down. No one on. One out. The cranks prayed and hurrahed for Dave to come through, which he did in a way as he made it all the way to second on a misplay by Parks. West Fisler, two-for-four on the day, was up. Hope hung on hope for those faithful to the

A's. But Fisler fouled out to McGinley. Two gone! The grimness of desperation gathered in the stands and oozed onto the field as Meyerle advanced to the plate. But Meyerle slapped a ball off Schafer's hands to reach on an error. The Athletic had the tying and winning run aboard with the ailing Ezra Sutton up.[59] What would decades later be called baseball's moment of Ruth had arrived. In this 1870s age of iron men, there was no substitution. A game could be called if a player died just before or during a contest,[60] but so far no player saw this as a sensible strategy to save his team from defeat (despite differing wishes from more than one owner and a multitude of fans). Sutton, rheumatic arm and all, would have to try to win and bear it.

The cranks were on their feet. Borden stared in at the eye-blackened McGinley, bravely standing behind the plate, staring bleakly back at him with his one good seeing eye. An error, a hit or a wild pitch and the game would be tied. A walk would load the bases. The possibilities sent shivers of joyful anticipation thrilling through the throng. This was it. There was no need for Borden to hurry his pitch. Baseball was often outside of time. Let the meaning of the moment meander through Sutton's mind. Let him weigh the responsibility settling on his shoulders, specially the rheumatic one. Sutton was an iron man going rusty. Borden stepped into pitching position. Thoughts like "Let me be calm, and he be not so calm" rushed through batter's and pitcher's minds. Borden whipped the ball in. The cranks were on their feet. The runners were racing away from their bases. Sutton swung. The crowd's noise rose like a Wagnerian crescendo and abruptly stopped. Sutton's bat struck the ball and sent a little half-pop, half-liner, half-hit looper to Borden, who caught it with the least of difficulty. It was the easiest catch of the day and it ended the contest. The first National League baseball game ever was over. It had taken two hours and five minutes to play.[61]

11

May Days

The National League had opened with betting booths gone and private police ejecting gamblers and touts from ballparks. Missing were signs posted by cranks at park entrances: "No game played between these two teams is to be trusted."[1] Whether it could be or would be (even if it should be) an icon of honesty was yet to be determined. Fortunately, most baseball followers were willing to give the new enterprise the benefit of the doubt and, perhaps more importantly, their half-dollars.

Baseball was changing. A large bulletin board against the fence in the Cincinnati outfield had been completed in late April so cranks could follow the inning-by-inning progress of other games in the league.[2] Cognizant of the fact Kentucky air and attitudes were only a few hundred yards across the Ohio River from Cincinnati, the Red Stockings' schedule had been arranged to avoid conflict with any major local or Louisville horse race.[3] Oddly, no arrangement seems to have been made by the Louisville management to avoid scheduling conflicts. With wagering a moral imperative in the Blue Grass country, it amazed some cranks that both Cincinnati and Louisville had followed Hulbert's edict in ordering a copious quantity of police to control betting and keep the gambling community, at least, out of their ballparks.[4]

Other sports, particularly horse racing and prizefighting, competed with baseball. But this was to be expected. The Cincinnati sporting fraternity was excited in late April by the announcement that Joe Goss, champion of England, had issued a formal challenge to fight Cincy's Tom Allen, champion of America, in a 24-foot ring for any amount from $500 to $5,000 a side. Local pride was extended to its utmost puffery, the *Cincinnati Enquirer* being the first newspaper to publish the challenge. Tickets were now available at Hawley's. The fight was slated for September, the site a secret. With no time to lose, the fistic fanatics hurled themselves into a frenzy.[5]

"He beat Jem Mace, that Goss," a boxing buff in the baseball crowd would most likely proclaim, in syllables of awe. No one in buff's vicinity, including buff, had ever seen Mace or Goss fight, but reputation preceded a prizefighter and if he was good, it preceded with the impact of a right hook.

There, of course, was plenty of baseball talk as well. Speculation on Harry Wright's status—alive, dead, in between—continued. The *Chicago Tribune* of April 29 reported that the *Cincinnati Enquirer* had published a report concerning the death of the beloved Harry. The *Tribune* stated that there was no truth in the story and that it was a hoax.[6] But reports and denials only fed the rumor that circulated around the league, churning its way from crank to crank. The story would gradually fade away as time passed. Players also had their continual cascade of conversational banality. The opposition might joke as they watched Cincinnati infielder Amos "The Darling" Booth scouring the near and far reaches of the park for hairpins, these particular objects being his and numerous other players good luck charms. The belief that finding a hairpin translated that day into a safe hit was so common that cranks mailed hairpins to their favorite players and some even spent pre-game time scattering pins on the field itself.[7] The power of the pin didn't seem totally lost on Booth, who hit .261 in 1876, but pin power failed him completely in 1877 when he hit .172.[8]

After Boston's 6–5 victory over Philadelphia had initiated the National League's first season, cranks around the circuit itched to see their boys of summer in meaningful action. There was just something about that first game that grasped the game's follower. It spurred the imagination into furious flights of fantasy, seducing the crank into believing that this may be the year. It happens every spring, bursting forth after the long dark weeks of winter. From the deepest well of American optimism, baseball's faithful draw hope and project a season of victory in a sky of eternal sun. Anyone who loveth baseball also loveth the coming of the spring. Cranks held this truth to be self-evident.

Crowds were expected to overpopulate the league's parks beyond their capacities on Tuesday, April 25. A throng of at least 10,000 was forecast for Louisville, where the Grays opened against Chicago. Abundant batches of people were also forecast for Cincinnati, where the Reds hosted the Browns of St. Louis, and for Brooklyn, where the Mutuals played the Scarlet Hose of Boston.

The Grays' home opener was something special. Cranks came to bear witness to the first major league game ever played in Louisville. There was also the added attraction of the Grays playing the highly rated Chicago White Stockings. But despite the attendant publicity and high hopes, the crowd estimations were about 6,000 over the mark. About 2,000 watched the game from inside the park and about 2,000 more viewed the happening from a hillside viewpoint.[9] The *Chicago Tribune* noted that this elevation commanded "a clear view of the game over a short fence.... The audience which did not pay was fully as large as that which did."[10] Under a lovely azure sky, feeling the softest zephyrs of the spring-tide (as the *Courier-Journal* would report the weather) wasn't far from heaven for a crank on the hill or in the park. The fact Chicago won 4–0 did nothing to dim the delight of the Louisville faithful. The powerful visiting squad was expected to win most of the time. Even though the Louisville locals howled and hoped for the Grays to conquer, it somehow reaffirmed the existence of order, stability and reality in the universe when the team that was supposed to win, won.

The St. Louis Browns were slightly favored in the pools at Cincinnati, where a crowd estimated at about 2,000 gathered. The press, while condemning the curse of wanton wagering on the integrity of baseball, contributed to its own lack of integrity by publishing the latest odds, mentioning where cranks could place a friendly or unfriendly wager and proudly printing the names of prominent people who were placing bets.[11] National League executives of a Hulbertian hue must have wondered how they'd ever eradicate gambling if it was continually being supported and glorified in the public prints.

The glow in Cincinnati over the 1876 baseball season was as sweet as spring sunshine as Cincy, a candidate for cellarhood, won 2–1 before about 2,000 fans, Cherokee Fisher turning in a four-hitter. The only ominous omen, even though the Red Stockings also won this one, was Cincinnati not getting a hit off St. Louis pitcher George "Grin" Bradley until the sixth inning. The *Louisville Courier-Journal* had, as early as April 25, before a pitch was hurled in anger, anxiety or anguish, proclaimed Bradley as the hardest man in the profession to bat against.[12]

Smiles came to the St. Louis players when the Cincinnati faithful screamed "Home run, Charley" each time Charles Gould came to bat.[13] The smiles portrayed the tolerating contempt of the "insider" who wonders at the incredulity of the uninitiated. Evoking Charles Gould to hit a round-tripper seemed a sacrilege when uttered in earshot of Cincinnati's real long ball hitter, Charlie Jones. The latter's power placed him (and the baseballs he hit) above and beyond any player on the planet. The Athletic's 142-pound George Hall got his homers by speed of foot, not mass of muscle. Although Jones, the 200-pound piece of muscle, had only broken into the National Association in 1875, playing briefly for Keokuk, he already had a reputation among many as a man of substantial strength, able to hit a ball higher, farther, and harder than anyone alive. Some of Charlie's spring training shots hit earlier in the year were rumored to be still making their way west.

Already injured Cincinnati catcher Dave Pearson became intimately acquainted with more agony when his hand came into pain-imparting contact with a wayward foul tip. Pearson's forefinger was rendered asunder … right down to the bone. He caught on, his finger shedding blood throughout the game.[14]

An oddity surfaced in the Mutual's first home game. Pitted against Boston, Cammeyer's crew was 100–80 favorites in the wagering over the previous year's National Association champion Boston. Betting might be a mug's game, an activity for those unacquainted with the laws of logic or the finer senses of sanity, but these were questionable odds. Was it 1875 all over again? Probably not. The Mutuals lost 7–6 to Boston as high winds and unfavorable weather led to the situation where "spectators could be counted only by the hundreds."[15] When he juxtaposed his gate receipts with the money the crowds that had crossed the entryways at Cincinnati and Louisville represented, Cammeyer must have concluded that he was cursed.

Boston's home opener came on April 29 at South End Grounds. A 4,000 to 5,000 strong throng watched the locals lose 3–2 to Hartford in 10 innings. Two days later, Boston traveled to Hartford for the Dark Blues' season home opener on May 1 to lose 15–8. Not an auspicious start for the defending champions, but an augury of promise for Hartford. Chicago's Cal McVey, one of the Big Four, was called home from the Chicago–St. Louis series after an April 30 telegram informed him that his three-year-old daughter, Lulu Marie, was dying.[16] This news made notification that one of the Chicago outfield fences had blown over in a heavy evening wind a matter of insignificance for the Chicago squad.[17]

In the 10 days between Boston's 6–5 opening day win over Philadelphia on April 22 and twilight of the 1st of May, crowds of cranks shunned the debilitating financial realities of a three-year-long depression[18] and came out in reasonable numbers.[19] It seemed 50 cents was a small price to pay for having a large piece of one's mind carried away from the sordid business of everyday economic reality into a fairy tale world where wins and losses had no long range effect on the almost cashless crank.

April ended with Chicago leading the league. They were undefeated in three games, having outscored the opposition 25–7 and posting two shutouts. This confirmed the consensus that the Pale Hose were the team most likely to win the pennant. Cincinnati (2–1) was second; Boston (2–2), third; Hartford, the Mutuals and the Athletic (all 1–1) were tied for fourth; and St. Louis (1–2) and Louisville (0–3) completed the standings. The surprise was not that the lowly rated Cincinnati's had actually won two of their first three games or that highly regarded Boston and St. Louis were in the depths of the second division, but that, with so few games played, anyone could get the least excited about any of the standings. Many did. Perhaps Hulbert's league was going to survive.

The league's, and particularly Chicago's, appeal was well illustrated on an arctic cold day in Cincinnati with a tooth-edged north wind suggesting it was February 2 not May 2. At home, stoves and furnaces glowed as every attempt was made to keep warm. But the icy atmosphere and even an occasional spray of near-freezing rain did not deter more than 5,000 Cincinnati cranks from coming out to watch Chicago defeat the locals, 15–9. Only the intense internal fire of enthusiasm for baseball and a helpful shot of smuggled in Scottish delight kept a plague of pneumonia from sweeping through the stands. Chicago, simply, was the circuit's cardinal draw. The athletic histrionics that made the game exceptional involved Clack, Jones and Barnes. Cincy's Clack popped up and out in three trips to the plate with the bases afoot with Red Stockings. Chi's Ross Barnes sent a fastball well beyond Cincy's Emanuel Snyder in left for the National League's first ever home run. Most of the 40 homers that would be hit in 1876 were of the inside-the-park variety.[20] Barnes' blast was one of those 40. The far fences of '76 guaranteed that few baseballs ever left the playing field. Home runs came on long hits and fast legs, not on short fences and base-circling strolls.[21] Cincy's Charlie Jones followed a few innings later with the longest hit ever seen in Cincinnati, Chicago or Kingdom Come. The ball sailed well over left-fielder Bob Addy's retreating body and receding hairline to come to earth under a group of carriages parked against the fence, more than 500 feet from home plate.[22]

The May 2 Chicago-Cincinnati game was marred by a number of roughs getting into the exclusive patron grandstand. Their smoking, cussing and imbibing prevailed since there was no one bold enough or in adequate authority to eject them.[23] It was a simple case of a few making it miserable for a multitude. The people sitting around the disrupters suffered in silence. Many would probably not to be found at the park on following days. Such glimpses of bygone years still gnawed at the patrons' patience. The absence of sufficient park police suggested the security system might be starting to break down, but no problems arose in following games at Cincy.

Grays catcher Charlie Snyder had a quantity of tissue along his left cheekbone crushed when a flesh-seeking foul tip ripped into his face, causing his nose and mouth to bleed profusely as Cincinnati was defeated 3–2 by Louisville on May 4. A frantic call for a doctor brought coroner Maley, the Cincinnati club's official medical officer, onto the field to administer to the living.[24] The more hysterical and histrionic in the crowd probably wondered why Snyder didn't just collapse in a heap so the coroner could do his job and declare him dead. Speculation of Snyder's being dead, near-dead, out cold on his feet, having suffered a delayed concussion and of demonstrating symptoms of a vertical dementia must have echoed through the crowd but died out when Snyder stayed in the game to catch. At least no one complained about the game being held up to call a coroner onto the field when nary a soul was dead.

Chicago's cranks rode the enthusiasm of backing a winner. Their team being in St. Louis, cranks in the Windy City gathered at Mansur's and Foley's where inning-by-inning results were posted.[25] Chicago was edged by St. Louis 1–0 on May 5 as George "Grin" Bradley blanked the White Stockings on two hits. His mates got Grin the game's only run in the first inning when, with one out, Chicago pitcher Al Spalding fielded an easy grounder from John E. Clapp and proceeded to throw the ball well beyond the catching capacity of Chicago first baseman John Glenn, or any other mortal. Singles by Mike McGeary and Lip Pike brought Clapp home. It was all the easily affable and batter-baffable Grin needed. With St. Louis using the softer ball that they preferred to put in play, it was almost impossible to transform a Bradley thrown ball into anything resembling a hard hit. He was also aided by a St. Louis man as umpire and a playing field that was still in critical condition recovering from a previous day's rain.[26] The score might have been higher for St. Louis if the vaunted Chicago defense hadn't saturated the field in stinginess. Paul Hines made an electrifying catch of Joe Battin's fly to center field and lightning-bolted the ball to first to double up Lip Pike,[27] a base runner equal to Chi's Ross Barnes, cheetahs and lightning bolts in coursing along a base path.[28] James White, Chicago's cunning catcher, made two clever plays to snag a pair of Browns at home plate. John Peters made several good plays, retiring all three St. Louis batters in the ninth inning.[29] It was a great game. If the National League could produce enough of these encounters of the exciting kind all would be well.

Hartford promptly topped the Athletic 5–3 on May 6 to move into a tie for first place with Chicago. Each team had won four and lost one. The race continued and, on reflection, this early spate of exciting games may have been the league's salvation. First appearances can, like first loves, grasp the heart. A substantial number of cranks may have fallen further in love with the National League in spring 1876. It was a time fraught with possibilities, a time of joyous anticipation as cranks pre-calculated the outcome of each day's game. "If we win today and they lose, then we'll be ..." has always been common conversation at the ballpark.

11—May Days

May 10 was Chicago's home opener, actually the last of the year's eight home beginnings. It pitted top-contending Chi against cellar-descending Cincy. The mismatch, which saw Chicago top Cincy 6–0, drew cranks by the horsecar load to eat, drink and be merry.[30] Chicago's 23rd Street Grounds was where soda and refreshment kiosks, promoted by Al Spalding, replaced hawkers walking back and forth through the stands.[31] By the 1870s, food, drink and scorecards were already a quarter-century-old baseball tradition.[32]

The directors of the Vigilant Base-Ball Association, who represented "Colored" players in the Cincinnati area, had met May 11 to elect an executive to promote their interests.[33] The Vigilants were ignored. The league had "no written policy regarding blacks, but precluded them nonetheless through a 'gentleman's agreement' among the owners."[34] The league felt it had enough troubles without allowing the encroachment of blacks into white man's ball. Unofficial league policy was "no blacks need apply."

Adding insult to the rash of injuries plaguing the catching fraternity, even catchers' wives began to come down with various ailments. Injured backstop Dave Pearson was forced to stay home in Cincinnati due to a severe illness that suddenly afflicted his wife.[35] Further contributing to Cincy's burden, the team limped into St. Louis on May 13 to lose 11–0. The St. Louis onlookers ooh-ed and ahhhh-ed as Cincinnati's Charlie Jones hit three cloud-seeking foul balls scraping sky aside as they left the park. Each went well over the left field fence. One of Charlie's clouts started at least 50 feet inside fair air space, but wound its way northeast, partially on the strength of the natural hyperbolic spin imparted to it by Charlie's bat and partly on the urgings of a strong wind.[36] Cranks went home talking about "Baby" Jones' long ball abilities. The 26-year-old North Carolinian was viewed by pitchers and cranks with awesome respect. Such strength as his was noticed, noted and appreciated. So what if it was a lopsided game, heroes were starting to emerge. Perhaps it was another fortunate flick of fate that the worst team in the circuit had one of the league's most awesome hitters to keep cranks coming.

May wasn't half over before death, the void beyond all human conception, touched the life of Cal McVey and his wife when their pretty, much adored baby daughter died. Lulu Marie McVey, age three, was laid to rest on Sunday, May 9.[37] The funeral was attended by a solemn cluster of mourners, including White Stocking players, who stood pondering the grim reaper's unpredictable path of pathos through old or young, rich or poor, man or woman, athlete or crank, good or bad. It just seemed so much more cruel and incomprehensible when the person was so young. Memories of childhood were very fresh among the saddened players; many had only recently been children themselves.

McVey had played, at the request of the White Stockings management, during part of his daughter's death bed ordeal.[38] It is unknown how Hulbert felt about this. Perhaps he and Spalding felt playing might take McVey's mind off his troubles. Perhaps Hulbert felt he couldn't overrule his manager's decision. Many attributions can be made, but very few can ever be validated. One thing was certain. Men like Spalding and Hulbert, actually all people, are able either to justify or forget their questionable actions over time.

The pennant race continued throughout May with Chicago keeping ahead by the thinnest of margins of games won (the only criterion that counted)—May 13, Chicago 8–1 (.889), Hartford 6–1 (.857); May 20, Chicago 10–2 (.833), Hartford 9–1 (.900); May 27, Chicago 12–3 (.800), Hartford 10–3 (.769); and June 3, Chicago 15–3 (.833), Hartford 12–4 (.750).

May 15 brought news of a revolutionary marvel being constructed in England. The Glaciarium Club was building a 37x24-foot "real ice" skating rink in London. The English engineers evidently alternated the condensation and evaporation of sulphurous acid to produce an intense cold that was imparted to a mix of glycerin and water, which never froze but circulated with ease and icy effect through a series of copper pipes. A simple flood of water over the network of pipes produced 2 1/4 inches of pure ice. An earlier built rink had used ether instead of sulphurous acid. The story noted that there was no limit to the extent to which areas of water may be thus frozen, and with real ice keeping down the temperature, "rinking" might be made agreeable even in tropical heat.[39] The practical limitations of economics and engineering were not something to dampen a 19th Century man's enthusiasm. Men like William Cammeyer, dependent on the dollars his outdoor rink brought in during the off-season, may have wondered how many winters it would be before these indoor ice arenas would be competing with their outdoor rinks. But farsighted innovators needed capital and America was in a depression. The Cammeyers of commerce could console themselves that it would be a while before ethered ice would become a problem. The English may have skated on iron skates as early as 1662, "after the manner of the Hollanders,"[40] but hockey as a winter spectator sport would not evolve until the 1890s.

On Thursday, May 18, Louisville bested Cincinnati 9–3 at home. Attendance was poor due to nearby horse racing, where the real national pastime, wagering, was in full stride. Charlie Jones rewarded the few who attended with one of his epic arcing home run blasts. Lou'ville's Will Hague and Joe Gerhardt also homered and Charles (Pop) Snyder made a brilliant one-handed catch.[41] The races again adversely affected attendance on May

20, a Saturday, usually the biggest gate of the week, as Cincinnati lost once again to Louisville, this time by a 3–1 margin. Interestingly, the visiting team from Cincinnati garnered more applause than the locals, feelings of their team's superiority breeding a modicum of chivalry among the Louisville cranks.[42] You can always act the sportsman when playing a vastly inferior opponent, the belief that your win is assured working wonders on your potential for courtesy.

A questionable bit of scorekeeping by Oliver Perry "O.P." Caylor, Cincinnati baseball writer, kept May 23, 1876, from going down in National League baseball history forever. Boston's hope and glory Joe Borden, who had pitched the first no-hitter in major league history the previous year in the National Association, threw an 8–0 win over Cincinnati. Caylor recorded Borden as giving up two hits, which made the game a nice, neat shutout and little else. But, decades later, examination of Caylor's scorecard by baseball historian Lee Allen found that the two hits Caylor recorded were actually walks. Someone else would get credit for the first National League no-no before season's end and it would be some time before the league's scorekeeping procedures would be standardized.[43]

In the eternal quest of government to deprive the governed of their cash, the aldermanic board of Louisville passed an ordinance that evening requiring every visiting club to pay a $25 per game show-license. The seven clubs instantly concluded that if the Grays wanted them to play in Louisville, the Grays could pay the tax themselves. The Louisville club didn't object to the tax, although they felt they were entitled to a liberal civic

Sportswriter Oliver Perry (O.P.) Caylor proved the pen was mightier than the pitch when he supposedly recorded two "walks" by Boston pitcher Joe Borden as two "hits" to negate Borden's pitching the first ever National League no-hitter. (Transcendental Graphics)

donation for the team having so thoroughly advertised the city abroad. The *Louisville Courier-Journal* did mention it was unlikely the visiting teams would pay and the Louisville club might have to foot the bill.[44] Little further was heard of the ordinance.

A crucial, critical three-game series in the pennant race opened in Hartford on May 23 as the Dark Blues hosted Chicago's White Stockings. This was the elixir the baseball buff yearned for, the drink the purple stained mouth quaffed in glee to its deepest satisfaction. This was Tommy Bond, Hartford's 5' 7½", 20-year-old heat-hurling youngster, pitted against Al Spalding, Chicago's 6' 1", 25-year-old veteran change-of-pace ace and one-time flinger of fast-moving fastballs.[45] This was tall vs. short, east vs. west, youth vs. experience, raw physical strength vs. mental cunning. It was Rome vs. Carthage in the sands of North Africa, England vs. Spain in the azure blue waters off Trafalgar, Napoleonic France vs. Czarist Russia in the snows before Moscow. It was also the conflict's core in all its contrasting themes.

A bright, sun-saturated sky combined with zephyrs of gentle air stirrings made it a magnificent day. People came into Hartford from small towns, villages and farms as far as 50 miles away for the game. The White Stockings were being referred to as the Chicago Giants, an appellation that reflected how they had been lifted above the statute of mere mortals even by the Hartford faithful. This essence of spectator sport, this titanic symbolic struggle, turned out to be a bit of a disappointment for Hartford's supporters. Chicago won 6–4. A Dark Blue depression prevailed as Hartford committed 11 errors.

May 24 dawned with Chicago alone in first, two games up, and off to New Haven to win a non-league fray 17–4 before the home side's largest crowd ever. It was just one of seemingly endless exhibitions that were imposed between the usual three-days-a-week schedule of league games. Hartford had a rare open day with neither a league nor an exhibition game scheduled.

The real business of baseball resumed on May 25. Hartford won 4–1, closing the gap between themselves and Chicago to one game. Tommy Bond let up four hits. His fastball, slow drag ball, sharp curve and puzzling trajectory-twisting cross balls stifled Chicago's batsmen.[46]

While Bond was besting Chicago, the *Cincinnati Enquirer* reported Boston's signing of veteran pitcher Dick McBride.[47] The 31-year-old McBride had played for the Philadelphia Athletic for 15 years, having been a member of the original nine in 1861. He'd amassed a 148–64 win-loss record over the previous five years in the National Association and had posted a 44–14 mark for the second place A's in '75. The *Hartford Courant* noted that Borden, the pitcher McBride would probably be replacing, had "too little command of the ball when he pitches with speed."[48] The *Boston Herald* argued that Harry Wright and Boston's management hadn't given up on Borden. Problem was the young man needed considerable coaching and was unsettling his co-workers with his inadequacies.[49] But McBride's hiring suggested Wright was having second thoughts about Joe Borden. Despite Borden's faultily recorded "no-hitter," the phenomenal one was proving a phenomenal failure.[50] His replacement, McBride, was a grasp into the past, an act of desperation by Boston. McBride had been removed from the Athletic roster in the middle of a game late in 1875 and hadn't be re-employed by the A's in 1876. He would post a 0–4 win-loss record for Boston in June '76 and be gone by month's end.[51]

Saturday, May 27 brought news of another savaging of the National League's reputation when Hartford's management, or more exactly mismanagement, issued an edict prohibiting the sending of telegrams from the field to any newspaper during the course of a game.[52] The net effect would prevent a ream of papers around the league from putting up inning-by-inning bulletins outside their offices until the contest was over. This idiocy, coming just before the third and final game of the Hartford-Chicago series, left a core of cranks outraged and, as might have been predicted, desirous of killing, in this case, the non-messenger as they turned their anger on the press. The *Hartford Courant* noted on May 30 that the Hartford newspapers were not withholding inning-by-inning scores on bulletin boards to sell more papers but because wires to fields were controlled by the team manager, who felt posting scores hurt attendance.[53] The *Courant* then defiantly announced that inning-by-inning scores would be bulletined at Heubloin's on Mulberry Street.[54] How the info would be obtained was not mentioned, the *Courant* being adamant in not revealing its sources.

Nearly 3,000 attended the Saturday, May 27 game, which Chicago won 8–1. The Dark Blues reverted to erring encounters with batted baseballs, committing eight miscues. Chicago hit when it counted, Hartford did not. The *Clipper* said that Chicago got "their hits in where they did the most good; while with the home-team it was the reverse, their hits generally being made after two men were out."[55] Result: Chicago's record 12–3, Hartford's 10–3.

The Dark Blues also lost the services of Bobby Ferguson, who came up lame. Manager Ferguson moved Bond to third base to cover for his absence and sent "Candy" Cummings to the mound. "His Sweetness" had been Hartford's starter in several exhibition games and seemed to have regained his prowess as a pitcher of remarkable distinction. But Chicago hit the veteran curveball specialist as easily as they had Bond, getting 12 hits to Hartford's nine.

Decoration Day, America's first major holiday of the baseball season, came on May 30. A mass of people, estimated as anywhere from 10,000 to 20,000, attended Chicago's first game against the Red Stockings at Boston's South End Grounds.[56] Bostonians, in every wheeled conveyance known to beast of burden, made their way to the ballpark long before starting time. Even a lumbering, creaking, once retired stagecoach was brought out to carry an overload of shouting, shrieking cranks. Coach and fours sped by carrying the city's most prosperous. Streetcars were jammed to suffocation. Seats in an express wagon sold at a premium. The fact that this was a holiday when Americans remembered their war dead by placing decorations beside the tombstones of their bravely departed seemed almost forgotten. The crowd was so immense that management had to order the gates closed to leave enough room on the field for the game to be played. But as soon as the cranks saw the "pearly" gates shutting before them, anger replaced excitement. Special police had their hands, fists and other faculties full keeping order as the crowd swarmed over the fences. The cranks came on and on until finally there was no more room for them in the roped off sections of the outfield or in the aisles of the bleachers. The populace in South End Grounds was reaching critical mass when the multitude finally stopped multiplying.[57] The vote was in — the N.L. was as popular as passion itself.

Any vestige of apprehension the "Big Four" had of animosity being aimed their way for deserting Boston for Chicago was dispelled as soon as they took the field to practice. A tremendous ovation swept skyward, its crescendos of cheers sending sound waves so high that clouds seem to ruffle into wisps as the noise reached stratospheric heights. This ecstasy of excitement subsided to a less lofty level of enthusiasm only to rocket back to atmospheric altitudes from time to time as the game progressed. It ended with Spalding pitching magnificently to lead Chicago to a 5–1 victory over the Hubbites.[58]

About 4,000 took in the Mutuals' win over Louisville in New York, but only 1,500 watched Hartford top lowly Cincinnati 6–0 at Hartford. A fine crowd graced a 7–3 St. Louis victory over the Athletic at Philadelphia in a game saddened by the announcement of the death of Thomas Miller, a change catcher for St. Louis. Miller died of kidney disease at his parents' home in Philadelphia on this day of remembrance.[59] He caught a non-league contest for St. Louis against Elizabeth, N.J., only a week previously, had seemed in the best of health and had gone to visit his parents while the St. Louis club was in Philadelphia.[60] Harry Wright's "death" had been a mix of rumor and fantasy, but Tom Miller's demise was of the real life-ending variety.

11—May Days

The deaths of Tom Miller and Lulu McVey underlined the terrible reality that death was visited upon the young, frequently and somewhat randomly in the 1870s. Tuberculosis, pneumonia and "fever" could strike with epidemic ease at any time while typhoid favored the spring, malaria came in the summer, and smallpox was the major winter woe.[61] Average life expectancy was increasing, but it would be 1900 before it even reached a high of 47.[62] This prevalence of death among the young, and the obviously low probability of living a long life, possibly made it a bit easier to accept, if death is ever easily accepted. It may also explain the ready acceptance of 1870s–style baseball. It was a game where catchers handled foul tips bare-handed and bare-faced, gloves were scorned, and protective equipment was minimal. Infielders risked septic spikings and every hard-hit ground ball and line drive had the potential of terminating a player's chances of contributing to the next generation's genetic pool.

Overall, however, cranks were patronizing the league's pavilions in ever-increasing numbers and murmurs of cheating appeared to be down. The chances of the league's survival was improving pitch by pitch, inning by inning, game by game.

12

Baseball Bustin' Out All Over

The crowd that accumulated for Chicago's win in the opener of their three-game series at Boston on May 30 had the Boston brass expecting record attendance for the second game. It was slated for Thursday, June 1, and if the crowd at Tuesday's contest was any indication of people to come, another overflow crowd should gather at South End Grounds. An official estimate of 12,000 cranks had passed through the Walpole Street gates on May 30 with about 2,000 failing to adequately fund their passage in. Despite this, Chicago's purse for the game was $1,690. It was the largest share ever given a visiting team. Total receipts had been $5,040.[1]

About 5,000, a very good crowd for a weekday game, took in the second game as Chicago won 9–3. But the Chicago team's glow of good feeling over the N.L.'s activities was shattered as the worst of news of the personal, painful kind surfaced. Cal McVey was laid out for a few moments after getting hit in the groin by a batted ball trying to exceed the sound barrier and Deacon White took an ugly foul tip in the forehead which left him with a picturesque lump.[2]

The St. Louis management announced the suspension of infielder Mike McGeary for allegedly throwing the team's 6–2 Saturday, May 27, game against the Mutuals at Union Grounds.[3] McGeary had made four errors that led to six Mute runs in two innings.[4] It was not the first time Mike had been charged with "crooked" play.[5] For those, like Hulbert, who reacted to any National League scandal with the same malevolent frustration a hungry hawk has when a rotund rodent escapes its grasp, it was the first "D" in big cap Disaster.

The war between the Hartford management and the city's press also went on as editors continued to post inning-by-inning scores on bulletin boards at newspaper offices.[6] A league basing its existence on purity and professional management could survive an occasional iniquity, but not a multiplication of transgressions by players or foolish bureaucratic blunders such as Bulkeley's continuing refusal to let Hartford scores be posted in places where cranks not attending a game gathered. The *Chicago Tribune*'s diagnosis was that it was a Bulkeley blunder, "One of the stupidest ideas that ever entered into the head of base-ball managers."[7]

Cincinnati snapped a 13-game losing streak with an 8–2 win over Hartford before a sparse gathering of about 400 at Hartford Grounds. St. Louis stopped the A's 17–0 and the Mutuals beat Louisville 5–1 to round out the day's work on June 1.

The ghouls of ignorance (catcher watchers) were rewarded Friday, June 2, when the inevitable once again occurred. A vicious foul tip smacked Hartford backstop Bill Harbidge's eye. The resulting injury kept the ghouls in attendance happy for a few moments and Harbidge sidelined for a week or two. Baseball in 1876 was still a blood sport.[8]

Outfielder Dave Eggler of the A's also went down in the first week of June. The damage to Dave was so severe some people present questioned whether he would survive. Struck in the spinal column by a neuron-numbing fastball that got away from Lou'ville speedball ace Jim Devlin, Eggler collapsed in a crush of excruciating pain. In critical condition, he was rushed to the hospital in the fastest wagon available. A few hours later, an emotion-neutered medical report mentioned Eggler was suffering from multiple hemorrhages, was in critical condition and probably would not play again this season, if ever.[9]

Grin Bradley took another step toward pitching prominence on Thursday, June 1, as he shut out the Athletic of Philadelphia 17–0. In late May, Bradley averaged less than one called ball an inning, throwing only 24 in 27 innings in a series against the Mutes.[10] Such control was an asset that could turn an ordinary pitcher extraordinary.

In Boston, cranks were amazed to see Red Stocking first baseman Tim Murnan outrun Chicago's claim to chain lightnin' Ross Barnes when he ran down and caught the quick-of-foot Barnes off first.[11] Barnes might be able to outrun most of the opposition most of the time, but he couldn't outrun all of the opposition all of the time. If Barnes ran like Eclipse, Murnan raced like Hambletonian. But some cranks wondered if either were as fast as the Browns' streak of excited electricity, Lip Pike. On such questions, the cranks' world revolved.

Smarting from a hissing they received from their hometown devotees in their June 1, 8–4 loss to Cincinnati, Hartford stopped Cincy 7–2 on June 3 as Bond held the Red Stockings hitless into the eighth before "Old Reliable" Charlie Gould and "Gentlemanly Bobby" Clack got a couple of hits for Cincinnati. Why the Connecticut customers were so dissatisfied with the Dark Blues, who were running neck-and-nape with first-place Chicago, was a mystery. The team was winning the vast majority of its games.[12] Was Bulkeley's battle with the Hartford press over the posting of scores sowing the wind with souring seed?

In things economic, the Athletic management suddenly extended their park's outfield fences upward by a considerable distance. They had learned that the owner of four houses opposite their 25th and Jefferson Grounds had realized a profit of $100 on four Louisville-Athletic games by selling rooftop space at 25 cents a person.[13]

By June 6, Chicago had played three league and three non-league games during the past week before 25,000 persons, a record that supposedly surpassed any attendance figure for a six-game series in the history of athletic sports in America.[14] It was "Hail Hulbert!" in Chicago. Ironically, fewer than 1,000 came out to watch his White Stockings top the Athletic 7–0 in Philadelphia on Tuesday, June 6. America's Centennial Exhibition was a formidable counter-attraction for anything going on in Philadelphia.

The McGeary issue seemed to have been settled. Mike was back playing, muffing two ground balls as Hartford beat St. Louis 8–4 at Hartford, but no accusations of wrongdoing emerged.[15]

Writers occasionally put glimpses of color in the gray columns of their papers. The *Courier-Journal* used headlines like "The Bluegrass Giants Win Another 3–1"[16] to attract attention. It was a small improvement over "Louisville Win 3–1." The Boston *Globe*, reporting on a Boston-Louisville game, took on the Louisville club's tailor and dry cleaner, noting the Grays "were attired in a conspicuously hideous uniform of white, with stockings surrounded by one broad band of dirty blue."[17] One enthusiastic reporter in a paper that wished afterward to remain anonymous described a shutout of the Chicago squad as "blanking the champions nine consecutive times."[18] The spirit was strong, but the execution weak. Sportswriting was two to three decades away from moving beyond the straight-laced style of cityside reporting into the style that would make household names of Grantland Rice, Ring Lardner and Damon Runyan.

Henry Chadwick, the epitome of 1870s baseball reporting, continued his Herculean effort to turn the writing profession into applied mathematics. Chad summarized everything and anything that could be reduced to numerical reportage: hits, at-bats, errors, earned runs, unearned runs, balls called, strikes, fouls ad Cooperstownium. Baseball by the numbers was Chad's forte.[19]

Comments concerning the competition among newspapers was almost as unprintable as the competition among players. On June 7, the *Cincinnati*

Enquirer noted that the bungling Associated Press made 18 errors in reporting Cincinnati's 8–2 win over Hartford on Tuesday, June 1. On June 9, the *Enquirer* asserted that the AP's agent in Boston must be related to John Morrill, noting that the man had a habit of reporting in detail each and every man catcher Morrill threw out attempting to steal second. Since the AP man evidently ignored mentioning any other backstop's steal-preventing activities, the *Enquirer* suggested the agent was two paragraphs beyond bias.[20] The *Courier-Journal* reprinted what three Boston newspapers said about a recent Boston-Louisville game. Not one of the three ever gave the game's score.[21]

June was a third gone when it was plainly evident that Boston's Joe Borden's future was becoming the substance of clouds. He was throwing so wildly that batsmen and umpires gyrated in turbulent terror dodging his errant throws. It was little wonder that Louisville completed a three-game sweep of Boston to move into fourth place in the league standings with 10 wins on June 10. Boston fell into a fifth place tie with Cammy's Mutuals, each having nine wins. Borden's job was close to closure. Harry Wright's hiring of Dick McBride was getting less and less criticism.[22] Charlie Gould of Cincinnati had to leave the club and return home due to a serious illness in his family in mid–June.[23] At the same time, Jim Devlin of Louisville was battling a severe bout of boils. Treatment was prayer, iodide of potassium and more prayer.[24] The *Louisville Courier-Journal* reported on June 12 that "The Philadelphia *Item* says the miserable playing and remarkable defeat of St. Louis by New Haven on Thursday last (June 8), had a queer and suspicious look, and that several of the St. Louis players are loudly denounced."[25]

Tuesday, June 13, saw Cincinnati's citizenry shocked by a rumor that four members of their ball club had been killed in a railroad accident near Philadelphia. A cyclone of blue-tainted air whirred skyward from various places of newspaper publication as frustrated reporters, who had spent hours trying to verify the story, finally got confirmation that it was pure fiction.[26] The source was never disclosed. A rumor later surfaced that the source of the hoax was discovered, murdered by a gang of enraged sportswriters, flattened to the width of a paper thin wafer under a 40-ton press and buried forever in a Cincy paper's photo morgue.

Statistics published in the middle of June indirectly suggested that defense was, as Chadwick continually chanted, the champion's best friend. Ranking of average base hits per game strung the teams out in almost inverse relationship to their standings in the won-loss column. The lowly Mutes, Lou'ville and A's were one-two-three in the league in base hits per game. Front-running Chicago was a modest fourth.[27]

A collage of events cascaded by as spring moved toward summer. A rainy day at Cincinnati brought out a crew to spread sawdust on the field.[28] Louisville's shortstop–field manager Chick Fulmer and wife lost an infant child and left with the remains for burial at home.[29] Joe Gerhardt, Lou'ville firstsacker, couldn't finish a game after being spiked by Hartford's Dick Higham.[30] Boston pitcher Joe Borden threw a tantrum when he encountered difficulties throwing baseballs against Cincinnati. Borden even admonished good-natured George Wright during his tirade.[31] Cincy's exec threatened to remove any male spectator boorish enough to smoke in the presence of a lady.[32]

The war over Hartford's press posting inning-by-inning scores continued. The Dark Blues' management's first move had been preventing Western Union from telegraphing the news. The press had countered by using Western Union's rival, the Atlantic and Pacific Telegraphy Company. A messenger would carry the results from inside the ballpark to an outside operator, who'd telegraph the vital info to all and sundry. But Hartford's management then began stopping the messenger. The press retaliated by putting a "spectator" in a "bought and paid for" reserved seat. The "spectator" wrote the result for each inning on a slip of paper, crunched it into the shape of a ball and tossed it over the nearest fence to a waiting messenger. Bulkeley's men then ordered the "spectator" to change his seat. He did, sitting where he could signal with his fingers so that the info still got out. The war escalated when the wires carrying the reports were severed by a cutter or cutters unknown. The press then turned to other sources of information, the Hartford cranks getting the bulletins via New York. The news was now going an extra 250 miles to get from its source at Colt's Meadow in Hartford to the bulletin board on Hartford's Mulberry Street.[33]

Wags asked if Bulkeley was unaware that the First Amendment to the U.S. Constitution firmly stated that "A baseball club shall make no law abridging freedom of speech, or of the press; or the right of the people peaceably to assemble inside or outside a ballpark to watch a game or read a linescore."

Bulkeley escalated the conflict further by personally refusing to sell an Atlantic and Pacific Telegraph Company representative a reserved seat to a Hartford-Lou'ville game. The wily rep went elsewhere, got a ticket, and supplied his summaries by throwing envelopes with the crucial info inside to a messenger boy outside the park. Witnessing this outrage, Bulkeley ordered a policeman to confiscate the latest envelope. But the boy's youthful feet outran the policeman's flatter foot bottoms. At this point, public opinion finally intervened, Bulkeley and the police being so fiercely booed. Bulkeley finally backed down and left the notemaker-to-messenger-boy passing combination intact for the rest of the game.[34]

The "leakage" of info from the confines of Hartford's ballpark was not the only thing troubling Morgan Bulkeley these fine, warm June days. Minuscule crowds of 200, 400, 600 and, occasionally, 800 were becoming common for the Dark Blues.[35] A Saturday, June 17, game that should have been a park packer — the Dark Blues, fighting day-to-day with the White Stockings for first place, against the usually popular Louisville — was played before a few cranks lost amid acres of unoccupied seats. Young Tommy Bond threw a one-hit shutout as the Dark Blues edged the Grays 1–0. While the Mutuals were attracting 5,000 cranks into Brooklyn's Union Grounds to see a 10–3 Chicago win over the Mutes, Bulk's boys weren't drawing more than 600 to see Bond at near-perfect form against the Grays. At home, Lou'ville would attract anyone within a two or three hour train ride of the team's park. Fanatics rode specials from Lexington and Frankfort to Lou'ville on a steady basis.[36] Bulkeley's autocratic attempts to muzzle the press was destroying his team's spectator base. He was probably alienating his fellow club owners by causing far too much trouble with the press. Perhaps most galling was that Bulkeley was the person they had voted in as league president.

The western clubs ended their first eastern swing as spring gave way to summer on June 21. The west and east had split their games 24–24.[37] The eastern clubs now went west. George Hall of the A's led the league with 49 hits with Barnes of the White Socks second at 43.[38] By June 24, Hall had three home runs and five triples.[39] The A's outfielder was challenging Charley Jones of Cincinnati for the league's "slugging" mantle. Hall was circling the sacks with stunning speed as his off-the-bat shots landed, bounded and rolled to far away places with strange, bounding frequency while Jones was sending rockets glaring red into twilight's last gleaming.

Despite Hall's, Barnes' and Jones' feats afield, corruption was afoot. This time, the big C's of corruption and curiosity once again combined to attract reporters and readers away from what was going on out on the diamond. The number of direct and, even more frequent, indirect charges of corruption leveled at Cammy and his Mutuals were mounting. To preserve what respectability he had left, Cammy had a standing offer of a reward for solid information concerning any possible corruption in his club. Not an atom of absolute proof had surfaced against any of the Mutuals until June 23 when New York pitcher Robert Mathews received an apparently innocent telegram postmarked Chicago and dated June 23.[40] It read: "I am in communication with Fred Seibert all day. If you want to say anything to him let me know, he requested me to let you know it. Yours, etc., D.H. Louderbeck."[41] Mathews realized the seemingly innocuous telegram's sinister meaning instantly. Fred Seibert sold pools on baseball games in New York. Mathews went directly to Cammy, who reacted to Louderbeck's telegram by composing a reply, not to Louderbeck, but to Seibert. It read: "No. 37 Dearborn Street, Chicago. June 23, 1876.—F.H. Seibert, New York. Write me at Washington-avenue Hotel, St. Louis, full particulars. All will be right. Robert Mathews."[42]

The next step in Cammy's inspired sting faltered. Instead of telegraphing Mathews, Seibert wired Louderbeck. This put no hard evidence in the hands of the righteous or even those who wanted to *appear* righteous. Whatever the Seibert-to-Louderbeck telegram said, it resulted in Louderbeck coming to see Mathews a few hours later at the Mutuals' stopover hotel on Washington Avenue in St. Louis. The pair, however, failed to connect. After two or three tries, Louderbeck left a note. It was not incriminating.[43] Finally, Mathews and Louderbeck met, but Louderbeck was as guarded as a knight of old, shielding everything he said so severely that nothing was accomplished. Cammy and Mathews again conferred, deciding to try another telegram. This one read: "CHICAGO, JUNE 24, 1876.— To F.H. Seibert, New York: Write fully what you want me to do, and what you will do. Don't send anyone to me, as I am afraid of 'Cammy.' R.M."[44] Seibert replied, but only to say he wanted Mathews to write him fully. The address now given was No. 214 Penn Street, Brooklyn. The last four words of the telegram gave Cammy and Mathews hope: "Will write as requested."[45]

Cammeyer still lacked any solid evidence against Seibert and Louderbeck. If he could get some, it would help change his image from myopic miser winking at a half-decade's corruption on his team to a crusader storming against the game's evil elements. The next three days ticked by on turtle time for Cammeyer. Finally, on June 27, Mathews got a letter dated June 26 from Seibert in New York. It was as incriminating as open corruption itself. Seibert outlined a cipher code by which Mathews could designate which teams to bet on. The Mutuals would be Anderson; St. Louis, Bertram; Louisville, Darling, etc. Seibert openly explained, "If you wish to buy St. Louis, say 'Buy Bertram'."[46] All messages were to be sent to George Howard, New York Turf Exchange.

Cammy had his solid evidence. He turned the material over to a *Herald* reporter. Papers were obviously better at publicity than police forces. A reporter went over to Seibert's pool room in Rutledge Street, Brooklyn, near Union Grounds, while the Mutual-Hartford game was under way. Seibert probably surprised the reporter with his frankness. "Yes, it's authentic. Publish it—if you like. Everybody understands that we in this business get everything of that kind we can. Cammeyer told me long ago he would try to trap me. He has succeeded at last. He has had a grudge against me for a long time because I refused to come here and sell pools on amateur races to benefit his grounds."⁴⁷ Then Seibert clinched his case, promising, "I can make an affidavit that I never in my life bet $50 upon a game of ball."⁴⁸ Cammeyer's attempted sting had turned into a self-inflicted wound. Now the accusations were aimed back at him.

Cammeyer was not the only man having problems in the dying days of June. Joe Borden and his 11–12 won-loss record had created a crisis in Boston. He would now be the Red Stockings' designated sitter. Signed to replace Spalding, Joseph Borden, or Josephus, couldn't seem to get anyone out. Some said he had changed his style. Others thought he had lost his cunning.⁴⁹ Whatever the cause of his incompetence, Borden was being put out to pasture. The Boston brass must have been fuming since they'd given Borden a $2,000 per year contract for three years. It was a poorly spent $6,000. Boston's officials and Borden came to an agreement and switched him from player to groundskeeper.⁵⁰ The affable Borden didn't seem to mind the change. "If they would not let him pitch for three years for $2,000 a year, then he would cut their grass for three years for $2,000 a year ... he knew a good job when he had one."⁵¹

By late May Boston was looking for a replacement for the highly paid Joe Borden, called "Josephus the Phenomenal" by the press prior to the 1876 season. He was throwing tantrums over his own inability to throw strikes by mid–June and would become the N.L.'s highest paid groundskeeper when Boston's management benched him in late June. (Transcendental Graphics)

Borden was not the only player to be put out to pasture by Saint Harry's club. Boston had wanted rid of Bill Parks since season's start but hadn't been able to figure a legal or illegal way to break his "unbreakable" contract. Then, a never-named Boston player persuaded a friend in New York to write Parks claiming to represent St. Louis and say they were interested in securing Parks' services. They would meet Parks in New York when the Browns came to Gotham and talk contract if Parks would jump his present contract and come down. They offered Parks $100 a month.⁵² Parks took his

.173 batting average, 29 game playing career and extensive ego, jumped ship, and rushed off to New York to find that no one in the St. Louis organization knew anything about the mysterious letter. The duped and "dumped" Parks realized he was about as unwanted on the Boston club as the British fleet had been in Boston harbor a century earlier. Being a slightly better thinker than a ballplayer, Parks swallowed his pride, returned to Boston, opened a barbershop and happily began depriving cranks of their hair.[53]

Competition for entertainment coinage began to seriously challenge the National League as the month of June went into its second half. The Quaker City Regatta began in Philadelphia.[54] The ponies were at the post at Belmont and Jerome Park and racing was getting three columns of space.[55] The second polo game of the Bennett Championship Cup in New York saw the Reds beating the Blues.[56] Cricket matches were attracting attention in New York, Chicago and elsewhere. The Centennial Billiard Tournament opened in New York with attendance being too much for Cammeyer's liking.[57] If Cammy's team had been in Boston, he would have complained about the anniversary observance on June 17 of the Battle of Bunker Hill, which was held in Boston while the Red Stockings were hosting St. Louis in an important series. If it wasn't cricket, it was a horse race and if not that, pedestrianism in the form of a four-mile foot race.[58] Something was always on. Why Cammeyer complained, Hulbert never understood; if you couldn't stand the heat, get out of the ballpark.

Hulbert was most concerned at present with getting people into the ballpark. Club members, who bought stock in the team, season's tickets or both, got scarlet carpet treatment at Chicago. For $15, an elite of 200 club members got a reserved seat in the grandstand for each of the White Stockings' 35 championship (1876 for regular season) games and all the team's non-league games.[59] As important, they also got access to the team's clubhouse—the epitome of elitism. Chicago's was, perhaps, the best example of this descent to decadence. It was located on the northeast corner of Wabash Avenue and 23rd Street,[60] two blocks from the Chicago ballpark. A two-story Gothic frame structure, it housed 14 rooms and a basement. Most delightfully, the exterior was surrounded by spacious verandas and sky-vaulting shade trees. It was an easy escape from the humid furnace heat that came upon Chicago each summer. Shade and breeze, success and contentment—all home and visiting club members could enter its pearly gates.

The inside of this palace of a place was as elegant as 19th Century opulence could afford and with great wealth concentrated in few hands, it could afford plenty. A double parlor to the left of the hall entrance was furnished with both taste and elegance, and served as a reading room. The best baseball papers from every city in the league were stocked and reader ready. A large saloon-parlor, complete with luxuriant carpets and furniture of blue silk upholstery no less, was a favorite room for many. Large bay windows, hanging baskets of flowers and vines, cages of chirping birds and sparkling globes containing frisky, fast swimming goldfish all combined in this age of bric-a-brac extravagance to give support to its being the Gilded Age.[61] The ballplayers, who were also welcome, preferred the basement billiard room. Their choice was probably influenced by their boyish enthusiasm and their need for activity more than anything else.[62]

In contrast to the league's various clubhouses, the parks where the teams played were usually of cut-rate quality. The location of the Chicago ballpark was similar economically and geographically to the sites of ball fields in all other National League centers. A league field was always on land that was cheap for purchase or hire, and that had immediate accessibility to public or private transport. Chicago's ballpark was about three miles south of the city's central core. It was a flimsy affair of cheap, green wood and inexpensive spikes and nails. Built a few fluffs of wind from the lakefront, the park would shake when the fluffs became more than puffs. A strong blow and it might collapse. It could be furnace hot in mid-afternoon when a game was in its early innings, cool and comfortable in the early evening and late innings when gentle breezes moved from lake to land. Chicago, with upper-class clubhouse and working-class ballpark, catered to what was usually called "the better class of citizen." What made them better was their possessing abundant bushels of cash.

Games started at times convenient to the local office worker, manager and such. The Chicago Board of Trade closed early, so games in Chicago started at 2:30 P.M. Since New York's contributions to the world of finance and commerce closed at a slightly later hour, the Mutuals began business at 3:30 P.M. In the fall, the times would be adjusted to accommodate the sun's insistence on setting earlier and earlier.

By late June, the Louisville club was exceptionally proud of its class of patrons. Doctors, lawyers, merchants and clergymen attended Grays games. When circuit and U.S. judges came, judiciously handing down their decisions on the rightness or "wrongness" of an umpire's decision, the press published news of their presence.[63] With the league starving for respectability, the caliber of customer was of the utmost importance. To survive, Hulbert's league had to distance itself from the disreputable image of a gambling-rife, alcohol-drenched, corruption-ridden sport the National Association had left in many people's memory. As June ended, the National League seemed to have stumbled on an audience mix that gave hope for its survival. It would all depend on continuing to build an image of respectability. The problem was that the best laid plans of mice and magnates often go awry.

13

Happy Birthday America

The *Louisville Courier-Journal* was noting in its editions that "Gentlemen who intend to take ladies to the Louisville park this afternoon, should not fail to secure seats in time. Reserved places may be had at No. 2 Tyler Block."[1] The *Courier-Journal* was talking of "The Great Game Today—Louisville vs. Mutuals."[2] Attendance promised to be very large.

This was the Fourth of July, 1876. It was the day climaxing America's first hundred years of existence. It was a day of patriotism and puffery, a good day to be American, especially if you were white; wealthy enough to be, at least, in the middle class; and healthy (a universal prerequisite for good days). The National League featured a full slate of games with New York at Louisville (as the *Courier-Journal* was extolling), Boston at St. Louis, the Athletic at Cincinnati and Hartford at Chicago. Despite the *Courier-Journal's* enthusiasm over New York–Louisville, the Hartford-Chicago encounter was the main event.

The crowd for the Dark Blues–White Stockings game was anywhere between 15,000 and 18,000,[3] the largest throng ever to witness a ball game in Chicago. The White Stockings had a 2–1 season's edge over the Dark Blues. Their rivalry was at its competitive peak. Hartford was coming into Chicago for a three-game series. This had sports journalists hurling hyperbole and puffery like pitchers throwing curves, change-ups and fastballs. Stupendous, gigantic, titanic, unbelievable, greatest, most important ever, most glorious! All the descriptive verbiage fit for a Wagnerian opera could be used. Both teams were vying at the entrance to Valhalla for admittance and so froth and forth. This series might be the *Gotterdammerung* for one of them. Chicago started the series with 25 wins; Hartford with 22. Each team had lost five. Since all that mattered were wins, the deep shade Blues had to sweep to tie things up. Tiers of seats extended entirely around the 23rd Street Grounds with not a spot unoccupied. Police were kept busy keeping persons off the playing field.[4]

Hundreds of miles and a time zone to the east, police were as occupied containing a large crowd clustered in front of the Dark Blues' clubroom on Main Street in Hartford. Spalding lost the coin toss. Hartford elected to bat second. An inning by inning update of the Hartford-Chicago game was posted on the club's bulletin board. The throng threatened to block the street as their numbers grew in quantity and enthusiasm. Excitement rose as the zeros kept coming up...

Chicago	0	0	0	0	0	0
Hartford	0	0	0	0	0	0

Chicago seemed to be the sloppy Socks on Independence Day 1876. Tightness, that knot of nerves that paralyzes the better senses, led to base runner Paul Hines being put out in Chicago's seventh. Anson sent a long fly to the outfield, Hines wandered away from third, hesitating. Should he go in or return to third? While he was debating the issue, the Hartford outfielder gathered in the ball and doubled the doubt-ridden Hines off third. Such tension cost Chicago throughout the contest. Only McVey hit Bond's offerings with any consistency or brutality.

The Hartford half of the seventh started well for Chicago as outfielder Paul Hines made a great catch of a high fly sent seeking sunlight and sky by Tommy York. Then Oscar Bielaski misplayed a Everett Mills liner sent his way and had the passing baseball elude his touch entirely. It was scored a hit since Bielaski, who would win no Oscars for fielding in '76, was ruled to have never touched the ball while it was airborne.[5] Catcher Jim White then dropped a third strike on Bill Harbidge, Hartford's and arguably the league's worst batsman. The usually fine-fielding White compounded his miscue by trying and failing to get Mills at second rather than throwing the lumbering Harbidge out at first. John Remsen followed with a double that bounded past a hurrying Hines in center and went into a crowd of cranks standing across the outfield. Remsen's crowd-rule double scored Mills with what turned out to be the winning run. John Burdock sent a pair of insurance runs across, hitting one just inside the left field foul line to score two more Dark Blues runners.[6] Chicago failed to score in the eighth or ninth.

The 3 in the midst of all those 0's stood out in splendor on the Hartford clubhouse scoreboard. The local lads had won. Cheers and hats went seeking stratospheric heights. Bond had thrown a five-hitter. The sweet sensation of victory chorused through the Hartford crowd. Club and league president and club owner Morgan Bulkeley (he had every title but king), whose interest in baseball was minimal at the most, broke precedent and actually sent a congratulatory telegram to Captain Robert Ferguson. Then Bulks, who felt food superior to baseball, provided a fine spread for him and his fellow directors to consume. For his players, he had words of praise; for his fellow directors he had dishes of plenty.[7]

While Hartford's faithful glowed, White Stockings fans back in Chicago glowered. Hartford was giving Chicago the race of their lives for first place. Most people interested in baseball had picked, and still were picking, Chicago to win it all, but it was far from a done thing. The faithful worried.

The New York–Louisville game featured a weather-wonderful day. A thin glaze of cloud softened the heat lines in the fierce face of ol' Sol and a cool, freshening and absolutely refreshing breeze wafted through the stands. For thousands, it was a treat to be outside the warm, stifling confines of the city's downtown core. Hours before the game, cars leading to the grounds were people-packed to the content of the horsecar company owners and discontent of the plodding company horses. All and sundry were on the way to the ballpark. People were rammed, jammed and crammed into a continual procession of horsecars, but few were finding the ride to the park unpleasant. The crowd was too buoyed up with holiday enthusiasm, patriotic fervor over being alive at the time of America's 100th birthday, and too full of good Kentucky bourbon, German beer and other self-carried refreshments to feel anything but great. You might not be able to buy a hard drink at the ballpark, but you could still bring it in, nicely circulating around inside you.

From 3 P.M. on, Louisville's Fourth Avenue lines began to have their problems. That is, the people waiting for horsecars on the lines began to have their problems. People wishing to board cars on Walnut, Chestnut and all the nut and non-nut streets further up the line intersecting Fourth had to wait till 3:45 before room on the cars began to appear. Some of the less patient realized the seemingly endless procession of crank-crowded horsecars would continue for some time and had simply taken things into their own legs and walked to the ballpark. Many unwilling to walk failed to see the game. Investigators, holding a postmortem of the debacle, concluded that the supply of cars simply fell far short of the demand. It was something everyone knew. "Investigations! Infestations! Indigestion!" muttered those who hadn't made it to the game. By 4 P.M., 5,000 people were inside the grounds and 2,500 more were outside in favorable viewing spots.[8]

Lou'villers wanted to see the Mutes' "Long Jim" Holdsworth, the dancing batter (he never seemed to stay still while at bat), hit one of his trademark line drives into the outfield. If the Mutes were going to get a horrific hit, it would be a tasty treat to see Holdsworth performing at his best and the anticipation of watching a Grays outfielder turning one of his rifle shots into an out was twice as delicious. That Grays pitcher Devlin would stifle Holdsworth's hitting ability would also prove most satisfactory for the hometown faithful. The awe of seeing the Gotham giants, advertised and believed as being threatening and savage, only to be overcome by the local hero was the story line of baseball. It was the theme of things gigantic that came between the mundane line scores and gray columns of statistics, making baseball something other than just a staged contest between mercenaries. It didn't seem to matter whether the opposing visitors were really awesome giants or not, one group of cranks would always believe or kid themselves that they believed the visitors really were giants. Other groups would be satisfied that the opposition was exotic and, therefore, interesting (even if they weren't exotic). Lou'ville would win 4–1. On some other day, the other side would win.

Elsewhere, the A's topped Cincy 6–3 at Cincinnati. The *Clipper* noted that nearly 3,000 persons, the "largest attendance of the season," witnessed the game.[9] The A's had a 3–2 lead going into the ninth, when "a couple of heavy showers caused a cessation of play for about an hour. Finally after a liberal use of sawdust, the umpire (Charles Daniels) decided that the ground was made fit to play on."[10] Cincy's Charlie Gould sent a long shot into center field that Athletic West Fisler, who slipped on the slick grass, failed to catch. Fisler's misfortune was soon followed by Philadelphia pitcher George Zettlein uncorking a wild pitch, "excusable on account of the greasy condition of the ball"[11] according to the *Clipper*, that moved Gould into scoring position. Henry Kessler's single into short left promptly brought Gould home with the tying run. Cincinnati was unable to put any more people across the plate and the game went into extra innings. The Athletic parlayed five singles into three runs in the top of the 10th and shut the Red Stockings down in the bottom half to get the win.

About 6,000 patrons at St. Louis watched Boston edge the Brown Stockings 4–3 in 12 innings to complete the Independence Day celebrations. About 30,000 paying customers, an astounding number for the time, had watched National League baseball that Fourth of July. The infant association was alive and well.

The eastern side of America, now as urbanized, industrialized and stabilized as old world Europe, was shaken Thursday, July 6, as the first news of the annihilation of George Armstrong Custer and five cavalry companies at some place on the western frontier flashed east. Talk of avenging the massacre dominated many a conversation. It didn't cross the consciousness of many easterners that the land to the west had been long settled, long inhabited and long civilized (albeit by a different civilization). The descendants of those who came fleeing religious prosecution were in no mood to tolerate the heathen landowners' claims to their religions, their lands or their way of life. In another era, the west would have been considered *lebenstraum* and the natives *untermenschen*.

There was no way of conceding that white cavalry units had been led into the massacre by a white incompetent, who was totally out-generaled by a superior Sioux mind. Perhaps deep in the unconscious recesses of the eastern mind was the gnawing near-realization that the brain inside is independent of the skin color outside. That nature doled out abilities in a sort of genetic lottery that spread the genes around about equally from group to group would have been a revelation of both stunning and shunning consequence.

Life and the National League went on. The second game of the Hartford-Chicago series on July 6 was highlighted by a tremendous first-inning shot that went from John Remsen's bat to some place far beyond the left field fence for a Dark Blues home run.[12] Some cranks believed it was still going two days later. The crack of Remsen's against the baseball set the tone for a 6–2 Hartford win. It gave Hartford a 3–2 lead in games played between the two clubs and disappointed 3,500 Chicagoans who attended the game. It moved Hartford to within one game of the front-running White Stockings. Had the Dark Blues claimed a forfeit in an earlier Mutuals game, which would have counted as a win, they would be tied with the mighty "Lads from the Lake."[13] The National League was less than a year old and already nice guys were beginning to finish according to Durocher.

The rumor mill was grinding once again on July 6. The latest story to seep insidiously into the public psyche brought the idea that Bradley and the Browns wouldn't try to win a game from Hartford if the Dark Blues could sweep the Socks. Bradley and the Browns' motive was supposedly intense hatred for the Chicago organization. Bradley and teammate Joe Battin were assumed to be headed for the A's in '77 to join Meyerle, Hall and Sutton to build the core of a potential Philadelphia pennant winner. Problem was whether the A's could meet even a couple of months of paydays if they loaded their lineup with high-priced help. A second rumor suggested the first was as silly as stupidity since the A's couldn't even afford the people on the seventh-place team they had now.[14]

Cincinnati ended a five-week and 13-game losing streak on July 6, defeating the A's 5–2 in 10 innings. It was a jolt of joy that Cincy cranks rarely experienced. The victory was only the second win in the team's last 25 games. After losing a Friday exhibition game in New Haven, Cincy made it two National League wins in a row as they stopped the Athletics 7–5 on the 8th. It would equal their longest win streak of the year. The July 6 Louisville press was adamant that there would be ample horsecars to the park for the day's game and pointed out that there wouldn't be any detention at the gates either.[15] The long days and warm weather now had Lou'ville starting their games at 4:00 P.M.[16] Cranks were off work, pleased to sit in the slowly cooling stadium and watch the sun stain the grass with a glowing warmth and a tainted, tinted yellowing light as young men in heavy flannels played baseball.

Saturday, July 8, dawned with Chicago having 25 wins to Hartford's 24. Since the Dark Blues had three more games left to play than the White Socks, the anxiety was high in both cities. By evening, Hartford still had played three fewer than Chicago, but the Lake lads were now ahead 26 wins to 24 after Chicago beat Hartford 9–3 as Cal McVey got the win. McVey started because Spalding was not considered to be effective against Hartford. Relegated to left field, Spalding contributed to Chicago's victory by making a fantastic one-handled running catch.[17] Dick Higham, the big-nosed, hard-nosed catcher for the Deep Blues, took an errant baseball in his *nasus externus* during the game. Fortunately, the ball came in contact primarily with the lower lateral and sesamoid cartilages of Higham's magnificent proboscis. The part of the ball that cracked against the upper part of Higham's

Cal McVey, one of the Big Four who jumped from Boston to Chicago in 1876, was one of three National League players who lost a child during the league's inaugural season. Pitching against Hartford was just one example of the value of McVey's versatility. McVey, shown in his Boston uniform, most likely in 1873 or 1874, was a formidable batter, only hitting below .300 once in a nine-year major league career. Catching, playing outfield and third base and pitching, McVey hit .347 and had a 5–2 win-loss pitching record in 1876. (Transcendental Graphics)

snout did the most damage. The "give" being less in this nasal part and the resistance being stiffer, the ball and nose parted company, both bruised, but only the nose spouting blood and coursing with pain.[18] Harbidge came in to catch and Higham took his nose into right field where he had considerably more time to react to any baseball leaving a bat. America was into its second century and baseball was back to runs, hits, rumors and injured catchers.

14

31 Innings, 2 or 3 Days, 1 Game

A remarkable game began Saturday, July 8, at Louisville.[1] For reasons known only to themselves, Cammeyer and the Mutuals wouldn't agree on Louisville's first choice of umpire, a gentleman named Welsh. A brief discussion followed and was terminated when John Morris of the previous year's Louisville club was agreed upon as arbiter.

The ritual coin flip went to hometown Louisville. The Grays elected to bat second and sent Jim Devlin striding confidently to the pitcher's point to face the lead-off batsman for the Mutuals, Jim Holdsworth. Umpire Morris called, "Play ball!"

The game proceeded with defense dominating until the Louisville half of the second. Scott Hastings, who had hit .295 in a five year National Association stint and who would see his career end after 20 games with Cincinnati in 1877, started things off with a single. Chick Fulmer moved the hurrying Hastings into scoring position with a single of his own. Mathews got the weak hitting Pop Snyder out only to let up a run-scoring single to Johnnie Ryan.

Lou'ville led until the Mutuals' third at-bat. After Joe Start grounded out, Fred Treacey hit that schoolyard commonality, the overtopped grounder that spits off the bat and rolls in an earth-anchored fury toward some infielder selected by chance to pit his defensive skill and speed against the grass-grabbing baseball. Treacey, hoping to make amends for his hapless bat work, dashed full throttle and out-streaked Somerville's toss, his right foot touching the bag a thin slice of a second before the thunk of the ball being tucked away in Joe Gerhardt's hard hands signaled its arrival. Jim Hallinan, a .279 hitter in the National Association, then ripped a liner into center. The ball went to ground and bounded into a confrontation with Hastings, who let it slip through his legs and skitter away. Treacey scored and Hallinan made third. The Mutes went up 2–1 when the following batsman, Bill Craver, grounded out Somerville to Gerhardt as Hallinan hoofed it home.

The production of runs stopped until the Mutes' sixth when, with two out and Brooklyn base runners Nate Hicks and Eddie Booth hugging second and third, the Grays' defense disintegrated. Ed Somerville fumbled Al Nichols' five-and-dime grounder and then threw high, wide and wild to Gerhardt at first. Hicks, who had hesitated off third, took off for home plate. Gerhardt recovered Somerville's errant throw and promptly added one of his own trying to get Hicks at home by throwing the ball over a leaping Snyder's uplifted arms. Booth, who hadn't hesitated, scored a few steps behind Hicks. Nichols wound up at third. The Grays' defense continued to dysfunction when "Long Jim" Holdsworth's easy fly was mishandled with monumental ineptitude by Hastings, who dropped the ball, letting Nichols score. The Battle of Hastings with Mutually struck baseballs was over. The score was Mutuals 5, Louisville 1.

It remained thus until the bottom of the ninth. Some Louisville onlookers became non-lookers as they filed out the exits making for the nearest horse-drawn streetcars. A fortunate few climbed aboard their own rigs and more than an unfortunate few more took a deep breath and started a long walk home to save the price of car fare so they might be able to pay to see another game on another day. Inside the park, the Mutuals were starting to pack their bats into their canvas carriers and prepare for the wagon ride back to the hotel. This made sense. Comebacks from four-run ninth-inning deficits were rare. They are, however, not completely impossible. A few Grays followers sat in a "Is this one or not one of those times?" kind of suspension, caught in a web of anticipation, hope and reluctance to leave.

Hastings opened the inning with a ground-gripping single past third-sacker Al Nichols. Perhaps in the bundle of a billion "ifs" – if Nichols had not been one of the more defensively inept third basemen – Hastings' shot might have been stopped and turned into the first of three outs. But awkward Al *was* playing third and Hastings *did* hit a hard shot Al's way. Up to the moment Hastings' hit came calling, Nichols had fielded third chances with the elegance and elan befitting a premier third baseman. But at this instance, Nichols reverted to form and absolutely failed to impede the passing baseball's progress into the outfield.

Shortstop Chick Fulmer, a man with a reputation for clutch-hitting, followed with a tremendous booming triple over Treacey in left. Hastings scored. Mutuals 5, Louisville 2. Some of the less faithful stopped filing out of the park and joined the more faithful who had remained in their seats. Only those of little faith continued to file out. The exodus ended abruptly when weak-hitting Somerville, who hit .211 in 1875 in the National Association and would hit .188 in 1876 in the National League, sent a long fly out to Treacey which scored Fulmer. Mutuals 5, Lou'ville 3. Snyder, about as incompetent a batsman as Somerville, hitting .236 over an 18-year major league career, squibbed a ground-gripping grass hugger past Nichols, who seemed to have abandoned any attempt at athletic endeavor at third. Hallinan, backing up Nichols, held Snyder to one base with a brilliant stop 30 feet behind third. The tying run was now advancing to the plate. The crowd's appreciation mounted in a chorus of clapping, cheering, whistling and whooping that became a crescendo of encouraging noise. It doubled in volume when Ryan, an excellent hitter, ripped a single to left, which moved Snyder to second. The rising roar was cut mid-octave when "Move up Joe" Gerhardt failed to live up to his nickname, flying out to Treacey.

Two out, two on, two runs down! Louisville's best — perhaps the league's best batter — .300-plus hitting Jim Devlin, a pitcher who could hit tons, was now at the plate. The essence of excitement cascaded through the crowd. This was crisis point. In another era, Mutuals pitcher Bob Mathews would have been long gone, replaced by a giant economy-size relief pitcher ready to ignite the atmospheric oxygen between pitcher's point and plate with his fastball. This, however, was 1876. Mathews was on his own, standing alone in middle of the infield, calm in the eye of the storm.

What happened next was the mix of foolishness and outrageous fate that is sometimes part of the joy in the enjoyment of baseball. Snyder, not the slowest sort of player who often makes catcher their position of priority, made a tactical error. Two runs down, his team's premier batsman at the plate, two men on, one in scoring position – in such a situation even the fastest fellow does not try to steal third. Getting cut down at third to end a game with your team's best at bat would be beyond embarrassment. But Snyder, not the fastest runner either, ran! The crowd roared in disbelief. Mutes' catcher Nate Nicks threw a strike to third. Snyder, still six to seven feet off base, was a cinch out but Nichols' fingers were thumbs, his coordination catastrophic. He muffed the ball, juggling it, then watched it fly away behind him to end in another back-up stop by shortstop Hallinan. The swift-of-mind Snyder didn't hesitate and hurried home. Ryan took second. Mutuals 5, Louisville 4.

The crowd was ecstatic. Snyder wasn't supposed to have stolen third, let alone score. The energy of excitement was alive and pulsing through the crowd. Cheers choked the air with noise. Devlin promptly sent Mathews' next offering outfield-bound. The ball greeted grass in deep left-center where Johnnie Ryan finally caught up with it in time to hold Devlin to a double as Ryan scored. Louisville 5, Mutuals 5.

The crowd was now back in the game. It didn't seem to deflate them much when Hague foul-flied out to Treacey, sending the game into extra innings. Most of the Lou'ville looky-Lous were still savoring the Grays' four-run surge to a tie.

The next six innings reverted to the defensive domain with goose egg following goose egg, inning after inning. The dusky depths of late Saturday evening found the game tied 5–5 after 15 innings. A rising moon had replaced a setting sun. The ability to see being limited to bats of a flighty kind and birds of a twilight feather, umpire Morris called a halt for the evening. It was three hours and 20 minutes since he'd said, "Play ball!" The stats showed Louisville with 17 hits to the Mutuals' 15; six errors to the Mutuals' nine; and five earned runs to the Mutuals' one. Louisville had left 14 runners stranded; Mutuals, 10. With Sunday a non-playing day, it only took a few minutes for the two managers to agree to replay the contest on the following Monday. A crowd of cranks, 18 players, an exhausted John Morris, who had umpired the contest, and a fatigued flock of press representatives left the park.

It was 44 hours and 40 minutes since Morris had called "Play ball" for Saturday's 5–5 marathon when Ezra Sutton, an active player with the Athletic club, was selected ump for the replay of Saturday's tie. This was analogous to having the Orioles' Rafael Palmeiro umpire a Red Sox–Yankees game today. Sutton was picked because it was Monday, an off-day for the usual umpiring candidate, because the A's were in town for a series to start Tuesday, because he was available and because the weather had turned kiln-like, making the job as attractive as a third-degree burn. The affable Sutton was probably the only man willing to take the job. The heat scorched the stands and the few fanatical cranks who turned out, probably no more than 700 in all, were slowly parboiled as the make-up game progressed. It was a wonder the players found the energy to play the game the way they did.

Louisville won the toss again and elected to bat second once more. The Mutes got a first-inning run when Jimmy Hallinan drove in a run with a surge of electrified baseball into left between Johnnie Ryan and the line for a long double. Devlin, who had tried to get Hallinan out with his fastball, shook his head in disgust. He had gone with heat and got burnt.

Louisville came back in their half of the first to score twice. The game would have been over if later-day rules had been in effect, but the game was a replay, scheduled for nine full innings. Lou'ville went up 3–1 in the fourth when Ryan, who had reached first on an error, scored on a series of singles by Snyder, Gerhardt and Devlin. There was an inkling of irony as the rally was started by the weak-hitting Snyder and was completed by the hard-hitting Devlin.

In the sixth, the home side Grays surged ahead 4–1 as Devlin bedeviled and beDevlined Mathews once again, sending Ryan, who had reached third on errors, home when he grounded out on a scorcher to third.

The Mutes got two unearned runs in the seventh. Devlin walked Hicks, gave up a single to Booth when the ball shot skyward on an unexpected bound over second-sacker Somerville's right shoulder, and then let Mathews follow with a hard hit to center which scored Hicks. After he got Al Nichols and Jim Holdsworth out, Devlin let up a single through second to "Old Reliable" Joe Start, which scored Booth to close it to 4–3. The Mutes were now only a run down.

The offenses fizzled until the Mutes' ninth when tragedy in the form of stark humiliation struck home. At a time when one of every six plays culminated in an error,[2] muffing a ball was not a cardinal or even an ordinal sin, but there was sometimes a wrong time to err. Snyder picked such a moment. The 22-year-old woefully weak hitter was a fine defensive prospect.

Ezra Sutton, an active player for the Philadelphia Athletic, was picked as arbiter for the Monday, July 10, part of a 31-inning game between the New York Mutuals and the Louisville Grays. (Transcendental Graphics)

He had hit .153 with his hometown Washington Nationals in 1873, the year he broke into the National Association, but managed to stay employed because of his catching capabilities. His future employment depended almost entirely on his defensive abilities. Any accumulation of errors could lead to Snyder's instant acquaintance with unemployment.

Snyder's physical faux pas came when Mathews, pitcher, second weakest regular with a bat in the Mutuals' line-up by .004 points, started the Mutuals' ninth by striking out. To Snyder's mortification, however, the ball detached itself from his hands, squirted away, and bounded toward the stands. Mathews, who had waved the ball bye-bye with his bat, realized he had a life when the ball eluded the security of Snyder's grasp. The little pitcher sped to first. Safe!

Al Nichols followed and picked this particular time to get one of the 38 hits, the lowest total for all Brooklyn batters, that he got all season, doubling between center fielder Hastings and right fielder Art Allison. That put runners on second and third with none out. Holdsworth promptly sent a long fly to Hastings that allowed Mathews to score, the only compensation for Lou'ville being Nichols getting caught off second trying to come back and tag up.

The gods of games had spun the wheel once again and the nine innings had again ended in a deadlock. Louisville and Brooklyn had now gone 24 innings to no decision.

Mathews and Devlin matched shutout innings for the next hour or more ... 25 innings, 26 innings, 27 ... 28 ... 29 ... 30 innings. Score today: 4–4. Score Overall: 9–9.

The Mutes' 31st or 16th inning started as if the skein of zeros might extend the game into a third day. The sky was darkening with the sun seeking the shelter of the faraway hills. Hicks went out to Devlin on a foul fly. Booth singled. Mathews flew out to Ryan. Two gone. Devlin was an out away from another "goose egg." But Al Nichols got another of his 38 season hits, a grounder that was hit so hard it went through third baseman William Hague as if he were a will-o'-the-wisp, an invisible specter. Booth was now on third, Nichols at first, Jim Holdsworth at bat. A good hitsman, Long Jim was no one to take lightly. He had hit over .300 in three of his four years in the National Association. Walk him and "Old Reliable" Joe Start would be up with the bases loaded. Devlin began to work Holdsworth with care. Trouble was, despite his brain being careful, his body was careless. Perhaps it was fatigue, but he got the ball in a space above the plate that allowed Holdsworth to extend his bulbous arms to their most powerful potentiality. Long Jim smashed the ball a county mile and several city blocks into right center. The ball roared over Hastings and Allison, ending its journey close to the fence, almost 500 feet away. Holdsworth, not the swiftest of foot, tired and weighed down by 10 pounds of sweat-soaked flannels, ended on third with a triple. He would hit only one other triple in 1876 and only four in a four-year N.L. career. Timing was vital to heroes. Singles by Start, Treacey and Hallinan would follow to give the Mutuals a four-run inning and Devlin a devil of a headache. It was 8–4, Mutuals.

The Grays mounted a rally in their half of the 16th that once again had would-be "leavers" lingering between seat and gate. Hastings singled. Fulmer struck out. Somerville singled. Then Snyder got a favorable bounce on a fair-foul and beat it out for a single, redeeming himself for the passed ball that had ignited the four-run Mutual rally. Hastings scored to make it 8–5. Hope lived eternal. It looked like Louisville just might send the game into more innings but Fred Treacey, unknowingly playing his last season of big league ball, made two brilliant running foul-bounce catches, one off Ryan, the other off Gerhardt. In later years, catching a foul ball on the first bounce would not be an out. If that rule had not been in effect, the game may have gone on for decades.

But it was over. Little Bobby Mathews and the Mutuals had bested big Jim Devlin and the Grays 8–5 (Monday's score) or 13–10 (overall score). The win had come after 31 innings. The second game had taken three hours and 15 minutes. The Mutuals had spent six hours and 35 minutes to get a "one" added to their win column. Dusk had descended.

Between the first pitch Saturday afternoon and the last "out" Monday evening, the earth, its inhabitants and the National League had aged by 51 hours and 15 minutes.

15

Striving to Be Second

On Tuesday, July 11, third-place St. Louis topped second-place Hartford 2–0. League-leading Chicago beat fourth-spot Boston 18–7. By the 16th of July, Chicago would be four games ahead of Hartford. The White Stockings would steadily pull away as the race for the 1876 pennant slowly melted into meaninglessness.

The St. Louis–Hartford race for second would be the focus of what interest there was left in National League baseball as the lazy languor of August settled over the eastern and midwestern United States. As 1876 wore on, the summer heat bronzed the players. It also caused the ground to bake into a concrete-like crust that made the hardest balls bound, rebound and confound fielders. The hot air and high humidity sometimes coupled with windless skies to make mid–July games oven-oriented exercises. The heat kept crowds down. Multitudes came out only to see Chicago play.

July was also the start of the annual mating season as club officials tried to sign players for the coming year.[1] Since talking face-to-face to a player (actually mouth-to-ear) was considered the most likely way to get the player to come over to your side, club reps moved from city to city talking to this and that coveted player. St. Louis had mounted such a vigorous campaign that complaints now circulated from owner to owner concerning their exuberant efforts. The crucial one seemed to be their pestering an unnamed pitcher to consider playing for the Browns in '77.[2] The unnamed one was already signed for '77 and had said so, as well as "no" to the St. Loo overtures. But St. Louis continued to proposition the unnamed one, raising the ante to $2,500 for the coming year.[3] Since there was no rule against such recruiting, there was not much that could be done. But if the National League directors decided to ban any tinkering with other people's players until season's end or make a player a team's exclusive property, then there would be an end to such mid-season meddling. With such ideas, the edge of the wedge to be called "No Free Agency" began to percolate in the brains of 1876 baseball people.

15—Striving to Be Second

There was also a complexity of personal concern in all this for Hulbert. The Chicago owner had secretly been negotiating with George (Grin) Bradley and was hoping to get Grin's signature on a '77 White Stockings contract.[4] It wouldn't have been the most sagacious move for Hulbert to advocate censuring St. Louis for something he himself was doing. Oddly, of all the teams sending people hither and thither after other people's players, the only team apparently abstaining from recruiting was Cammeyer's Mutuals. The Mutes were also the only club issuing absolutely no news about signings for '77.[5] Hulbert and other owners must have wondered why.

The St. Louis 2–0 shutout over Hartford on July 11 was the first time Bulkeley's boys had been blanked. It gave credence to those writers predicting St. Louis would finish above the Dark Blues and squelched the silly rumor that St. Louis would lose to Hartford simply to spite Chicago.[6] Two days later, St. Louis and Bradley again shut-out Hartford, this time by a 3–0 score. Chicago meanwhile continued to beat Boston, 18–7 on the 11th and 11–3 on the 13th.

The first inkling of what Hulbert, last year's most successful raider, thought about the seeking of next season's staff halfway through the present season appeared in Meacham's material in the *Chicago Tribune* on July 12. Hulbert felt it foolish for clubs to be shuffling after '77's players this early in the '76 season.[7] The story suggested that the mighty Socks wouldn't change more than a man for '77.[8] Owners and officials around the league must have wondered why Hulbert, who had built a potential champion on piracy, was suddenly down on raiding. Some may have asked if the old hypocrite was afraid someone might pull a coup and capture a few of his Chicago stars for '77.

The miserable hot swelter of sweat July called "weather" took its toll on attendance, except in Chicago where neither heat nor humidity seemed to bother cranks or players. The Chi cranks' enthusiasm and elan seemed to insulate the Lake City onlookers from the heat, while the players' very physical conditioning made them immune to the weather's super-heated attempts at aggravation.

The specter of suspicious happenings in seasons past sent shivers along the spines of several sweltering owners on July 15. It concerned the Mutes-Cincy game and the pools. Betting on the Mutuals-Cincinnati game had swung $20 to $15 in favor of Cincy.[9] With a 6–29 record, Cincy didn't seem to warrant a 4-to-3 edge in odds against the 14–20 Mutuals.[10] Most reporters probably felt that if Cincinnati won a dozen games in '76, the earth would quake in disbelief.

The strange switch of odds brought about by a flood of money suddenly backing hapless Cincinnati raised more than Chadwick's interest and ideas. Every reporter in town worth his salt and even a few not worth theirs were instantly on the story, asking questions here, there and everywhere. It was not long before the press learned that a group of gamblers were making no secret of having "fixed" the game so that Cincinnati would win. Management's close association with the press insured that the owners soon were informed. A frantic telegraphing to Cammeyer and Co. by league officials suggested that any sign of play not approaching an all-out effort by the players or any "turning a blind eye" by Cammeyer would lead to the severest of consequences.[11]

The upshot was that if a conspiracy had existed, it failed to materialize. The Mutes won 8–6. A group of gamblers, moaning their copious losses on the game, probably left grumbling about there being no trusting anyone these days. The N.L.'s integrity was saved from little more than casual scrutiny, however, because St. Louis was hosting Hartford in the third game of their crucial three game series as the Browns and Blues battled for exclusive control of second place.

16

No No

In 1876, as today, the business of baffling batters depended primarily on disturbing the batsman's timing, perception and predictive abilities. To accomplish all or any of these, a pitcher had to offer the batsman variations of velocity, trajectory and, within the space the batsman designated, location from pitch to pitch, thus presenting a tossed salad of speed, movement and illusion. The prime businessman on a warm, sultry July 15 was St. Louis starter George Washington Bradley.

Being known as "Grin" Bradley suggested he was rarely more than a half-smile away from a laugh. His picture, however, glaring back at us from those early days of camera communication suggests "Grim" Bradley may have been a more accurate moniker. Grin Bradley's nickname belied a serious, savagely determined inner Grinless Bradley, a man who wanted to play and to win as much as anyone alive, a man who played baseball for 18 years, came back from a year's suspension (1885) and willingly worked as a change pitcher and a third baseman to stay in the game.[1] In a league where the average player rose about 5' 9½" above the ground and weighed in at about 170½ pounds, Grin, at 5' 10½" and 175 pounds, was the heaviest and the third tallest regular pitcher in the league.[2] Grin was a big man, perception always being partial to its time and place.

John Remsen, one of the five Brooklyn-born batsmen in the Hartford lineup, was first to face the St. Louis Smile on this Ides of July in what was, presumably, just another game. The nearly-six-foot, 189-pound outfielder had one of the most essential qualities required of a leadoff batsman — speed. His primary deficit was a certain impurity as a hitter. Remsen had spent four years in the National Association collecting 256 hits in more than a thousand at-bats for an anemic .247 BA. He made up for this inadequacy by frequently reaching first on bobbled ground balls. A rapidly racing Remsen quickly approaching first base had the effect of making an infielder try to speed up the fielding process, oftimes to bobble the ball and sometimes to lift his hands before the ball arrived and thereby miss it entirely. Even when successfully stopping the ball, an infielder trying to get Remsen at first often tried to get rid of the ball before it was securely in hand. Worrying made hurrying, turning haste into waste. Remsen was having an up year in '76. He would end the season with a respectable .275.

John Burdock, another Brooklyn-born Dark Blue, batted second. Burdock had been Remsen's teammate since both broke into the National Association in '72 with the old Brooklyn Atlantics. After two years with the Atlantics, the pair had played for Cammeyer's Mutuals in '74 and had come north to Hartford in '75. The 5' 9½", 158 pound Burdock had established himself as a better batsman than Remsen, hitting .265 over four N.A. seasons. Unlike the quintessential number two batter, Burdock batted right-sided. Since he would play from 1871 to 1885 before trying his hands at hitting from the left side,[3] Burdock was likely quick of foot in his younger years and probably quite capable of hitting to his off-field as a right-handed batter. The ability to hit behind the runner was probably recognized as a requirement of number two men fairly soon after Alex Cartwright roweled out the first diamond in American dust in 1846. Afield, Burdock was "one of the first premier second basemen"[4] in the National League.

Although nicknamed Grin, George Bradley appears to scowl in this photograph. He led the National League with a 1.23 earned run average, pitched a league-leading 16 shutouts and is officially recognized as pitching the first National League no-hitter, throwing a no-no against the Hartford Dark Blues on July 15, 1876. His feat was barely recognized at the time. Many papers did not mention that his 2–0 victory was a no-hitter. (Transcendental Graphics)

The number three man in the Hartford order was England's contribution to both baseball and corruption — Dick Higham. His shadowy past (he was suspected of throwing both the odd, and even, game) would be eclipsed by his shadier future. He would be expelled from baseball in 1882 while working a scam as an N.L.

umpire.⁵ That he would survive so long was a testimony to the minuscule moral fiber of baseball executives. Hulbert compromised his code of cleanliness in diffidence to the likes of the Dark Blues' Higham. For Hulbert, it was always a balance between expedience and ethics. Like Lincoln, who was ready to save the union without freeing a single slave, Hulbert was willing to keep the National League operational without jailing a single Higham. Ethics aside, Dick was a good batsman. Despite cyclical variations in his dedication to ardent play, Higham had hit a healthy .288 over five years of National Association play with Cammeyer's Mutuals, the Lord Baltimores and Hulbert's White Stockings. At least Higham was no longer with Chicago, leaving Chicago's Socks a slight bit cleaner. As an athlete, Higham was an ideal number three hitter. He could hit with regularity and power. He would lead the league in '76 and '78 in doubles. With Remsen a potential league leader in bases on balls ('78), Hartford had above average run producing possibilities.

The Dark Blues' clean-up man was Robert Ferguson, a 31-year-old Brooklyn-born veteran and former president of the National Association. Ferguson hit .243 in the National Association, and would bat .271 in the National League for an overall .261 BA in his 14-year playing career. Interestingly, only 15.5 percent of his 625 National League hits went for extra bases. This represented a slugging average of .323, suggesting that he was not a formidable force in the cleanup spot. Charley Jones, Cincinnati's and the league's acknowledged power pack in 1876, would have a .443 slugging average in a six-year American Association and five-year National League career. In 1876, 25 of Jones' 79 hits were for extra bases (a 31.5 percent average) and his 11-year major league total of 323 extra base hits came on 1,101 total hits (a 29.3 percent average). George Hall, Philadelphia's answer to Jones, would have a .492 National League slugging average before being expelled from the league in 1877. In 1876, 25 of Hall's 98 hits or 25.5 percent were for extra bases. The 5' 7", 142-pound Hall was a creature of speed. Of Hall's 185 major league career hits, 22 or 11.9 percent were doubles, 21 or 11.4 percent were triples and 5 or 2.7 percent were home runs. The half-inch under six foot, two pounds over 200 Jones was a beast of the powerful kind. Of Jones' 1,101 major league hits, 170 or 15.4 percent were doubles, 98 or 8.9 percent were triples and 55 or 5.0 percent were home runs. Compared to Jones, Ferguson was a pale shadow of a slugger. Ferguson, big league baseball's first switch hitter, might have been better placed as a number two man, but the man who made up the lineup made him number four. That man was the Hartford manager, and Robert Ferguson was the Hartford manager. Ferguson's contemporaries "characterized him as competitive, authoritative, intelligent, rule-wise, short-tempered, tactless...."⁶

The assessment of Fergy's peers could very well be correct. He was dexterous at bat and fast afoot, and, if he were quick of mind, his designating himself as the clean-up hitter was probably an act of ego more than anything else.

Brooklyn-born (it seemed to be a requirement to make the Hartford roster) J.J. Norton hit fifth in the Hartford order. J.J. played shortstop and any other professional position under the name Tom Carey. Playing under an alias was not the rarest of practices in the 1870s. Many people viewed ball playing as an activity barely distinguishable from the criminal.[7] The 27-year-old middle infielder had hit .283 over five N.A. seasons while playing for the Fort Wayne Kekiongas, Lord Baltimores, Mutuals and Hartfords. Although the 5' 8", 145-pound Carey (nee Norton) was a singles hitter, he would accumulate 102 RBIs on a lifetime 288 major league hits. Not bad for a man with a slugging average of .293 over four N.L. years. Tommy Bond, who batted sixth when pitching, was starting in July 15's game. Ireland's contribution to big-time ball was younger than spring training. Bond, now 20, had broken in with the Brooklyn Atlantics in '74 as a blaze-balling 18-year-old and had transferred to Hartford in '75, where he added a twisting, snarling curve to his power pitching.[8] Bond and the legendary breaking ball artist Candy Cummings gave the Dark Blues a formidable pitching staff, 1870s style.

Brooklyn-born (where else?) Tom York came seventh in the Hartford order. The left-handed hitting York was also probably misplaced in the Hartford batting order. York would amass 10 homers, 57 triples and 174 doubles in his major league career. Those 10 homers, 57 triples and 174 doubles added to 241 extra base hits—meaning 32.5 percent of all York's hits went for extra bases. If not cleanup, at least number two seemed a natural batting spot for York. This, however, did not seem so to manager Ferguson. How can anyone seem so wrong, cranks must have wondered. Anyone with the ability to get an extra base hit for every two of his singles and hit 57 triples and 10 home runs in an era when almost all homers were inside-the-park pokes must have spoken speed and whispered power from the time he first broke in.

Everett Mills, 31-year-old first baseman, slow of foot, was playing out his final season as a premier league player and hitting eighth. Good with the wood, Mills would post a lifetime .281 average, but, at 31, Everett wasn't forever. Some folks would be beginning to feel that Mills' best days were to the rear of his fading uniform. Others would be of the "once a hitter, always a hitter" mind and believe Ferguson should place Everett higher in the batting order.

Bill Harbidge, the young Dark Blues catcher, hit ninth in the order.

16—No No

The first left-handed catcher,[9] Harbidge must have been more than adequate defensively behind the plate since he showed little promise while standing with bat in hand beside it. In '75 he broke in with Hartford, batting .216. In later years, wags might point out that Harbidge actually improved his batting performance in '76, raising his average to .217. He would post an eight-year career average of .248. Alternating with veteran catcher Doug Allison, who hit .274 in five National Association years and .232 in five National League years, Harbidge was an offensive liability better hidden in the lowest echelon of any batting order.

This, then, was the lineup Bradley faced on this beautiful midwest afternoon. The Hartford lineup might not have been the most cleverly conceived, but as the game progressed, it would become apparent that any arrangement of Hartford batsmen would have been inadequate for the task. Bradley was simply sensational from start to finish that day.

A baseball's flight from pitcher to catcher is influenced by the arm of the pitcher and the laws of physics. There was probably never a batsman now or then who knows that the density and fluid velocity of the air and the circumference of the ball down to the 18th decimal place all contribute to how the sphere progresses. It might be esoteric to argue that the effect of the flow of air over the ball is described by something called the Reynolds number, which is proportional to the density of the air, its fluid velocity and the size of the object. It is inversely proportional to the viscosity of the fluid the ball is immersed in (in physics, air acts as the fluid). Or that air resistance is *smaller* for turbulent flow than for a smooth flow of air. Or that the orientation of the stitches on the ball affects the drag coefficient, which depends on the velocity through the value of the Reynolds number.[10] All this is so much physics. All the batter knows is that the damned (if not possessed) ball somehow eluded his bat once again.

The batter has "a fraction of a second to learn the speed, location, and type of pitch."[11] On average today it takes four-tenths of a second for the ball to get from the pitcher's hand to the catcher's glove. The distance is 15½ feet longer today than it was in 1876 and the ball is thrown overhand. But the reaction time needed to track, target and thump a passing baseball is most likely very similar despite the difference in pitching distance, throwing technique and such. Today's fastpitch softball is probably the closest analogy to 1876's baseball. The anecdotal evidence is legend and is supplemented by some hardcore empirical data. Considerable hype over the years has boasted how a speed demon softball pitcher could strike out just about anyone. In 1937, pitcher Johnny "Cannonball" Baker blew three swift ones past Ruth in a batting-pitching demo. Ruth is reputed to have said, "I can't see them long enough to get the bat around." A year later,

Ruth faced another softball hurler, Hardy Brownell, who deliberately threw three bad balls wide of the plate, then struck out Ruth on two heaters and a change. Ruth admitted he hadn't been able to see the fastpitch heat.[12] In 1962, Ted Williams got one base hit and one foul ball off 40 pitches by Joan Joyce (reputedly one of the greatest female softball pitchers ever). Williams' bat didn't get acquainted with any of the other 38 pitches. Joyce's fastball has been reportedly clocked at over 100 miles per hour. Frankie Frisch advocated that baseball batters face softball pitchers for the first two weeks of spring training to hone their reflexes. In 1991, Pete Rose went 2-for-6 in a softball game. He was thrown off by the slow pitch and felt he would have done better against a diet of fastballs.[13] In a head-to-head (arm-to-arm?) comparison between Steve Barber of the Baltimore Orioles and Bill Massey of the Clearwater Bombers, baseball hurler Barber's best fastball was timed at 95.55 miles per hour at the end of its 60 foot, 6 inch trajectory (actually, more likely 55 foot). Softball pitcher Massey's underhanded pitch over a 46-foot distance was timed at 98.8 m.p.h. The timing was done using a 50-frame-per-second camera.[14] The data suggests that the difference in difficulty between 1870s and present-day batting is minimal. In both situations, the batter has a fraction of a second to learn the speed, location, and type of pitch and about two-tenths of a second to swing the bat.[15]

The old idea of keeping your eye on the ball isn't exactly as accurate (or easy) as it sounds. When the eye has picked up the ball after it has left the pitcher's hand, about one quarter of a second is left for the batter to swing. The eyes follow the ball for a few hundredths of a second at a time as the brain, that marvelous three and one-half pound piece of worm meat that makes us human, does a miraculous thing. Since the eyes can't move fast enough to track the ball, the brain calculates the trajectory, speed, position in space, et cetera of the oncoming ball in less than a hundredth of a second. It then jumps the eyes ahead to that spot in time-space where it predicts the ball will be. These eye movements, called saccades, probably occur about four or five times as a ball bores down from 45 feet away. To top this, the brain tells the body not only whether to swing, but where to swing. It is quite obvious that any late deviation of the ball from its predicted path or any miscalculation of mind and eye and the bat will contact nothing more than several millions of airy molecules as the ball bores by.[16] It's a beautiful act, whether or not we have the least appreciation of the elegant physics involved. All the important things happen in msec's (milliseconds). In modern-day baseball, "it requires about 460 msec for a ball (at 89 mph) to travel from the pitcher to the plate ... the MT of the bat (the time from the first movement of the bat until it reached the plate) was about 160 msec, so that the bat started moving 160 msec before the ball reached the plate; this is equivalent to about 21 ft. (6.4m) of ball travel."[17]

The crux of all modern-day research on batting is that the batter has to make all the decisions about the nature of his swing by the time the ball, moving at about 90 mph, has traveled about 43 feet, more than half the total distance to the plate.[18] A batter has between 140 and 160 msec to swing the bat.[19] The closer he is to 160, the nearer he is to becoming a civilian. This means the difference between success and failure occurs in a time zone of 0.020 second. As Dad told all of us, "Be quick."

Neither Bradley nor his Hartford adversaries knew any of these realities of physics and human performance. The batters were aware of only one reality: they could neither hit Bradley's ball nor wipe the smile off Grin's face on July 15.

Bradley combined the abilities of a straight pitcher like Al Spalding, considered by many the best in the game, and the ingenuity of a breaking ball specialist like Candy Cummings, the consummate chucker of curves.[20] The actual ball that Bradley threw when pitching in St. Louis was of a soft, mushy consistency. Referring to the "putty ball" the St. Louis management always picked as the game ball at home, the *Chicago Tribune* noted that it was "dumpty ... instead of responding with a click when hit, it simply gave a dull thud like a chunk of mud. The hardest pounding could not drive the sphere anywhere in particular ... hard hitters entirely failed to make any impression on it."[21]

It is likely that when Bradley threw his "straight" ball as hard as he could, he did so holding the sphere with his two forefingers and thumb. Bradley's blazer probably did not progress toward the plate as quickly as Bond's or as Spalding's did when Albert G. was younger. Biographical notes on Bradley don't emphasize his being an 1870s Walter Johnson, Bob Feller or Nolan Ryan. Bios on Bond[22] and Spalding[23] do mention their ability to considerably hasten the ball's journey past opposing batters. Bradley was most likely a master of the mix, showing the batsman a variety of speeds, a variation of locations and sudden last-second changes in a baseball's progress to the plate. Even an average fastball appears to be moving very rapidly when it's presented to the batsman amongst slow, slower, to almost stalled pitches, especially those that bend away from the bat at the last instant. This has been the repertoire the fastball/curveball pitcher has shown batters for more than a century and was most likely Bradley's menu of offerings on July 15.

As any baseball buff knows, the three-dimensional space occupied by the ball on its arrival at the plate can also be varied. A batter standing well forward in the batter's box, placing his body bare inches from the plate and having the tendency to move forward in the act of striking, is often a setup for a quickly moving pitch hugging the inside corner of the plate. If the same batter stands far away, the heater on the outside is indicated. These theoretical realities are all very well, but in the real world, out on the diamond, the pitcher has to put the theory into practice and throw 'em where the bat ain't. On July 15, Grin got theory and practice to agree.

Bradley's curve was probably not the swift out-shoot. Held like the "straight" fastball, the ball was cradled tightly between forefingers and thumb, but released with a quick snap of the wrist with the hand turning over as much as possible.[24] Few pitchers in the 1870s threw it. The problem was making the ball break with any consistency coupled with a certain amount of difficulty with throwing it where a pitcher wanted it to go. Bradley is not always mentioned among the 1870s curveball hurlers.[25] If Bradley had a swift out-curve, it is likely his name would have become linked with this hard-to-handle rarity.

Bradley could have thrown the in-shoot, letting it go off the ends of his forefingers, putting more speed on it than on the "swift" out-curve and sending it straight down the middle for the first 43 feet, his grin turning to a smile as the ball suddenly deviated in on right-handed batters.[26] This early curve—or more accurately, screwball—would not be in the batsman's bunch of expectations and would lead to considerable Hartford fluster, fury and frustration. But whether out-shoot or in-shoot or both, Bradley must have thrown his curve with befuddling finesse, propelling the ball past the plate in the worst possible place for a batter to make the best contact.

As the game wore on, the ball was dented and dimpled by contact with bat, fence, the boards in the bleachers and the grandstand. Ushers retrieved it faithfully for further use when the occasional crank hesitated in throwing it back. It was chewed up by a dozen scrapes with gravel on the sidelines or base paths. The ball, always used for the entire game[27] unless lost in a distant patch of scrub usually growing 450 to 500 feet from the fence (and only proclaimed "lost" after a hunt and seek session lasting at least five minutes), was much maligned by game's end. This gradual distortion of shape, this change from a regular round surface allowed a crafty pitcher like Grin to alter its course toward the plate with more and more deviousness. The bruised and battered ball often took its own course toward the waiting batsman. The immutable laws of physics are as predictable as death and taxes, but not to batsmen, and the mutated ball always followed these universal axioms of science, twisting and spinning its way past a tentative thrust of bat with annoying regularity.

Bradley weaved an assortment of pitches past the wielders of ash, willow and hickory. A dozen batters would be downed as the ball was scooped up en route to the outfield by an intervening infielder who relayed the ball to first baseman Herm Dehlman before the runner arrived.. Four more were out on balls hit directly to Dehlman, who ended the proceedings himself. The remainder went out on air balls when one St. Louis fielder or other intervened between gravity and grass to arrest their descent. Left fielder Ned Cuthbert caught two; center fielder Lip Pike, one; third baseman Joe Battin, two; second sacker Mike McGeary, three and catcher John Clapp, three. In between, Clapp erred three times, shortstop Dickey Pearce twice, Bradley, Battin and Dehlman, once each, allowing eight Dark Blues to reach first on errors.

The game lasted one hour and 50 minutes. St. Louis, scoring solo runs in the first and second innings, won the game 2–0. It was a no-hitter—the National League's first—and Bradley's third straight shutout. He had blanked Hartford 2–0 and 3–0 in the two games prior to his no-no masterpiece.[28]

Coverage of the no-hitter was almost non-existent; a pitcher rendering a foe hitless was not considered an event of the least significance in 1876. Newspapers reported the National League's first official no-hit, no-run game in the epitome of understatement. Stories were short. Bradley's no-hitter was not even mentioned in most papers. In many stories, Bradley's name only appeared below the linescore. Some stories even criticized Bradley's efforts. "St. Louis sportswriters gave much ink to the Browns' third straight shutout over Hartford that week, noting only deep into their stories that it was a no-hitter. One next-day report of the no-hitter included a shot that the Browns would be higher than third in the standings if 'such weak and rare hitters as Bradley' had done more with the stick."[29]

The lead on the no-no "story" in the *Chicago Tribune*, the unofficial voice of Hulbert and the National League, said:

> ST. LOUIS-HARTFORDS
> Special Dispatch to the Tribune.
> ST. LOUIS, July 15.—The Hartfords were for the third time this week whitewashed by the St. Louis club today. The batting of the Hartfords was execrable, not a single hit being made off Bradley....[30]

The latter sentence implied the lack of hitting was a result of poor batting, not anything that Bradley had done. The *Trib* did note that only three putouts were made by the St. Louis outfield (two in left field by Edgar [Ned] Cuthbert and one in center field by Lip Pike). The infield accounted for 21 putouts—Mike McGeary tallying three POs at second base; Joe Battin, two at second, and Herman Dehlman, 16 at first. That left three POs for the St. Louis battery, most likely of the fly ball, pop-up and line drive variety. The 1870s was not an era when a dominant hurler would post 10 or 12 strikeouts over nine innings. It was an era when pitchers got very little credit for getting batters out, throwing shutouts and such.

A reprint from the hometown *St. Louis Republican* in the *Louisville Courier-Journal* mentioned the Browns had only let up nine hits in three games over a total of 27 innings against Hartford and ignored mentioning that the third game was a no-hitter.[31] The *Louisville Courier-Journal* itself simply reported the St. Louis club had whitewashed Hartford. A careful-eyed crank might have noted a six-point line below the line score which read: Base hits—St. Louis 6; Hartford 0.[32] The *Hartford Courant* didn't even cover the game until its July 18 edition and then the *Courant* featured Hartford being whitewashed for three straight games.[33] The *Louisville Courier-Journal* cited the *Republican* talking of the Browns' three shutouts in a row, noting that "Such a thing has never happened in the history of the game."[34] In a 13-line story, the *Chicago Tribune* reported the Hartfords had been whitewashed and did mention that not a single safe hit had been made off Bradley, but its mention in the lead wasn't given any particular place of significance in the rest of the story.

Whether Bradley's effort was really the first National League no-hitter is still debated. Boston's Joe Borden threw a 4–0 no-no for the Philadelphia Pearls against Chicago on July 24, 1875, in a National Association contest. That was big league baseball's first no-hitter, but Borden may also have pitched the National League's first no-hitter on May 23, 1876. Cincinnati newspaperman O.P. Caylor, the lone official scorer, may have demonstrated that the pen is not only mightier than the sword, but also mightier than the bat, when he supposedly recorded two "walks" given up by Borden as two "hits." Some sportswriters and N.L. officials disagreed with Caylor's categorizing walks as hits, but "since then, enough doubt has been cast on Borden's effort against Cincinnati to erase his honor of tossing the first National League no-hitter."[35] Scorekeeping was simply not universally uniform in the 1870s. Only God and the ghosts of '76 know if Borden was sinned against.

17

Dog Days[1]

By mid–July Sirius, the dog star, was definitely in ascendancy. The weather was hot and humid. The National League Championship was down to a three-way race between Chicago, Hartford and St. Louis. Chicago and Hartford were three and three against each other as were Hartford and St. Louis, while St. Louis and Chicago were two and two. There seemed to be little to choose between them. The numbers could be crunched and munched and reams of data on runs and hits calculated, correlated and extrapolated, but such analysis didn't offer much insight, except, perhaps, that offense wasn't everything. The A's were second in runs scored and second in hits, but seventh in the standings. With George Hall, Levi Meyerle and Ezra Sutton as hitsmen, the A's could certainly mount a formidable offense. Hartford, on the other hand, was well down in runs scored (fifth) and hits (sixth) and yet were in second place in the standings, with five fewer wins and two more losses than Chicago. The other clubs pretty well matched their runs and hits with their position in the N.L. standings.[2]

Chadwick, who continually emphasized the importance of pitching and defense, certainly seemed to be correct. Chicago's Al Spalding (47–12, 1.75 ERA), St. Louis' Grin Bradley (45–19, 1.23 ERA) and Hartford's duo of Candy Cummings (16–8, 1.67 ERA) and Tommy Bond (31–13, 1.68 ERA) were definitely the cream of the crop. Perhaps Louisville's Jim Devlin (30–35, 1.56 ERA, league-leading 122 strikeouts) could be placed in the same corral. Hitting was important, of course. The seventh-place A's might have George Hall second in base hits with 62, and Levi Meyerle sixth with 56. Cellar-sited Cincinnati might have Charley Jones 11th with 52 hits, but first place Chicago had Ross Barnes leading with 77; Paul Hines, fourth with 59 and John Peters, fifth with 58. In hits per game, Chicago had five players in the top nine. Maybe Chadwick should reconsider his partiality to pitching and defense. Then again, maybe not.

By July 16–17, Hartford was headed back east. The western swing had not helped Hartford in their struggle with Chicago for first spot. The Dark Blues had gone 6 and 5 while the White Stockings were winning 9 and losing 3. Hartford continued to pick up nicknames if not wins. The kinder class of sportswriters now referred to them as the "Dark Blue Nutmegers" while the more sarcastic citizens of the press called them the "Would-be-invincibles."[3]

Raiding and attempts at raiding continued through July despite editorial protests as to its questionable morality. Cincinnati's Si Keck telegraphed Tim Murnan of Boston to come and join his Ohio club in '77 for $2,000 a year. Murnan declined the offer.[4] About the same time, N.T. Appolonio of Boston was openly going after St. Louis outfielder Joe Blong for the coming season.[5]

The mystery of Harry Wright's non-death at the end of April was finally cleared up. A New Haven reporter admitted he was the source of the unintended hoax. He admitted that, delighted over a rare New Haven victory over Wright's Boston club, he had sent the line "Harry Wright is dead" over the wire. To him, it meant that Wright's Boston team had been beaten by New Haven. His inept stab at communication had unwittingly set sequences of obituaries and soliloquies magna cum laude in motion concerning the dearly non-departed. The now startled reporter had refrained from explaining his faux pas from sheer embarrassment.[6] Presumably, the quality of New Haven baseball was only matched by the quality of New Haven reporting.

The canine king of the dog days seemed to have arrived on Tuesday, July 18, as the temperature went equatorial and the humidity oceanic beneath a clear blue sky at Brown Stockings Park in St. Louis. The heat and Cincinnati's lack of competitive potential kept the crowd down to around 200. Bradley's being within an "out" of another no-hitter before Cincy went into hit mode garnered little attention in the press. The focus was Charley Jones' hitting a crashing double with two out and light-hitting Amos "The Darling" Booth following with a run-scoring single to sabotage Bradley's shutout as St. Louis won, 5–1. That Jones, whose muscles were evidently made for wild horses, beasts of burden and grizzly bears, was featured was understandable. In 1876, 32 percent of Jones' hits would be for extra bases. He was Cincinnati's premier player.

A new tragedy became evident in the playing ranks of the National League by mid–July. Cherokee Fisher's boy, Charley, was dying in a Philadelphia hospital. Time would soon be up for another National League player's child.[7]

By July 18, the clubs were beginning to compare their home and away share of the gate with great care. St. Louis management was cognizant of having paid out twice as much to Hartford as they received for playing in Hartford, and the Louisville executive was aware the share they handed Hartford was almost four and one-half times as much as Louisville received in Hartford.[8] Who said Hartford was such a bonanza to play against on the road? The directors of the two western clubs probably wondered if the Dark Blues shouldn't be replaced by another club. In other St. Louis–Hartford news, John Remsen, the Deep Blues' fine center fielder, signed to play for the Browns in '77. Salary: $2,500.[9]

The blistering hot weather continued to keep attendance down. The players were bronzed by the sun settling none too sedately on their skin for the past two weeks. The summer heat was lethal to many city dwellers. The *New York Times* ran its usual daily roundup of the effects of the long, hot summer, listing four deaths, 15 prostrations and one person driven insane from sun-stroke and heat on July 13.[10] Such reports followed day after day. Attendance fell. If riding to the ball park in a sweat-smelling, human-humid horsecar wasn't deterrent enough, sitting in the searing sun, which always seemed to shine onto your seat or into your eyes, probably was. Even if shade shadowed your spot, the air under the grandstand roof could be as stifling as a Puritan's Sunday code.

One of the worst examples of big-league baseball was presented for the National League public on Saturday, July 22, as Chicago defeated Louisville 30–9 in Chicago. Hulbert and friends must have sat in sweltering disbelief and simmering disgust. The contest included 37 errors, 10 wild pitches and six passed balls. The *Louisville Courier-Journal* declared Louisville's performance the worst ever by a pro team.[11] The only excuse for the error-filled debacle, aside from genetic ineptitude, was a heavy wind that favored the offense. Neither the humidity nor heat — it was 89 degrees Fahrenheit — was unusual. Playing an unfamiliar position was probably the culprit since the Louisville battery was particularly miscue-minded. Pitcher J.J. Ryan made 11 errors, 10 of which were wild pitches that counted as errors in 1876, and catcher Winfield Scott Hastings made 10, six of which were passed balls that also counted as errors in '76. Johnny Ryan was primarily an outfielder. He appeared in six National Association games for New Haven in 1875, winning one and losing the rest, and this July 22nd appearance was his lone attempt at being a National League pitcher. Hastings was an outfielder, second baseman and sometime catcher, a versatile veteran but not a master craftsman at any position. Hastings fought the Battle of the Backstop that July 22. League officials could only find comfort in the knowledge that the average crank's memory wasn't any longer than that of the average voter. Such exhibitions of erring tended to be forgotten as soon as a well-played game came along.

The possible "transfer" of Lip Pike from St. Louis to Cincinnati was hinted at in the papers.[12] Now that Jack Remsen of Hartford had been engaged to play for St. Louis in '77,[13] Pike's presence in center field was superfluous. He was apparently unwanted and unappreciated, despite his sizzling speed, sure hands and .300-plus statistics as a batsman. Replacing Pike with Remsen made neither common nor uncommon sense. Pike had more speed than a light beam and was one of the best defensive outfielders to occupy major league grass.[14] Remsen hit .247 in four N.A. years and was on his way to a .275 season in 1876. Pike hit .321 in five N.A. years and was in the midst of a .323 season in '76. So why should St. Louis want rid of him? Remsen simply didn't seem fair exchange for Pike. One simple reality might explain a lot: Lip Pike was Jewish.[15] But St. Louis had hired Pike knowing full well his religious affiliation. He had played in the old National Association for Troy (1871), Baltimore (1872–73), Hartford (1874) and St. Louis (1875). Both the knowledgeable and the naïve believed there had to be another explanation, but what it was remained beyond public knowledge or comprehension.

An outfielder with a .300 bat and light beam speed, Lipman (Lip) Pike was dropped at season's end in 1876 by St. Louis either because he had questioned the honesty of St. Louis player-manager Mike McCreary or because of his religious faith. Pike, the first Jewish player in both the National Association and the National League, was replaced by Hartford's weak-hitting Jack Remsen. (Transcendental Graphics)

Monday, July 24, was a memorable day for many cranks who were becoming tired of being baked, fried and refried as one hot day seared past another. The temperature dropped in Louisville, falling to a cool 70 degrees Fahrenheit. The foolish thought it was a suggestion that the sweltering season of sunstroke might have ended. The less foolish thought correctly. It was simply a break in the series of summer sizzlers. The cranks talked incessantly about the change in the weather and of a Charley Jones home run that got lost in the outfield grass in Saturday, July 22's game. The more critical of Cincinnati's cranks probably questioned why Red Stockings manager Charlie Gould continued to bat power-hitting Charley Jones in the leadoff slot.[16] To many, it didn't make sense.

The Louisville press continued to criticize Chapman's Grays, even when Lou'ville stopped a seven-game St. Louis win streak, defeating the Browns 7–4 at St. Louis' Grand Avenue Park on July 22. A classic quote from an unknown Louisville player reflecting on past failures and not the present victory was featured in the day's report. Waxing poetic, the unnamed Grays player noted that "bad plays, like buzzards, follow one another in black procession until they make a perfect array of ugly things about a single hideous carcass of a game."[17] Louisville had let up 48 runs in two games to Chicago, losing 18–0 on July 20 and 30–9 on July 22 as far as the *Chicago Tribune* was concerned and 30–7 if you believed the *Louisville Courier-Journal*.[18] Humiliation seemed to blend with the daily humidity to bring baseball to its knees in popularity.

The Pike story continued to stay in the daily columns. A St. Louis *Republican* story reprinted in the *Louisville Courier-Journal* of July 25 scolded the Browns' management for losing the best batter, swiftest base runner and one of the finest fielders. An altogether conscientious player, Pike was liked by 19 of 20 St. Louis spectators. His loss, according to the *Republican*, was "due to personal dislike and prejudice and not incompetency."[19] Remsen, despite his high salary, was never a superior player to Pike. Pike had out-batted John J. in '73, '74 and '75 and was ahead of him in '76 as well. Why let him go then? The answer may have been the less than friendly relations that existed between Lip Pike and Mike McGeary of St. Louis. Pike had been quoted in the New York and St. Louis press accusing McGeary, who had been under suspicion for shady play earlier in the year, of throwing a recent game against the Mutuals. Maybe that was it. Pike thought so.[20] Hulbert, in his drive to establish a clean league, wanted rid of the McGearys if they were guilty. He just could be. He was on Concannon's '75 Philadelphias and had been accused of questionable play.[21] Hulbert did not like these accusations that went unproven and not acted upon. There would have to come a time when the league had a president who would step in and who, after a fair trial, would either clear or "convict" the accused. Since Bulkeley wasn't inclined to act, accusations only hurt the league. Simply put, to accuse was to abuse. Hulbert knew the script for '76 was slowly being written, event by event, in the annals of bad publicity. He didn't like it. Most league officials agreed. It was better to leave well enough alone. See no evil, once again, seemed a solution since it meant print no evil.

By the final week of July, the press was commenting on the possible future moves of Cammeyer and his New York Mutuals. Q of the day was: Would the New York–Brooklyn team remain in the league in 1877? Cammy had been in the amusement purveying business for more than a decade and former times had been better than present times. Like all people on the planet except the psychotic, he was not fond of losing money and was finding that operating in the red was becoming a habit.[22] People in the New York–Brooklyn area didn't seem overly interested in whether his Mutuals prospered or perished anymore. The area population being so large, there were always a few cranks coming through the gates of Union Grounds; but now they were getting fewer and fewer. The Mutuals were an infirmary for the lame, halt, corrupt and incompetent.[23] Cammy's budget only allowed the signing of such players. He made money in the shoe business,[24] but ran his ball club on a shoe string. Mutual players like Bill Craver had dubious reputations,[25] but who else could play second base as well as Craver for what Cammy could pay. Unless upbraided by higher authority, Cammy usually looked the other way when one of his players took too much drink or pocketed a little betting money to supplement his meager pay.

Cammy didn't have many options for '77. Since Hicks, Mathews, Hallinan and Start were already committed to other clubs, not many of the Mutes' present players would be back. This decimation of the team's roster led to his first option. His receipts wouldn't allow him to put together a full nine of experienced players, so Cammy could only field the best team of youngsters he could find. He simply was unable to match the bids of wealthier organizations or those willing to court immediate bankruptcy by borrowing against tomorrow's gate receipts.[26] But if Cammy made an accommodation with Bulkeley, as was rumored, the entire Hartford team could play in his Union Grounds in '77.[27] It was not a fantastic idea. Bulkeley probably wouldn't object. The Dark Blues were having trouble meeting their pay schedule.[28] Six of the team's 12 players were New Yorkers. Bulkeley, who was making public protests claiming that Hartford would stay in Hartford, had been signing his players to contracts with himself, not the Hartford Baseball Club.[29] Bulks might not have more than an iota of interest in baseball, but he was keenly interested in matters of business. There was, of course, the possibility that Bulks would move the Dark Blues to Providence, another attractive option. It had three times the population of Hartford.[30] But New York–Brooklyn was as populated an area you could find anywhere. It seemed the only two options Cammeyer had for keeping a ball team in Brooklyn–New York was to field a team of youngsters or rent out his grounds to Hartford.[31] He might even manage the Dark

Blues[32] or he could manage Si Keck's Cincinnati nine for him whether or not Hartford used his Union Street Grounds.[33] Finally, retiring from the field was not an unattractive option. Cammy wasn't getting any younger. This last alternative may have been even more attractive to him on July 25 as Boston routed the Mutes 11–1.

A minor triumph in the National League's battle for respectability came during the last week of July when George Bechtel, who had played 14 games for the Grays and two for the Mutuals so far in 1876, was finally expelled from the league. The reason involved his having too amorous a relationship with alcoholic beverages.[34] Bechtel had not been a run-of-the-mill outfielder. He had hit .278 over five years in the National Association with the Athletic, Mutuals, Philadelphia White Stockings and the Philadelphia Centennials. Clubs didn't like to cut hitters of Bechtel's standing. But the Grays and then the Mutes concluded his .200 average so far in 1876 was not an aberration, but an indication that his potential didn't warrant toleration of his drinking. Bechtel had returned to and hung around Lou'ville for two weeks after his release from the Mutes, pestering baseball people, demanding a re-hearing to which the authorities finally agreed to listen. Bechtel vehemently denied that he had been intoxicated in New York. He even introduced new evidence to back his claim of innocence. As a compromise, the league directors reinstated him and he supposedly went off to finish the season at Jackson, Michigan, which was ostensibly, except for its paychecks, an amateur team.[35]

A flurry of lopsided games didn't help league attendance in late July. On Wednesday, July 26, Chicago pounded pathetic Cincinnati 28–3 at Chicago in a batting bonanza as the White Socks got 31 hits. Boston pounded out 22 hits while beating the Mutuals 18–6 in Beantown two days later. The Mutes got 12 hits of their own. Chicago continued to pulverize Cincy, getting 23 hits to Cincy's 10 in a 17–3 non-contest on July 27. Pitching prevailed at Grand Avenue Park in St. Louis where Louisville bested St. Louis 4–2. Devlin let up nine and Bradley, six hits.

Lip Pike, the man who could move from first to second faster than the spark of an electric arc, formally announced having signed to play next season for the Cincinnati Reds. He now told the press that he was not retired from St. Louis for expressing the opinion that Mike McGeary sold a game St. Louis had played against the Mutuals in Brooklyn.[36] Cincinnati's citizens reveled in the news of the Red Stockings acquiring the St. Louis speedster for '77, but soon sobered concerning the formal announcement of William "Cherokee" Fisher's release from the '76 squad. The *Hartford Courant* printed a less than savory insinuation, stating that "Fisher resigned by request," then added, "He was too much of a beer pitcher."[37]

Other papers mentioned Fisher had been released for "quaffing too many intoxicating draughts"[38] or made similar references to alcoholic indulgences. They didn't mention Cherokee's release was also brought about by his non-toxic pitching. Fisher's 4–20 win-loss record and 3.03 ERA didn't compare favorably with the league's other regular hurlers. Everyone in baseball knew boozers who won almost always kept their jobs and that boozers who lost found themselves unemployed. Jobs rested on win-loss, not drink–no drink decisions. Fisher's release came a day before he learned that his boy, Charley, was in declining health and dying. Fisher could be forgiven if he increased his internalization of alcoholic substances in the days that followed.

The Browns beat Louisville 7–0 Saturday, July 29, at St. Louis on another Bradley one-hitter, Chick Fulmer getting the only Grays hit, a very lucky and questionable one. The press was more interested in the way Eddie Haley, the song and dance artist, performed as umpire than Bradley almost throwing a second no-hitter. The only hit off Bradley was a Fulmer pop that should have been caught before it dropped between McGeary and Blong. Bradley somehow finished the game with a grin.

The *New York Herald* continued to give baseball less than enthusiastic press as July drew to a close. Other papers around the league promptly reprinted the *Herald's* unsympathetic utterances, especially when its reporters referred to Hulbert's beloved baseball as the National Wastetime.[39] The *Herald* had long charged that professional baseball players had an itching palm for on-coming baseballs and in-coming cash. It often asserted that games were frequently fixed, baseball being allegedly controlled by a clique of gamblers whose friends brought in bets to the local poolroom operator. It openly stated that club managers were afraid to investigate in case they found what they did not want to find and consequently had to print the truth. See no evil continued to mean publish no evil. And it argued that two-thirds of the country's interest in baseball had eroded away over the past six or seven years. Now 1,000 to 1,200 cranks came when 6,000 to 7,000 used to attend. What was most frustrating about the *Herald's* harangues was that they were correct. Hulbert's attempt to purge baseball of its seamier element was far more surface than substance. Publicity, in the form of stories that revealed the dark side of baseball, was bad if the culprits were not "brought to justice," a euphemism for "booted out of the league."

The press continued to spend considerable reportorial time and editorial space on the idea that the Hartford club would move from Hartford to Brooklyn in 1877.[40] The Hartford newspapers covered the story as expected, arguing that Hartford would stay in Hartford. The papers cited that there was no need for the Dark Blues to move. Attendance was down in Hartford due to the general depression[41] that was affecting every city in the league, but Hartford's receipts still covered all expenses. Bulkeley continued to claim to have no plans to move his Dark Blues. They would stay and play in Hartford in '77.[42] What else could he say at this moment in time? He still had seats to fill in '76 and those seats were in Hartford. But then again, maybe it was premature for anyone to think of moving the Dark Blues.

The *Hartford Times*, mixing economics and athletics, expressed its profound distaste for the way ballplayers were demanding abominably high salaries and its dislike of their custom of engaging themselves for next year before finishing this year's obligations. Could a player signed with team A for '77 continue to play at top form for team B for the rest of '76, especially when playing for B against A? The *Times* didn't think so.[43]

In a happier modality, Dave Eggler, his spinal injuries healed, returned to active play with the Athletic, the dire forecasts by the medics of his never playing again being grossly incorrect.[44]

Dog day baseball continued, featuring humidity and heat, shade seeking and sunburn. The *Courier-Journal* noted that the temperatures on the seats on the right side of the field at Lou'ville park were often too high for comfort.[45] To the Romans, Sirius rising was an ill omen amid a summer of scorching sunshine; to the Egyptians, it was the life-giving flood of the Nile; and to 1876 Americans, it was the browning of infield grass, the baking of boards and benches in ballpark seating areas and a bit of discomfort amid the entertainment called baseball.[46] It was a long, long time to September and the cooling caress of autumn.

18

The Runs of August

Between the 30th of June and 30th of July, Chicago won 11 of 13 games to stand atop the National League with 35 wins and 7 losses. Since only the number of games won counted in the race for the pennant, the White Stockings had an eight-win lead over St. Louis and a 10-win lead over Hartford. In modern terms, the standings were:

	W	L	Pct.	GB
Chicago	35	7	.833	—
Hartford	25	10	.714	6½
St. Louis	27	14	.659	7½
Boston	22	19	.537	12½
Louisville	18	24	.429	17
New York	15	24	.385	18½
Philadelphia	11	26	.297	21½
Cincinnati	6	35	.146	28½

The White Socks' .833 record was as sizzling as the summer weather, which remained hot.

The popularity of N.L. baseball was melting in Philadelphia where the game appeared as dead as the winter of '75-'76. The Centennial was its chief executioner. The Athletic's administrators were being cast as pallbearers. President T.J. Smith had put management in the hands of Al Reach at the start of the year. Reach survived a short sojourn before giving way to A.H. Wright, who was manager, club secretary and no improvement on any previous front office occupant.[1]

The White Stockings, however, were still drawing multitudes. Concerning the upcoming Chi-Lou'ville series, the *Louisville Courier-Journal* said, "[It was] the last chance to see the great Chicagos ... we advise every one to go out and witness to what a degree of perfection the game has at last been brought."[2]

At Louisville, attention focused on a tiny variant that might turn the upcoming games to its favor. The Southern City powers noted that the coming contests between the Grays and the Whites would have the advantage of the Grays picking the game ball. The White Socks, playing at home, had always selected a lively ball. The Grays would go for the deadest ball.[3] A moribund baseball could negate Chicago's edge in both batting and fielding. Hard hit ground shots bounding across the infield a tad slower should allow the slightly slower infielder to get to them and make the putout at first. Line drives should proceed away from the plate at a slightly slower speed giving the slightly less adept fielder a bit longer to make a catch. The soft sphere should simply bring the two teams closer together in on-field ability. At least, that was the theory.[4]

The Louisville ballpark had undergone a few changes since Chicago last visited the Grays' grounds. A recently built addition extended about 50 feet north of the grandstand, the space being used as an entranceway, and was now full of snorting equines and black carriages crammed with paying customers. The northern and western fences had been extended upward to at least 16 feet, effectively eliminating a number of express wagons packed and stacked with boys, each paying a dime to the driver-owner for a perch, lining up along the outside of the formerly low fences to watch the Grays at play. The Louisville management had seen that this bunch of freeloaders (or bastion of free enterprise depending on your point of view) was no longer cutting into the team's gate receipts. Any conveyance entering the outfield area now had to go through the newly provided entranceway and, of course, pay for the privilege. It was, perhaps, a matter of opinion, but a final difference in the park since Chi's last visitation appeared to be a lengthening of the grass in the deep outfield areas.[5]

Despite Louisville's ill-groomed outfield and selection of a sphere about as solid as a transparent apple, Chicago had little trouble inaugurating August with a 15–7 win. The sportswriter for the *Louisville Courier-Journal* succinctly noted that to beat Chicago, Lou'ville would need a ball as dead as a nine and quarter-inch lump of mush.[6] Chicago went on to take two of three games from the Graying Louisvilles. Despite this propensity to better their opponent time after time, the White Socks continued to be roundly cheered as a visiting team wherever they went. This held in Louisville as much as anywhere else.[7]

Enthusiasm abounded in Louisville during the series. Despite threatening weather and a previous night's rainstorm that suggested to some a possible sodden, unplayable field, about 1,000 fanatics watched Louisville defeat Chicago 4–2 in the second game. The *Courier-Journal* couldn't contain itself, repeatedly referring to the contest as the Greatest Game Ever Played at Louisville.[8] Hulbert came down to catch the contest in the crank meaning of the word. He was quoted in the *Courier-Journal* that the dead ball was killing baseball. The *C-J*'s reporter noted that Lou'ville preferred its chances with the lifeless ball.[9]

The popularity of the White Stockings was keeping the National League alive — at least, in Louisville — during these days of summer heat. Louisville's Fourth Avenue Railway added cars to their service to have enough to handle traffic to and from the ballpark for these early August Chicago games.[10] Chicago drew 2,000 customers into Indianapolis' new grounds earlier in the year for a friendly, meaningless game.[11] Where Chicago went, cranks were bound to follow.

The rumor mill noted that George Hall, the home run king of the A's, would be with St. Louis in '77. The *Cincinnati Enquirer* noted that it was "an excellent idea to hire a Hall."[12] Although the line was worth a parcel of praise by the author's editor, the story didn't turn out to be true. Hall, who would play for Louisville in '77, probably would wish it had been. At the end of the '77 season, Hall would be suspended for life along with three other Grays — Jim Devlin, Al Nichols and Bill Craver — for dumping games.

The fate of William "Cherokee" Fisher, Cincinnati chucker and heavy drinker, came to its final settlement. Sometime earlier "The Fish" had reportedly resigned and reportedly been suspended, now it was time to report the veteran pitcher had been released.[13] His status had evidently been in limbo. On the negative side, Fisher didn't have a winning record (51–64) when Cincy first got him. The positive part had been that he had experience. On the sarcastic side, the more savage critic could conclude that it was experience losing. He did pitch for two winning teams, going 9–3 for the Lord Baltimores in 1872 and 22–18 for Philadelphia in 1875. But he was 30 years old and wasn't with a winner now. So William Charles Fisher, who relied on pinpoint control and who had the misfortune of pitching for the worst team in the National League, was destined to finish the season with the team George Bechtel had been exiled to, Jackson, Michigan.[14] The fact that Fish drank like a Fisher was actually irrelevant. Losers were leavers.

The *Cincinnati Enquirer* received a petition bearing 2,000 signatures during Fish's suspension which urged Cincinnati rehire him for the coming year.[15] Cincy owner Si Keck, however, rejected all appeals to resurrect Fisher, who materialized at the Cincinnati ballpark in the official capacity as umpire before going north to Jackson. Fisher was given an "A" by all onlookers, the *Enquirer* reporter extolling Fisher as "an excellent umpire."[16] The fact Cincy lost 10–3 to St. Louis did not seem to affect the crowds' appreciation of the pitcher-turned-arbiter.

The battle in the league standings along with the heat and humidity was combining with accumulating injuries to wear teams down. The

18 — The Runs of August

Mutes, for an aching example, were down to nine regulars.[17] The race of most interest was now between the Dark Blues and the Browns. Everyone was conceding the whip pennant to the White Stockings, whose superiority had moved from the apparent to the absolutely obvious.

High court was held this fine first day of August in Hartford as management investigated the team's play during its recent western trip. Accusations abounded. The controversy revolved around the comments of Tommy Bond, the team's young, outspoken pitcher. Manager Bob Ferguson seemed implicated. Rumor was that the turmoil was splitting the team asunder.[18] It would be some time before the Bond-Ferguson battle would be resolved. Meanwhile, Bond's chain lightning deliveries were decimating the club's backstopping staff, which was truly black and blue, three of the Dark Blues catchers being presently disabled.[19]

The talk on the second day of August concerned the shooting of Wild Bill Hickok, the famed frontiersman, who had evidently been shot in the back in Deadwood, South Dakota, by a person unknown. Judging from the talk of the day, the popularity of firearms to baseball seemed to parallel directly the difference between the velocities of bullets and baseballs.

A record in Cincinnati baseball was scrawled in the settling dust by game's end the following day. For the first time in the history of professional baseball in Cincy, the home club failed to score a run as St. Louis and Grin Bradley blanked the sorry Cincy side 10–0 behind a two-hitter that was scored as a four-hitter, as O.P. Caylor continued to record "walks" as "hits."[20] The game could have been even more lopsided. Cincy's Will Foley elevated himself above and beyond gravity's grasp to make a superhuman one-handed catch that ended an inning and kept two or three more St. Louies from scoring. All this was viewed by about 200 patrons who occupied the Ohio Valley sweatshop that was Cincy's ballpark in late summer. These cranks must have been of the dedicated sort. Enduring a sit in the sun this sweltering day was an act of devotion and dedication more to the National game than the National League. The pitcher-poor (a newcomer called Dory Dean was proving a flop) Red Stockings were without their only real gate attraction. Charley Jones, slugger supreme, was in bed with a severe fever and a cluster of aches and agonies.[21]

Chicago and Louisville got involved in a temper-tampered tilt in Louisville. Rain began to drip down on the river city's park sometime in the fourth inning. Umpire Charles Houtz ignored a league rule that stated: "Should rain commence to fall during the progress of a match-game, the umpire must note the time it begun, and *should it continue for five minutes* he shall, at the request of either captain, suspend play. Such suspended game shall not be resumed until, in the opinion of the umpire, the ground is in fit condition for fair playing."[22] This would not have been a problem if the clouds had cooperated and kept the remainder of the rain to themselves, but clouds being clouds, and gravity being what it is, the rain continued to come down in cascading crescendos of wet. Umpire Houtz refused to suspend play. By then it was the fifth inning and the rain was plummeting earthward in rivers. Chicago was at bat and leading 4–1. Chicago batsmen instantly attempted to go out, but Louisville recognized this ploy and refused to put anyone out. As a result Chicago, rather reluctantly, scored five runs. With Houtz refusing to suspend play, a stalemate followed with hotter heads prevailing and players on both teams going Vesuvius. Houtz eventually awarded the White Stockings the game 9–0. Louisville protested. Amazingly, it was all settled amicably later that evening, the teams' captains agreeing to replay the contest the following Monday. Not so amazingly, the rain hardly left a trace of cool upon the land. Many a player had a tough time sleeping that night. An argument between men could be forgotten, adversaries could forgive, but the hot weather was a wolf of a different breed.

On Friday, August 4, St. Louis held second place with 29 wins to Hartford's 27 victories. Hartford had 27 wins in 37 starts for .729 to St. Louis' 29 wins in 43 games for .674. No one spoke of a race for the whip pennant anymore. The seven other sides in the league had conceded the flag to Chicago, who had a habit of losing one, then winning four or five, losing one, then winning six or seven, and so forth.

In non-baseball circles, Philadelphia sports followers were buzzing about a return prizefight having been arranged between young Billy Walker and Jimmy Weeden on or about August 30 in the vicinity of Philadelphia.[23] Since prizefighting was illegal, the papers printing news of the upcoming event was, in the strictest sense of the law, something akin to publishing a story that the local bank would be robbed sometime in the next few weeks.

With his players feeling the cumulative effects of day after day of sizzling summer weather when even rainy days steamed with humid heat, manager John Chapman got the signature of St. Louis Reds' Dan Collins on a Grays' contract as Louisville regrouped for the remainder of the season.[24] Collins would play seven games for the Grays, batting .143 during his 15 minutes of fame. Collins' materialization on the Grays' roster Saturday, August 5, accompanied Lou'ville's first win over championship-bound Chicago in nine tries. Unfortunately, a very heavy rainstorm Friday evening and continually threatening weather Saturday morning kept the afternoon attendance clustering near 1,000. The Grays' grounds, however, were correctly touted as the best drained in the league so the game was playable. Chicago's groundskeeper might have disagreed as to the grounds' drainage rating as the game progressed, however. The spongy turf cushioned sharp grounders into routine outs and slowed the fleet feet in White Socks to "You're out" speed.[25] The 4–2 Louisville victory helped turn the columns of the Louisville papers into a glowing Gray print complete with crowing commentaries.[26]

John Morris had taken over from Houtz as umpire. After the rhubarb of the last Louisville game, Houtz's interest in umpiring had gone wanting. The baiting of umpires was becoming a problem. If it continued, the "kill the umpire" crowd would cause an acute shortage of arbiters.[27]

The Mutuals extracted a 4–1 decision that same Saturday from the Dark Blues on a furnace-hot Hartford field. The Hartford executive expected a fine turnout to see Joe Start and Jim Holdsworth of the Mutes who had signed to wear Dark Blue in '77. Outfielder Holdsworth, with hands of surety, led the league in least errors by any player, having committed but 10 miscues in 40 games. The appeal of seeing Start, Holdsworth and the Mutes was evidently limited: between 600 and 1,000 patrons attended.[28] It may have been just as well. Robert "Baltimore Bobby" Mathews, the 25-year-old right-hander — who at 5' 5½" and 140 pounds probably had to spell his name with one "t" since carrying another "t" would be enough to put him in risk of a hernia or slipped spinal disc — pitched for the Mutes. He blanked the Dark Blues for eight of nine innings, letting up a solo run in the eighth. The loss was exceedingly depressing, turning Hartford an even darker shade of blue. Hartford scored the only earned run in the game, committed three fewer errors than the Mutuals and stranded five runners to the Mutes' three. The stranded Hartford runners must have charged around through manager Ferguson's mind well into the night before sleep relieved him of his waking nightmare.

The Hartford press pacified any fears that the loss of Remsen and Mills to foreign fields in '77 would not be amply made up by the signing of Start and Holdsworth. A carefully compiled comparison of the four men was published showing that in total games, runs, base hits, putouts and errors the pair of newcomers was equal to or better than the pair leaving the club. Career data for Start and Holdsworth showed that the Hartford newsmen actually underrated the potential worth of Start and Holdsworth. Their lifetime career records would later show that Start, .295 in 16 major league years, and Holdsworth, .285 in eight years, were definitely better at bat than Mills, who didn't play in the N.L. after 1876, or Remsen, who had a .239 average over 10 years. The Hartford news people, of course, only had data up to August 1876.

Baseball club owners must have shuddered when they scanned the staid *Philadelphia Inquirer*, which still devoted more space to cricket than baseball. Louisville upset Chicago 4–2 on Saturday, August 5, in a whale of a game, but on Monday, August 7, the *Inquirer* relegated the game to two and one-half lines followed by eight and one-half inches of cricket and rowing.[29] The owners knew that baseball would never go anywhere if sports scribes emulated the *Inquirer*. The press had to cover N.L. games with proficiency, panache and plenty of space for the league to be successful.

Si Keck must have sighed as his eyes searched the Cincy Grounds for people — paying people — on Tuesday afternoon, August 8. Cincinnati was hosting Chicago, but the magic that had attracted crowds of cranks in Louisville had gone "poof!" in Cincy. The first time Chicago visited Cincinnati, the stands had been packed with anywhere from 4,000 to 5,000 patrons. The next Chicago series in Cincy saw the crowds drop to between 1,200 and 1,500 fans. Now, in August, not even league-leading Chicago could bring people in to see a game at Cincinnati. Fewer than 150 people watched Chicago beat Cincinnati 13–3. The game put the feasibility of Cincinnati using Dory Dean as a replacement for the departed Cherokee Fisher in further jeopardy, as the White Stockings racked up nine base hits in the first inning off the latest Red right-hander. Dean might be a hometown boy from the Cincinnati suburb of Cumminsville who had pitched for the local Blue Stockings the previous summer, but for all their faults, baseball moguls never sinned on the side of sentimentality. Cincy's management went back to hurler hunting.

Elsewhere, Bradley continued to baffle opposing batsmen as St. Louis stopped Louisville 3–0 on a one-hitter. Grin had a smile and a no-hitter for 8⅓ innings before Joe Gerhardt cracked an air-splitting record-wrecking line drive into right field to erase both the smile and the no-hitter. The *Louisville Courier-Journal* didn't mention Bradley's one-hitter until the last graph. The newspaper suggested he pitched well and made several excellent stops of hard hit grounders.[30] The unimportance of the pitcher as a pitcher continued to be alive and well.

The rarely used Ross ball, for instance, was decidedly the deadest baseball made, so dead and moribund that most teams had long since said eulogies over it and left it buried in the graveyard of rejected baseballs. The Mahn ball was slightly more alive. Some players said you could barely hear its heart beat with a stethoscope. Frustrated foes of St. Louis felt much of Bradley's success was due to St. Louis' always opting for a genuine Ross ball in all their home games.[31] St. Louis officials didn't deny that the Ross ball's lack of recoil aided the team's fielders and thereby Grin Bradley, but that didn't mean Bradley wasn't capable of stopping batsmen with a livelier baseball. Bradley's road record wasn't much different from his performance at home.

By the second week of August, the decline and falter of the Athletic had become serious. Management already owed its players back pay ranging from $200 to $500 each on that year's contracts and a parcel of hard cash on the previous year's as well. At season's start, the A's executive had priced the club's shares (which came with free tickets) so low they amounted to little more than payments for season seats. The result was large crowds, but little money. Now, the pain was plain: expenses had not been met by gate receipts. The A's stared bankruptcy straight in the IOUs. Neither tourists nor Philadelphians came in any quantity to their games. One source told the *Chicago Tribune* that the Athletic wouldn't be able to complete the schedule and definitely wouldn't be coming west for their final series.[32]

Their expected demise might be filled by letting Indianapolis or New Haven into the league in '77. Spalding said there would be fierce opposition to their admission.[33] The A's could re-organize over the winter and play next year under some other name — Puritans, Pennsylvanians, Quakers, it didn't matter — but the A's by any name would still be the A's.[34] The idea that the National League might have to go without a team in Philly in '77 was becoming a definite possibility, but even if the Athletic managed to survive, a financially feeble team in a different uniform was still an economically anemic enterprise.

Hot, simmering August air seemed to shimmer over Philadelphia on the 8th. The darting, dancing deliveries of long Lon Knight, the tall, thin reed, weren't particularly difficult to meet as Hartford got 10 hits enough to edge the Athletic 3–1. Knight's effectiveness may have been slowly sapped away by the day's searing heat as he let up two runs in the ninth when Hartford broke a 1–1 tie. Why the heat was one-sided in its effect, be–Knighting Lon, but not draining Hartford hurler Tommy Bond's arm of energy and effectiveness, was left for physiologists of a latter age to explain.

On August 9, the Dark Blues topped the A's 9–1, taking advantage of accumulating hand hurts affecting young Athletic backstop Edward West (Whitey) Ritterson. The *Chicago Tribune* noted that he "gave out in the eighth inning and the home nine had only to hit the ball and get [sic] first to get home."[35] By then Ritterson's hands were not a sight for sore eyes, but for a doctor's. Hartford mounted an assault on the A's catcher in the last two innings, scoring three in the eighth and four in the ninth, primarily on Ritterson's errors.

The contest between the Athletic and the Mutuals showed there was still considerable amateurism in the press and in the National League. The *New York Times* reported that "Nealy Phelps, the ticket-taker at the gate, and a good ball player in any position, was induced to go behind the bat and catch for Knight's swift and wild delivery."[36] The lack of professionalism in the National League was the Athletic being unable to field a catcher and having to use the Mutuals' "last string" backstop. The amateurism in the press was *The Times* referring to Neal as a good ball player in any position. Phelps made 10 errors, five putouts and got one assist. The Mutuals won 9–7, but no A complained. Cornelius Carman Phelps would play only one other game that year, going 0-for-4 for the A's. His total major league career would include 10 games and five hits in 39 trips for a .128 batting average spaced over five years of non-play. Phelps' brief big-league career was almost as short as his life. He would die at age 45 in 1885.

Hartford played Bridgeport Thursday, August 10, losing this meaningless exhibition 9–8. They came home with smiles beaming after learning from the wire services that Louisville had topped St. Louis 4–2.

A certain devilment cut loose as the warm evening followed the blistering, burning day. Colonel J.P. Joyce, the former Cincinnati Red Stockings manager, told the youngest reporter on the press corps his stock story for the naïve and uninitiated. The general idea was that high salaries would ultimately kill baseball. Eventually all the best players would be on one club, as they almost were now. Joyce condemned the excessively high salaries the players were presently receiving. Then he grinned, letting the benevolence of a smile hide the malevolence of a mind. But the eager young man took notes with uncritical enthusiasm, his mind on a scoop, nothing else. Joyce suggested that the league should allow no players to be re-engaged at the end of each season. Their names should be put into eight boxes. There would be a box for catchers and pitchers since they tended to work together, a box for first basemen, a box for second basemen, and so on. Each manager would draw from each box and would be bound to retain the players he pulled from the boxes. In this way, chance would render the teams more equal, results of games would be less certain and crank interest would be deeper than the ocean between America and the old countries.[37]

Joyce's tongue-in-cheek proposal sounded good. Trouble was: how would you ever get rid of a player you pulled out of the hat if he were over the hill? Joyce's rules would argue you had to keep what you got. It could be a formula for an old player's home. And what incentive would there be to develop players? To scout them out? No one would want to put out time and money tracking down a good prospect only to have his name put into a hat for anyone to chance upon. And what about pay? If you had to play the player, he could hold you up for anything. This was the core problem with such ideas. They've only been in the oven for half the time necessary and thus come out half-baked. But they certainly sounded good enough to print. Francis C. Richter of *The Sporting News* of Philadelphia would put out a serious proposal called the Millennium Plan in 1887[38] that contained ideas similar to those set forth in jest by Joyce.

Over in Cincinnati, the lowly Reds' general manager George Keck, owner Si's brother, had been refusing to identify the great unknown pitcher he was supposedly bringing out for a tryout. The guess by the press was that it would be someone named Pratt and that he would be a flop. They would be correct on at least one count. George Keck's unknown would take a "Pratt fall." The gentle people of the press still wanted to know who'd be pitching for Cincy come game time on Saturday, August 12, and pressured a befuddled and bothered George Keck, who finally announced that the Red Stockings would introduce Dale Williams as a starter on Saturday.[39] Press conjecture about Pratt had been wrong. It was also incorrect that Keck's eyes were on Edward Sylvester "The Only" Nolan. The latter, a supposed phenom, was presently pitching for the Columbus Buckeyes.[40] It was rumored that Nolan had been offered $2,200 a year to pitch for Boston.[41] He would not surface in the National League until 1878, when Indianapolis would enter the league. He turned out to be only another feared fable of "might be," as he posted a 23–52 win-loss record over five years (1878, 1881, 1883–1885). Baseball talk was, as usual, the speech of rumor and speculation, good-natured cynicism and agitated anticipation.

The Saturday, August 12, game between Cincinnati and Chicago confirmed George Keck's word as Dale Williams appeared, pitched and became the latest Red Stocking sacrifice at the pitcher's point. Williams, a swift throwing youngster, pitched a nine-hitter as Cincinnati lost 5–0 to Chicago before a crowd of about 1,000, approximately three times greater than any recent Cincy crowd. Williams, whose delivery was very similar to the departed Fisher's, had arrived in Cincinnati from Indianapolis at 4 A.M. on the morning of the game. He demonstrated good control, a deceptive curve and an inability to get batsmen out with any regularity. Despite the defeat, the Cincinnati press gave him a good review. This was probably due to a need not to speak ill of the newly arrived and alive, possibly reinforced by the fact Williams was another hometown Cincinnati boy. On Sunday, August 13, the teams rested. The *Louisville Courier-Journal's* treatment of the series was a testament to the quaintness of the era and their story on the St. Louis–Louisville final game was a lulu. The 3–0 St. Louis win in the August 8 opener saw "The home nine defeated in an uninteresting and doleful game."[42] The 4–2 Louisville triumph in the August 10 second game was "baseball in all its beautiful perfection ... the prettiest contest of the season."[43] The August 12 finale was the epitome of 1876 reporting:

the eight hundred people who were present at the last game of the season between the Browns and the Louisvilles were treated to a delightful exhibition. The game Tuesday was comparatively tame and uninteresting, owing altogether to the weak batting of both clubs, that of the home nine in particular. The one Thursday was a decided improvement, the batting being much better and the fielding almost faultless, while that of yesterday was the most interesting and exciting of the lot, average work being done with the ash, while the fielding was simply excellent.[44]

The Saturday game seems to have been a case of "Ask not what your pitcher can do for your team, but ask what your fielders can do to stop the opposing team."

On Monday the 14th, the Dark Blues showed the benefit of an off-day of R and R — repose and renewal — by besting the Athletic 5–4 in a contest that saw each team get a dozen base hits. This was the day the war between President Bulkeley and the *Hartford Times* ended.[45] No armistice had been signed, but Bulkeley had withdrawn his objections and was letting the papers gather and send out inning-by-inning scores to be posted in appropriate places around town. Something done as routine around the league by the press had finally been allowed by the league's austere president.

The A's executive stared at the receipt figures of the club's recent eastern road trip this mid–August afternoon. The figures sat on the page in black ink, evenly spaced like headstones in the team's cemetery ledger: Boston, nothing exceeding $100 a game; Hartford, the El Dorado of visiting clubs, gate shares of $18 and $22; New York, $50.[46] It was a grave situation.

The monthly meeting of the Athletic Baseball Club was held at No. 1–108 Sansom Street as usual that evening. Since the last meeting, the A's had won seven and lost 20. Things got ugly when for some reason known only to himself and God, Frank Mills, an A's director, tried to have the press ejected from the meeting. Mills' motion, duly seconded, was defeated 25 to 5. Director Charles Sperling had the dishonor of officially announcing that only $24.86 was left in the A's till, treasury and bank account. The Athletic members appointed 15 men to oversee their future.[47] Newsmen saw it as a case of the broth being spoiled even before too many crooks ... er ... cooks could get at it. It didn't pay to anger the gentlemen of the press by threatening them with ejection.

The executive concluded that the season had been both an athletic and a financial failure for their Philadelphia entry. In placing blame, the directors avoided citing competition from the Centennial Exhibition or crank disinterest due to the A's being mired so deep in seventh place that only a totally inept Cincinnati team, which had only won six games, kept the Athletic out of the cellar. They concluded that the principal cause of their woes was their having been big-hearted and honest enough to pay the club's debts from the past year. The directors evidently felt it had been foolish to have paid the piper, each convinced that had they shucked their responsibilities and not paid their debts, the season would have been an entirely successful one.[48] This novel approach to business ethics probably allowed them to feel guiltless about the accumulation of this year's debt. Their guile guaranteed they would sleep undisturbed.

The next day was hardly an hour old when, a few minutes after 1 A.M. Tuesday, August 15, the Cincinnati team filed, displaying a mix of fatigue, frustration and froth, onto the train at Columbus. Their fatigue was from the late hour and the hard game they had played against the Columbus Buckeyes. Their frustration was from the upset of learning that although general manager George Keck had engaged berths by telegraph on the Louisville sleeper, said berths were already occupied by slumbering passengers when the train pulled into Columbus. The froth was from the whole maddening circus of playing for a cellar-dwelling team whose management, George Keck in particular, couldn't even get proper travelling accommodations for its players. Leave-it-to-George meant misery for Cincinnati. The Red Stockings, forty winks from sleep and forty-one miles beyond good morale, were forced to stay awake or sleep sitting all night. The train puffed into Louisville at 11 A.M. Tuesday.[49] Perhaps as a consequence of their travails of travel or perhaps because they were the league's creatures of the cellar, the Cincinnati side suffered a horrendous 17–5 loss to Louisville. Williams was hit with ease. Seven of Louisville's 17 runs being unearned, and the Reds' five runs coming on three safe hits and six Louisville errors, suggested miserable fielding by both sides. It was a game void of elegance and gracefulness. The statistics were appallingly unpleasant for the die-difficult Cincy cranks. Louisville got six doubles, 10 earned runs and 29 total bases. Cincinnati tallied five pass balls and three wild pitches, just to mention two of their less appealing statistical accomplishments. Such was life in last place.

Rumor continued from mouth to ear around the league. The latest concerned the distinct possibility that Indianapolis and New Haven would both be admitted to the National League in '77.[50] Cranks, already sweltering in the summer humidity and heat, were experiencing more hot air. Thoughtful observers wondered just how many more times rumor was wrong than right. Another rumor suggested that the former baseball editor of the *Hartford Times*, John G. Belden, would take over management of the Dark Blues in '77. The press suggested that the decision was President Bulkeley's alone to make and that he couldn't make a change that would improve on the work manager Bob Ferguson was doing. The *St. Louis Times*, no relation to their Hartford namesake, agreed.[51]

An announcement late in the day stated that Joe Borden, the dashed hope of the Boston Red Stockings for a big year in '76, had finally been released, joining Cherokee Fisher in the deposed pitcher bin. Rumor, that ubiquitous, underlying current of communication that seemed to seep and slither through the league in a constant, carefree flow, suggested Borden would be pitching for St. Louis in '77.[52]

The injury of the week didn't come on the baseball field, but on civilian soil. Hartford first baseman Everett Mills sustained one of those silly but serious injuries that athletes are occasionally prone to, when a bottle of soda pop he was holding suddenly burst, sending glass shearing into skin, bone, arteries, veins and such parts of flesh that seem especially ill-equipped to receive such instant and painful visitations. Mills would almost lose his little finger in the spray of razor-like glass shards.[53] He would survive to play another day.

Hartford manager/League President Bulkeley issued one of his rare suggestions this August evening, asking each club to contribute $250 to make up a fund for the detection of crooked play. What Bulkeley had in mind for the fund remained a mystery. A reward? The hiring of a Pinkerton? Bulks' announcement didn't say.[54] League owners had long dismissed Bulkeley as anything more than a figurehead presence of a president. He was now only a talking figurehead.

19

Summertime and the Livin' Ain't Easy

The ides of August came and went, if that was the proper title for the 15th day of the eighth month. Chicago, St. Louis and Hartford were contending the top three spots in N.L. competition. Boston, Louisville and the Mutuals were running fourth, fifth and sixth respectively, but Boston and Louisville had little respect for the Mutes. The Athletic was a distant seventh and Cincinnati appeared to have fallen through the cellar into a sub-basement some place south of competitiveness. By nightfall on August 15, the standings were:

	GP	W	L	Pct.*	T
Chicago	49	40	9	.816	0
St. Louis	47	32	15	.681	0
Hartford	45	31	13	.705	1
Boston	44	25	19	.568	0
Louisville	52	21	28	.429	3
Mutuals	44	18	25	.419	1
Athletic	48	12	35	.255	1
Cincinnati	47	6	41	.128	0

*Based on W-L record, tie games excluded.

The papers in 1876 didn't publish team win-loss percentage, the pennant being based solely on number of wins. Depending on a Chicago crank's coefficient of comfort, Hulbert's White Stockings looked a near-certain pennant winner; the Athletic and Cincinnati, absolute cinches for next to last and last place. The Grays and the Mutes seemed serious contenders for fifth, especially if the team's win-loss percentages (an indication of potential to win) and the Mutuals' eight games in hand were taken into consideration. Boston had a lock on fourth (it was just a case of throwing away the key) and a remote chance of finishing higher, being six wins back of Hartford and seven back of St. Louis. The quest for second place was a coloring contest: Would it be Brown or Dark Blue?

Chadwick reported that Cincinnati and Louisville had come up with a novel idea to start their back-to-back late August series—they agreed to let Cincy bat first for their three games in Lou'ville and for Lou'ville to bat first when they played three in Cincy.[1] The home team batting second was not set in stone in 1876.

On Thursday, August 17, Si Keck lived up to his reputation as a disagreeable human being as he continued his non-deliberate, but increasingly effective, campaign to alienate all and sundry from his friendship.[2] Si the Butcher watched a torrential rain pelt down between 2:30 and 3 P.M., just before his Cincinnatis were to take the field against Louisville. Then a bright, basking shark of a sun slipped out from behind a blob of cloud and began to roast the Cincinnati grounds. Standing on the edge of the steaming green field, Keck decided the field wouldn't be dry until 4:30 or 5 P.M. He quickly concluded the cranks wouldn't wait that long. An exhibition game scheduled for the next day at Frankfort could be postponed since league games were supposed to be played on make up days if the need arose.[3] Today's rain meant the need was arising. Despite objections by umpire and players, both opposition and friendly, and in spite of verbal indications to the contrary from the crowd, Keck's decision stood. The meatpacker–baseball team owner put one more wedge of animosity between himself and the cranks, who had come so far to see so little.

While Si Keck was losing friends and failing to influence people, Grin Bradley continued to pace N.L. pitchers, throwing yet another one-hitter as St. Louis blanked Chicago 3–0 at Grand Avenue Grounds. A hot furnace of a cloudless day kept the St. Louis crowd huddling under the grandstand or beneath hand-held newspaper pages that turned the bleachers into a shining sea of gray on white. The 3,500 who braved the humid heat were treated to a delight of a game. Spalding and Bradley matched brains and brawn, in-shoots and out-shoots until St. Louis scored three runs in the top of the ninth and Bradley blanked the White Hose in the bottom half to secure the one-hit St. Louis victory. Bradley's bid for a second no-hitter was squelched by a looping single by Jim "Deacon" White.

The only other real news of August 18 was a cryptic announcement out of Boston that the Red Stockings had officially released the already retired Joe Borden from its roster. Joseph was now going to be a phenomenal groundskeeper—if not at grass cutting, perhaps at pay.[4] It was rumored he'd be tending Boston's playing field for a major league pitcher's salary.

Third-place Hartford and fourth-place Boston began a home-and-home series on Saturday, August 19, that could be crucial for both clubs.

To have even a cat in a dog's den chance of grabbing third place from the Dark Blues, the Red Stockings would have to sweep, or come close to sweeping, all six games.[5] The only other way was for Hartford to go into freefall, which wasn't likely. Only the most faithful of the Boston faithful could expect this. They did not have long to have their highest hopes squelched as Hartford edged the Red Stockings 5–4 behind the hard-throwing Tommy Bond's seven-hitter. Jack Manning, trying to fill in the pitching post left by the departure of the inept Joe Borden, threw a four-hitter for Boston. It was most disappointing for the Boston cranks, and even more disappointing for the newsmen who saw a potential string of stories if Boston could have, at least, won five straight from Hartfords and set up a dramatic all-important sixth game.

More than 6,000 flowed into Grand Avenue Grounds, St. Louis, on Monday, August 21, to bear witness to an argument-infested game with Chicago that combined debating, most elegant; oratory, both elegant and inelegant; and foul-mouthed epithets, all inelegant. Chicago seemed strangely surly from the game's commencement, constantly criticizing the umpiring of Will Walker of Cincinnati.[6] Things came to bursting point in the ninth when a sharp hit by Ned Cuthbert of St. Louis brushed the body of homeward hurrying teammate Mike McGeary. After striking McGeary, the ball went bounding by White Stocking third-sacker (nee post) Adrian Anson and McGeary scored. Chicago immediately claimed obstruction, maintaining the interference was intentional.[7]

The rule governing McGeary's confrontation with the passing baseball read that a runner proceeding from base to base who is hit by the ball is only out if he *purposely* gets in its way.[8] Being of the proper psychological intuition to divine another person's intentions, the umpire was the designated decision maker. Umpire Walker, a youngster, perhaps due to nine innings of needling from Chicago or due to the crowd presently roaring obscene threats, mystically decoded McGeary's inner motivations and decided Mike had touched the baseball unintentionally, rejected Chicago's pleas and ruled the run legitimate.[9] A grinless Bradley, an upset Mike McGeary and a furious Joe Battin of St. Louis instantly and angrily joined an equally grinless Adrian Anson, equally upset Al Spalding and equally furious Jim White of Chicago in a heated conversation with the umpire. The ballplayers were joined by a crowd of the pro–St. Louis persuasion who gathered around argument central. All pleaded their side's case in emotional extremities beyond control. The air around home plate was bluer than that of the sky above and so hot that any hawk circling overhead couldn't help but be swept thousands of feet upward on the resulting thermal. After arguing some more about how McGeary had kept third-sacker Anson from fielding the ball by deliberately kicking it, Spalding stormed off the field, taking his team with him, preferring to sulk in the shade than play out the meaningless half-inning in the blazing heat.[10] The St. Louis faithful probably left the game debating whether their team had won 9–0 on a forfeit or by the "actual" 7–6 score.

As might be expected, Meacham's final story of the incident in the *Chicago Tribune* said that McGeary deliberately kicked the ball away from Anson's hands, and, laughing at what he had done, ran home. Then, according to the *Tribune*, young Walker, the umpire, called McGeary out on interference, but reversed his decision when a number of no longer spectating spectators converged on him with the remainder of the St. Louis crowd roaring obscene threats in the background.[11] The *St. Louis Times* saw it quite differently: the ball was hit so hard McGeary couldn't avoid it. The *Times* simply concluded that Chicago was upset because they couldn't stand a third straight loss to St. Louis.[12]

St. Louis executive S. Mason Graffen erupted over Meacham's duplicity when he read through the various editions of the *Tribune*. Meacham's first filed story evidently said McGeary's obstruction was accidental and that St. Louis was entitled to the game, while his later special to the *Tribune* said McGeary purposely kicked the ball and that Chicago was defeated by a howling mob exerting pressure on a youthful umpire.[13] The angry Mr. Graffen was rumored as looking to punch in at least one of Meacham's two faces.

On August 20 and 21, the *Louisville Courier-Journal* considered the Grays' remaining games with Boston and concluded the big fellows from the South had a good chance of

Frail, 120-pound William Arthur (Candy) Cummings, one of baseball's earliest curve ball pitchers, came off the bench with a 7–8 record to become Hartford's principal pitcher in late August 1876. He took over for temperamental youngster Tommy Bonds, who had a 31–13 record, and kept the Dark Blues in a neck-and-neck race with St. Louis for second place. (National Baseball Hall of Fame Library, Cooperstown, N.Y.)

grabbing fourth place from the New Englanders.[14] The *C-J* reporter was probably influenced by Louisville's 4–1 win over the western Red Stockings on August 18, when, for the first time, the Grays played the entire game without making an error. They also won on August 19. To give some credence to the papers' predictions, Lou'ville would win, 6–3, over Cincy. The day before, Hartford had stopped Boston 10–4. The Hartford win was fraught with worry for the Dark Blue management. Pitcher Tommy Bond, the club's "Asa" or "Ace," depending on whether or not you remembered Asa Brainard, was out with a sore arm. While mixing a curve with his blistering fastball, Bond had strained the tendons in his forearm beyond immediate repair.[15] It was an effect curveball pitchers would discover to their despair for years to come. Candy Cummings, who'd been tossing breaking stuff for years, filled in admirably. No one knew it yet, but it would be the last game Bond would ever pitch for Hartford. A smoldering and savage dispute between Bond and Hartford manager Bob Ferguson on the one hand, and, evidently, Bond and Cummings on the other, was cascading toward an inevitable resolution.

On Tuesday, August 22, cranks were led to believe that Boston's latest attempt to replace Borden as a pitcher (not groundskeeper), Lowell hurler Curry Foley, would start this sultry afternoon against Hartford. Foley failed to materialize on this or any subsequent afternoon in '76. The amateur team he played for simply refused to release him.[16] Charles Joseph "Curry" Foley did not appear in '77 or '78 either. He would make his debut three seasons later starting a few games for Boston in '79. Since he would win nine and lose nine that year, it is probably just as well for Boston and Foley that he did not come to the fore in late '76. In a way, Foley might as well have pitched. Ferguson, often billed as the "King of the Third Base," made five errors to help give Boston a win over his Hartford nine. The *Courant* suggested Ferguson take himself aside and scold himself as severely as he talked to any of his players committing anything resembling an error. What Bond may have said about the performance of Ferguson, a man he had already accused of questionable play in previous games, went unreported. Fred "Tricky" Nichols, temporarily engaged after being released by New Haven, pitched in place of Foley for Boston.

At Chicago, the Windy City Wonders, using their usual lively ball, stopped St. Louis 12–2 to continue their undisputed claim to first place. The boisterous ball employed by the White Stockings evidently befuddled the St. Louis defense as the Browns, used to working with the dodo-dead sphere employed at their Grand Avenue Grounds, made 18 fielding errors. Lou'ville opened their series at Cincinnati with an 8–0 victory to complete the day's action.

A few games were played between August 23 and September 4, but, in general, it was an off time when the teams devoted their skills to excelling in exhibition games. Later generations would wonder at the wisdom of these arrangements, asking why the N.L. simply didn't double its scheduled number of league games and forsake the small-change exhibition games they played by the dozen throughout the year. The answer echoing back from the past would upbraid the arrogance of the present-day holder of hindsight. Attitudes in 1876 were in transit. Two decades of free-spirited interaction between pro, semi-pro and amateur could not be shucked in a single afternoon or a single season. It probably would not have been politic for the National League to have totally split its relations with the many hundreds of non-league clubs. If alienated, the better of the bunch could easily group together and become a rival force. It simply wouldn't be good business to break ground for a potentially rival league.

The mills of rumor continued to grind out a succession of stories debating Philadelphia's ability to stay solvent. The *Hartford Courant* covered the Athletic club's August 14 meeting, reporting that the directors admitted the season had been a failure.[17] The *Cincinnati Enquirer* concluded that it was "hardly probable that we shall see the Athletics out west again this year."[18] As time passed half the press seemed to remember Sperling's announcement at the team's meeting that the A's had only $24.86 in the team's coffers,[19] while the other half seemed to have let Sperling's pronouncement evaporate into some kind of accounting amnesia.

A story surfaced in late August predicting that fewer than eight teams would compete in the National League in '77. It was accompanied by word of a possible new association being formed. The information was reprinted in papers around the league. This was the spinoff from speculation surrounding the A's predicament.[20] The prestige of the National League went to a new low as the latest debacle adorned the public prints.

Boston's George "Foghorn" Bradley, who had been pitching for the Live Oaks of Lynn, was Harry Wright's right-hander du jour as the "Replacement for Borden" campaign continued on August 25 against the Mutuals. The 21-year-old native of Milford, Massachusetts, tossed a three-hit victory in his debut. Foghorn's first success against major league competition was more sensation than substance. Despite having the same name as St. Louis' best, this George Bradley would prove to be something else again. Foghorn was evidently no Grin. It was, perhaps, of interest that Foghorn was one of the pitchers the hapless Keck brothers had been trying to land for Cincinnati.[21] Although they probably moaned about not signing him, they need not have fretted. He would win 9 and lose 10 for a Boston club that was far superior to Cincinnati before he exited stage right from the baseball scene.

Gaps in the Cincinnati communication network coupled with an anomaly in the weather led to a near empty home park on August 25. The catastrophe began about 1:00 P.M. when heavy rains dumped sufficient water on the downtown sections of the city to flood the streets, turning thoroughfares into morasses of mud.[22] The deluge, however, was a local affair, so localized that only the downtown area was soaked. The ball grounds were dry and in splendid playing condition. When neither the Louisville team nor cranks appeared at the park as game time neared, someone put one (the downtown storm) and one (the accompanying belief that it must have drenched the park) together and sent telegrams off to the appropriate clubs that the game was on.[23] The press was also notified and runners were sent around to taverns and meeting places to scrounge up as many cranks as possible. A small sum of patrons arrived in time for the game. Their attendance was amply awarded as Louisville and Cincinnati played one of the most brilliant games of the season. Louisville played for 10 innings without making an error.[24] This was an utter rarity in the 1870s, since an error occurred on average every sixth play in the National League.[25] Any team playing an errorless game stretched the limits of probability to the mind-boggling, awing the audience. Louisville cranks who saw the affair were so amazed that they almost forgot that Cincinnati, so acquainted with adversity that winning was almost a lost art for them, played so well that they registered a 3–1 victory after 11 innings. Fortunately, the press played the game up and the management debacle down. The latter was no news being good news for the National League.

The *Louisville Courier-Journal*, still as enthusiastic about baseball as ever, displayed the buoyant elan of a newspaper covering big league baseball for the first year, and sent two reporters along with vice-president Charles Chase of Louisville to cover the final Cincinnati-Louisville game Saturday, August 26. The newspaper boasted that the next day's paper would have the same full coverage as a home game.[26] The occasion was the anniversary of the opening of Cincinnati's Avenue Grounds, a park placed so distant from downtown Cincinnati that it was considered beyond civilization. The year-old Avenue Grounds were so far from the Cincinnati business district they could only be reached by carriage or a special train.[27] The Red Stockings didn't fare any better than usual on their park's first anniversary day. Louisville defeated the troglodytic cellar dwellers 3–2.

The defensive gem of the game was Snyder's great one-hand catch of a fly that hugged the air above the foul line until he intercepted it to end the fourth inning. It had set off a flurry of fantastic cheering. Snyder's extreme modesty caused him to sneak in along under the pavilion fence as he came in from the field, but the crowd rushed down onto the edge of the field and gave Snyder such an ovation that the young man almost died from embarrassment.[28] A hero devoid of the brashness of youth was a hero indeed. Elsewhere on this sizzling, searing August 26, the nadir of crank interest seemed to have been reached when a few hundred true believers watched the Mutuals win 10–9 over Boston at Cammy's Union Grounds.

It was so hot and humid in the midwest that many Chicagoans probably thought Lake Michigan had boiled over and steamed into the city. Chicago's management decided to drop right fielder Oscar Bielaski.[29] The press had concluded weeks previous that Oscar was not a big "O" or even a little "O," but simply a zero.[30] Bielaski would be replaced by the presently impressive Fred Andrus.[31] None of Chicago's executives would win any Oscar excising Bielaski for Andrus. He would hit .306, going 11-for-36 in eight games in 1876, but would play only one more major league game in his life, batting 1-for-5 in a game in 1884. St. Louis won the game 8–6, the significant part being Bradley's beating Chicago on a six-hitter using the White Stockings' lively ball. It suggested he'd be a worthwhile addition to the Socks in '77 and that his pitching success did not just stem from his using the St. Louis–preferred mush ball.

Scandal struck the league in late August. Reality replaced rumor and it became general knowledge that Tommy Bond accused Dark Blues manager Robert Ferguson of selling Hartford's game on Saturday, August 19, in Boston and their Saturday, August 12, game in Philadelphia, as well as two or three games against the Mutuals.[32] Ferguson had forced the issue, denying Bond's charges in an open letter to the editor in the *Hartford Times*. Reprints in papers like the *Louisville Courier-Journal* gave the affair prominence around the league.[33] The fire-breathing Bond asked for his release, but the Hartford brass, headed by Morgan Bulkeley, refused to let him go.[34]

Sometime in the lingering summer of late August, New Haven, the team that had aspired to National League status and that had argued elegantly for admission, supposedly folded.[35] Without the players, many lost to the National League, without the prestige that went with being a big-league team, and without the population to draw enough support for even an ex-major league team, the demise of New Haven's dream of returning to the game's "top tier" was inevitable. The city would never return to big-league ball, but, as Mark Twain would have said, reports of New Haven's death were greatly exaggerated.

The race for second spot between St. Louis and Hartford was coming down to dreadlock over possible deadlock time. The St. Louis schedule saw the Browns playing two road games each against the Mutuals, the A's, Boston and, on September 15 and 16, Hartford. The Dark Blues were at home against Louisville, Cincinnati and Chicago before meeting St.

Louis. Backers of the Browns saw it as a possible collage of catastrophe, a make-or-break business for road-bound St. Louis, who'd be playing eight straight on alien soil while the Hartfords were playing at home. Cranks for the Hartford club saw things differently. Aside from Cincinnati, a fiercer phalanx of foes was coming to dine on Candy Cummings and the Dark Blues. Louisville was a better club than New York and Chicago was much better than Boston. At least the Browns and Blues would have a chance to separate themselves from each other when they met in a pair of mid–September games and there still would be a month of baseball left after these mid-month set-to's.

On a more cerebral plane, talk of replacing the base hit in the statistics columns in 1877 with the number of times a player reached first, whether by error, walk or safe hit, circulated around the league's press tables.[36] The idea was to make players play for the club by running out every hit, which some weren't doing lately.[37] It was the basis for the presently used "On-Base Percentage," a statistic that years later elevated players like Eddie Stankey, who led the National League in walks three times, to prominence. Stankey played for the Chicago Cubs, Boston Braves, St. Louis Cardinals and Brooklyn Dodgers between 1943 and 1953, amassing a lifetime batting average of .268 and an on-base percentage of .410.

By Monday, August 28, an enraged Bobby Ferguson was asking for Bond's release from the Hartford club,[38] but club president Morgan Bulkeley was evidently not a man to move in haste even though dissention tore through the Hartford ranks like a steel plough through prairie grass.

As if the Bond business wasn't woe enough, the league's troubles continued to compound. The *St. Louis Globe-Democrat* predicted that the Athletic would not be back for '77[39] and, in other news, Spalding was quoted as saying there would be fierce opposition to the admission of New Haven, Indianapolis and other aspiring teams. The *Globe-Democrat* pointed out that a movement to form a second association was quietly going on. These associationists would charge 25 cents a game and bind themselves not to play any National League clubs. The teams most likely to be in the association would be the Columbus Buckeyes, Pittsburgh Alleghenys, Detroit Aetnas, Harrisburgs, New Castle Neshannocks, St. Louis Red Stockings, Memphis Red Stockings and other crack teams from the east. A bit at the bottom of the story suggested that certain gentlemen in Chicago—Chicago?—and Philadelphia were interested in placing first-class teams in the new league. The whole thing sounded like a rewrite of Chadwick's monster league that would be big enough to have each team play each other once and not get finished till three days after Christmas 1899.

Tuesday, August 29, was a bad day for National League teams if non-league games were taken even semi-seriously. The Standards of Wheeling topped Cincinnati 11–7, which could be stomached considering Cincy's placing in the standings, but it was harder to swallow Syracuse's 4–1 besting of Boston and some Canadian team called the Maple Leafs winning 9–7 or 10–9, depending on which newspaper you wished to believe, over the St. Louis Browns.[40]

Hartford's Tommy Bond reversed his position on August 31 and withdrew all charges against Bob Ferguson, pleading the immaturity of youth for his outburst. He was probably telling the truth. Not many 20- to 21-year-olds have lived the 50 or 60 years needed to gain the wisdom of maturity.[41]

As of September 1, 1876, Chicago had 41 wins; St. Louis, 35; Hartford, 33; Boston, 30; Louisville 24; the Mutuals, 18; Athletic, 13; and Cincinnati, 8. A few math-minded cranks must have realized that Lou'ville need only win 17 of their remaining 17 games while Chicago lost all their remaining 16 for the Grays to grab a tie for first with the White Stockings. The Mutuals were in even better shape, needing to win only 23 of 24 while Chicago again lost every one of their remaining contests to force a tie. If the Mutes won all their remaining games while the Chi's lost all theirs, the Mutes could win it all. Fantasy and fandom were already fellow travelers in the 1870s. Actually, the Mutes and Grays had about as much chance as the A's or Cincy to catch Chicago. The Athletic had to win 28 of 19 games and Cincy, 33 of their remaining 21 games while the White Stockings lost all theirs. But that was the mathematics of imagination.

20

Days Dwindling Down

Conceived in February, born in April, the infant National League was nearing the end of its initial year by September. The press, even when just doing its job, was at its dismal best in describing how attendance was declining. The *Chicago Tribune* cited the *New York Clipper* griping about poor attendance at eastern games.[1] The weather may have been unpleasant, but bigger crowds had come out in worse weather. Perhaps out of frustration, the league-loyal *Chicago Tribune* attacked editors who viewed baseball in its better times as "ten thousand idiots assembled to observe eighteen lunatics quarrel over base-ball."[2] Of all the papers, the *Louisville Courier-Journal* was, at least, practical about the decline, assigning its race reporter to cover baseball for the rest of the month.[3] If league-loyal Louisville was fleeing the field, was mass desertion far behind?

The truth was in the gate receipts. Hulbert had come to the unhappy conclusion that his Chicago club would probably be the only team to turn a profit in 1876.[4] Why he should be so sad over his competitors' financial failings might be a mystery to many of his business world friends, but not to any baseball man. Pro baseball was a business, but there might be no business like it. Unlike the railroad owner whose business could boom if his chief competitors went under, in baseball a club owner could go bust if his chief competitors collapsed. This need for a healthy, wealthy clutch of competitors was paramount. The other clubs' lack of solvency could mean they might lose players to outlaw teams and if the rumors were true and the Athletic and the Mutuals were to violate a most essential tenet of the league by refusing to come west to play out their schedule, only six teams, two eastern and four western, would be left in the National League.[5] The two biggest cities in the league would have been expelled for refusing to complete their western swing and would be prime territories for a rival association to set up shop in opposition to the National League. Hartford would need to replace the Mutuals in New York.

Friday, September 1, and Saturday, September 2, were not blue-letter baseball days as prizefighting took press attention. The Jimmy Wheedon and Billy Walker prizefight held August 31 near Pennsville, New Jersey, had ended with Wheedon being declared winner and Walker, whose non-fighting name was Philip Koster, being declared dead. The sheriff had tried to interfere long before the fight and Walker reached their end, but the crowd intervened. The deceased's body was found in the evening on Salt Wharf at Greenwich Point. The newspapers published full details of the incident and sort of celebrated Walker's wake by noting that Joe Goss and Tom Allen were set to meet somewhere near Cincinnati on Thursday, September 7.[6] The *Cincinnati Enquirer* ran a story noting, "All who wish to attend will do well to remember that ... genuine tickets can only be obtained from Eph Holland at the Empire Saloon."[7] Wheedon, along with an entourage of people associated with the fight's arrangements, was eventually arrested, convicted and sent to jail.[8] Prizefighting might be illegal, gross and barbaric, but it made for popular reading.

In New York, a beleaguered Cammeyer, already down to his pocket bottoms in debt, had to accept the utter humiliation of his crew losing a 3–1 decision to the Resolutes. It was the second time during the 1876 season the Mutes had been beaten by an "outside professional" organization. Cammy couldn't have relished the outcome. It was not a thing that translated into increased ticket sales.

In the race for second place, St. Louis and Hartford stayed neck-and-neck, collar-to-collar as each won on September 5 and 6. St. Louis stopped the Mutuals 9–0 and 4–3, while Hartford beat Louisville 6–1 and 6–3 at Hartford.

Perhaps the biggest news, if what already was in the public domain for weeks then finally officially confirmed could be called news, was the announcement in early September that Tommy Bond's contract, which had extended into 1877, had been formally annulled by the Hartford club. Despite Bond having issued an apology, ill feeling still festered in plaguelike prominence between young Tommy and manager Bob Ferguson.[9] Bond was quoted as having said he would not play with Hartford as long as Ferguson stayed with the club.[10] It had been another eruption of youthful impulse, unhampered by any semblance of maturity. It left the Hartford executive with little choice. Cummings was chucking curves very well, while the idled Bond was pitching dissension. Shortly after the formal announcement, a wire whisked a note of interest around the league. Bond, aching arm and all the rest of him, was listed as playing third base for New Haven in a September 6 exhibition against Cincinnati.[11] The resourceful Bond had evidently been signed by New Haven seconds after Hartford dismissed him. The reportedly defunct New Haven team was still in the baseball business.

The reason Bond went to New Haven was not difficult to deduce. Legally, he had not just been released. The league had suspended him and Hartford had seen to it that his salary was forfeited. Bond had been in limbo, unable to play for any league team during the remainder of the 1876 season unless the league executive re-instated him. His pay withheld, his appetite intact, he was in monetary need. So he quickly latched on to the non-league New Havens. On September 12, the *Louisville Courier-Journal* had an item on Bond possibly going to St. Louis in 1877 for a goodly amount of "sugar."[12] The next day the *Courier-Journal* reported that Bond had signed with Boston for 1877 and the day after that, the Louisville paper reported that Bond had "certainly signed with the Bostons for next season."[13] As long as Bond didn't play for Boston, St. Louis or any N.L. team in '76, he'd be fine. The league had to be flexible. Hulbert and friends were well aware of the increasing number of empty seats, each one representing an unsold ticket. Bond could therefore play with New Haven for the present. The New Haven team wasn't under the National League's jurisdiction. All would be fine. Bond could pitch for any non–N.L. or N.L. club he wished in '77. His choice was Boston. He would play for the National League entrant from 1877 through 1881.

Neither the majority of cranks not availing themselves of the uncluttered confines of the horsecars nor the rows of uninhabited choice seats at the local ballpark seemed to have any effect on the promoter mentality of many scribes in the baseball press. Despite all this and perhaps because the regular season was winding down, the *Cincinnati Enquirer* and *Louisville Courier-Journal* were advocating as early as the first week of September that a baseball tourney be staged in Louisville in late October. Cincinnati, Louisville and a few non-league teams were to be invited. What was to be done about late autumn weather or how the onlookers were to be induced to watch a meaningless series of games was not mentioned in the public prints.[14]

The most significant occurrence in early September was almost overlooked by the press corps. Only a few eyebrows rose when Chicago and St. Louis announced they would play an exhibition on Cammeyer's Union Grounds in Brooklyn on September 8.[15] This was a thunderbolt reduced to a spark in the gray columns of the sports section. It suggested something strange was afoot and yet the usually paranoid press, which could conjure a conspiracy from seeing Hulbert and Cammeyer passing each other on the way to a refreshment stand, didn't seem to notice the announcement's possible importance. Teams didn't suddenly agree to play each other on foreign fields. Why should Chicago and St. Louis wish to make Cammeyer their landlord even for a friendly game? Why were they so anxious to put money in Cammeyer's clutches? Was Hulbert that desperate to keep New York in the league? There had to be a big story behind this. Its time for telling simply wasn't September 6. Perhaps the eyes of the editors, and even the brains of the best, were not truly focused on baseball.

The biggest excitement in sports in early September was boxing. The prizefight between Joe Goss and Cincinnati's Tom Allen was slated for September 7. The bout was to take place across the state line in Kentucky, not more than 50 to 100 miles from Cincinnati. The *Philadelphia Inquirer* noted that in order to prevent the Goss-Allen prizefight from taking place, Kentucky's governor had telegraphed sheriffs to be alert and to arrest all persons violating the law.[16] The lawmen must have read these wires with a certain amount of astonishment. What did the governor think their job was if it wasn't to arrest violators? Goss would win the September 7 fight on a foul.

News of the holdup of a Northfield, Minnesota, bank by Jesse James' gang and a subsequent wild chase after the gang by a citizens' posse would also have the wires whistling most of the day. When it came to headlines, violence and mayhem held the patent.

Stockholders met the evening of September 7 at Louisville headquarters on Jefferson Street to elect their 1877 directorate. Sam Casseday, Jr., the club's secretary and treasurer, read his report. The club was reasonably financially sound, something not common to the National League. W.N. Haldeman, A.V. DuPont, Thos. Sherley, Nicholas Finzer, Charles Chase, George Speed and Charles Johnston were elected directors. Haldeman ended the night as president, Chase, vice-president, and Casseday, secretary-treasurer.[17]

A Hartford-Cincinnati rainout of Friday, September 8, led to a dilemma and eventually to a piece of National League baseball history. To finish the series and get in the rainout, Cincinnati would have to stay over till Monday. But this would double the cost of room and board, bringing the hotel bill to $88. Such a sum would most likely exceed any share of a Monday game that Cincinnati would receive.[18] Needing as many chances to win as possible to close the gap between themselves and St. Louis in the race for second place, the Hartford management wrestled with the problem of getting the game in and keeping expenses to a minimum. Finally, someone thought of playing two games on Saturday, September 9, weather allowing. Officials from Hartford and Cincy agreed that the first game would be in the morning, the second in the afternoon. There would be plenty of time to clear the Hartford ballpark and refill it between games.[19]

They might as well have been back-to-back as in a doubleheader since cranks at the first game were few and those at the second even fewer. The morning game attracted about 100 spectators, hardly enough to count as a crowd, while the afternoon contest drew about 200.[20] But Saturday, September 9, 1876, did go into baseball history, National League and otherwise, as the first time two professional teams played two games against each other in one day.

The first tilt took one hour and 45 minutes to play and was won by home team Hartford 14–4. The *Courier-Journal* noted that for "the first time in the history of the League a championship game was played at half past ten o'clock in the morning."[21] The game was a misery for Cincinnati as Dale Williams, not one of those paper-produced phenomenal pitchers the press loved to glorify, was batted all over the field. Some shots seemed likely to leave Hartford's ball park and land somewhere in Kentucky, perhaps Ludlow, Williams' birthplace, a quiet hamlet across the Ohio River from Cincinnati.[22] Although among pros an excuse is only an invitation for abuse, Williams could have complained. His arm was already hurting from previous work even before he started to pitch the morning contest.[23] As a result, his fastest efforts seemed slower than the Second Coming, approximating a dimension of time reserved for snails, slugs, turtles and such creatures of sloth-style speed. Making 23 hits, Hartford's hitters put so much wood on the ball that the sphere's cover began to take on a hickory hue. Dandy "Candy" Cummings did a respectable job of holding the Red Stockings to four runs on 11 fairly well scattered hits.

The afternoon contest saw Hartford make one change in their lineup: York replaced the light-hitting Harbidge in centerfield. All 5' 9" and 120 pounds of Cummings were again at the pitcher's point for Hartford. This frailest of fellows was opposed by another Cincinnati hometown hopeful, Dory Dean, a 5' 10", 160-pound presence who looked stronger, more athletic and simply more dominant than the faint-of-figure Cummings.[24] Dean's fastball went from his hurler's hand hellbent for catcher's grasp. Problem was, after the first three or four innings, Dean's ability to throw the ball with voracity or velocity deteriorated to the point where his pitches were slower than Williams' snail ball was in the first game. As a result, Dean let up 10 hits and eight runs. Cummings worked another graceful nine innings, again scattering 10 hits, allowing four runs and winning the second game. The last half of the twin bill took two hours and 15 minutes, Candy taking a little more time in this one. After all, anyone as fragile of physique as Cummings was entitled to take a wee bit longer over the last nine of the 18 innings he pitched over a stretch of seven hours. At Philly, St. Louis bested the Athletics 15–2 before 200 fans to keep the race for second place as close as a couple of lovers at sunset.

Theoretically, whether the two games played on Saturday, September 9, between Hartford and Cincinnati constituted the first true doubleheader is a matter of semantics. If the definition of a doubleheader is based on number of games played in a single day, it was the first. If the definition is dependent on cranks paying one admission for the two games, then it was not. Since each game required a separate admission, they were considered separate happenings in the 20th century and not baseball's first twin bill. The 21st century verdict is not in.

21

Westward No! The Mutes and A's

St. Louis and Hartford continued their neck-and-nape race for second place as mid–September neared. The Browns, on the road in Philadelphia, kept in contention by beating the Athletic on Monday, September 11. Bradley didn't allow an A to reach first base until the eighth inning, throwing a six-hitter for the 15–2 win. On September 12, the dark-shaded Blues were at home, edging league-leading Chicago in the opening game of the White Stockings' final eastern series. The game was a diamond gem. In an era when fielding was the principal spectacle, the "Hartford outfielders made the finest display as a whole because of the many fly catches"[1] they came up with. For the Chi side, second baseman Ross Barnes grabbed a ground ball off Ferguson's bat while racing full tilt away from first base, then pivoted while on the dead run and threw a dart to Cal McVey at first for a half-step out. It was a play even Hartford cranks appreciated. Of course, they could only afford to be a wee bit generous, as the Dark Blues' victory was matched by a 5–2 St. Louis win over Boston.

The *Chicago Tribune* had for some time been advocating a three-game series between St. Louis and Chicago to settle the Western Championship. The *Tribune* disclosed that St. Louis had already agreed to play a 10-game exhibition series with Chicago. As was the custom in the news business, the *Louisville Courier-Journal* reprinted the story and, as was also a custom of the fourth estate, commented. The *Courier-Journal* noted that St. Louis agreed solely for the purpose of putting money in its treasury.[2] As far as the *Trib* was concerned, calling it a championship series would make things more meaningful. Chi had won the pennant, but St. Louis had won six of 10 games from Chicago. Cranks were supposedly still speculating who was best. The *Tribune* reacted in typical press fashion, continuing the inter-paper publicity, noting that the *St. Louis Republican*'s man bitterly denied that St. Louis agreed to any such championship series, and then spent "some space in asserting that the series is only for the gate money."³ The *Trib* went on: "The championship of the country is settled by games won, and it is a fair inference that the championship of the West be settled in the same way. The Chicagos have won 23 games in the West and the St. Louis have won 19."⁴ The *Trib* also noted that it was the intention of the Chicago club to give their "chief antagonists another shy [*sic*] at the Western championships, but, if they refuse it, well and good: Chicago will carry the name of 'Western Champions' as well as float the pennant which indicates the championship of the country."⁵

September 13 saw the rumored new baseball association actually being formed in New Haven. Fifty shares were sold to establish a capitalization of $2,500.⁶ That was probably between 10 to 20 times less than the worth of most National League teams in 1876 "when a franchise could be founded for less than $50,000 and an annual team budget of $25,000 was adequate."⁷ The new association claimed to have only modest hopes of maintaining a reasonable level of minor league ball in the coming years.

The following day, September 14, ushered in the month's major on-field event. It was the showdown series between the second-running Browns and the third-place Dark Blues. The two teams had occupied their respective places in the standings for more than six weeks. If Hartford was going to catch St. Louis or if St. Louis was going to break free of the pursuing Dark Blues, this was the time.

Despite the importance of the game, only 600 of Hartford's citizenry showed up. It was not a good sign for baseball. The game itself was a good one. With the score knotted at 2–2 in the ninth, St. Louis came to life with a string of base hits climaxed by Pike's three-run double that cleared the bases of Browns. When Remsen bobbled McGeary's searing shot down the third base line, Pike moved from third to home in several blinks of a cat's eye to insure a 6–2 St. Louis victory.

St. Louis and Hartford met again two days later. New Haven resident George Seward, very recently an outfielder for St. Louis and having played 24 games for the Browns in '75, was chosen to umpire the contest. That Bob Ferguson would permit an ex–Brown to officiate a key game may have left many Hartford cranks puzzled. Ferguson's propensity to folly might be common knowledge "cranked" around the circuit, but stupidity was not considered a conduit to suicidal silliness. The game was won 6–4 by St. Louis. The prevailing cause was evidently as much Seward's bias as anything done by the Browns or not done by the Dark Blues.⁸

Elsewhere, a few eyebrows were raised as Cincinnati easily hit Mathews and won 9–6 over the Mutuals at New York on September 16. After the Mutes had beaten Cincy in their last encounter, these geniuses thought that Cammy's crew was certain to repeat the process and accordingly put out their money at "the unwarrantable odds of $100 to $40."9 Expecting the Mutuals to win wasn't their mental misfire. Putting their money at risk on unreasonable odds was. The upset Cincy win cost these Mutual backers $2.50 for every $1 they put up.

Chadwick discussed recent verbal aggressions, possibly transgressions, of Hartford's disposed Tommy Bond in the *Clipper* on the 16th. Evidently "Bond had insulted Ferguson in the United States Hotel, Hartford, recently and, in the presence of Mr. Bulkeley, made charges of unfair play against him."10

Chadwick went on to explain that Bond was suspended when he was unable to provide proofs of his charges, or to substantiate them in some other way. His pay was forfeited and his contract with Hartford for 1877 annulled. The accusatorily verbose Tommy, trying to show his word was his bond, had provided his rationale, or more precisely his lack of rationale, for uttering the ill-advised remarks concerning Hartford manager Bobby Ferguson's integrity as an honest player in the *Hartford Times*, which was conveniently reproduced in Chad's *Clipper*. The crux of Bond's defense was that "whatever charges of 'crooked' play or wilfully losing games were made by me [Bond] *were entirely unfounded* and made in a moment of excitement."11 Perhaps the egoistic Bond, who was no doubting Thomas when it came to his self-concept as a great pitcher, felt Hartford might be besting St. Loo if he were only back with the Dark Blues. His contriteness may have come from the realization that his mouth, and not his arm, had removed him from the pennant picture.

As mid–September came and went, the question of whether the Mutuals or the Athletic or neither would meet their obligations and make their scheduled western swing became of paramount importance. It was the biggest threat yet to the league's integrity.12 The two teams had ignored their obligation to complete their last swing west in the moribund 1875 National Association and the executive overseers of the National Association had, in turn, ignored their own obligation to do anything about the Mutuals' and A's transgressions. They did mouth the usual threats for public consumption.13 Now in '76, Hulbert and friends were talking to press and public of imposing the same old sanctions. Cammeyer was rumored to feel Hulbert would never expel his Mutuals. Speculation was that Hulbert was just grandstanding and would do nothing. It seemed the more Hulbert and his western execs talked, the more Cammeyer seemed to disbelieve them. The westerners were casting themselves with the wolves who, howling for sheep's blood but not attacking, were unwittingly reversing the old fable. Cammeyer and company didn't believe they'd ever bite. It was a new twist on "Crying Wolf."14

G.W. Thompson, the new president of the Athletic, moved to negotiate with Hulbert, sending the Chicago boss a letter offering a possible solution. Thompson openly admitted the A's wouldn't be able to come west a second time, but invited Chicago to come to Philadelphia to complete the games. He pled injuries to his key players, heavy debts and loss of gate receipts.[15] It cost a team about $20,000 a year to play a full season. The Athletic had accumulated receipts of $11,643, leaving the team a little over halfway to the total needed with about three home games left. Funds for their final western swing were nonexistent.[16] Unlike other clubs, the Centennial Exposition had drawn cranks away from the Athletic's ballpark. The A's also had to contend with the city's usual rowing events.[17]

Thompson offered 80 percent of the gate receipts to Chicago and St. Louis if the two western clubs came to Philadelphia instead.[18] The problem was, as implied by the financial shortfall, the Athletic weren't drawing enough cranks to give the offer any substance. An offer of 80 percent sounded good, but 80 percent of a few dozen dollars wouldn't even pay Chicago's or St. Louis's train fare, let alone either club's hotel and food bills. Finally, on the moral plane, the Mutuals and A's were violating one of the key principles Hulbert and friends had been advocating for more than a year. If the National League didn't act, it would be going down the same path as the National Association and taking its credibility with it.

Shortly after receiving Thompson's plea for a bargain, Hulbert and friends got a note from Cammeyer which was short and to the point. On account of straitened finances (financial hardships, in common English), the prospect of small gate receipts and so forth, the Mutuals couldn't come west again.[19] The Mutuals of New York were a different kettle of boiling water to the Athletic of Philadelphia. To begin with, the Mutes represented the nation's biggest city. In fact, the New York–Brooklyn population was greater than the population of several of the remaining National League cities combined. Cammeyer just might concoct a rival league that could, given time, put the struggling National League out of business. The western owners knew that Cammeyer's Mutuals had an even flimsier case than the pathetic, if not apathetic, Athletic. But business was business. The Mutuals, despite their unsavory reputation, had been allowed into the National League. Then, questionable hirings and even more questionable games had gone unquestioned. Such was Gotham's power—massive population, newspaper center, telegraphic hub and steady—albeit small at times—attendance despite an image bent toward the corrupt. There was always potential there, the basis for a baseball bulwark to be built.

Hulbert decided to bite at least the tip of the bullet as far as the Mutuals were concerned. With St. Louis owner Charles Fowle agreeing, Hulbert offered Cammeyer a $400 guarantee each from Chi and St. Loo if the Mutes would come and play two games in Chicago and three in St. Louis in the space of a week.[20] It was a compromise. If Cammeyer accepted, it just might keep New York in the league and could, despite a bit of controversy, be smoothed over in the press. For Hulbert, it was an ultimate sacrifice of principle to solve a practical reality. A National League without New York might not survive.[21] Cammeyer's reply was courteous, curt and calamitous. He rejected their offer.[22]

Even today it is difficult to explain why Cammeyer turned down the generous Chicago–St. Louis offer. The $400 guarantees and even the lowest estimate of what the Mutuals would have gotten in gate receipts in Louisville, Cincinnati, St. Louis, Chicago, and in exhibition games in Indianapolis, Columbus, and assorted other cities should have more than paid for the Mutuals' entire trip. There had to be a reason other than money. What was it? The *Chicago Tribune* suggested the reason was Cammy's certainty of belief that Hartford would be moving to his Union Grounds in Brooklyn in 1877.[23] Hulbert and Cammeyer may have been further removed from each other's modes of reasoning than might be expected of a couple of businessmen. Both had built their enterprises on moderate risk-taking, making money by their wits and learning from their mistakes. Hulbert had made his money in the coal, grain[24] and the grocery business.[25] He seems to have been a "self-made" man.[26] Cammeyer, already a man of inherited wealth, had shot to prominence early in the sports business, first as a skating rink owner, then on the strength of a reasonably clever idea: enclose a ball field and they will come — with money. The few times they threatened to stop coming, Cammeyer simply came up with another clever idea. But Cammeyer, being the son of one of the nation's leading leather merchants, was already wealthy when he began to charge people for the privilege of skating on his Union Grounds rink.[27] The rags-to-riches as compared to riches-to-riches businessman could just possibly be fellows of a differing feather. Cammeyer miscalculated the strength and determination of Hulbert and his followers. Believing the expense of traveling to Chicago et al. for the final few series of the 1876 season was likely to produce a loss, Cammeyer refused to bring his Mutuals to the west.[28] It would turn out to be the biggest mistake Cammeyer, who loved his Mutuals, would make.

September attendance was pathetic for the eastern teams, 150 being the average number of cranks through the gates in Boston, Philadelphia, Hartford and New York. That was not even sufficient to pay a visiting team's hotel bills. The Mutes and Athletic were playing out their eastern obligations void of enthusiasm or elan.[29] The *New York Times*' coverage, when it did turn to baseball, suggested the epidemic of non-excitement that must have exhibited itself in the eerie semi-silence within the Union Grounds.[30] A *Times* headline for an August 19 game in which the A's made 22 errors and the Mutuals committed eight suggested the declining quality of A and M athletic performance:

> MUFFIN CONTEST AT PHILADELPHIA—THE ATHLETICS PLAYED WORSE THAN THE MUTUALS—CONSEQUENTLY THE LATTER WON THE GAME.[31]

The coverage didn't improve as the year aged. Close to a month later, on September 15, the Mutes edged Cincy 2–1 at Union Grounds before 400 cranks. The *Times* noted that the "game was uninteresting, there being but one brilliant play throughout, a one-hand catch by Kessler."[32] The *Times* was now describing the Mutuals' Booth as wretched at second and Hallinan as unable to function creditably at short. Besides inadequate pros, Cammeyer was putting amateurs (John Maloney and Michael Hayes) on the playing field in Mutual garb and the *Times* was sarcastically comparing these fill-ins in a favorable light with the pros. Maloney played two games in 1876 for the Mutuals and one game in 1877 for the Hartfords of New York, going 3-for-11 for a .273 B.A. Hayes played five games for the Mutuals in 1876, hitting 3-for-21 for a .143 B.A. To make matters even worse, the Mutes were sitting in sixth place with nowhere to go. The idea of Hartford moving into the Union Grounds in 1877 must have been very comforting for Cammy. Adding to both New York's and Philadelphia's financial woes was a spate of cold, disagreeable weather that settled along the Hudson and Delaware Rivers. Even the double-covered lively Reach ball, favored by the Athletic, reacted like a lump of iced lead.[33] September rain seemed to precede or threaten to precede every game. G.W. Thompson wrote a letter pleading the A's case to Hulbert and the western clubs in mid–September.[34] Louisville topped the A's 3–0 on or about the same day before fewer than 150 people as Lou'ville's Jim Devlin threw a one-hitter. George Hall, the A's best hitter, singled to spoil Devlin's no-no.

The press was not helping the A's cause much. What was being printed could be pretty grim. The fourth estate, outside of Philadelphia, routinely referred to the Athletic management as bloodsuckers and unscrupulous scalawags.[35] The moribund National Association did not survive a consistently bad press and neither could any league, including the National, regardless of whether the press was being over pessimistic or simply telling the truth. Even where the press did keep the faith, the message wasn't inspiring. The September 18 edition of the ever-faithful *Courier-Journal* concluded that Louisville had to win all six of its remaining games and that Boston had to lose five of their eight for Louisville to even tie for fourth.³⁶ Such facts did not inspire crank interest. By September 19, most papers were devoting more space to horse racing than baseball. In some papers, baseball news was becoming a series of short telegraphic messages: No one named on September 19 to succeed S.M. Graffen as St. Louis' manager. Treasurer McManus is presently running the front office. Louisville's Snyder suffered a severe ankle injury in an exhibition game three weeks ago. Hobbling on crutches....³⁷

Then there were the real negatives: the accusations and counter-accusations that painted baseball a murky gray. The latest came when an unnamed person accused Lou'ville's Jim Devlin of not playing to win in the September 16 Louisville-Athletic game. The press of September 20 carried a rebuttal from pitcher Devlin. Zettlein had pitched for the A's. Louisville won 7–6 in 10 innings, yet someone still accused Devlin of bedevilment.³⁸ The game was marked by eight Louisville errors—four by shortstop Chick Fulmer, but none by Devlin. It was also marked by the oddity of Devlin catching a foul-tip that rebounded off the head of Louisville catcher Bill Holbert. Who knew if the accusation was accurate? Without proof, you couldn't kick anyone out of the league, but with publication, you could kick hell out of the league.

There were not sufficient souls at the A's monthly meeting September 20 for a quorum. The Committee of 15 reporting on the affairs of the club had not concluded their labors. A Louisville reporter said they were engaged in a vain hunt to find more than 15 cents in the A's treasury. He was probably closer to the truth than to the humor he intended.³⁹

The young men of Boston and Hartford went west. The young men of New York and Philadelphia stayed home. The dice had been tossed. Thompson of the A's was reported as having resigned. Most of his players would join other clubs⁴⁰ but, as time would tell, he wasn't going to give up. He began plans for a campaign that would keep his A's in the league despite their violation of the league rules.

Luck, that coy name given chance, played its part in the fortunes of a small group of Louisville players who wanted to take a Friday train back from Pittsburgh and an exhibition contest, but were persuaded to take the following train. The first train, the one they would have taken, ended in a twisted metallic heap on the Pan-handle Road with many passengers severely mangled, some to death.⁴¹ The misfortunes of the injured and dead and the bad news for their friends and relatives had bypassed the Louisville players, relatives and followers. Perhaps it was just best to say the Louisvilles had been lucky.

It was not long, however, before bad news concerning National League baseball came back into prominence. The papers were soon noting that St.

Persuaded to take a later train back home from Pittsburgh, several Louisville Gray's baseball players avoided death by train wreck in late September 1876. Top row, from left: Scott Hastings, Jim Devlin, Charlie Synder. Middle row: John Carbine, Bill Hague, Chuck Fulmer, Jack Chapman, Joe Gerhardt, Art Allison. Bottom row: George Bechtel, Johnny Ryan. (Special Collections: Photographic Archives, University of Louisville)

Louis player Joe Blong had umped a game up in Pittsburgh and tried to give the game to St. Louis. "Tried" was the operative word since Pittsburgh's Allegheny team beat St. Louis 4–3 despite Blong's allegedly biased umpiring.

The suspicious side of human endeavor reared its questioning head again on Friday, September 22, as problems arose in a Boston-Chicago game at Chicago. The betsmen of New York, acting on a tip, had wagered heavily on the Bostons. This oddity was followed by some strange behavior exhibited in the seventh inning by the pool-sellers who declared, "Sorry, all bets are off." It was a time akin to the point in a race where the horses are driving for the wire. After considerable wrangling, the situation was restored to some semblance of sanity by a person known only as "McMan," who decided the pool-sellers had to pay up. "McMan's" ability to settle the matter attested to his fantastic powers of persuasion, an ability found now and then in the bookmaking world even today. Chicago won 12–0. The pool-sellers paid up.[42] The suspicious, on hearing of this latest hubbub in the New York betting parlors, concluded that it was probably a case of a "fix" coming "unfixed."

Saturday, September 23, was a stupendous day for the '75 National Association Champion Boston team. The long-suffering Red Stockings, decimated by Hulbert's four-player raid, depressed by the failure of highly touted Joseph Borden to come through as an even adequate pitcher and mired in fourth place, finally defeated Chicago 10–9. Excited over their win after nine straight failed attempts, the Bostons danced around the field, flinging their caps toward the clouds. No sound of fury from the Chicago crowd scaled the skies, but, lo and be-hear, cheers came forth. A group could be magnanimous if it supported the side winning 90 percent of its games and certain to take the whip pennant.[43]

On Monday, September 25, the *Brooklyn Argus* asked its readers if professional baseball organizations couldn't be suppressed next season.[44] The *Argus* didn't ask if the U.S. Constitution couldn't also be suppressed.

Chicago cinched the first National League championship on Tuesday, September 26, at their 23rd Street Grounds, defeating Hartford 7–6. The Dark Blues scored four runs in the bottom of the ninth, but stopped putting people across the plate a run short.[45] Chicago would complete its season two days later, topping Hartford 16–10 and filling many a White Stocking with happy feet. The rest of Chicago's schedule had only games slated with the A's and Mutuals.

As September slipped toward a close, the '76 season was quietly coming to its termination. It was not an ending envisioned by anyone craving excitement, increased crowd interest or overflowing club coffers. The press was still shortening its baseball coverage, mirroring the cranks' declining interest. Talk was mainly about whom or who would play with who or whom (there wasn't a sportswriter alive who was absolutely certain which was correct usage) next year.[46]

What could have been a crowd-pleasing climax, the final two games between St. Louis and Hartford at St. Louis were pretty well dampened at that point by the "games won" rule and not winning percentage deciding league placement. St. Louis cranks felt that their club, with 42 wins, was safely ahead of Hartford with only 38 wins. Since the two games between the pair were in St. Louis, the outcome seemed all but decided. St. Louis citizenry were not interested in the fact that Hartford was tied for third spot with Boston, each with 38 wins. If a percentage of wins over games played system had been employed, the St. Louis grounds might have been packed with paying customers. If St. Louis, at 42–18, were to lose both games and thereby be 42–20 or .677, Hartford, presently at 38–20, would be 40–20 or .666, only .011 behind. The Hartford games after that would be park-packers. Some league officials probably cursed having kept Chadwick's pennant determining statistic of "games won" in place for 1876. As it was, St. Louis won 5–2 on Thursday, September 28, and Hartford triumphed 4–1 on Saturday, September 30. The rumor that Hartford would move to Brooklyn in '77 also surfaced again.[47]

Louisville went into their last September game with a 4–4 record for the month and a 28–33 mark for the year. Their opponent was Boston, which was 38–25 overall and untouchably positioned in fourth spot. With only a smattering of games left in their schedule, less than nine since the A's and Mutes were refusing to come west, the Grays had no hope of finishing higher than fifth. They were also in no danger of finishing any lower since the self-idled Mutes sat in sixth with a 21–34 record. The Boston game would seem to have all the appeal of whitewashing a fence. But as Mark Twain was so smartly surmising in those days, there were always those who could find joy in the oddest of activities. For the few hundred cranks who came out to the Louisville ballpark, there was the attraction of a ride on an uncrowded horsecar, a better-than-usual seat in the stands, a chance to have a good gab with a friend, quick and courteous service at the refreshment stand, and so forth. A seemingly meaningless game could thus become a *gemutlich* experience even on a cool, cloudy day.[48]

September ended with a throwing contest in Indianapolis as an adjunct to a Cincinnati exhibition game. Will Foley of Cincinnati won with a throw measured 348 feet on the fly.[49] There seemed little left for October except back room squabbles over the fate of New York and Philadelphia, the outcome of which could make or break any fledging new league.

22

The Many Misters of October

October dawned, bringing a gloomy sky and a chilly chunk of icy weather that was too cold for the comfort of cranks or competitors. The latter in summer uniforms shivered under a cloudy sky, the former sat inactive under the grandstand's shadows, chilled to the marrow no matter how attired.[1]

Rivals for second spot, St. Louis and Hartford, split a pair, the Browns winning 5–2 on the 29th and the Dark Blues being the dominant color on the 30th with a 4–1 win as September ended. Despite the weather, Louisville took to the fields of October in neat, new uniforms. Heads topped by white caps of a different shape than their previous hair covers, legs encased in solid blue stockings, the Grays seemed well tailored if ill-named.[2] In an odd move, the *Chicago Tribune* advocated formation of a western league.[3] Was Hulbert floating another trial balloon through the good and willing services of Lewis Meacham? In New York, the fall racing season opened Monday, October 2, at Jerome Park as a herd of hooves momentarily trampled the Mutes and Cammeyer into coffin and grave.[4]

In chilly weather fit only for seals, sea lions and other furred folk, St. Louis bested Boston 5–3 Tuesday, October 3. An exceptionally large and extremely cold crowd attended. The size of the crowd and the thermometer fluid both shrank as the game progressed. It was a December day that dropped like a block of ice into early October. The cold was widespread. A small assembly of thermally challenged cranks, a trio of half-frozen scorers and reporters watched Hartford beat Louisville 11–2. By game's end, only a few refrigerated fanatics were left in the stands. They may have been frozen to their benches and unable move. Few of these chilled cranks, along with the ice-coated players and frostbitten scorekeepers who remained at contest's end, could remember the score a half-hour after the game was over.

Next day, Hulbert journeyed north along Lake Michigan to Milwaukee to watch his Chicagos defeat the West Ends of Milwaukee 10–7. The trip had been worthwhile. The West Ends gave their distinguished visitors 60 percent of the gate receipts, paid for all the pre-game advertising, and played in a nice little park (seating capacity 1,000). Like any other team in the ball business, the Milwaukees had horsecars to carry spectators right to the playing field.[5]

Nostalgia prompted the Socks to journey southwest into Iowa to play Marshalltown, a tiny town on the Iowa River, about 60 miles northeast of Des Moines, for another exhibition. This journey to Anson's birthplace was a present from Hulbert to his most muscular power hitter. The Chicagos delighted the locals, who came in from their sod huts, log houses and other assorted prairie dwellings to see the gods of baseball. The far-flung country folk felt a certain aura surrounding these men of big league stature who played in far away places with odd-sounding names like Chicago and Cincinnati. Only having read about and never having seen these men, readers both young and old elevated these unseen heroes to godlike status. Millions of American boys had sat abed, gleaning the latest from the sports columns, reading about the exploits of a Barnes or a McVey, a Spalding or an Anson. Pennant races would be followed in this way for generations. The reader placed these men in the company of his other print borne heroes, the giants of pulp fiction, the great ones of lore and legend. Such games are nothing short of profound religious experiences. It was the daylight of the gods.

It was only fitting that Chicago defeated the local nine 35–7 on October 3. It can safely be said the crowd, naive and not jaded by big city familiarity with big time sport, enjoyed every minute. An infielder might make three or four putouts without an error in a league game any day of the week, but that would be far, far away in huge cities many of these people had never seen. A league game may have been meaningful in the sense of helping decide league position, but a game in Chicago or St. Louis did not have the same spiritual sensation, the awing uplift provided the true believers of Marshalltown.[6]

A debacle of almost farcical dimension occurred in Cincinnati while Chicago was downing Marshalltown. The Columbus Buckeyes arrived in Cincinnati to find no one at Gibson House had any knowledge of a reservation of rooms for them or a pair of games they were to play. A quick glance through the local papers and a short sortie through the downtown wire outlets and the usual haunts of baseball's faithful quickly revealed the games were neither known of nor advertised. Contacting Cincy's Si Keck, the Buckeyes' manager found a considerable misunderstanding existed between the Buckeyes and the Red Stockings. Someone in the Cincinnati executive had fouled out as a communicator. To make the most of a bad thing, bulletins were hurriedly posted at various points in the city and the game was played. No more than 30 or 40 people attended. Columbus won 5–1. It was typical Cincy mismanagement. The Buckeyes must have pondered on the so-called superiority of the National League. In contrast, more than 5,000 watched Chicago top the Brown Stockings 2–1 in St. Louis the next day. The game was touted by some reporters as the first game of a best-of-something series for the Championship of the West. Interest in the series quickly petered out and only four games were played.[7]

Louisville's Grays played their last game of the season on Thursday, October 5, before a half-frozen throng of scorers, reporters and cranks. Hartford won 11–2 to move within four wins of St. Louis. The game meant zilch to Louisville, but everything to Hartford, who needed every win they could garner if they were to reach their hoped for destination: second place.

Chadwick was predicting in mid–October that Hartford would attain their goal and beat out St. Louis for second spot. He noted that the Dark Blues were playing well as a team, something they had not been doing in the first half of the season. He eluded to the cliques that had formed behind Cummings and Bond. As far as Chadwick was concerned, due to this Hartford lost games that they should have won. When Bond was removed, Chadwick argued, the club played better because the team was working as a whole.[8] Any denial of Chadwick's charges was guaranteed to make many people believe the charges were definitely true. Chicagoans must have cringed at the idea that Hartford might not have put out 100 percent since it tarnished their team's tremendous pennant-producing season. The St. Louis faithful would not be enamored by these Chadwickian ideas either. Privately, many players and most executives must have felt Chadwick's comments could be embarrassingly correct. Chadwick's prominence as a reporter was not based on any foolish sentiment. The man knew baseball.[9]

After ending September with that 4–1 win over the Brown Stockings in St. Louis and taking a pair from the Grays 6–0 and 11–2 at Louisville on October 4 and 5, an upcoming three-game series with utterly inept Cincinnati was crucial to Hartford. The Dark Blues were on a roll, having won three in a row. Maybe they could catch the Browns after all. Enthusiasm was epinephrine-inspired in Hartford, but disinterest dominated the Cincinnati scene. The Hartford hordes, watching the bulletin boards at home, went wild as the Dark Blues took a 7–4 series opener from the Red Stockings on October 6. The *Cincinnati Enquirer* reported, "In the ninth inning [pitcher Dory Dean] was hit in the groin by a red-hot liner from [Tom] York, but pluckily assisted [first baseman Charlie] Gould in putting his man out, after which he was overcome with the accident."[10] Players would not wear protective cups until 1915, 39 years after Dean's encounter with York's line drive.[11]

Hartford continued to roll, taking 11–6 and 11–0 wins from Cincy on October 7 and 9, to extend their road streak to six straight. The Browns had 45 wins and 19 losses by October 9 with a game left to play against Cincinnati, but the team had also gotten involved in a meaningless exhibition series with Chicago. The first game on Oct. 5, won 2–0 by Chicago, drew 4,000 people and considerable cash into the Browns' ballpark. St. Louis never got around to playing that last game with Cincinnati. Hartford returned east and played three more, defeating the Mutuals 3–0 at Brooklyn's Union Grounds on October 17, and Boston 5–0 and 11–1 on October 20 and 21 at Boston. The Dark Blues finished the season with a eight-game winning streak on the road for a total of 47 wins and second place.

But Hartford's win total of 47 and St. Louis' 45 didn't completely settle the issue over second place. When the Mutuals and the A's reneged on coming west, St. Louis had been unable to play six games against them. St. Louis had missed a chance to win any of those games. If they had played and won three of them they would have topped Hartford's win total. Hartford in the east didn't have such problems, the Mutuals and A's played them. How much St. Louis' superiority in win-loss percentage dwelt on people's minds was also unknown. The second-place Dark Blues had a 47–21 record for .691 and the third-place Brown Stockings, a 45–19 record for .703. Since the league based place of finish on number of games won, St. Louis' edge in percentage was irrelevant. The press was more concerned about whether to revise the standings by removing games involving the defaulting Mutuals and defecting A's. The *Hartford Courant* had confidently been printing revised standings every day based on deletion of A's and Mutes games.[12] Other papers followed suit, but it was a moot point which standings should prevail. In the end, the argument stopped when even casual analysis revealed that the relative standings of the league's remaining teams was pretty well the same whether A's and Mutes games were counted or not. Hartford had a 4–4 record against the Mutuals and a 9–1 record against the A's. Erasing their games against the A's and Mutes left Hartford with one more win than St. Louis. The league office ended the conjecture by declaring Chicago the winners and printing a finished set of standings with the Mutuals and A's included.[13]

From September 11 on, Hartford had won 13 games to St. Loo's six. Hartford's management strategy of struggling to get every possible Dark Blues game in led to the Dark Blues playing 19 games to St. Louis' eight in the final weeks of the campaign. That was 11 more games than the

Browns played. It would have been of little value except that Hartford finished the season with a nine-game winning streak. Hartford finishing with two more wins than St. Louis also made the unplayed St. Louis–Cincinnati game moot; a Browns victory would leave St. Louis a win short.

Chadwick, who sprinkled his writings with considerable mathematical data, came up with a chart of Boston's month-by-month record that was of considerable interest. Any reader quick to calculate and quicker to contemplate relationships not overtly observed would have noted that splitting the Red Stockings' record in two revealed that Boston had played a remarkably fine second half. The April-May-June totals for Harry Wright's crew was 14 and 16 (a .466 percentage) while their July-August-September-October totals were 25–14 (a healthy .641 percentage). It took little imagination to realize that the Red Stockings had vastly improved from season's start to finish. Harry Wright's highly touted "Boston plan" for training players to function as a unit worked. Chicago used it for that matter. Chadwick praised it as the basis of "scientific" play. Its only drawback was that it took time to train new players to perform according to any plan, the "Boston plan" being no different.[14] It was, perhaps, lucky the season ended when it did for Chicago, St. Louis and Hartford, or Boston might not be in fourth place. It was also perhaps fortunate that Boston had not gone south during the winter of '75-'76 to train and thereby open the season ready to run over everyone.

A particularly scathing Chadwick story came out on a cloud-cluttered October 14. The story was bleak and wounding. Chad lampooned the National League's executive (a plural nom de plume mainly meaning the singular William Ambrose Hulbert) for its season-long hypocritical conduct. The trouble with the story was that, once again, Chadwick was essentially correct. Chadwick pointed out that the National League moguls had thrown Concannon's Philadelphias out in February for alleged dishonesty only to re-engage the team's most notorious offenders, saying: "We thought it was best to forgive them their crooked ways, and to trust to the stringency of our League laws to make them play straight this season."[15]

This quote probably burnt like a coal from the forge of hell itself into Hulbert's very being. Chadwick went on to argue that there was more crooked play than ever throughout the 1876 season by players of more than one league club. Chadwick was going a bit far, but 1876 certainly hadn't been a season polished with purity. Chad argued that although absolute and direct proof of fraud was impossible, conclusive proof could come by circumstantial evidence. Much maligned as proof, conclusions based on circumstantial evidence often were shown to be valid. He pointed out that a verdict of "guilty" was most likely true when players frequented the haunts of gamblers, showed an interest in pool-selling operations, associated with men who lived by pool-gambling; and, most importantly, when they committed errors at opportune times for the success of a pool-ring arrangement.[16]

Chadwick's list of "guilt by correlation" concepts were quite impressive, especially the last point — those errors that coincided with pool-selling profits. Chadwick went on to argue that errors by Start (Mutuals), Fisler (Athletic), Wright (Boston), Clapp (St. Louis), Spalding (Chicago), Fulmer (Louisville), York (Hartford), Gould (Cincinnati) and about 20 other players would simply be errors since these were men of marked integrity. It was a different matter, however, when players with a history of unfavorable associations committed errors key to a game's outcome.[17] It was an argument that wouldn't stand too tall in court, but the cranks weren't in court, although most were as judgmental as any juror. Chadwick advocated that the league throw out all those men marked by the code of Cain. Until this was done, Chadwick concluded, people by the thousands would go out to Gotham's distant Prospect Park to see a legitimate contest between a couple of amateur nines of limited talent while a pitiful 50 or so spectators would attend the professional farces at Union Grounds.[18] The only problem for Chadwick's formula for cleansing baseball was that the game was played in the United States and the country had a Constitution that looked down on little things like guilt by association, unfair dismissal and such.

If Hulbert, fueled by these Chadwickian chronicles, was in a foul mood, it was soon mollified when an autographed contract came in the mails from George "Grin" Bradley. The St. Louis ace had signed with Chicago for 1877. With Spalding as a back-up, and almost his entire 1876 pennant winning team returning, William A. had every right to believe his White Stockings would be winners for some seasons to come. Catcher Jim White might take some R & R — resign and return to Boston — and outfielder Bob Addy might play for Cincinnati in 1877, but John Glenn, Paul Hines, Cal McVey, John Peters, Adrian Anson and Ross Barnes would all be back.[19] Hulbert's confidence may have explained his not overreacting to the wheeling and dealing being done in the months prior to season's end.

Hindsight, that old rascal that makes many a foolish man think he is a genius, was not in Hulbert's grasp. No one could fault him for the blossoming of Bond as a pitcher at Boston (40–17) or of future Hall-of-Famer Jim O'Rourke (.362) coupling with the departed White (.387) to give

Boston a one-two-three combination that was invincible in 1877. Hulbert, perhaps, should have seen that the abolition of the fair-foul rule for the '77 season would cut the speedy Barnes to mortal size.[20] Barnes would never hit above .300 again, posting .272, .266 and .271 averages as his career crashed over the next three years in comic-tragic fashion. No one, including Hulbert, could have expected the Chicago White Stockings to finish below .500, ending fifth in a six-team league in '77 after their brilliant '76 season.

Back in Cincinnati, sports scribe Caylor was continuing his random observations on the just finished season. He wrote that Cincinnati finished last for a number of reasons and the complete number could be counted under the heading "poor management." Booth, Foley and Pearson were moved from position to position so that none of them got used to playing a permanent position. Consequently, they made a rash of errors. Sweasy stayed at second and had an excellent fielding record for the second half of the season. George Keck, owner Si's brother, had no more ability to run a baseball club than a vegetarian had to run a meatpacking house. Foley would have made a good captain, but they appointed Chapman.[21]

With the Mutuals and Athletic literally gone, the composition of the 1877 National League was of paramount concern to most cranks. Of course, Hartford might be able to fill Cammeyer's ballpark. Philadelphia was more difficult. With the A's gone, it would be silly to deal Concannon in. He could still be a threat if given the opportunity. There was one small or, perhaps, not so small, selfish consideration for Hulbert to get the A's out of the league. Grin Bradley, the ace pitcher he had wooed away from St. Louis for '77, was beholden to the A's, having signed with them before signing with Chicago.[22] All was legal since the A's were supposedly defunct and destined for ejection from the league. But if the A's were reinstated, Bradley might be an Athletic in '77. Hulbert's decisions often gave Chicago an edge on the sharp side.

The wisdom of playing non-league games was discussed by several club members during the fall. The papers covered these games fairly enough, but there was an underlying psychological effect concerning these contests that worked against the National League teams. A win by a non-league team over a National League club was outstanding news and well-remembered, but National League teams were expected to win, so their wins were not news of significance and were easily forgotten. There was another problem. Chadwick had calculated that league clubs lost 37 exhibition games in 1876. They probably won far more; "but Chadwick, demonstrating his prejudice against the League's claims of superiority, never tabulated their wins."[23] Chadwickian copy of this sort didn't inspire a crank's faith in the National League. With the league down to six teams for 1877, any elimination or reduction of non-league games was out of the question. Each team would need every game it could arrange to keep solvent. Hulbert, although he didn't like the idea, went along with the practice of filling-in-the-days between league games with exhibitions. Oddly, the idea of doubling or tripling the number of regular season games didn't seem to have surfaced.

The league's rulers also agreed to retain the requirement that placed the responsibility for reporting each player's statistics in the hands of the club's executive. Each owner sent a copy of his team's stats to Nick Young, National League secretary in Washington, D.C.,[24] and a second copy to Henry Chadwick at the *Clipper* for the final compilation.[25]

Speedster Ross Barnes, shown in an 1874 studio photograph, was one of the Big Four who jumped from Boston to Chicago in 1876, where he had a career season. The 145-pound second baseman won the National League batting championship, batting .429 and getting 138 hits in 66 games for an average of 2.09 hits per game. (Transcendental Graphics)

Statistics for the '76 Chicago White Stockings showed that Barnes topped the league in batting with 138 hits in 66 games. Eight of Chicago's "regulars" had hit over 30 percent of the time they batted and only one player, Oscar Bielaski, had failed to average more than a hit per game. The Socks had hit for a team batting average of .337, posted a team fielding average of .882, scored an average of 9.36 runs a game,[26] won 52 and lost 14 for a dazzling .788 percentage. Individually, Ross Barnes had led the league in at least eight offensive categories: runs (126), hits (138), triples (14), total bases (190), walks (20), batting average (.429), slugging average (.590) and on base percentage (.462). Paul Hines tied Hartford's Dick Higham and teammate Barnes in doubles with 21. Jim White led in RBIs (60). In fact, the top five RBI men in the league wore white socks: White (60), Hines (59), Barnes (59), Anson (59) and McVey (53). Eight Pale Socks batted over .300. The club had completely dominated the league. Despite all this offensive prowess, Henry Chadwick attributed Chicago's success to their excellent fielding; only catcher White had averaged more than one error per game (and that was fine fielding for a backstop). Chad was probably correct. It was an era when 60 percent of runs scored were unearned,[27] the club that gave away the least runs being most likely to win. Of the 3,066 runs scored in 1876, 1,201, just over 39 percent, were earned. By the 1890s 70 percent were earned, by the 1920s, 80 percent and by the late 1970s, about 88 percent. In 100 years, major league baseball changed from a game where about three unearned runs were scored for every two earned runs in 1876 to about one unearned run crossing the plate for every nine earned runs.[28]

Study of the data summarizing the 10 games St. Louis and Chicago played showed St. Louis had won the series 6–4; out-hitting the Socks 99–94. Throughout the season, Chicago's offense dominated:

	BA	SA	RS
Chicago	.337	.417	624
Hartford	.267	.322	429
St. Louis	.259	.313	386

St. Louis was happily dominated by Grin Bradley, who completed 63 of 64 games, winning 45 and losing 19 for a .703 average. He posted a 1.23 earned run average, best in the league, and he recorded 16 shutouts, another league-leading statistic, representing more shutouts than Bond and Spalding put together. In fact, Bradley would lead the league in lowest opponent batting average (.228), lowest opponent on base percentage (.242), fewest hits per game (7.38) and most wins above team wins (22.5). He was beyond doubt the pitcher of the year. Spalding had the most wins (47) and best winning percentage (.797). This was probably more a result of the eight men out on the field with him than Spalding's superlative pitching. His earned run average was 1.75, but 1.75 put him fifth of the eight regulars who pitched in 1876. Bradley (1.23), Devlin (1.56), Cummings (1.67) and Bond (1.68) were better. Any of the four, pitching for the White Socks, could have accompanied Chicago to the pennant.

The bottom line, however, was Chicago's attendance. It had been excellent; a total of 82,000 filed through the club's turnstiles.[29] Boston brought in 64,500, which for a fourth place finisher was quite good.[30] Total league attendance was recorded as 343,750 or about 1,300 per game. It was not bad for the league's first year.[31] Maybe the National League would survive four or five more years if all went well.

The season also ended with a lot of talk about having a regulation ball for 1877. The home club's right to use the ball it preferred had lost considerable favor. Most people wanted a lively ball. Al Spalding was already anticipating cash in the Spalding Sporting Goods accounts with his plan to gain the contract to provide an official ball for the 1877 season.[32] If he got the contract, his baseballs would ostensibly compete with those manufactured by Reach and by Wright & Ditson, but all were under Spalding's control. By 1900, the man *Sporting Life* called "The Big Mogul" would also head the Bicycle Trust.[33]

Several major achievements had been brought about by the end of the National League's first year. The nucleus of six baseball clubs had been run on reasonably sound business principles. None of the N.L. clubs except Chicago, if you believed one set of figures, none but Chicago and Boston, if you believed another set of accounts, made any money in 1876.[34] Unbeknown to anyone, 1876 was the fourth year of a six-year depression.[35] When prosperity returned, the businesslike foundation would mean club profits and league stability. A side effect, probably not envisioned by even the most avarice-eyed owner (none were that clever), of placing the clubs firmly in the hands of entrepreneurs and not players meant that when prosperity came, the players would get a vastly reduced share of the profits than they would have had under the old cooperative arrangement. Hulbert, of course, could argue that there would have been no profits if the old cooperative endeavor had remained. Whether he was considered correct or not depended on the perceiver's socio-economic and political attitudes.

Hulbert hadn't been able to eliminate the less respectable from baseball, but the gambling group no longer prowled the stands and grounds of the various baseball parks. This lowered profile of baseball's betting connections and, combined with no games on Sunday and no liquor being sold on any day, gave glimpses of a game dedicated to promoting pureness.

With winter coming, the foliage leaving the trees and the wind beginning to bite, the players dispersed to the four corners of Northeastern America. A few remained in the cities they had played for, some even continuing to work for their baseball boss. In Cincinnati, Amos Booth, Henry Kessler and Charlie Gould were put to work in and about Si Keck's pork house. Charley Jones, who left to visit his parents in Indiana, was expected to return to learn the pork business. Clack returned to his trade of brush making. Their lot was typical of most National Leaguers.[36]

An event eventually to become of some concern to the entrepreneurial custodians of pro baseball occurred on the night of November 23, 1876, at Massaoit House in Springfield, Mass. A small group of college men gathered, representing the universities of Princeton, Harvard, Yale and Columbia, to form the Intercollegiate Football Association.[37] A second American game was being formalized this icy evening by an ex-pitcher named Walter Camp.[38]

23

Hail Hulbert!

Shortly after enjoying a stupendous noonday meal on Wednesday, December 4, 1876, the delegates to the first annual meeting of the National League of Professional Base Ball Clubs filed into the parlors of Cleveland's Kennard House. The meeting had originally been scheduled to begin Monday, December 2, but the delegates quickly and informally realized they had very little business to transact and they would not need to get together till Wednesday.[1] The arrangement suited everyone: the pragmatic (since it was practical), the conniving (since it gave them more time to connive and thereby control the various outcomes of the meeting), the placid (since they would go along with anything), and the naive (since they didn't know any better and couldn't imagine anyone imposing an agenda on anyone else).

A circular aimed at the general public was sent out by the directorate. It was a propaganda piece touting the National League's commitment to clean, high caliber play and to its unending efforts against the gambling elements who would corrupt America's sacred pastime.[2] This piece of puffery impressed no one and even depressed a few, but the majority of cranks probably approved of it.

The men at this meeting controlled the destiny of the National Baseball League. Among the group were N.T. Appolonio and Harry Wright of Boston; William Hulbert, A.G. Mills and Albert Spalding of Chicago; Charles Chase and C.W. Johnstone of Louisville; Charles A. Fowle of St. Louis; Josiah L. Keck of Cincinnati; Robert Ferguson of Hartford (Bulkeley's proxy); Nick E. Young of Washington (the league secretary); and an unwanted G.W. Thompson of Philadelphia.[3] The latter, although as welcome as a wart, was not a man to give up easily. He had come to argue the A's case for staying in the league. Two men were blatantly "visible" by their absence: Morgan G. Bulkeley, the president of the National League, and William Cammeyer, manager of the Mutuals, the team representing America's most populous city.[4] Neither man's absence was a complete surprise.

Bulkeley was voluntarily leaving baseball to increase his fortune in insurance and further his career in politics. Cammeyer was exiting from the league knowing Union Grounds, his ballpark, would be inhabited by Hartford's Dark Blues and managed by Ferguson in 1877.[5] Cammeyer, age 55, was retiring from baseball. His fortune was assured from his father's leather business, the Cammeyer Shoe Company, and a major league team was paying rent to use his beloved Union Grounds. Although Cammy had made his money in leather, his heart had been beating in his ballpark. A Cammeyer obituary (he died in 1898) observed that "almost to the day of his death [Cammeyer] spoke reverently of its many triumphs."[6]

After appointing Appolonio the chairman, the first order of business was the proposed expulsion of the Mutuals and Athletic. The board comprising Appolonio of Boston, Ferguson (Bulkeley's proxy) from Hartford, Chase of Louisville and Fowle of St. Louis—two from the east and two from the west—would consider the expulsion requests and make recommendations on how the league should act.[7] It was a neat process for Hulbert. If the Mutes and A's were cast aside, the Chicago power broker wouldn't be in the forefront of the group expelling them. Appolonio, Ferguson, Chase and Fowle would have forced them out, not he.

The first flash of foment came in the considering of the A's case. G.W. Thompson argued for the Athletic's retention before a stone-faced assembly. He had much to explain. A letter from George W. "Grin" Bradley, Adrian C. Anson and Joseph V. Battin argued they had contracted to play in 1877 for the Athletic, believing the team was solvent. The club, however, was bankrupt. It had failed to pay its own players, the western clubs' their share of gate receipts, and had a treasury bereft of funds, being over $6,000 in debt. Bradley, Anson and Battin said they wanted to be able to play for a club capable of fulfilling its contracts.[8] It was unfortunate for the A's that two of the three complaining players were closely affiliated with Chicago and Hulbert. The White Stockings wanted Bradley and Anson for '77, and also wanted the hated A's out on principle. After all, the A's, like the Mutuals, had violated the rule that a team should complete all league games that were reasonably possible to complete. Although the Mutes sent no representatives, Cammeyer had recognized the hopelessness of his team's position, sending a letter that said, "It was no use for the League to have rules if it did not enforce them."[9]

Thompson entered a document, signed by all members of the Athletic Base-Ball Club, on behalf of the Philadelphia team. Thompson pointed out that the Athletic boasted a record for responsibility and honorable dealing in all its relations, second to no club in the National League. It was an old argument; when in trouble blatantly blow your own horn and deny doing anything wrong. If the A's were so responsible and so honorable, why hadn't they met their obligations and come west? Thompson went on to argue that the Athletic organization dated back beyond any other club in the league and again emphasized that its influence had always been for honesty and honor. Finally, he said that the A's had a disastrous season, all beyond the team's control. The team had to combat the Centennial Exposition, along with disease and injuries to several key players. Eggler and Sutton had been walking wounded most of the year. The team — out of a sense of honor — had assumed and paid off an old debt of $5,600.[10]

He was making a point. If you took the A's $6,000 debt at the end of this year and subtracted their $5,600 debt at the end of '75, it became clear the team had almost broken even. To break even with the competition the A's had in Philadelphia in '76 was no mean feat. It boded well for financial success in '77 when there'd be no Centennial. But an active A's in '77 would mean Chicago would be without Bradley and Anson. When the A's Thompson was finished, A.G. Mills took the floor. Mills, a Chicago director, would reply for the western clubs. "Hulbert's spokesman, weasel of the week, never thinks for himself," Thompson may have thought, but he would have most likely been incorrect. Hulbert did not have to tell Mills what to say. He only had to know how vehemently and sincerely Mills' own mind had come to the conclusion that the A's should be expelled. A true believer was far better than a robotic mouthpiece any day. Mills completely annihilated Thompson's arguments, delivering a scathing attack that one National League member later told a reporter "was a fitting obituary for that swindling organization."[11]

The board ruled by unanimous vote of 4–0 to refer the matter to the National League clubs at large and recommended that both the Mutuals and Athletic baseball clubs be expelled.[12] In a few minutes a vote was taken and it was over. G.W. Thompson was soon walking down the steps of Kennard House. Cammeyer had been correct in not coming. It had been a woeful waste of time. The league vote on both teams had been unanimous, 6–0.[13] G.W. probably wondered if anyone had listened to him. He left, his thoughts as dark as anthracite.

The uncontested Mutuals' release from the fold was an easy matter. No one challenged the formal demand by the western clubs that the naughty New Yorkers be expelled. Cammeyer had capitulated and withdrawn from the field. It seemed uncharacteristic of the old miser until you thought of his personality. Cammy was, in truth, penny wise and pound foolish (or, in American, cent clever and dollar dumb). To save a few bucks, he had reneged on taking his team west and in so doing had saved a few shekels while losing his team. The expulsion of the Mutuals was not as drastic as it appeared. In fact, it wasn't drastic at all. Hartford agreed to play their games in Brooklyn. The team would be Hartford in name only.[14]

The directors made the Athletic's expulsion a little more palatable to the Philadelphia cranks by agreeing to try to get a club to represent Philadelphia. Hartford's agreement to move was exceptionally satisfying.[15]

A number of amendments to the league constitution were passed. Perhaps the most interesting was a provision that was made for admission of new clubs at any time before the start of a season. This would keep the outsiders' hopes up. Aspirants were always less critical of the organization they wished to join. The league could always squelch any applicant they wished to keep out. As a further sop to the outsiders, an interesting mechanism was put into the works. One club could be admitted to the league without a vote, upon proper application to the secretary. The catch was that the team had to win a series of games during the previous season against National League competition that afforded a fair test of the aspirant's merits.[16] It was better for the outside teams who wanted to get in to think they had a chance and it was even better for them to compete to get in. If a club ever made it through the league's new tortuous test of merit, it really would be a club worth letting in. The new trial by combat format would also take some of the danger out of the better outside clubs getting together and forming their own league to try and rival the National League.

The lingering problem of deciding the final standings of the clubs in the 1876 season required logic, diplomacy and a feel for public perceptions. Charles Fowle of St. Louis asked that the games that the Mutuals and A's had not played be counted as defaults and scored as victories for the opposing side. If this were agreed upon, St. Louis would be second-place finishers, topping Hartford by having won one more game.[17] Otherwise, Hartford would take the runner-up spot. If the two eastern clubs voted one way and the four western clubs another way, the split between east and west might widen. No one wanted that. After all, the league had just booted two eastern teams out. Keeping in mind that not even the Shadow knows what was in the minds of the men present, the men present, probably as much to keep the peace and insure there would be a league in 1877, decided only to assign a position to one club and declared that Chicago was the official pennant winner.[18] The league left it to the newspapers to assign second place to the team of their choice, Hartford or St. Louis. Chadwick's *Clipper* listed the top three finishers as Chicago, Hartford and St. Louis.[19]

The board then settled a few player complaints in typical bureaucratic style. Devlin had asked that his contract with Louisville be declared annulled because of alleged unfair treatment in the matter of salary.[20] The board voted to allow Devlin to withdraw his complaint and implied that there should be no reprimand from his club.[21] Ferguson had presented a complaint against Tommy Bond asking for the pitcher's expulsion since the terrible one had made sustained, unsubstantiated inflammatory remarks about fellow players. Bond had countered with a retraction. A "no jurisdiction" decision was an excellent solution for the league since it kept both players in its fold and swept under the rug the messy business of an investigation finding anything nasty for the press to publish about the National League.[22] Every executive in the National League knew that an exposed sin was far more repulsive than an unexposed transgression. See no evil, hear no evil, report no evil was still the watchword.

A number of procedural and technical problems were hashed over as the meeting proceeded. The directors had a tremendous row over how umpires should be selected.[23] Although umpires always seemed to inspire arguments, there was no disagreement over how little they should be paid. One estimate was that it would be $800 a year and expenses.[24] It was finally decided that three men in or near each city in the league would be named at the start of the season as an umpiring corps. Which of the particular three would ump the game in any particular city would be chosen by lot three hours before game time. Unfortunately, the club officials couldn't agree on acceptance of three names for any of the six cities except Mike Walsh, John Morris and Dan Devinney,[25] who'd work Lou'ville. The matter was referred for solution to a special committee of two: Harry Wright and William Hulbert.[26]

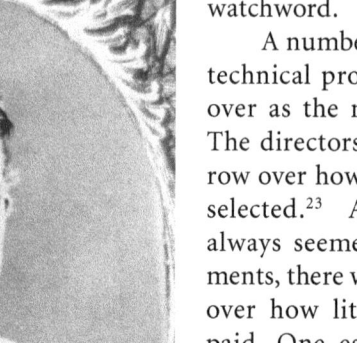

Albert Goodwill Spalding, shown in a 1872 Boston uniform, was the leader of the Big Four who jumped from the Boston Red Stockings to Chicago in 1876. He not only pitched Chicago to the first National League pennant, but worked with William Hulbert to help found the National League. Always the entrepreneur, Spalding got the rights to sell the National League's first official baseball by providing an endless supply of baseballs to the National League owners. (Transcendental Graphics)

Spalding's baseball was adopted as the National League's official ball.[27] It was to be of the same size and weight as the '76 ball, to have a double cover and a core of one-ounce hard rubber. It insured a lively, hard, uniform sphere and, therefore, an increase in spectator excitement.[28] Spalding's offer to supply the league with free baseballs and to pay the National League a dollar for every dozen of his baseballs it used as long as he was allowed to call his ball the "official league ball" was easily agreed upon. Not able to believe their good fortune at getting paid for accepting an endless supply of free baseballs, the National League owners had instantaneously agreed. To add further lucre to the Spalding bank account, the league granted his sporting goods company the contract to publish the league's annual guidebook.[29]

A security system was instituted concerning the official balls. All would be examined by the league secretary, tested and approved. Each would be packed in paper and foil, and sealed in a box not to be opened until delivered to an umpire just before a game.[30] The tight security surrounding the care and transport of the league's official baseballs had been long in coming. Close guardianship guaranteed that a Cherokee Fisher clone wouldn't paddle the ball for a couple of hours before a game began to make it soft and mushy.[31]

Bases were made 25 percent larger. They would now be 15 inches on each side. Home base would be moved up into the diamond.[32] The sides of the plate would now form a portion of the foul lines.[33] The toss of the coin for first innings was eliminated. The home team would always bat first from now on.[34] The umpire's "weather watch" was eliminated.[35] A game must be now called after 30 minutes of rain.[36] Fair-fouls were abolished.[37] A batted ball hitting a runner would now immediately put the runner out.[38] A base runner could now pass behind a fielder who obstructed his path in an attempt to field a batted ball. The base paths were ruled the property of the defense. A fielder touching a runner to put him out must now hold onto the ball. If he dropped it, the runner would be safe.[39] A new rule reflecting a concern with speeding up the game (some of which lasted up to two hours or more) seemed like a contradiction of concepts. A batsman who was given a base on called balls would be entitled to the walk if he ran to first, but could be fielded out if he walked to first.[40] Thus, a walk in 1877 would be a kind of "run."

In things financial, the men at the meeting decided that each club would now be required to use a self-registering apparatus connected to a turnstile to indicate exactly how many persons got into each ground for each game. The visiting club would get 15 cents (30 percent of the gate) for each paying person entering.[41]

The league tightened its icy grip on the players. Any player exhibiting "indifferent" or "careless" play could have his pay withheld or his contract cancelled.[42] Showing its concern for things of both greater and lesser significance, the league noted that players would be charged $30 each for their uniforms. Fifty cents was to be deducted from a player's salary for each day a player was absent while on the road.[43] As for the health of the participants, it was decided that a player couldn't be substituted except for an injury after the second inning rather than the fourth.[44]

The crucial league presidency election was another influential interlude featuring a masterpiece of manipulation and a calculated gamble by Hulbert, the league's mastermind, who cheerfully nominated Boston's N.T. Appolonio for president. The nomination had hardly been seconded when Appolonio arose, thanked his nominator and seconder, and declined the honor. Appolonio indicated that it was doubtful he would be associated with Boston for another year. The *Louisville Courier-Journal* noted that Appolonio's health was "retirement material."[45] With Hulbert's eastern nominee gone, the possibilities were probably down to one, Bill Hulbert, or two, Hulbert or the saintly Harry Wrighteous. The rest were no threat: Cincinnati's Si Keck, too abrasive a personality to garner any votes; Hartford's Robert Ferguson, too many debacles when he was National Association president; or Louisville's Charles Chase and St. Louis' Charles Fowle, neither in the league long enough, both relative unknowns. In five minutes, Hulbert was nominated and unanimously elected president. Nick Young was re-elected secretary.[46] His salary was increased to $500 per year.[47]

After two days the National League directors concluded the league's first annual meeting. The members left, their minds on the upcoming 1877 season. Chicago was expected to win it all once again. The press was now treating the league with little rancor. Even Chadwick was coming around to the positive. The image of a cleaner, more honest circuit was emerging. Hulbert could only conclude that if the National League were to last five more years, this had to be its finest hour.

Epilogue: Extra Innings

Two executives (Morgan G. Bulkeley and William Ambrose Hulbert), one sportswriter (Henry Chadwick) and six boys of summer 1876 (Adrian Anson, William Cummings, Jim O'Rourke. A.G. Spalding, George Wright and Harry Wright) are in Baseball's Hall of Fame.

Eight other 1876 players received at least one nominating vote: Doug Allison (1), Ross Barnes (3), Joe Battin (1), Tommy Bond (1), Cal McVey (1), Lip Pike (1), Jack Remsen (1) and Jim (Deacon) White (1).[1]

Hulbert was president of the National League from 1877 to 1882. He was not enshrined in Cooperstown until 1995.[2] He died on April 10, 1882, from heart disease and was buried in Graceland Cemetery on Chicago's North Side. Wrigley Field would be built only two blocks away.[3]

Slugger Charley Jones would bother batters for years before retiring with a .299 lifetime batting average, 170 doubles, 98 triples and 55 home runs, all hit in an era of far distant fences and more dead than lively baseballs. He was blackballed from the National League in 1880 and would conclude his career in the American Association, the "Beer and Whisky League" that rivaled the N.L. in the 1880s.

For 1876's most dominating pitcher, George "Grin" Bradley, 1876 would be a career season. Sixteen of his 28 lifetime shutouts came in 1876. He would pitch for eight years, posting a very ordinary 138–125 lifetime win-loss record. Other players would have various fates. Albert Spalding became a league executive and sporting goods magnate. Weak-hitting William Harbidge of Hartford, the first left-handed catcher in baseball history, who worried constantly about his chances of staying in the National League, happily played for eight years before being retired. He finished with a lifetime batting average of .248. Bob Ferguson, baseball's first switch-hitter[4] and maligned early executive, found favor as an umpire in later years.[5] Amos "The Darling" Booth, the infielder who collected hairpins hoping they would translate into hits, saw his second career as a mounted policeman in Cincinnati end when a wild, erratic ride terminated with his horse being thrown into a Cincinnati canal.[6]

Chadwick was awarded a lifetime annual pension by the National League in 1894, presented at the White House by Theodore Roosevelt in 1904, and was writing on baseball until his death in 1908.[7] Cummings retired from professional baseball in 1878, learned the painting and wallpapering business while continuing to play baseball at the amateur level, ran his own decorating business in Athol, Massachusetts, for 32 years and passed away at age 75.[8]

The fact that three players—Cal McVey, Charles "Chick" Fulmer and William "Cherokee" Fisher—would lose a child during the season was probably not exceptional. Many children didn't make it to adolescence in an era when the average life expectancy was 43.4 years, about 60 percent of what it is today.[9]

One year to the day after the National League's inception, a fat, furry rodent in Pennsylvania would give new meaning to National League's founding day. Poking his head from his burrow, this original Punxsutawney Phil forecast just how long it would be before the baseball season would begin. Phil's annual predictions made February 2 more famous as Groundhog Day than the National League's birthday.[10]

There being no happily ever after in reality, the National League troubles were by no means over as 1876 ended. The International Association of Professional Base Ball Players, a new player's league, was formed in 1877 in opposition to the National League.[11] By late summer 1877, a hippodroming scandal involving four Louisville Grays threatened to rip apart what Hulbert and friends had brought together. Four Grays—Jim Devlin, George Hall, Al Nichols and Bill Craver—would be expelled for life.[12]

Hartford's Dark Blues would, as rumored, move to Brooklyn in 1877 and play at Cammeyer's Union Grounds. They would be known as the Hartford Brooklyns or Brooklyn Hartfords depending on whim and wag. It is unknown how certain Hulbert was that his 1877 National League would have a team in the New York–Brooklyn area when he expelled Cammeyer's Mutuals from the N.L. in December 1876.

The National League would wallow in hypocrisy, corruption and sanctimony for many more years for, like all human endeavors, the National League was fraught with all the foibles of an imperfect species. Hulbert's league was certainly not the house that truth built. It was an association forged through time by very human human beings for motives no more pure or impure than have motivated the building of many institutions. Blacks would be excluded for 71 years. Only gradually would the legacy of

Hulbert become less and less corrupt. The league brought in the reserve clause on September 29, 1879, and set the stage for decades of player-owner animosity.[13] Baseball would be run in ruthlessness for decades under management's iron fist.

The league's survival provided a place in the summer sun aspired to by millions of youngsters. In 1876, Willie Keeler was a wee four-year-old, John McGraw was three, Honus Wagner was two, and, most representative of the thousands of men who have played in the N.L., Jeremiah Nops (72–41 W-L record over a six-year career, went 20–6 for Baltimore in 1897) was one. Mordecai "Three-fingered" Brown and Rube Waddell were born in 1876. For these infants, a league was waiting, just as it waits today for youngsters who can be seen throwing, catching and batting baseballs on sun-saturated fields.

The young men who charged across the National League's diamonds of 1876 are all gone now. They are only ghosts; gray graceful figures running forever through our collective memories. Few were great players, most were mediocre by today's standards and some were downright crooked, but to all these young men and to William Hulbert and his executive confreres, we owe our thanks. They helped solidify an institution that has meant so much to our nation and which has filled decades of American summers with joy.

Chapter Notes

Preface

1. Seymour, *Baseball: Early Years*, pp. 78–81.
2. Rader, *Baseball: A History of America's Game*, pp. 40, 42.
3. Golenbock, *Wrigleyville*, p. 18. Baseball historian Fred Lieb is cited as describing Hulbert as "Albert Spalding's mouthpiece."
4. Bartlett, *Bartlett's Familiar Quotations*, p. 313.

Chapter 1

1. Smith, *Pioneers of Baseball*, p. 42.
2. Anson, *Ball Player's Career*, p. 92.
3. Rosenberg, *They Gave Us Baseball*, p. 16: "A colleague once described Hulbert as a man with a 'magnificent physique, commanding presence, strong personality and endowed with a powerful intellect, keen logic, and impressive directness of speech ... essentially a leader among men....'"
4. Anson, *Ball Player's Career*, pp. 92–93.
5. *Baseball Century*, p. 26.
6. William E. Akin, "William A. Hulbert" in Tiemann & Rucker, *Nineteenth Century Stars*, p. 65.
7. Rosenberg, *They Gave Us Baseball*, p. 16: Hulbert became club president after Chicago finished seventh in 1874.
8. Seymour, *Baseball: Early Years*, p. 59.
9. Thorn & Palmer, *Total Baseball*, p. 701: Chicago finished the 1875 season with a 30–37 win-loss record.
10. Jim Devlin, Richard Higham and George Zettlein were three members of the 1875 Chicago team who gained notoriety during their career.
11. *Baseball Century*, p. 26.
12. Voigt, *American Baseball*, p. 61: Hulbert was owner of a coal dealership. Ryczek, *Blackguards*, p. 133: Hulbert was a driving, energetic proprietor of a grocery and coal business. Holtzman & Vass, *Chicago Cubs Encyclopedia*, p. 296: Hulbert was a successful grain and coal merchant.
13. Ryczek, *Blackguards*, p. 134: "Hulbert was of a different breed than the club executives who composed the ruling board of the N.A. He had never played baseball and viewed the professional version of the sport as a vehicle for making money, rather than as a source of recreation or civic pride." Ryczek, p. 248, attributes this information to a letter from Harry Wright to Bob Addy. The date was illegible.
14. Seymour, *Baseball: Early Years*, p. 128: Hulbert sanctioned the use of Pinkerton's to guard against attempts to throw league games.
15. Seymour, *Baseball: Early Years*, p. 59, p. 75. Contrary to Seymour, *Dickson Baseball Dictionary*, pp. 200–201, defines hippodroming as the practice of promoting baseball with stunts (e.g., John L. Sullivan as an umpire).
16. *Baseball Century*, p. 25. Voigt, *American Baseball*, pp. 20–21: The elimination of revolving was crucial to the recognition of professional baseball as a legitimate business. This was also Chadwick's line of argument. Voigt noted that "years later, major league baseball solved this problem by insisting on a reserve clause ... but in these formative years the revolving evil remained as a crucial stumbling block to the orderly and profitable promotion of big-time baseball."
17. Voigt, *American Baseball*, pp. 53–54.
18. Reidenbaugh, *100 Years*, p. 7.
19. Reidenbaugh, *100 Years*, p. 7.
20. Seymour, *Baseball: Early Years*, pp. 139–140: Hulbert could be haughty, having a high and mighty attitude toward the American Association when it was established. Seymour, *Baseball: Early Years*, p. 212: "Hulbert was a strong executive who ran the League and, as one newspaper said, made it what it was. His decisive actions against recalcitrant clubs and dishonest players show his forceful personality.

Notes — Chapter 1

He steered the League safely through its first grim years."

21. John M. Ward, "Is the Base-Ball Player a Chattel?" *Lippincott's*, vol. 20, 1887, p. 8 cited in Melville, *Early Baseball*, p. 125.

22. McCullough, *From Cartwright*, p. 49: "No matter what Hulbert's true intentions were, in one fell swoop he did, in fact, clean up baseball and create a respectable new league."

23. McCullough, *From Cartwright*, p. 50.

24. Vincent, *Mudville's Revenge*, p. 139.

25. *New York Times*, March 28, 1872, in Rader, *American Sports*, p. 69.

26. Rice, *Seasons Past*, p. 27: Every National Association team was on the verge of bankruptcy in 1875. Ryczek, *Blackguards*, p. 214: The drawing power of Hulbert's Chicago team, Concannon's Philadelphias and Cammeyer's Mutuals became virtually nil as the 1875 season progressed.

27. Rader, *American Sports*, p. 114: Hulbert had the support of the western clubs that resented the eastern domination over the NAPBBP—National Association of Professional Base-Ball Players (usually referred to as the National Association).

28. Nemec, *Great Encyclopedia*, p. 65.

29. Nemec, *Great Encyclopedia*, p. 83.

30. Spink, *National Game*, p. 18.

31. Hulbert letter of Dec. 5, 1875, to Campbell Bishop: "I see no great objection to giving papers friendly to us an inside view." He was certain that they could trust the *Chicago Tribune*, *Louisville Courier-Journal* and the *Cincinnati Enquirer*.

32. Voigt, *American Baseball*, p. 54.

33. Smith, *Pioneers of Baseball*, p. 15: Harry Wright was "respected by everyone, always just and fair, and loved by veteran ballplayers and youngsters alike."

34. Nemec, *Great Encyclopedia*, p. 6: "Many club nicknames in the early years of baseball were singular."

35. Jones, *Former Major League Teams*, p. 24.

36. Ryczek, *Blackguards*, pp. 209–215. Jones, *Former Major League Teams*, p. 24.

37. Maher & Ivor-Campbell, "William Henry Cammeyer" in Ivor-Campbell et al., *Baseball's First Stars*, p. 21.

38. Ryczek, *Blackguards*, p. 119.

39. Spink, *National Game*, p. 18.

40. Bartlett, *Familiar Quotations*, pp. ix, 374.

41. Hulbert letter of Feb. 10, 1876, to Charles Fowle of St. Louis.

42. Melville, *Early Baseball*, p. 77.

43. Conglobate: to form or collect into a ball or rounded mass.

44. Dickson, *Dickson Baseball Dictionary*, p. 183: Baseball's most illiterate message was authored by Miguel (Mike) Gonzales in spring 1924 with a four-word telegraphic message assessing the capabilities of Moe Berg. It read, 'Good field, no hit.'

45. *Clipper*, Feb. 12, 1876, p. 362.

46. *Louisville Courier-Journal*, May 9, 1876, p. 4.

47. *Louisville Courier-Journal*, May 9, 1876, p. 4.

48. *Clipper*, Oct. 23, 1875, cited in Ryczek, *Blackguards*, p. 212.

49. McCulloch, *From Cartwright*, p. 48.

50. Voigt, *American Baseball*, p. 54: Chadwick wrote: "Almost every team had its 'lushers'...." There was no machinery to enforce any rule against drinking. The National Association councils were packed with players, who, holding key positions, had little disposition to act.

51. Maher & Ivor-Campbell, "William Henry Cammeyer" in Ivor-Campbell et al., *Baseball's First Stars*, p. 21.

52. Seymour, *Baseball: Early Years*, p. 48.

53. Maher & Ivor-Campbell, "William Henry Cammeyer" in Ivor-Campbell et al., *Baseball's First Stars*, p. 21.

54. Lowrey, *Green Cathedrals*, p. 39.

55. Lowrey, *Green Cathedrals*, p. 114.

56. Lowrey, *Green Cathedrals*, p. 10.

57. Seymour, *Baseball: Early Years*, p. 25.

58. Seymour, *Baseball: Early Years*, p. 16.

59. Rice, *Seasons Past*, p. 7.

60. Adelman, *A Sporting Time*, pp. 148, 159. Gershman, *Diamonds*, p. 11.

61. Adelman, *A Sporting Time*, p. 150.

62. Shannon & Kalinsky, *Ball Parks*, p. 4.

63. Shannon & Kalinsky, *Ball Parks*, p. 4.

64. Shannon & Kalinsky, *Ball Parks*, p. 5.

65. Shannon & Kalinsky, *Ball Parks*, p. 5.

66. Frank V. Phelps, "Robert V. Ferguson (Old Fergy)" in Tiemann & Rucker, *Nineteenth Century Stars*, p. 43: Ferguson's "peers characterized him as competitive, authoritative, intelligent, rule-wise, short-tempered, tactless...."

67. Shannon & Kalinsky, *Ball Parks*, p. 5.

68. Nemec, *Great Encyclopedia*, pp. 66, 71. The Atlantics lost their final 31 games of 1875, dropping out of the National Association with a win-loss record of 2–42. Orem, *Baseball from the Newspaper Accounts*, p. 242: The Atlantics were $5,000 in debt.

69. McCulloch, *From Cartwright*, p. 114.

70. Tygiel, *Past Time*, p. 16.

71. Tygiel, *Past Time*, p. 16.

72. Vincent, *Mudville's Revenge*, p. 138.

73. Vincent, *Mudville's Revenge*, p. 138.

74. McCulloch, *From Cartwright*, p. 248.

75. McCulloch, *From Cartwright*, pp. 248–249.

76. Mark Alvarez, "William Henry Wright (Harry)" in Ivor-Campbell et al., *Baseball's First Stars*, p. 178.
77. Seymour, *Baseball: Early Years*, p. 72.
78. Wheeler & Baskin, *Cincinnati Game*, p. 24.
79. Wheeler & Baskin, *Cincinnati Game*, p. 120.
80. Rosenberg, *They Gave Us Baseball*, p. 6.
81. McCulloch, *From Cartwright*, pp. 289–290.
82. Ryczek, *Blackguards*, p. 200.
83. Ryczek, *Blackguards*, p. 202.
84. Voigt, *American Baseball*, p. 42.
85. Voigt, *American Baseball*, p. 42.
86. Ryczek, *Blackguards*, p. 206.

Chapter 2

1. Seymour, *Baseball: Early Years*, pp. 77–78.
2. Wheeler & Baskin, *Cincinnati Game*, p. 21.
3. Wheeler & Baskin, *Cincinnati Game*, p. 21.
4. Nemec, *Great Encyclopedia*, pp. 9–10.
5. Appel & Goldblatt, *Baseball's Best*, p. 350.
6. Ryczek, *Blackguards*, p. 135: The *Chicago InterOcean* described how Wood lanced an abscess on his left thigh, then, with infected fluid on the blade, accidentally stabbed himself in the right leg, which, in turn, became infected. Then, while doctors were trying to set the leg, the bone snapped, cutting an artery. By the time the entire operation was done, Wood had lost his right leg.
7. Robert L. Tiemann, "James Leon Wood" in Ivor-Campbell et al., *Baseball's First Stars*, p. 174.
8. Nemec, *Great Encyclopedia*, p. 697.
9. *Cincinnati Enquirer*, Aug. 30, 1876, p. 8.
10. Appel & Goldblatt, *Baseball's Best*, p. 350.
11. Golenbock, *Wrigleyville*, p. 15.
12. Voigt, *American Baseball*, p. 62.
13. *Baseball Century*, p. 26.
14. Dickey, *History of National League Baseball*, p. 4.
15. Peterson, *The Man Who Invented Baseball*, p. 178.
16. Dickey, *History of National League Baseball*, p. 4.
17. Appel & Goldblatt, *Baseball's Best*, p. 350.
18. Picture of White in Tiemann & Rucker, *Nineteenth Century Stars*, p. 135.
19. Spink, *National Game*, p. 90: White led the N.A. in fielding percentage in 1871 and 1875 and the N.L. in 1876. Spink, *National Game*, p. 92: White was "one of the speediest throwers, as well as a great batsman ... [he] was a really great player...."
20. Nemec, *Great Encyclopedia*, p. 39.
21. Frederick Ivor-Campbell, "Calvin Alexander McVey" in Tiemann & Rucker, *Nineteenth Century Stars*, p. 92.
22. James, *Bill James Historical Abstract*, p. 13.
23. Spink, *National Game*, p. 190.
24. Spink, *National Game*, p. 190.
25. Seymour, *Baseball: Early Years*, pp. 77–78.
26. Maher & Ivor-Campbell, "William Henry Cammeyer" in Ivor-Campbell et al., *Baseball's First Stars*, p. 21.
27. Maher & Ivor-Campbell, "William Henry Cammeyer" in Ivor-Campbell et al., *Baseball's First Stars*, p. 21.
28. Maher & Ivor-Campbell, "William Henry Cammeyer" in Ivor-Campbell et al. *Baseball's First Stars*, p. 21.
29. Maher & Ivor-Campbell, "William Henry Cammeyer" in Ivor-Campbell et al., *Baseball's First Stars*, p. 21.
30. Orem, *Baseball from the Newspaper Accounts*, p. 232: The Mutuals would not go west at the end of the 1876 season.
31. *Chicago Tribune*, Feb. 13, 1876, p. 12.
32. Orem, *Baseball from the Newspaper Accounts*, p. 232.
33. Seymour, *Baseball: Early Years*, p. 69.
34. Frederick Ivor-Campbell, "Henry Chadwick (Chad, Father of Base Ball)" in Ivor-Campbell et al., *Baseball's First Stars*, p. 26. Appel & Goldblatt, *Baseball's Best*, pp. 66–67.
35. Appel & Goldblatt, *Baseball's Best*, p. 66.
36. Frederick Ivor-Campbell, "Henry Chadwick (Chad, Father of Base Ball)" in Ivor-Campbell et al., *Baseball's First Stars*, p. 26.
37. *Chicago Tribune*, Feb. 20, 1876, p. 10 and April 2, 1876, p. 5.
38. Thorn & Palmer, *Total Baseball*, p. 681; Thorn et al., *Hidden Game*, p. 681.
39. Frederick Ivor-Campbell, "Henry Chadwick (Chad, Father of Base Ball)" in Ivor-Campbell et al., *Baseball's First Stars*, p. 26.
40. *Chicago Tribune*, Feb. 20, 1876, p. 10.
41. Seymour, *Baseball: Early Years*, p. 69.
42. *Baseball Century*, p. 26. Bartlett, *Baseball and Mr. Spalding*, pp. 73–78.
43. *Baseball Century*, p. 26.
44. Dickey, *History of National League Baseball*, p. 5.
45. Bartlett, *Baseball and Mr. Spalding*, pp. 73–78.
46. Appel & Goldblatt, *Baseball's Best*, p. 350: By 1877, most pitchers were throwing curves.
47. Morse, *Sphere and Ash*, p. 34: The origin of the curve is unknown. Morse lists several 1875 "Minor League" curveball pitchers. Seymour, *Baseball: Early Years*, p. 63: Fred Goldsmith claimed to be the originator of the curve, but he, himself, had credited Charles

Avery, a Yale pitcher, with its invention in the 1860s.
48. James, *The Bill James Historical Abstract*, p. 12: George Zettlein was reputed to be a very hard thrower at the start of the 1870s. Al Spalding threw very hard, but Tommy Bond was probably the fastest. Kaese, *The Boston Braves*, p. 25: Bond was one of the first successful curveball pitchers and was sometimes called the Father of Modern Pitching.
49. Morse, *Sphere and Ash*, p. 34.
50. Nemec, *Great American Baseball Team Book*, p. 7: Spalding could neither throw nor hit a curveball.
51. Morse, *Sphere and Ash*, p. 34.
52. William E. McMahon, "Albert Goodwill Spalding," in Ivor-Campbell et al., *Baseball's First Stars*, p. 154.
53. *Baseball Century*, p. 26.
54. Dickey, *History of National League Baseball*, p. 5.
55. Seymour, *Baseball: Early Years*, p. 78.
56. Bartlett, *Baseball and Mr. Spalding*, p. 76.
57. Dickey, *History of National League Baseball*, p. 5. *Baseball Century*, p. 26: The Big Four "played out the season in New England, devastating the rest of the Association. Their outstanding play left no charge for hippodroming."
58. Golenbock, *Wrigleyville*, p. 16.
59. Bartlett, *Baseball and Mr. Spalding*, p. 76.
60. Thorn & Palmer, *Total Baseball*, p. 703: The A's finished seventh in 1876.
61. William E. McMahon & Robert L. Tiemann, "Adrian Constantine Anson (Capt., Uncle, Pop)," in Ivor-Campbell et al., *Baseball's First Stars*, p. 3.
62. Appel & Goldblatt, *Baseball's Best*, p. 11: Anson was basically a line-drive hitter. Thorn & Palmer, *Total Baseball*, p. 936: Anson hit .329 over a 22-year National League career. He was 6', 227 lbs. He covered little ground and was never an accomplished fielder, starting his career at third base and moving to first, where he played most of his career. He made 58 errors in 1884.
63. Burns, "The Chicago Cubs," *Sport*, Sept. 1950, p. 27.
64. Appel & Goldblatt, *Baseball's Best*, p. 11.
65. Appel & Goldblatt, *Baseball's Best*, p. 11.
66. Appel & Goldblatt, *Baseball's Best*, p. 12.
67. Dickey, *History of National League Baseball*, p. 4.
68. Anson, *Ball Player's Career*, p. 83.
69. Appel & Goldblatt, *Baseball's Best*, p. 11: Spalding, with Boston and Anson, with the Athletic, became friends over the years from 1872 on. Dickey, *History of National League Baseball*, p. 4.
70. Anson, *Ball Player's Career*, p. 92.
71. Astor, *Baseball Hall of Fame 50th Anniversary Book*, p. 21.

Chapter 3

1. Voigt, *American Baseball*, p. 51. Thorn & Palmer, *Total Baseball*, p. 701.
2. Baker, *Sports in the Western World*, p. 159.
3. Baker, *Sports in the Western World*, pp. 160–176.
4. Anson, *Ballplayer's Career*, p. 92.
5. Voigt, *American Baseball*, p. 63.
6. Seymour, *Baseball: Early Years*, p. 78.
7. Ward, *Baseball: An Illustrated History*, p. 27. Seymour, *Baseball: Early Years*, pp. 128–129.
8. Nemec, *Great Encyclopedia*, p. 70.
9. Seymour, *Baseball: Early Years*, p. 67.
10. Vincent, *Mudville's Revenge*, p. 134.
11. Voigt, *American Baseball*, p. 61.
12. Vincent, *Mudville's Revenge*, p. 132.
13. Vincent, *Mudville's Revenge*, pp. 134–135.
14. Vincent, *Mudville's Revenge*, p. 132.
15. William E. Akin, "William A. Hulbert" in Tiemann & Rucker, *Nineteenth Century Stars*, p. 65. Rader, *Baseball: A History of America's Game*, p. 40.
16. William E. McMahon, "Albert Goodwill Spalding," in Ivor-Campbell et al., *Baseball's First Stars*, pp. 154–155.
17. Vincent, *Mudville's Revenge*, p. 123.
18. Vincent, *Mudville's Revenge*, p. 134.
19. Vincent, *Mudville's Revenge*, p. 131.
20. Frank V. Phelps, "Robert V. Ferguson (Old Fergy)" in Tiemann & Rucker, *Nineteenth Century Stars*, p. 43.
21. Dickey, *History of National League Baseball*, p. 5. *Baseball Century*, p. 25.
22. Dickey, *History of National League Baseball*, p. 5.
23. Nemec, *Great Encyclopedia*, p. 84.
24. Twombly, *200 Years*, p. 82.
25. Furnas, *The Americans*, pp. 638–639.
26. Nemec, *Great Encyclopedia*, p. 84.
27. Harper, *How You Played*, p. 278.
28. Gershman, *Diamonds*, p. 28.
29. Seymour, *Baseball: Early Years*, p. 82.
30. Voigt, *American Baseball*, p. 64.
31. *Chicago Tribune*, Oct. 24, 1876, in Sullivan, *Early Innings*, p. 92.
32. Thorn & Palmer, *Total Baseball*, p. 701.
33. St. Louis Plan — Commission 1969. Website of St. Louis, Missouri, organization/heritage/history.
34. Kirsch, *The Creation of American Team Sports*, p. 231.
35. Ralph Horton, "Henry Van Noye Lucas" in Tiemann & Rucker, *Nineteenth Century Stars*, p. 81.
36. Seymour, *Baseball: Early Years*, p. 79:

Hulbert and Fowle would be appointed a committee of two with full power to act for the four western clubs and given the job of going east to negotiate with the eastern teams they wanted to include in the new league.
37. Melville, *Early Baseball*, p. 76.
38. *Chicago Tribune*, Feb. 7, 1876, p. 7.
39. Fox, *Big Leagues*, p. 198.
40. Emery & Emery, *The Press and America*, p. 221.
41. *Spalding's Baseball Guide 1876*, p. 44.
42. Hulbert letter of Jan. 28, 1876, to Fowle.
43. Alvarez, "William Henry Wright (Harry)" in Ivor-Campbell et al., *Baseball's First Stars*, p. 178.
44. Voigt, *American Baseball*, p. 43.
45. William E. McMahon, "Albert Goodwill Spalding" in Ivor-Campbell et al., *Baseball's First Stars*, pp. 154–155.
46. Melville, *Early Baseball*, p. 77. Melville spells the Boston owner's name as Appolonio. *Spalding's Official Baseball Guide, 1876*, p. 42, spells it Apollonio.
47. David Pietrusza, "Morgan Gardner Bulkeley" in Ivor-Campbell et al., *Baseball's First Stars*, p. 15.
48. *Chicago Tribune*, Feb. 9, 1876, p. 3.
49. Dickey, *History of National League Baseball*, p. 5.
50. Lucas & Smith, *Saga of American Sport*, p. 182.
51. Hulbert letter of Sept. 14, 1876, to Fowle, cited in Melville, *Early Baseball*, p. 87.
52. Ryczek, *Blackguards*, p. 212.
53. Fox, *Big Leagues*, p. 198.
54. Seymour, *Baseball: Early Years*, p. 81.
55. Seymour, *Baseball: Early Years*, p. 82.
56. *Chicago Tribune*, Feb. 20, 1876, p. 10.
57. Seymour, *Baseball: Early Years*, pp. 15, 21, 22: The Knickerbocker Baseball Club of New York was organized in 1845. The Gothams were formed in 1850, the Eagles and Empires in 1854. The New York four were joined in the mid-1850s by four Brooklyn teams—the Excelsiors, Putnams, Eckfords and Atlantics.
58. Seymour, *Baseball: Early Years*, p. 25.
59. Shannon & Kalinsky, *Ball Parks*, pp. 41, 44.
60. Lowry, *Green Cathedrals*, p. 39. Fox, *Big Leagues*, p. 186: The Mutuals were a very popular team long before they moved to Brooklyn. They played before large crowds at Elysian Fields, Hoboken, in the early 1860s.
61. Riess, *City Games*, p. 197.
62. Sullivan, *Early Innings*, pp. 92–95.
63. Deutsch et al., *Scrapbook History of Baseball*, p. 10. Appel & Goldblatt, *Baseball's Best*, p. 350.
64. *Baseball Century*, p. 26.

Chapter 4

1. *Chicago Tribune*, Oct. 24, 1875, in Sullivan, *Early Innings*, p. 92.
2. Seymour, *Baseball: Early Years*, p. 78. The *Chicago Tribune*, Feb. 4, 1876, would attribute Meacham with originating the organizational plan for the National League. Years later, in 1882, when Hulbert died, the *Tribune* argued that Hulbert, together with Meacham, matured the plan of the National League.
3. Hulbert letter of Dec. 4, 1875, to Campbell Orrick Bishop. Hulbert letter of Dec. 7, 1875, to Charles Chase. Hulbert letter of Dec. 8, 1875, to St. Louis baseball executive (probably Bishop). The name is obscured.
4. Hulbert letter of Nov. 8, 1875, to Chase: "I can safely say the St. Louis people are ready to join us."
5. Hulbert letter of Nov. 8, 1875, to Chase.
6. Hulbert letter of Nov. 8, 1875, to Chase.
7. Krieghbaum, *Facts in Perspective*, pp. 190–192. Over half a century ago, communications experts and psychologists had summarized a basic seven kinds of propaganda. Reading through Hulbert's letters of 1875–1876 suggests Hulbert used them all. The seven techniques are: 1. Name Calling—bad names applied to whatever the propagandist wants his audience to reject or condemn. 2. Glittering Generalities—situations are identified with broad, accepted ideals and "virtue words." 3. Transfer—symbols of authority, sanction, and prestige that arouse emotions are attached to things the propagandist wishes to promote. 4. Testimonial—note that well-known individuals endorse the idea to be sold. 5. Plain Folks—creating impression that the subject of the message is just common folk like the rest of us and is incapable of guile and deceit. 6. Card Stacking—facts, illustrations, and statements carefully selected to make the maximum (positive or negative) impression. 7. Band Wagon—everybody is doing it (supporting us).
8. Hulbert letter of Nov. 8, 1875, to Chase.
9. Hulbert letter of Nov. 8, 1875, to Chase.
10. Hulbert letter of Nov. 8, 1875, to Chase.
11. Hulbert letter of Nov. 8, 1875, to Chase.
12. Hulbert letter of Dec. 4, 1875, to Bishop.
13. Spalding letter of Dec. 7, 1875, to Chase.
14. Hulbert letter of Dec. 8, 1875, to unknown western executive.
15. Hulbert letter of Dec. 8, 1875, to unknown western executive.
16. Golenbock, Peter, *Spirit of St. Louis*, pp. 6, 8: Bishop was a talented amateur player who ended his career in 1867 to open a law practice. Bishop helped draw up the league's constitution, the first schedule, wrote the initial

player's contracts, and formulated the entire program.
17. Hulbert letter of Dec. 4, 1875, to Bishop.
18. Hulbert letter of Dec. 4, 1875, to Bishop.
19. Hulbert letter of Dec. 4, 1875, to Bishop.
20. Hulbert letter of Dec. 7, 1875, to Fowle.
21. Hulbert letter of Dec. 7, 1875, to Fowle.
22. Hulbert letter of Dec. 7, 1875, to Fowle.
23. This was found in an 1875 file as a P.S. to a letter by Hulbert to an unknown person.
24. Hulbert letter of Nov. 16, 1875, to Chase.
25. G.W. Thompson letter of Oct. 30, 1875, to Hulbert.
26. Thompson letter of Oct. 30, 1875, to Hulbert.
27. Hulbert letter of Nov. 5, 1875, to Thompson.
28. Hulbert letter of Nov. 5, 1875, to Thompson.
29. Hulbert letter of Nov. 5, 1875, to Thompson.
30. William E. McMahon & Robert L. Tiemann, "Adrian Constantine Anson (Capt., Uncle, Pop)" in Ivor-Campbell et al., *Baseball's First Stars*, p. 5.
31. McMahon & Tiemann, "Adrian Constantine Anson (Capt., Uncle, Pop)" in Ivor-Campbell et al., *Baseball's First Stars*, p. 5.
32. McMahon & Tiemann, "Adrian Constantine Anson (Capt., Uncle, Pop)" in Ivor-Campbell et al., *Baseball's First Stars*, p. 4.
33. Seymour, *Baseball: Early Years*, p. 78.
34. Seymour, *Baseball: Early Years*, p. 79.
35. Voigt, *American Baseball*, p. 62.
36. Spink, *National Game*, p. 18.
37. *New York Times*, Jan. 30, 1876, p. 2. Voigt, *American Baseball*, p. 62.
38. *New York Times*, Jan. 30, 1876, p. 2.
39. Rice, *Seasons Past*, p. 28.
40. *Baseball Century*, p. 26.
41. Seymour, *Baseball: Early Years*, p. 60.
42. *Baseball Century*, p. 26.
43. Nemec, *Great Encyclopedia*, p. 84.
44. Seymour, *Baseball: Early Years*, p. 82.
45. Orem, *Baseball from the Newspaper Accounts*, p. 244.
46. Seymour, *Baseball: Early Years*, p. 81.
47. Orem, *Baseball from the Newspaper Accounts*, p. 244.
48. Seymour, *Baseball: Early Years*, p. 81.
49. Voigt, *American Baseball*, pp. 89–90.
50. *Spalding's Baseball Guide, 1876*, pp. 38–39.
51. Voigt, *American Baseball*, pp. 89–90.
52. *Baseball Century*, p. 26.
53. Ryczek, *Blackguards*, p. 226.
54. Voigt, *American Baseball*, p. 63.
55. David Q. Voigt, "The History of Major League Baseball," in Thorn & Palmer, *Total Baseball*, p. 10.
56. *Baseball Century*, p. 27.
57. Spalding letter of Dec. 7, 1875, to Chase.
58. Chase letter of Oct. 23, 1875, to Hulbert.
59. Rader, *Baseball: A History*, p. 30.
60. Allen, *Cincinnati Reds* p. 9.
61. Allen, *Cincinnati Reds*, pp. 5, 7.
62. Mott, *American Journalism*, p. 463: A trial run was launched on Christmas Day 1875. The first regular issue appeared Jan. 3, 1876.
63. Mott, *American Journalism*, p. 442.

Chapter 5

1. Seymour, *Baseball: Early Years*, p. 79; Reidenbaugh, *100 Years*, p. 3.
2. Seymour, *Baseball: Early Years*, p. 78.
3. Levine, *A.G. Spalding*, p. 23.
4. Kaese, *Boston Braves*, p. 5.
5. Alvarez, "William Henry Wright (Harry)" in Ivor-Campbell et al., *Baseball's First Stars*, p. 178.
6. Seymour, *Baseball: Early Years*, p. 69.
7. Alvarez, "William Henry Wright (Harry)" in Ivor-Campbell et al., *Baseball's First Stars*, p. 178.
8. Appel & Goldblatt, *Baseball's Best*, p. 398.
9. Voigt, *American Baseball*, p. 62.
10. Appel & Goldblatt, *Baseball's Best*, p. 52.
11. Appel & Goldblatt, *Baseball's Best*, p. 52.
12. *Chicago Tribune*, Feb. 4, 1876, p. 5; Feb. 13, 1876, p. 12.
13. Melville, *Early Baseball*, p. 86.
14. Melville, *Early Baseball*, p. 86.
15. Melville, *Early Baseball*, p. 87.
16. Seymour, *Baseball: Early Years*, p. 81.
17. Anson, *Ball Player's Career*, p. 93.
18. Seymour, *Baseball: Early Years*, p. 81.
19. Seymour, *Baseball: Early Years*, p. 77.
20. Voigt, *American Baseball*, p. 21.
21. Somers, *The Rise of Sport in New Orleans, 1850–1900*, p. 150.
22. Seymour, *Baseball: People's Game* p. 7.
23. Seymour, *Baseball: People's Game*, p. 7.
24. Lucas & Smith, *Saga of American Sport*, p. 127.
25. Seymour, *Baseball: Early Years*, p. 83, quotes Spalding saying, "The genius of our institutions is democratic. Base Ball [sic] is a democratic game."
26. Vincent, *Mudville's Revenge*, p. 14.
27. Guttman, *Sports Spectators*, p. 111.
28. Guttman, *Sports Spectators*, p. 116.
29. Maher & Ivor-Campbell, "William Henry Cammeyer," in Ivor-Campbell et al., *Baseball's First Stars*, p. 21.
30. Ryczek cited in Maher & Ivor-Campbell, "William Henry Cammeyer," in Ivor-Campbell et al., *Baseball's First Stars*, p. 21.
31. Ryczek cited in Maher & Ivor-Campbell, "William Henry Cammeyer," in Ivor-Campbell et al., *Baseball's First Stars*, p. 21.

32. Seymour, *Baseball: Early Years*, p. 75.
33. Orem, *Baseball from the Newspaper Accounts*, p. 232. *Chicago Tribune*, Feb. 9, 1876, p. 3, noted that the Atlantics did not lose much money, getting a good share of their money from the gambler's pool-box.
34. *Chicago Tribune*, Feb. 13, 1876, p. 12.
35. Wheeler & Baskin, *Cincinnati Game*, p. 27.
36. Lucas & Smith, *Saga of American Sport*, p. 181.
37. Wheeler & Baskin, *Cincinnati Game*, p. 19.
38. Wheeler & Baskin, *Cincinnati Game*, pp. 23, 28, 48: Brainard's delivery was described as "chain lightning" with expert placing.
39. Seymour, *Baseball: Early Years*, p. 75.
40. James, *Bill James Historical Baseball Abstract*, p. 10.
41. Baker, *Sports in the Western World*, p. 147.
42. Baker, *Sports in the Western World*, pp. 146–147.
43. Seymour, *Baseball: Early Years*, p. 76.
44. Orem, *Baseball from the Newspaper Accounts*, p. 206.
45. Hulbert letter of Nov. 8, 1875, to Louisville vice-president Charles Chase.
46. Vincent, *Mudville's Revenge*, p. 133, noted: "The announced objectives were only a ruse."
47. Orem, *Baseball from the Newspaper Accounts*, p. 244.
48. *Clipper*, "A Startling Coup d'Etat," in Sullivan, *Early Innings*, p. 96.

Chapter 6

1. Voigt, *American Baseball*, p. 63.
2. Voigt, *American Baseball*, pp. 35–36.
3. Dickey, *History of National League Baseball*, p. 5.
4. Rader, *Baseball: A History*, p. 36.
5. *Spalding's Baseball Guide, 1876*, p. 5.
6. *Clipper*, Feb. 12, 1876, p. 362.
7. *Spalding's Baseball Guide, 1876*, p. 41.
8. *Clipper*, Feb. 12, 1876, p. 362.
9. *Chicago Tribune*, Feb. 13, 1876, p. 12. Deutsch et al., *Scrapbook History of Baseball*, p. 9.
10. *Clipper*, Feb. 12, 1876, p. 362.
11. Orem, *Baseball from the Newspaper Accounts*, p. 245.
12. *Clipper*, Feb. 12, 1876, p. 362.
13. *Chicago Tribune*, Feb. 4, 1876, p. 5. *Spalding's Baseball Guide, 1876*, pp. 43–44: Gave names of proxies held and mentioned in the *Chicago Tribune*, but on p. 23, *Spalding's Guide* had Hulbert and Fowle carrying proxies for John Joyce, Cincinnati; Charles Chase, Louisville; and Nathaniel Hazard of St. Louis.
14. *Chicago Tribune*, Feb. 20, 1876, p. 10: Chadwick was "the whine of a little man who was not admitted" and was the "self called 'Father of the Game!'"
15. Voigt, *American Baseball*, p. 63.
16. Reidenbaugh, *100 Years*, p. 5.
17. Seymour, *Baseball: Early Years*, p. 80.
18. Rader, *American Sports*, pp. 115–116.
19. Seymour, *Baseball: Early Years*, p. 79.
20. *New York Clipper*, Feb. 12, 1876, p. 362.
21. Seymour, *Baseball: Early Years*, p. 80.
22. Rader, *American Sports*, p. 115; Spears & Swanson, *History of Sport and Physical Activity in the United States*, p. 105.
23. Rosenberg, *They Gave Us Baseball*, p. 20.
24. Voigt, *American Baseball*, p. 66.
25. Voigt, *American Baseball*, p. 64.
26. Seymour, *Baseball: Early Years*, p. 85.
27. Rice, *Seasons Past*, p. 29.
28. Deutsch et al., *Scrapbook History of Baseball*, p. 9.
29. *Spalding's Baseball Guide, 1876*, p. 37.
30. *Chicago Tribune*, Feb. 13, 1876, p. 12.
31. *Spalding's Baseball Guide, 1876*, p. 37.
32. *Chicago Tribune*, Feb. 13, 1876, p. 12.
33. Deutsch et al., *Scrapbook History of Baseball*, p. 9.
34. *Spalding's Baseball Guide, 1876*, p. 32.
35. Deutsch et al., *Scrapbook History of Baseball*, p. 9.
36. Seymour, *Baseball: Early Years*, p. 69.
37. Wheeler & Baskin, *Cincinnati Game*, p. 24.
38. Wheeler & Baskin, *Cincinnati Game*, p. 24.
39. Alvarez, "William Henry Wright (Harry)" in Ivor-Campbell et al., *Baseball's First Stars*, p. 178.
40. Rader, *Baseball: A History*, p. 42.
41. Rosenberg, *They Gave Us Baseball*, p. 18.
42. *Spalding's Baseball Guide, 1876*, pp. 22–23.
43. Jerry Mallory, "Sol White and The Origin of African American Baseball," in Dreifort, *Baseball History from Outside the Lines*, p. 62.
44. Rader, *American Sports*, p. 95.
45. *Spalding's Official Baseball Guide, 1876*, p. 24.
46. David Pietrusza, "Morgan Gardner Buckeley" in Ivor-Campbell et al., *Baseball's First Stars*, p. 15.
47. Appel & Goldblatt, *Baseball's Best*, p. 52–53.
48. Rosenberg, *They Gave Us Baseball*, p. 20.
49. Voigt, *American Baseball*, p. 66.
50. Gold & Arhens, *Golden Era Cubs*, p. 3.
51. Seymour, *Baseball: Early Years*, p. 84.
52. *Clipper*, Feb. 12, 1876, p. 362.
53. Seymour, *Baseball: Early Years*, p. 84.
54. Ryczek, *Blackguards*, pp. 6, 59, 66, 71, 99–101, 103, 131, 133, 147.
55. Seymour, *Baseball: Early Years*, p. 83.

56. *Spalding's Baseball Guide, 1876*, p. 8; Voigt, *American Baseball*, p. 66.
57. *Spalding's Baseball Guide, 1876*, p. 18: The proposed National League rule for 1876 set the championship season to run from the 15th day of March to (and including) the 15th day of Nov..
58. *New York Times*, Feb. 3, 1876, p. 8.
59. *Louisville Courier-Journal*, Feb. 3, 1876, p. 4.
60. *Chicago Tribune*, Feb. 4, 1876, p. 5.
61. *Chicago Tribune*, Feb. 13, 1876, p. 12.
62. *Baseball Century*, p. 27.

Chapter 7

1. *New York Times*, Feb. 3, 1876, pp. 1, 8.
2. *New York Times*, Feb. 7, 1876, p. 2.
3. *Chicago Tribune*, Feb. 4, 1876, p. 5.
4. Vincent, *Mudville's Revenge*, p. 136: Argued that opposition to the new league could be found in cities with National League franchises and that press reaction to the new league was generally unfavorable.
5. *Hartford Times* in *Clipper*, Feb. 12, 1876, p. 362.
6. *Philadelphia Item* in Louisville *Courier-Journal*, March 17, 1876, p. 4.
7. *St. Louis Globe-Democrat* in *Clipper*, Feb. 12, 1876, p. 362.
8. *St. Louis Globe-Democrat* in *Clipper*, Feb. 12, 1876, p. 362.
9. *Clipper*, Feb. 12, 1876, p. 362.
10. *Clipper*, Feb. 12, 1876, p. 362.
11. *Philadelphia Times* in *Chicago Tribune*, Feb. 7, 1876, p. 7. The *Tribune* noted that the *Philadelphia Times* was the only Philadelphia paper that consistently covered baseball.
12. *Chicago Tribune*, Feb. 9, 1876, p. 3: Reported the *New Haven Register* referring to the National League as a ring and saying that if New Haven was not admitted, the club would challenge the existing eight National League teams and would prove to be one of the best.
13. *New York Times*, March 12, 1876, p. 2.
14. *New Haven Register* in New York *Clipper*, Feb. 12, 1876, p. 362.
15. *New Haven Union* in *Chicago Tribune*, Feb. 9, 1876, p. 3: Argued that the New Haven team had paid advance money to the men engaged, had complied with the rules of the association, had gone to a joint stock plan, had a lease on a playing grounds, had gone to the expense of fixing it up for baseball, and that this was known by the other teams.
16. *Chicago Tribune*, Feb. 9, 1876, p. 3.
17. *Clipper*, Feb. 12, 1876, p. 362.
18. *Clipper*, Feb. 12, 1876, p. 362. Adelman, *A Sporting Time*, p. 151.
19. *New Haven Register* in *Clipper*, Feb. 12, 1876, p. 362.
20. *Chicago Tribune*, Feb. 20, 1876, p. 10: By Feb. 20, Chadwick's *Clipper* was the only New York sporting paper objecting to the new league.
21. Bartlett, *Baseball and Mr. Spalding*, p. 104.
22. Voigt, *American Baseball*, pp. 62–63.
23. Frederick Ivor-Campbell, "Henry Chadwick (Chad, Father of Base Ball)" in Ivor-Campbell et al., *Baseball's First Stars*, p. 26. Chadwick's invention of the box score is challenged in Dickson, *Baseball Dictionary*, p. 68. Dickson notes that New York *Herald* sportswriter Michael J. Kelly is believed by some critics to be the originator.
24. Ivor-Campbell, "Henry Chadwick (Chad, Father of Base Ball)" in Ivor-Campbell et al., *Baseball's First Stars*, p. 26.
25. *Chicago Tribune*, Feb. 13, 1876, p. 12. Although not mentioned by name, sufficient references in the text identify the frequently used "Old Veteran" nickname as being a sobriquet for Chadwick.
26. *Clipper*, Feb. 19, 1876, p. 370: There was a "fully attended and enthusiastic meeting of the Philadelphia Club" on Feb. 10. A spirit of resistance to the inconsistent and arbitrary action of the National League was evident.
27. *Clipper*, Feb. 12, 1876, p. 362.
28. *Chicago Tribune*, Feb. 20, 1876, p. 10: Chadwick could be contradictory. After a long time of being "uncomplimentary" to the management of the Philadelphia club and its players, the *Clipper* (the whole concern, paper, editor, and all) got into bed with Philadelphia. Protestations of honesty endorsed Zettlein, Meyerle, Craver et al.
29. Vincent, *Mudville's Revenge*, p. 137.
30. *Clipper*, Feb. 12, 1876, p. 362.
31. *Clipper*, Feb. 19, 1876, p. 371.
32. *Clipper*, Feb. 5, 1876, p. 357.
33. *Clipper*, Feb. 12, 1876, p. 362.
34. *Clipper*, Feb. 12, 1876, p. 362.
35. *Clipper*, Feb. 19, 1876, p. 371.
36. *Clipper*, March 26, 1876, p. 406.
37. *Clipper*, Feb. 19, 1876, p. 371.
38. *Clipper*, Feb. 12, 1876, p. 362.
39. *Clipper*, Feb. 12, 1876, p. 362.
40. "Baseball Notes" in *Clipper*, Feb. 12, 1876, p. 362.
41. *Chicago Tribune*, Feb. 4, 1876, p. 5.
42. *Chicago Tribune*, Feb. 4, 1876, p. 4: The ideas of the new association were precisely those recommended in the *Tribune* of Oct. 24, 1875.
43. *Chicago Tribune*, Feb. 13, 1876, p. 12: It didn't matter where the idea of the new league originated as long as both sides—east and west—were satisfied with the new arrangement.

44. *Clipper*, April 22, 1876, p. 26.
45. *Clipper*, March 25, 1876, p. 406; *Chicago Tribune*, Feb.. 27, 1876, p. 9.
46. Reidenbaugh, *100 Years*, p. 7. Seymour, *Baseball: Early Years*, p. 83. *Louisville Courier-Journal*, Feb. 23, 1876, p. 4: It took two votes from fellow teams to kick a team out of the National League in 1876.
47. Seymour, *Baseball: Early Years*, p. 88.
48. Dickey, *History of National League Baseball*, p. 5.
49. Gershman, *Diamonds*, p. 28: "No team could sign a player who violated the [league] constitution or had been discharged, dismissed, or expelled by another league club. In other words, the league began with a formal blacklist."
50. Gershman, *Diamonds*, p. 28.
51. Vincent, *Mudville's Revenge*, p. 134.
52. *Chicago Tribune*, Feb. 13, 1876, p. 12; Feb. 20, 1876, p. 10.
53. *Clipper*, Feb. 19, 1876, p. 370.
54. *Clipper*, Feb. 12, 1876, p. 362.
55. *Clipper*, Feb. 12, 1876, p. 362.
56. Voigt, *American Baseball*, p. 70.
57. Bartlett, *Baseball and Mr. Spalding*, p. 85.
58. Rice, *Seasons Past*, p. 29.
59. Seymour, *Baseball: Early Years*, p. 86.
60. *Chicago Tribune*, Feb. 23, 1876, p. 8.
61. *Chicago Tribune*, Feb. 8, 1876, p. 2: The Chicago Foot-ball Club had regular meetings at Tremont House and planned to play the 23rd Street Club in their usual place, White Stocking Ball-grounds, on Washington's birthday.
62. *Chicago Tribune*, Feb. 13, 1876, p. 12.
63. *Chicago Tribune*, Feb. 20, 1876, p. 10.
64. Sullivan, *Early Innings*, p. 90.
65. Melville, *Early Baseball*, p. 77.
66. *Chicago Tribune*, Feb. 27, 1876, p. 9.
67. *Louisville Courier-Journal*, Feb. 20, 1876, p. 4: Higham had been an unreliable player for every club he played for in the past two or three years. *Louisville Courier-Journal*, Feb. 27, 1876, p. 3: Reprinted Higham's letter to the *Clipper*, further sending the story around the league.
68. *Chicago Tribune*, Feb. 27, 1876, p. 9.
69. *Chicago Tribune*, Feb. 27, 1876, p. 9.
70. *Chicago Tribune*, Feb. 27, 1876, p. 9: One negative vote at any other time than an annual meeting was sufficient to exclude a team from gaining league membership.
71. *Chicago Tribune*, Feb. 27, 1876, p. 9.
72. *Clipper*, Feb. 26, 1876, p. 378.
73. *Clipper*, April 22, 1876, p. 26.
74. *Clipper*, April 1, 1876, p. 3.
75. *Clipper*, March 10, 1876, p. 394.
76. *Chicago Tribune*, March 5, 1876, p. 12.
77. *Clipper*, April 8, 1876, p. 13.

78. *Clipper*, Feb. 12, 1876, p. 362; March 18, 1876, p. 402; April 18, 1876, p. 13. Melville, *Early Baseball*, p. 81.
79. Melville, *Early Baseball*, p. 103.
80. *Clipper*, March 11, 1876, p. 394.
81. *Clipper*, March 11, 1876, p. 394.
82. *Chicago Tribune*, March 5, 1876, p. 12. New Haven had withdrawn. The remaining National Association teams were Kleinz (Philadelphia), Centennials (Philadelphia), Quickstep (Wilmington, Del.), Active (Reading, Pa.), Niahannock (Newcastle, Pa.), Baltimores, Atlantics, St. Louis Red Stockings and the New Haven Stars.
83. *Clipper*, March 25, 1876, p. 406.
84. *Clipper*, Feb. 26, 1876, p. 378.
85. Adelman, *A Sporting Time*, p. 176. The National Association's nominating committee unanimously opposed admission of any club composed of one or more colored persons.
86. Kirsch, *The Creation of American Team Sports*, p. 212.
87. *Clipper*, Nov. 19, 1870, p. 258 in Kirsch, *The Creation of American Team Sports*, p. 212.
88. *Clipper*, Nov. 26, 1870, p. 260.
89. Adelman, *A Sporting Time*, p. 176.
90. Bowman & Zoss, *Diamonds in the Rough*, pp. 138–139.

Chapter 8

1. Wheeler & Baskin, *Cincinnati Game*, p. 33, p. 48.
2. Voigt, *American Baseball*, p. 100: "When his request for a release was refused by Hulbert and Spalding, Anson sulked and refused to practice. But while standing by in street clothes and watching the team practice, the urge to play overcame his bitterness."
3. *Chicago Tribune*, Feb. 17, 1876, p. 2, noted that Hines was in full daily practice in the gymnasium, and that McVey had arrived "in excellent shape ... almost too heavy ... a blemish which a little preparatory work will remove."
4. Seymour, *Baseball: Early Years*, p. 64.
5. Gershman, *Diamonds*, p. 44.
6. Gershman, *Diamonds*, p. 12.
7. Seymour, *Baseball: Early Years*, p. 64.
8. Seymour, *Baseball: Early Years*, p. 63.
9. Twombly, *200 Years*, p. 81, 211: Harvard catcher Fred Tyng wore a mask in 1875. Being able to position himself closer to the batter, Tyng threw Yale and Princeton runners out quite easily. He was called a sissy and a cheat. By 1877, the mask was patented, but it was not adopted universally. *Baseball Century*, p. 212: The year the chest protector became catcher's gear was 1884. Clark, *Sports Firsts*, p. 4: Padded gloves (mitts) for catchers were around by

1891. Wills, *Sports Illustrated*, June 12, 1989, p. 97 reported in an article "Safe at Home" that protective cups weren't standard fare for catchers until 1915.
  10. Seymour, *Baseball: Early Years*, p. 64.
  11. Ballard, *Sports Illustrated*, April 5, 1989, p. 116: "Before antibiotics, blood poisoning was an ever-present threat to limb and life."
  12. Seymour, *Baseball: Early Years*, p. 64.
  13. *Louisville Courier-Journal*, April 22, 1876, p. 4: Anson was not recognized as a superstar in 1876.
  14. Thorn & Palmer, *Total Baseball*, p. 936: Andrus would play nine major league games; Anson, a future Hall-of-Famer, tallied 2,276.
  15. *Louisville Courier-Journal*, April 22, 1876, p. 4.
  16. *Louisville Courier-Journal*, April 22, 1876, p. 4.
  17. Ryczek, *Blackguards*, pp. 197–198.
  18. *Clipper*, April 8, 1876, p. 13.
  19. Kaese, *Boston Braves*, p. 7: "When pitchers started bending [the ball], George's batting average nose-dived."
  20. Wheeler & Baskin, *Cincinnati Game*, p. 22: George stole seven bases in one game.
  21. Twombly, *200 Years*, p. 51.
  22. Wheeler & Baskin, *Cincinnati Game*, p. 27.
  23. Voigt, *American Baseball*, p. 78.
  24. Bernard J. Crowley, "James Henry O'Rourke (Orator Jim)" in Ivor-Campbell et al., *Baseball's First Stars*, p. 124: Harry Wright told O'Rourke that the "Puritans of Beantown [who backed the team financially] will not stand for the name O'Rourke." Voigt, *American Baseball*, p. 84: O'Rourke later became a lawyer.
  25. Furnas, J.C., *The Americans*, p. 84.
  26. *Chicago Tribune*, Feb. 9, 1876, p. 3.
  27. Twombly, *200 Years*, p. 78: Feeder was a term from rounders. The feeder's duty was to set up the situation to put the ball in play, that is, let the batter hit the ball.
  28. Appel & Goldblatt, *Baseball's Best: Hall of Fame Gallery*, p. 119. McBride, *High and Inside*, p. 154, attributes Cummings' nickname "Candy" to his being fond of sweets.
  29. Appel & Goldblatt, *Baseball's Best*, p. 119.
  30. Nemec, *Great Encyclopedia*, p. 25.
  31. *Clipper*, April 8, 1876, p. 13.
  32. *Clipper*, Feb. 12, 1876, p. 365.
  33. Reidenbaugh, *100 Years*, p. 7.
  34. Seymour, *Baseball: Early Years*, p. 66. *Louisville Courier-Journal*, Feb. 27, 1876, p. 3: "Memphis wants a good player to occupy the position of pitcher on a first-class nine now being formed.... This is a good opportunity for a good pitcher who wishes to make an engagement. Address H.F. Smith, 224 Madison Street, Memphis, Tenn."
  35. *Clipper*, Feb. 5, 1876, p. 357.
  36. *Clipper*, April 8, 1876, p. 13.
  37. *Clipper*, April 8, 1876, p. 13.
  38. Voigt, *American Baseball*, p. 27: "Wright bore down hard on training. He worked the men hard, but he also taught them useful tactics that welded them into an efficient machine."
  39. Voigt, *American Baseball*, p. 42. Wright was "one of the first to perceive the fatal effect of too rigid a policy of player discipline." He knew managing involved human relations.
  40. *Clipper*, April 8, 1876, p. 13.
  41. *Clipper*, April 8, 1876, p. 13.
  42. Rader, *Baseball: A History*, p. 40.
  43. Phil Brown, "William H. Craver," in Ivor-Campbell et al., *Baseball's First Stars*, p. 41.
  44. *Clipper*, April 8, 1876, p. 13.
  45. *Clipper*, April 8, 1876, p. 13.
  46. *Clipper*, April 8, 1876, p. 13.
  47. Thorn & Palmer, *Total Baseball*, p. 1104 and Nemec, *Great Encyclopedia*, p. 685: Both spell Fisler's first name "Wes." Overfield, J.M., "Weston Dickson Fisler" in Tiemann & Rucker, *Nineteenth Century Stars*, p. 44, used "West."
  48. Wheeler & Baskin, *Cincinnati Game*, pp. 29, 133: Gould, a Cincinnati native, was a local hero.
  49. Wheeler & Baskin, *Cincinnati Game*, p. 133: Jones was the N.L.'s first slugger and the first player to hit two homers in one inning.
  50. Wheeler & Baskin, *Cincinnati Game*, p. 16: Bob Addy, in 1877, was the first man to steal a base sliding.
  51. Wheeler & Baskin, *Cincinnati Game*, p. 90.
  52. *Clipper*, April 8, 1876, p. 18.
  53. Gray, *Anatomy*, p. 386–390n.
  54. Levine, *A.G. Spalding*, p. 28. Smith, *Illustrated History of Baseball*, p. 51.
  55. Appel & Goldblatt, *Baseball's Best*, p. 350. Gold & Ahrens, *Golden Era Cubs*, p. 5.
  56. *Clipper*, April 8, 1876, p. 13.
  57. *Clipper*, April 28, 1876, p. 13.
  58. *Clipper*, April 8, 1876, p. 13.
  59. *Clipper*, April 8, 1876, p. 13.

Chapter 9

  1. *Clipper*, Feb. 5, 1876, p. 357.
  2. Sample clips from the *Clipper's* editions of April 15, 22 and 29, 1876, show the National League teams posting a 20–1 win-loss record against Picked Nines.
  3. *New York Times*, March 26, 1876, p. 2.
  4. *Clipper*, April 29, 1876, p. 34.
  5. Gershman, *Diamonds*, p. 12.
  6. *Clipper*, April 8, 1876, p. 10.
  7. Wheeler & Baskin, *Cincinnati Game*, p.

28. *Clipper*, April 1, 1876, p. 3; April 8, 1876, p. 10.
8. *Clipper*, April 15, 1876, p. 18.
9. *Clipper*, April 8, 1876, p. 13.
10. Wheeler & Baskin, *Cincinnati Game*, p. 28.
11. *Louisville Courier-Journal*, April 29, 1876, p. 4.
12. *Louisville Courier-Journal*, April 30, 1876, p. 1.
13. *Chicago Tribune*, April 2, 1876, p. 5.
14. *Cincinnati Enquirer*, May 6, 1876, p. 5.
15. *Cincinnati Enquirer*, April 13, 1876, p. 8.
16. Wheeler & Baskin, *Cincinnati Game*, p. 239.
17. Wheeler & Baskin, *Cincinnati Game*, p. 200.
18. *Cincinnati Enquirer*, April 16, 1876, p. 1.
19. *Cincinnati Enquirer*, April 24, 1876, p. 8.
20. *Cincinnati Enquirer*, April 24, 1876, p. 8.
21. *Clipper*, April 22, 1876, p. 26.
22. *Louisville Courier-Journal*, April 18, 1876, p. 4.
23. *Louisville Courier-Journal*, April 18, 1876, p. 4.
24. *Louisville Courier-Journal*, April 20, 1876, p. 4.
25. *Louisville Courier-Journal*, April 20, 1876, p. 4.
26. *Louisville Courier-Journal*, April 20, 1876, p. 4.
27. *Hartford Courant*, April 8, 1876, p. 2.
28. *Louisville Courier-Journal*, April 17, 1876, p. 4.
29. *Clipper*, April 8, 1876, p. 13.
30. Seymour, *Baseball: Early Years*, p. 64.
31. Wheeler & Baskin, *Cincinnati Game*, pp. 48, 84: Jim (Deacon) White claimed that he was the first catcher to use a padded glove. The year was 1872.
32. Wheeler & Baskin, *Cincinnati Game*, p. 48.
33. Clark, *Sports Firsts*, p. 4.
34. *Cincinnati Enquirer*, April 15, 1876, p. 8; April 16, 1876, p. 1. Pearson was the spelling used in the *Enquirer*, Pierson the spelling in Thorn & Palmer, *Total Baseball*, p. 1380.
35. *Chicago Tribune*, April 16, 1876, p. 6.
36. *Clipper*, April 22, 1876, p. 29.
37. *Louisville Courier-Journal*, April 21, 1876, p. 4.
38. *Hartford Courant*, Feb. 9, 1876, p. 2.
39. *Hartford Courant*, Feb. 5, 1876, p. 2.
40. *Clipper*, April 8, 1876, p. 13: Chadwick had Shandley as the Mutes' starting centerfielder in a team "which in individual playing strength, is not surpassed by any other now in the arena." *Spalding's Baseball Guide, 1876*, p. 44: listed James J. Shandley on the nine-man roster of the 1876 Mutuals.

41. *Chicago Tribune*, Feb. 8, 1876, p. 2.
42. *Spalding's Official Baseball Guide, 1876*, pp. 42–44.
43. *Chicago Tribune*, April 21, 1876, p. 8: Initially reported that comment on the multicolor caps was most favorable. Bartlett, *Baseball and Mr. Spalding*, p. 97: Noted the scheme was actually an absolute failure.
44. *Chicago Tribune*, April 21, 1876, p. 8.
45. *Louisville Courier-Journal*, April 21, 1876, p. 4
46. Thorn & Palmer, *Total Baseball*, p. 1007: Carbine, who had played 10 games in 1875 in the National Association, appeared in seven games in 1876, his only National League season, for Louisville. He hit .160, going 4-for-25.
47. *Chicago Tribune*, April 23, 1876, p. 4.
48. Nemec, *Great Encyclopedia*, p. 85.
49. *Clipper*, April 29, 1876, p. 34.
50. *Chicago Tribune*, April 23, 1876, p. 4.
51. Nemec, *Great Encyclopedia*, p. 85.

Chapter 10

1. Lowry, *Green Cathedrals*, pp. 10, 27, 68.
2. Thorn & Palmer, *Total Baseball*, pp. 703, 640, 792, 842, 892.
3. Lowry, *Green Cathedrals*, p. 68.
4. Gershman, *Diamonds*, p. 30.
5. Black & Garland, *History of Fashion*, p. 286.
6. Collins, Robert, *Age of Innocence 1870/1880*, p. 64.
7. *Chicago Tribune*, Dec. 24, 1876, p. 3.
8. Thorn & Palmer, *Total Baseball*, p. 701.
9. Nemec, *Great Encyclopedia*, pp. 65, 67.
10. Philips, Frank, "David Daniel Eggler" in Ivor-Campbell et al., *Baseball's First Stars*, p. 57.
11. *Clipper*, April 29, 1876, p. 34.
12. Wheeler & Baskin, *Cincinnati Game*, p. 22.
13. Deutsch et al., *Scrapbook History of Baseball*, p. 10.
14. Deutsch et al., *Scrapbook History of Baseball*, p. 10.
15. Appel & Goldblatt, *Baseball's Best*, pp. 305–306.
16. Thorn & Palmer, *Total Baseball*, p. 1367.
17. *Clipper*, April 22, 1876, p. 26.
18. Jack Kavanagh & Frederick Ivor-Campbell, "John E. Manning (Jack)" in Ivor-Campbell et al., *Baseball's First Stars*, p. 100.
19. *Clipper*, April 22, 1876, p. 26.
20. Kaese, *Boston Braves*, p. 19.
21. Kaese, *Boston Braves*, p. 18: Borden was a "Morning Glory." He flopped.
22. Thorn & Palmer, *Total Baseball*, p. 936.
23. Thorn & Palmer, *Total Baseball*, p. 936.
24. Appel & Goldblatt, *Baseball's Best*, p. 396.
25. Wallace, *Baseball Anthology*, p. 52.

26. Thorn & Palmer, *Total Baseball*, p. 1037, and Nemec, *Great Encyclopedia*, p. 720: Both spell the A's catcher's name Coon. *Clipper*, April 29, 1876, p. 34, and *Louisville Courier-Journal*, April 25, 1876, p. 4: Spell his name Coons.
27. Nemec, *Great Encyclopedia*, p. 89.
28. Appel & Goldblatt, *Baseball's Best*, p. 396.
29. Kross, *American Economic Development*, p. 10.
30. Appel & Goldblatt, *Baseball's Best*, p. 39.
31. *Clipper*, April 29, 1876, p. 34.
32. Appel & Goldblatt, *Baseball's Best*, p. 39.
33. Dickey, *History of National League Baseball*, p. 7.
34. Nemec, *Great Encyclopedia*, p. 85.
35. *Clipper*, April 29, 1876, p. 34. *Baseball Century*, p. 39.
36. *Clipper*, April 29, 1876, p. 34.
37. *Clipper*, April 29, 1876, p. 34.
38. *Spalding's Baseball Guide 1876*, p. 306.
39. *Spalding's Baseball Guide 1876*, pp. 5, 25.
40. *Baseball Century*, p. 39.
41. Thorn & Palmer, *Total Baseball*, p. 1336 and Voigt, *American Baseball*, p. 332: Used the spelling Murnane. *Clipper*, April 29, 1876, p. 34: Used the spelling Murnan.
42. *Clipper*, April 29, 1876, p. 34.
43. *Clipper*, April 29, 1876, p. 34.
44. *Baseball Century*, p. 39.
45. Larry R. Gerlach, "Umpires" in Thorn & Palmer, *Total Baseball*, pp. 465–469: The practice of using arm signals to indicate balls and strikes, safe and out, etc., was popularized in the early 20th century by William "Bill" Clem, generally regarded as the greatest umpire in history. Joseph M. Overfield, "William Ellsworth Hoy (Dummy)" in Tiemann & Rucker, *Nineteenth Century Stars*, p. 64: Regarding William (Dummy) Hoy, "It has been written, though possibly apocryphal, that Hoy was responsible for hand signals by umpires. Lee Allen, in *Hot Stove League*, wrote that Cy Rigler started this practice. Rigler did not come into the majors until 1905, two years after Hoy had retired." Nemec, *Great Encyclopedia*, pp. 154, 192, 774: Ed (Dummy) Dundon, who pitched for the Columbus Buckeyes of the American Association in 1883–84, forced umpires to use signals. This was five years before Hoy began his major league career with the Washington Nationals of the National League in 1888.
46. *Clipper*, April 29, 1876, p. 34.
47. Gray, *Anatomy*, p. 824.
48. *Clipper*, April 29, 1876, p. 34.
49. *Clipper*, April 29, 1876, p. 34.
50. *Clipper*, April 29, 1876, p. 34.
51. *Baseball Century*, p. 39.
52. *Clipper*, April 29, 1876, p. 34. Thorn & Palmer, *Total Baseball*, p. 1278: Manning's given name was Jack, although he used John.
53. *Louisville Courier-Journal*, April 25, 1876, p. 4.
54. *Clipper*, April 29, 1876, p. 34.
55. *Clipper*, April 29, 1876, p. 34.
56. *Louisville Courier-Journal*, April 25, 1876, p. 4.
57. *Louisville Courier-Journal*, April 25, 1876, p. 4.
58. *Baseball Century*, p. 39.
59. *Clipper*, April 29, 1876, p. 34.
60. *Clipper*, Feb. 12, 1876, p. 362.
61. *Clipper*, April 29, 1876, p. 34.

Chapter 11

1. Twombly, Wells, *200 Years*, p. 82.
2. *Cincinnati Enquirer*, May 2, 1876, p. 8: The bulletin board was at 50 West Front Street near the bridge.
3. *Cincinnati Enquirer*, April 23, 1876, p. 1.
4. *Cincinnati Enquirer*, April 23, 1876, p. 1; *Louisville Courier-Journal*, April 24, 1876, p. 4.
5. *Cincinnati Enquirer*, May 13, 1876, p. 8; April 21, 1876, p. 8; April 28, 1876, p. 8.
6. *Chicago Tribune*, April 29, 1876, p. 6.
7. Wheeler & Baskin, *Cincinnati Game*, p. 94.
8. *Cincinnati Enquirer*, May 13, 1876, p. 8; April 21, 1876, p. 8; April 28, 1876, p. 8.
9. *Louisville Courier-Journal*, April 26, 1876, p. 4.
10. *Chicago Tribune*, April 26, 1876, p. 1.
11. *Chicago Tribune*, May 6, 1876, p. 2: Chronicled the wagering activities of gamblers, telling who was down on his luck, who had to walk home from a distant city, and such.
12. *Louisville Courier-Journal*, April 24, 1876, p. 4.
13. *Clipper*, May 6, 1876, p. 42.
14. *Cincinnati Enquirer*, April 28, 1876, p. 8.
15. *Clipper*, May 6, 1876, p. 45.
16. *Louisville Courier-Journal*, May 2, 1876, p. 4.
17. *Cincinnati Enquirer*, May 8, 1876, p. 8. *Louisville Courier-Journal*, May 13, 1876, p. 1.
18. Kross, *American Economic Development*, p. 10: The depression lasted from 1873 to 1878.
19. *Chicago Tribune*, April 25, 1876, p. 5: 2,000 were present when the Athletic beat Boston 20–3 on April 24. *Chicago Tribune*, April 26, 1876, p. 1: 2,000 were at Chicago when Chicago defeated Louisville 4–0 on April 25.
20. Shannon & Kalinsky, *Ball Parks*, p. 59.
21. Shannon & Kalinsky, *Ball Parks*, p. 9: "As the game and the men who played it outgrew the confines of the older ballpark, the explosive drama of the homerun came to the fore.

The lively ball and the shrinking ballpark made this change possible."
22. *Cincinnati Enquirer*, May 3, 1876, p. 8.
23. *Cincinnati Enquirer*, May 4, 1876, p. 8. Contained in a letter to the Base-Ball Editor.
24. *Cincinnati Enquirer*, May 5, 1876, p. 8. *Louisville Courier-Journal*, May 5, 1876, p. 4; May 6, 1876, p. 1.
25. *Louisville Courier-Journal*, April 27, 1876, p. 4.
26. *Chicago Tribune*, May 6, 1876, p. 2.
27. *Clipper*, May 13, 1876, p. 51.
28. *Cincinnati Enquirer*, July 24, 1876, p. 8.
29. *Clipper*, May 13, 1876, p. 51.
30. *Clipper*, May 20, 1876, p. 61: The game drew 5,000.
31. Adomites, "Concessions" in Thorn & Palmer, *Total Baseball*, p. 669.
32. Shannon & Kalinsky, *The Ball Parks*, p. 8.
33. *Cincinnati Enquirer*, May 12, 1876, p. 8.
34. Tygiel, "Black Ball" in Thorn & Palmer, *Total Baseball*, p. 548.
35. *Cincinnati Enquirer*, May 9, 1876, p. 8.
36. *Cincinnati Enquirer*, May 15, 1876, p. 5.
37. *Louisville Courier-Journal*, May 13, 1876, p. 1.
38. *Cincinnati Enquirer*, May 15, 1876, p. 5.
39. *New York Times*, May 15, 1876, p. 5, citing story in the *London Standard* of May 4, 1876.
40. Baker, *Sports in the Western World*, p. 87.
41. *Louisville Courier-Journal*, May 19, 1876, p. 4; *Cincinnati Enquirer*, May 19, 1876, p. 8; *Clipper*, May 27, 1876, p. 67.
42. *Louisville Courier-Journal*, May 21, 1876, p. 1.
43. Nemec, *Great Encyclopedia*, p. 69. *Louisville Courier-Journal*, May 25, 1876, p. 1.
44. *Louisville Courier-Journal*, May 30, 1876, p. 3.
45. William E. McMahon, "Albert Goodwill Spalding" in Ivor-Campbell et al., *Baseball's First Stars*, p. 54; Thorn & Palmer, *Total Baseball*, pp. 1605, 1941; Bob Richardson, "Thomas Henry Bond (Tommy)" in Tiemann & Rucker, *Nineteenth Century Stars*, p. 15.
46. *Hartford Courant*, May 26, 1876, p. 2.
47. *Cincinnati Enquirer*, May 25, 1876, p. 5.
48. *Hartford Courant*, May 16, 1876, p. 2.
49. *Boston Herald* in *Hartford Courant*, May 20, 1876, p. 3.
50. *Hartford Courant*, May 16, 1876, p. 2.
51. Robert L. Tiemann, "James Dickinson McBride (Dick)" in Ivor-Campbell et al., *Baseball's First Stars*, p. 101.
52. *Hartford Courant*, May 27, 1876, p. 2.
53. *Hartford Courant*, May 30, 1876, p. 2.
54. *Hartford Courant*, June 1, 1876, p. 2.
55. *Clipper*, June 3, 1876, p. 75.
56. *Cincinnati Enquirer*, May 31, 1876, p. 8: Reported 20,000 attending. *Clipper*, June 10, 1876, p. 85: "Some twelve thousand people took advantage of the opportunity to attend." *Louisville Courier-Journal*, June 1, 1876, p. 4: Not less than 10,000 people attended and thousands failed to gain admittance. *New York Times*, May 31, 1876, p. 2: The game was "witnessed by 20,000 people, two-thirds ... were within the grounds."
57. Anson, *Ball Player's Career*, pp. 95–96.
58. Anson, *Ball Player's Career*, p. 96.
59. *Cincinnati Enquirer*, June 1, 1876, p. 8.
60. *Louisville Courier-Journal*, May 31, 1876, p. 4.
61. Kross, *American Economic Development*, p. 45.
62. *Encyclopædia Britannica*, 1960, vol. 14, p. 52.

Chapter 12

1. *Louisville Courier-Journal*, June 3, 1876, p. 4.
2. *Louisville Courier-Journal*, June 3, 1876, p. 4.
3. *Cincinnati Enquirer*, June 1, 1876, p. 8.
4. *Louisville Courier-Journal*, June 3, 1876, p. 4.
5. *Louisville Courier-Journal*, May 31, 1876, p. 4. *Hartford Courant*, June 1, 1876, p. 2.
6. *Hartford Courant*, June 1, 1876, p. 2.
7. *Chicago Tribune*, June 8, 1876, p. 5.
8. *Hartford Courant*, June 3, 1876, p. 2.
9. *Louisville Courier-Journal*, June 6, 1876, p. 4.
10. *Hartford Courant*, June 3, 1876, p. 2.
11. *Cincinnati Enquirer*, June 7, 1876, p. 8.
12. *Louisville Courier-Journal*, June 2, 1876, p. 1; June 4, 1876, p. 1; June 5, 1876, p. 4.
13. *Louisville Courier-Journal*, June 6, 1876, p. 4.
14. *Louisville Courier-Journal*, June 6, 1876, p. 4.
15. *Hartford Courant*, July 7, 1876, p. 2.
16. *Louisville Courier-Journal*, June 9, 1876, p. 4.
17. *Boston Globe* in *Louisville Courier-Journal*, June 10, 1876, p. 4.
18. *Louisville Courier-Journal*, June 10, 1876, p. 4: The paper was the *Boston Globe*.
19. *Clipper*, June 10, 1876, p. 83: Chadwick summarized a three-game series between the Mutuals and Louisville with an extensive amount of statistical material. He listed each Louisville batters' times at bat, base hits, games played and total fielding errors and hits,

earned runs, balls called, strikes, and fouls let up by Louisville pitcher Jim Devlin and Mutual hurler Bobby Mathews. He also provided a summary of the scores of all games played each month, league standings, win-loss records of west teams vs. east teams, earned runs, total hits for each game, and a summary of the best played games for the month involving N.L., semi-pro and amateur teams. Box scores filled page after page of the *Clipper*, detailing games as diverse as Chicago vs. Boston and Howard Athenaeum vs. Globe Theatre. Howard won 35–12 on June 2 at Boston.
20. *Cincinnati Enquirer*, June 9, 1876, p. 8.
21. *Louisville Courier-Journal*, July 10, 1876, p. 4.
22. *Louisville Courier-Journal*, June 10, 1876, p. 4.
23. *Cincinnati Enquirer*, June 10, 1876, p. 8.
24. *Cincinnati Enquirer*, June 22, 1876, p. 8.
25. *Louisville Courier-Journal*, June 12, 1876, p. 4.
26. *Cincinnati Enquirer*, June 14, 1876, p. 7.
27. *Louisville Courier-Journal*, June 12, 1876, p. 4.
28. *Cincinnati Enquirer*, June 21, 1876, p. 8.
29. *Cincinnati Enquirer*, June 22, 1876, p. 8.
30. *Cincinnati Enquirer*, June 24, 1876, p. 8.
31. *Cincinnati Enquirer*, June 25, 1876, p. 1.
32. *Cincinnati Enquirer*, June 26, 1876, p. 8.
33. *Hartford Courant*, June 13, 1876, p. 2; June 14, 1876, p. 2.
34. *Hartford Courant*, June 14, 1876, p. 2.
35. *Hartford Courant*, June 2, 1876, p. 2: June 1 game — Cincinnati 8, Hartford 2, A — 400; June 5, 1876, p. 2: June 3 game — Hartford 7, Cincinnati 2, A — 200; June 7, 1876, p. 2: June 6 game — Hartford 8, St. Louis 4, A — 600; June 9, 1876, p. 2: June 8 game — Hartford 6, St. Louis 3, A — 200; June 12, 1876, p. 2: June 10 game — Hartford 7, St. Louis 0, A — 800; June 14, 1876, p. 2: June 13 game — Hartford 4, Louisville 0, A — 400; June 15, 1876, p. 2: June 15 game — Hartford 6, Louisville 1, A — 400. This represented an attendance of 3,000 for seven games — an average of 429 cranks per game for a team that went 6–1 in wins and losses, and won six games in a row.
36. *Louisville Courier-Journal*, June 22, 1876, p. 1.
37. *Hartford Courant*, June 21, 1876, p. 2.
38. *Hartford Courant*, June 21, 1876, p. 2.
39. *Hartford Courant*, June 24, 1876, p. 2.
40. *Louisville Courier-Journal*, July 27, 1876, p. 4.
41. *Louisville Courier-Journal*, July 27, 1876, p. 4.
42. *Louisville Courier-Journal*, July 27, 1876, p. 4.
43. *Louisville Courier-Journal*, July 27, 1876, p. 4.
44. *Louisville Courier-Journal*, July 27, 1876, p. 4.
45. *Louisville Courier-Journal*, July 27, 1876, p. 4.
46. *Louisville Courier-Journal*, July 27, 1876, p. 4.
47. *Louisville Courier-Journal*, July 27, 1876, p. 4.
48. *Louisville Courier-Journal*, July 27, 1876, p. 4.
49. Kaese, *Boston Braves*, p. 15.
50. Kaese, *Boston Braves*, p. 19.
51. Kaese, *Boston Braves*, p. 20.
52. Kaese, *Boston Braves*, p. 20.
53. Kaese, *Boston Braves*, p. 20.
54. *Philadelphia Inquirer*, June 19, 1876, p. 2.
55. *New York Times*, June 11, 1876, p. 12.
56. *New York Times*, June 18, 1876, p. 12.
57. *New York Times*, June 16, 1876, p. 10.
58. *Clipper*, July 8, 1876, pp. 115, 117.
59. *Chicago Tribune*, March 5, 1876, p. 12.
60. *Chicago Tribune*, May 14, 1876, p. 7.
61. *Chicago Tribune*, May 21, 1876, p. 2.
62. *Chicago Tribune*, April 2, 1876, p. 5.
63. *Louisville Courier-Journal*, June 6, 1876, p. 3.

Chapter 13

1. *Louisville Courier-Journal*, July 4, 1876, p. 8.
2. *Louisville Courier-Journal*, July 4, 1876, p. 8.
3. *Louisville Courier-Journal*, July 5, p. 4, 1876: Reported that a crowd of 12,000 attended.
4. *Hartford Courant*, July 8, 1876, p. 2: Cited the *Chicago Inter-Ocean* saying that the exact number of people could not be estimated accurately, but the *Courant* reporter guessed anyway, estimating the crowd between 15,000 and 18,000.
5. *Chicago Tribune*, July 6, 1876, p. 1: Bielaski muffed York's outfield fly. *Hartford Courant*, July 8, 1876, p. 2: Bielaski simply made an error of judgment.
6. *Hartford Courant*, July 8, 1876, p. 2. *Clipper*, July 15, 1876, p. 125.
7. *Hartford Courant*, July 6, 1876, p. 2.
8. *Louisville Courier-Journal*, July 5, 1876, p. 4.
9. *Clipper*, July 15, 1876, p. 125.
10. *Clipper*, July 15, 1876, p. 125.
11. *Clipper*, July 15, 1876, p. 125.
12. *Chicago Tribune*, July 7, 1876, p. 8: Called the home run "Remsen's lucky hit in the first inning."
13. *Hartford Courant*, July 7, 1876, p. 2.
14. *Hartford Courant*, July 7, 1876, p. 2.

15. *Louisville Courier-Journal*, July 6, 1876, p. 1.
16. *Louisville Courier-Journal*, July 8, 1876, p. 4.
17. *Hartford Courant*, July 9, 1876, p. 1; July 10, 1876, p. 2.
18. *Hartford Courant*, July 9, 1876, p. 1; July 10, 1876, p. 2.

Chapter 14

1. The re-creation of the two-part game was constructed from several newspaper accounts. The *Louisville Courier-Journal* of July 9 and 11, 1876, was particularly useful due to its detailed account of much of the game's action (e.g., Booth's grounder hit straight at second base took an unexpected bound over Somerville's right shoulder).
2. Thorn & Palmer, *Hidden Game of Baseball*, p. 193. This does not count "battery errors" such as passed balls and wild pitches, which were called errors in 1876.

Chapter 15

1. The *Louisville Courier-Journal* ran a number of stories on various attempts at raiding. *Courier-Journal*, July 15, 1876, p. 4: Noted that a *Chicago Tribune* article mentioned that a St. Louis director came to Chicago to sign Chicago players for 1877. The director boldly walked up to one of the best Chicago players and offered him $3,000 a year and captaincy of the St. Louis team. When the player refused, it went to $4,000, and when he refused again, it went to $6,000. The *Tribune* concluded that the Chicago management thought all this rushing around to sign players was ridiculous. *Courier-Journal*, July 17, 1876, p. 14: The Chicago player offered the $4,000 (the $6,000 bid seemed to have been forgotten by the *Courier-Journal* reporter) was Ross Barnes. Thorn & Palmer, *Total Baseball*, p. 948: Barnes hit .429 in 1876 and .272 in 1877, his batting average dropping primarily due to elimination of the fair-foul hit rule. *Courier-Journal*, July 17, 1876, p. 4: Cincinnati owner Si Keck telegraphed Boston's Tim Murnan at Chicago, offering him $2,000 to play for Cincy in 1877.
2. *Louisville Courier-Journal*, July 3, 1876, p. 4; *Chicago Tribune*, July 14, 1876, p. 2.
3. *Louisville Courier-Journal* in the *Clipper*, July 15, 1876, p. 123.
4. *Clipper*, July 15, 1876, p. 123: Bradley had signed with the Athletic for 1877.
5. *Clipper*, July 22, 1876, p. 131.
6. *Clipper*, July 15, 1876, p. 123: The idea that St. Louis would play into the hands of the Hartfords to spite Chicago was "probably foundationless, for while they would like to whip Chicago themselves, the St. Louis Club, we reckon, do not care about helping an eastern nine at the expense of the West." *Cincinnati Enquirer*, July 15, 1876, p. 8: "We don't observe that St. Louis is 'throwing' any games with the Hartfords this week." *Louisville Courier-Journal*, July 14, 1876, p. 4: The rumor was wrong that St. Louis would purposely lose three games to Hartford merely to spite Chicago. The *Enquirer* attributed the rumors to smart "Alicks" and "Smartys."
7. *Clipper*, July 15, 1876, p. 123: Henry Chadwick agreed with Hulbert, writing, "There is ample time between the first of December of one year and the first of February of another ensuing year to make all necessary contracts for a new nine." He urged a rule prohibiting "club managers from engaging a player—by verbal or written contract, until the actual close of the existing season."
8. *Louisville Courier-Journal*, July 14, 1876, p. 4: Attributed the *Chicago Tribune* and, thereby, Hulbert, as feeling it was foolish for clubs to be shuffling after players for next year in July. It was hoped that not more than one new man would appear on the Chicago roster for 1877.
9. *Louisville Courier-Journal*, July 18, 1876, p. 4.
10. *Chicago Tribune*, July 16, 1876, p. 3.
11. *Louisville Courier-Journal*, July 18, 1876, p. 4; *Cincinnati Enquirer*, July 18, 1876, p. 8.

Chapter 16

1. Jim Rygelski, "George Washington Bradley" in Ivor-Campbell et al., *Baseball's First Stars*, p. 9.
2. Thorn & Palmer, *Total Baseball*, p. 1609: Height and weight statistics are based on 89 players, listed in Nemec's *Great Encyclopedia*, pp. 92–97, 684–804, who appeared in 10 National League games or more in 1876.
3. Mark S. Sternman, "John Joseph Burdock" in Ivor-Campbell et al., *Baseball's First Stars*, p. 16.
4. Sternman, "John Joseph Burdock" in Ivor-Campbell et al., *Baseball's First Stars*, p. 16.
5. Larry R. Gerlach, "Richard Higham" in Ivor-Campbell et al., *Baseball's First Stars*, p. 77.
6. Frank V. Phelps, "Robert V. Ferguson (Old Fergy)" in Tiemann & Rucker, *Nineteenth Century Stars*, p. 43.
7. Seymour, *Baseball: Early Years*, p. 124: "Rough-and-ready, swashbuckling characters ... played professional baseball" even in the 1880s.

8. Kaese, *Boston Braves*, p. 25.
9. Clark, *Sports Firsts*, p. 7.
10. Adair, *Physics of Baseball*, pp. 6–7.
11. Monteleone & Gola, *Louisville Slugger Ultimate Book of Hitting*, p. 85.
12. Dickson, *Worth Book of Softball*, pp. 78–79.
13. Dickson, *Worth Book of Softball*, pp. 101–103.
14. Dickson, *Worth Book of Softball*, pp. 103–104.
15. Monteleone & Gola, *Louisville Slugger Ultimate Book of Hitting*, p. 86.
16. Klein in Landers & Christina, *Psychology of Motor Behavior and Sport—1977*, pp. 246–253.
17. Schmidt, *Motor Control and Learning*, p. 372.
18. Schmidt, *Motor Control and Learning*, p. 372.
19. Schmidt, *Motor Control and Learning*, p. 373.
20. *Chicago Tribune*, Nov. 5, 1876, p. 10.
21. *Chicago Tribune*, May 4, 1876, p. 5.
22. Bob Richardson, "Thomas Henry Bond (Tommy)" in Tiemann & Rucker, *Nineteenth Century Stars*, p. 15.
23. William E. McMahon, "Albert Goodwill Spalding" in Ivor-Campbell et al., *Baseball's First Stars*, p. 155.
24. Morrill, *Batting and Pitching Illustrated*, p. 27.
25. Jim Rygelski, "George Washington Bradley" in Ivor-Campbell et al., *Baseball's First Stars*, p. 9.
26. Morrill, *Batting and Pitching Illustrated*, p. 27.
27. Nemec, *Rules of Baseball*, p. 41.
28. *Chicago Tribune*, July 12, 1876, p. 2; July 14, 1876, p. 2.
29. Jim Rygelski, "George Washington Bradley" in Ivor-Campbell et al., *Baseball's First Stars*, p. 9.
30. *Chicago Tribune*, July 16, 1876, p. 3.
31. *Louisville Courier-Journal*, July 18, 1876, p. 4.
32. *Louisville Courier-Journal*, July 16, 1876, p. 1.
33. *Hartford Courant*, July 18, 1876, p. 2.
34. *Louisville Courier-Journal*, July 18, 1876, p. 5.
35. Nemec, *Great Encyclopedia*, p. 69.

Chapter 17

1. *New York Times*, July 15, 1876, p. 8: There was "considerable difference between standard authorities as to the beginning and end of *dies caniculares*, or dog days." The contending sequences included: July 3 to Aug. 11, July 15 to Aug. 20, July 24 to Aug. 24, and the latter part of July to Sept. 1.
2. *Chicago Tribune*, July 16, 1876, p. 3; *Hartford Courant*, July 20, 1876, p. 2.
3. *Louisville Courier-Journal*, July 16, 1876, p. 1.
4. *Louisville Courier-Journal*, July 17, 1876, p. 4.
5. *St. Louis Globe-Democrat* in *Louisville Courier-Journal*, July 20, 1876, p. 1.
6. *Louisville Courier-Journal*, July 17, 1876, p. 4.
7. *Cincinnati Enquirer*, July 18, 1876, p. 8.
8. *Louisville Courier-Journal*, July 18, 1876, p. 4.
9. *Louisville Courier-Journal*, July 23, 1876, p. 1.
10. *New York Times*, July 14, 1876, p. 5.
11. *Louisville Courier-Journal*, July 24, 1876, p. 4.
12. *Cincinnati Enquirer*, July 24, 1876, p. 8: Pike had signed with Cincinnati. The *St. Louis Republican* was quoted in the *Louisville Courier-Journal* on July 18, 1876, p. 4, stating that it was doubtful if Pike would be retained by St. Louis and adding: "Everyone in St. Louis, who judges Pike by his actual play, will desire to see him at center field next year."
13. *Louisville Courier-Journal*, July 23, 1876, p. 1.
14. *Cincinnati Enquirer*, July 24, 1876, p. 8: St. Louis' Pike, Chicago's Ross Barnes and the Mutuals' Jim Hallinan were the fastest trio in baseball.
15. Collett, *Cincinnati Reds*, p. 17: Pike was the first known Jewish player in professional baseball.
16. *Chicago Tribune*, July 19, 1876, p. 5; July 21, 1876, p. 5; July 23, 1876, p. 7.
17. *Louisville Courier-Journal*, July 26, 1876, p. 4.
18. *Louisville Courier-Journal*, July 21, 1876, p. 4; July 25, 1876, p. 4.
19. *St. Louis Globe-Democrat* in *Louisville Courier-Journal*, July 25, 1876, p. 4.
20. *Louisville Courier-Journal*, July 25, 1876, p. 4.
21. Richard Puff, "Michael Henry McGeary," in Ivor-Campbell et al., *Baseball's First Stars*, p. 104.
22. *Chicago Tribune*, July 23, 1876, p. 7.
23. *Louisville Courier-Journal*, July 25, 1876, p. 4.
24. Maher & Ivor-Campbell, "William Henry Cammeyer" in Ivor-Campbell et al., *Baseball's First Stars*, p. 21.
25. *Louisville Courier-Journal*, July 25, 1876, p. 4.
26. *Louisville Courier-Journal*, July 25, 1876, p. 4.

27. *Cincinnati Enquirer*, July 19, 1876, p. 8: A rumor that Hartford would play in New York–Brooklyn in 1877 had surfaced. *St. Louis Globe-Democrat* in the *Louisville Courier-Journal*, July 20, 1876, p. 1: It was now a fact Hartford would be transported bodily to Brooklyn in 1877 and would probably play under the management of Bulkeley and Cammeyer.
28. *Louisville Courier-Journal*, July 25, 1876, p. 4.
29. *Louisville Courier-Journal*, July 31, 1876, p. 4; July 25, 1876, p. 4.
30. *Louisville Courier-Journal*, July 25, 1876, p. 4.
31. *Louisville Courier-Journal*, July 25, 1876, p. 4.
32. Jones, *Former Major League Teams*, p. 70: Bulkeley was team president and Bob Ferguson was the manager of the Hartford Dark Blues, who played in Brooklyn in 1877.
33. *Cincinnati Enquirer*, July 26, 1876, p. 8: Reported the rumor that Cammeyer would manage Cincinnati in 1877.
34. *Louisville Courier-Journal*, July 25, 1876, p. 4; *Chicago Tribune*, July 23, 1876, p. 7.
35. *Chicago Tribune*, July 23, 1876, p. 7.
36. *Hartford Courant*, July 28, 1876, p. 2.
37. *Hartford Courant*, July 28, 1876, p. 2.
38. *Louisville Courier-Journal*, July 19, 1876, p. 4.
39. *New York Herald* in *Louisville Courier-Journal*, July 27, 1876, p. 4.
40. *Louisville Courier-Journal*, July 31, 1876, p. 4.
41. Smith, H. R. *Economic History of the United States*, p. 327.
42. *Louisville Courier-Journal*, July 31, 1876, p. 4.
43. *Hartford Times* in *Louisville Courier-Journal*, July 30, 1876, p. 4.
44. *Cincinnati Enquirer*, July 26, 1876, p. 8.
45. *Louisville Courier-Journal*, July 29, p. 4.
46. Berman, Bob, "Two Dog Night," *Discover*, Jan. 1994, p. 23.

Chapter 18

1. *Chicago Tribune* in *Louisville Courier-Journal*, Aug. 8, 1876, p. 4.
2. *Louisville Courier-Journal*, July 31, 1876, p. 4.
3. *Louisville Courier-Journal*, Aug. 1, 1876, p. 4.
4. *Louisville Courier-Journal*, Aug. 1, 1876, p. 4.
5. *Louisville Courier-Journal*, Aug. 2, 1876, p. 4 and Aug. 7, 1876, p. 4.
6. *Louisville Courier-Journal*, Aug. 2, 1876, p. 5.
7. *Louisville Courier-Journal*, Aug. 2, 1876, p. 4.
8. *Louisville Courier-Journal*, Aug. 6, 1876, p. 1.
9. *Louisville Courier-Journal*, Aug. 6, 1876, p. 1.
10. *Louisville Courier-Journal*, Aug. 3, 1876, p. 4; Aug. 6, 1876, p. 1.
11. *Chicago Tribune*, Aug. 2, 1876, p. 2: "Fully 2,000 persons were in attendance...."
12. *Cincinnati Enquirer*, Aug. 1, 1876, p. 8.
13. *Cincinnati Enquirer*, July 18, 1876, p. 8: Fisher had resigned the day after he learned that his boy, Charley, was dying.
14. *Louisville Courier-Journal*, Aug. 3, 1876, p. 4.
15. *Cincinnati Enquirer*, Aug. 1, 1876, p. 8.
16. *Cincinnati Enquirer*, Aug. 2, 1876, p. 8.
17. *Hartford Courant*, Aug. 2, 1876, p. 2.
18. *Chicago Tribune* in *Louisville Courier-Journal*, Aug. 1, 1876, p. 4.
19. *Louisville Courier-Journal*, July 31, 1876, p. 4. *Chicago Tribune* reprint in *Louisville Courier-Journal*, Aug. 1, 1876, p. 4.
20. *Cincinnati Enquirer*, Aug. 4, 1876, p. 8; Aug. 5, 1876, p. 2: S. Mason Graffen, manager of the St. Louis club, credited his men with a base hit on a walk, and would give them the benefit of it in his club averages at the end of the season.
21. *Cincinnati Enquirer*, Aug. 4, 1876, p. 8; Aug. 5, 1876, p. 5.
22. *Louisville Courier-Journal*, Aug. 4, 1876, p. 5.
23. *Philadelphia Inquirer*, Aug. 4, 1876, p. 3.
24. *Louisville Courier-Journal*, Aug. 5, 1876, p. 4.
25. *Louisville Courier-Journal*, Aug. 5, 1876, p. 4.
26. *Louisville Courier-Journal*, Aug. 5, 1876, p. 4: Ran a stack of heads, including:
    Our Boys Did It With Their Little
    Bats, While Devlin Completely
    Dazed Their Opponents
27. *Louisville Courier-Journal*, Aug. 5, 1876, p. 4.
28. *Hartford Courant*, Aug. 7, 1876, p. 2: Placed the crowd at 600. *Chicago Tribune*, Aug. 6, 1876, p. 7: Estimated crowd at 1,000.
29. *Philadelphia Inquirer*, Aug. 7, 1876, p. 2.
30. *Louisville Courier-Journal*, Aug. 9, 1876, p. 4.
31. *Louisville Courier-Journal*, Aug. 11, 1876, p. 4.
32. *Chicago Tribune* cited in *Louisville Courier-Journal*, Aug. 8, 1876, p. 14.
33. *St. Louis Globe-Democrat* in *Louisville Courier-Journal*, Aug. 24, 1876, p.1.
34. *Chicago Tribune* in *Louisville Courier-Journal*, Aug. 8, 1876, p. 4.

35. *Chicago Tribune*, Aug. 10, 1876, p. 1.
36. *New York Times*, Aug. 11, 1876, p. 8.
37. *Cincinnati Enquirer*, Aug. 9, 1876, p. 5; Aug. 10, 1876, p. 8.
38. Dickson, *Dickson Baseball Dictionary*, p. 261.
39. *Cincinnati Enquirer*, Aug. 15, 1876, p. 8.
40. *Cincinnati Enquirer*, Aug. 15, 1876, p. 8. John J. Miller, "Edward Sylvester Nolan (The Only Nolan)," in Ivor-Campbell et al., *Baseball's First Stars*, p. 121.
41. *Louisville Courier-Journal*, Aug. 3, 1876, p. 4.
42. *Louisville Courier-Journal*, Aug. 9, 1876, p. 4.
43. *Louisville Courier-Journal*, Aug. 11, 1876, p. 4.
44. *Louisville Courier-Journal*, Aug. 13, 1876, p. 1.
45. *Louisville Courier-Journal*, Aug. 14, 1876, p. 4.
46. *Louisville Courier-Journal*, Aug. 15, 1876, p. 1.
47. *Philadelphia Press* in *Louisville Courier-Journal*, Aug. 19, 1876, p. 4.
48. *Hartford Courant*, Aug. 17, 1876, p. 3.
49. *Cincinnati Enquirer*, Aug. 20, 1876, p. 8.
50. *Cincinnati Enquirer*, Aug. 14, 1876, p. 8.
51. *Hartford Courant*, Aug. 17, 1876, p. 3.
52. *Hartford Courant*, Aug. 18, 1876, p. 3.
53. *Cincinnati Enquirer*, Aug. 16, 1876, p. 8.
54. *Chicago Tribune*, Aug. 13, 1876, p. 3.

Chapter 19

1. *Clipper*, Aug. 26, 1876, p. 171.
2. Wheeler & Baskin, *Cincinnati Game*, p. 200. Josiah Keck was a ruthless, all bottom-line businessman. His lack of empathy for others got him little public sympathy.
3. *Louisville Courier-Journal*, Aug. 18, 1876, p. 4.
4. *Louisville Courier-Journal*, Aug. 21, 1876, p. 4. Randy Linthurst, "Joseph Empley Borden" in Tiemann & Rucker, *Nineteenth Century Stars*, p. 16.
5. *Clipper*, Aug. 19, 1876, p. 168: "The Bostons are looming up as rivals for third position, and they are not so far off the Hartfords...."
6. *Hartford Courant*, Aug. 22, 1876, p. 2.
7. *Louisville Courier-Journal*, Aug. 22, 1876, p. 4.
8. *Spalding's Baseball Guide 1876*, p. 37: "Any base-runner who shall in any way interfere with or obstruct a fielder while attempting to catch a fair fly ball or a foul ball, shall be declared out by the umpire with or without appeal. If he wilfully obstructs a fielder from fielding a ball, he shall be similarly declared out, and, if he *intentionally* kick, or let the ball strike him, he shall be declared out" [emphasis added].
9. *Louisville Courier-Journal*, Aug. 22, 1876, p. 4; Aug. 23, 1876, p. 1.
10. *Louisville Courier-Journal*, Aug. 22, 1876, p. 4; *Hartford Courant*, Aug. 26, 1876, p. 2.
11. *Chicago Tribune* in *Louisville Courier-Journal*, Aug. 23, 1876, p. 1.
12. *St. Louis Times* in *Louisville Courier-Journal*, Aug. 23, 1876, p. 1.
13. *Louisville Courier-Journal*, Aug. 25, 1876, p. 1.
14. *Louisville Courier-Journal*, Aug. 20, 1876, p. 1; Aug. 21, 1876, p. 4.
15. *Hartford Courant*, Aug. 22, 1876, p. 2. Richardson, "Thomas (Tommy) Henry Bond" in Tiemann & Rucker, *Nineteenth Century Stars*, p. 15.
16. *Hartford Courant*, Aug. 22, 1876, p. 2; Aug. 23, 1876, p. 3.
17. *Hartford Courant*, Aug. 17, 1876, p. 3.
18. *Cincinnati Enquirer*, Aug. 24, 1876, p. 8.
19. *Louisville Courier-Journal*, Aug. 19, 1876, p. 4.
20. *St. Louis Globe-Democrat* in *Louisville Courier-Journal*, Aug. 24, 1876, p. 1.
21. *Cincinnati Enquirer*, Aug. 28, 1876, p. 8.
22. *Louisville Courier-Journal*, Aug. 26, 1876, p. 4.
23. *Cincinnati Enquirer*, Aug. 26, 1876, p. 8.
24. *Louisville Courier-Journal*, Aug. 26, 1876, p. 4, and *Cincinnati Enquirer*, Aug. 26, 1876, p. 8, both reported the attendance as being 200 patrons. The *Louisville Courier-Journal*, Aug. 27, 1876, p. 1, changed its crowd estimate to 1,200 cranks. Judging from the three stories, the 1,200 estimate was most likely an error.
25. Thorn et al., *Hidden Game of Baseball*, p. 193: This 1-to-6 ratio does not count battery errors like passed balls and wild pitches which were counted as errors in the 1870s.
26. *Louisville Courier-Journal*, Aug. 26, 1876, p. 4.
27. *Louisville Courier-Journal*, Aug. 21, 1876, p. 4; Aug. 27, 1876, p. 1. Allen, *Cincinnati Reds*, p. 10: The park was on the site of what was later Chester Park.
28. *Cincinnati Enquirer*, Aug. 27, 1876, p. 6.
29. *Hartford Courant*, Aug. 26, 1876, p. 2. *Louisville Courier-Journal*, Aug. 20, 1876, p. 1.
30. *Louisville Courier-Journal*, Aug. 24, 1876, p. 1.
31. *Hartford Courant*, Aug. 26, 1876, p. 2. *Louisville Courier-Journal*, Aug. 20, 1876, p. 1.
32. *Hartford Times* cited in *Louisville Courier-Journal*, Aug. 26, 1876, p. 4.
33. *Hartford Times* cited in *Louisville Courier-Journal*, Aug. 27, 1876, p. 1.

34. *Louisville Courier-Journal*, Aug. 26, 1876, p. 4.
35. *Hartford Courant*, Aug. 21, 1876, p. 2.
36. *Louisville Courier-Journal*, Sept. 3, 1876, p. 4.
37. *Chicago Tribune*, Aug. 20, 1876, p. 3.
38. *Cincinnati Enquirer*, Aug. 28, 1876, p. 8.
39. *Cincinnati Enquirer*, Aug. 28, 1876, p. 8.
40. *Cincinnati Enquirer*, Aug. 30, 1876, p. 8; *Chicago Tribune*, Aug. 29, 1876, p. 2. *Enquirer* had it 9–7 for the London, Ontario, Tecumsehs. *Tribune* had it 10–9.
41. *Louisville Courier-Journal*, Aug. 31, 1876, p. 4.

Chapter 20

1. *Chicago Tribune*, Sept. 3, 1876, p. 3.
2. *Chicago Tribune*, Sept. 3, 1876, p. 3.
3. *Louisville Courier-Journal*, Sept. 25, 1876, p. 1.
4. Nemec, *Great Encyclopedia*, p. 89.
5. Levine, *A.G. Spalding*, p. 50.
6. *Clipper*, Sept. 9, 1876, p. 187: Published an advance concerning the Goss-Allen fight two days after the fight was over. The weekly *Clipper* had gone to press before Sept. 7.
7. *Cincinnati Enquirer*, Sept. 2, 1876, p. 8.
8. *Clipper*, Sept. 9, 1876, p. 187; Nov. 18, 1876, p. 266.
9. *Louisville Courier-Journal*, Sept. 9, 1876, p. 4; *Chicago Tribune*, Sept. 9, 1876, p. 6.
10. *Louisville Courier-Journal*, Sept. 10, 1876, p. 4.
11. *Clipper*, Sept. 16, 1876, p. 197. *Louisville Courier-Journal*, Sept. 9, 1876, p. 4.
12. *Louisville Courier-Journal*, Sept. 12, 1876, p. 4.
13. *Louisville Courier-Journal*, Sept. 13, 1876, p. 4; Sept. 14, 1876, p. 4.
14. *Louisville Courier-Journal*, Sept. 6, 1876, p. 4.
15. *Louisville Courier-Journal*, Sept. 7, 1876, p. 4: Reported Chicago and St. Louis would play an exhibition game on Union Grounds in New York City. *Chicago Tribune*, Sept. 7, 1876, p. 5: The game was going to be the first of a series for the Western Championship.
16. *Philadelphia Inquirer*, Sept. 7, 1876, p. 1.
17. *Louisville Courier-Journal*, Sept. 7, 1876, p. 4; Sept. 8, 1876, p. 4.
18. *Louisville Courier-Journal*, Sept. 11, 1876, p. 4: Ran a detailed accounting of the projected costs and income.
19. *Louisville Courier-Journal*, Sept. 11, 1876, p. 4.
20. *Louisville Courier-Journal*, Sept. 11, 1876, p. 4.
21. *Louisville Courier-Journal*, Sept. 11, 1876, p. 4.
22. Nemec, *Great Encyclopedia*, p. 4.
23. *Louisville Courier-Journal*, Sept. 11, 1876, p. 4.
24. Thorn & Palmer, *Total Baseball*, p. 1662: Charles Wilson (Dory) Dean pitched in 30 National League games in 1876, his only year in the majors. His win-loss record was 4–26. Nemec, *Great Encyclopedia*, p. 90, noted that Dean's .133 winning percentage was the worst ever by a pitcher in one year who was involved in a minimum of 20 decisions. Dean later became an outstanding tennis player. Cummings (p. 1656) had a 145–94 record for six years in the National Association and National League. Nemec, *Great Encyclopedia*, p. 772, wrote that Cummings was described as "frail," but, pp. 24–25, was also "considered by some historians to have invented the curveball. He threw the best curve of his day."

Chapter 21

1. *Hartford Courant*, Sept. 13, 1876, p. 2.
2. *Chicago Tribune* in *Louisville Courier-Journal*, Sept. 12, 1876, p. 4.
3. *Chicago Tribune*, Sept. 17, 1876, p. 8.
4. *Chicago Tribune*, Sept. 17, 1876, p. 8.
5. *Chicago Tribune*, Sept. 17, 1876, p. 8.
6. *Hartford Courant*, Sept. 14, 1876, p. 3.
7. Holtzman & Vass, *Chicago Cubs Encyclopedia*, p. 295.
8. *Hartford Courant*, Sept. 18, 1876, p. 2.
9. *New York Times*, Sept. 17, 1876, p. 5.
10. *Clipper*, Sept. 16, 1876, p. 194.
11. *Clipper*, Sept. 16, 1876, p. 194.
12. Melville, *Early Baseball*, pp. 84–85.
13. Melville, *Early Baseball*, pp. 84–85.
14. Shannon & Kalinsky, *Ballparks*, p. 5.
15. Seymour, *Baseball: Early Years*, p. 88.
16. Dickey, *History of National League Baseball*, p. 9.
17. Seymour, *Baseball: Early Years*, p. 88.
18. *Chicago Tribune*, Sept. 14, 1876, p. 5, reprinted G.W. Thompson's letter of Sept. 11, 1876, to W.A. Hulbert.
19. Melville, *Early Baseball*, p. 85.
20. Seymour, *Baseball: Early Years*, p. 88.
21. Melville, *Early Baseball*, p. 85.
22. *Louisville Courier-Journal*, Sept. 28, 1876, p. 4.
23. *Chicago Tribune*, Sept. 24, 1876, p. 3.
24. Holtzman & Vass, *Chicago Cubs Encyclopedia*, p. 296.
25. Ryczek, *Blackguards*, p. 133.
26. Holtzman & Vass, *Chicago Cubs Encyclopedia*, p. 296: Hulbert was wealthy by his early 40's.
27. Maher & Ivor-Campbell, "William Henry Cammeyer," in Ivor-Campbell et al., *Baseball's First Stars*, p. 21.

28. Shannon & Kalinsky, *Ballparks*, p. 5.
29. *New York Times*, Aug. 20, 1876, p. 12.
30. *New York Times*, Sept. 17, 1876, p. 5.
31. *New York Times*, Aug. 20, 1876, p. 12.
32. *New York Times*, Sept. 16, 1876, p. 8.
33. *Cincinnati Enquirer*, Sept. 13, 1876, p. 2.
34. *Chicago Tribune*, Sept. 14, 1876, p. 5.
35. *Louisville Courier-Journal*, Sept. 18, 1876, p. 1.
36. *Louisville Courier-Journal*, Sept. 18, 1876, p. 1.
37. *Louisville Courier-Journal*, Sept. 19, 1876, p. 4.
38. *Louisville Courier-Journal*, Sept. 20, 1876, p. 1.
39. *Louisville Courier-Journal*, Sept. 20, 1876, p. 1.
40. *New York World* in *Louisville Courier-Journal*, Sept. 24, 1876, p. 1.
41. *Louisville Courier-Journal*, Sept. 24, 1876, p. 1.
42. *Hartford Courant*, Sept. 25, 1876, p. 2. *Chicago Tribune*, Sept. 25, 1876, p. 5.
43. *Louisville Courier-Journal*, Sept. 25, 1876, p. 1. *Chicago Tribune*, Sept. 24, 1876, p. 3: Although Chicago "played by no means a perfect game, it should not be charged to them that they played badly enough to lose ... [the game was] stolen away by a series of outrageous decisions ... rules ... repeatedly transgressed by the umpire ... especially in the matter of calling balls and strikes. A curious reporter [kept count] and noted time and again that George (Foghorn) Bradley and Manning were allowed to pitch five and six balls without any call at all ... in the eighth inning ... Spalding hit a ball on the foul line and started up the dust and lime. It was called foul.... Sec. 11 of Rule 5 commands such hits to be called fair."
44. *Hartford Courant*, Sept. 25, 1876, p. 2.
45. *Louisville Courier-Journal*, Sept. 28, 1876, p. 4: The win made Chicago's "chances for the pennant certain." The story consisted of one four-line paragraph and a box score of the game.
46. *Louisville Courier-Journal*, Sept. 29, 1876, p. 1: Reported the *Boston Globe* speculating on who would be available if the A's did disband at season's end. Eggler, Meyerle and Fisler were considered top candidates to be picked up by other N.L. clubs. The *Hartford Courant* said it was not settled without doubt that Chicago's Jim (Deacon) White would play with Boston the next year.
47. Melville, *Early Baseball*, p. 85.
48. *Louisville Courier-Journal*, Oct. 1, 1876, p. 1: Boston defeated Louisville 6–5 while "a gloomy sky and chilly weather drew out a rather small crowd."
49. *Cincinnati Enquirer*, Oct. 2, 1876, p. 6.

Chapter 22

1. *Louisville Courier-Journal*, Oct. 1, 1876, p. 1.
2. *Louisville Courier-Journal*, Oct. 2, 1876, p. 4.
3. *Chicago Tribune*, Oct. 1, 1876, p. 7.
4. *Louisville Courier-Journal*, Oct. 4, 1876, p. 1: The horses were also running at Mystic Park in Boston (and probably a number of other tracks) by Oct. 4.
5. *Clipper*, Oct. 14, 1876, p. 229.
6. *Chicago Tribune*, Oct. 4, 1876, p. 5: Chicago got 25 hits and made five errors. Marshalltown got nine hits and made 14 errors.
7. *Hartford Courant*, Oct. 6, 1876, p. 2: Reported the score as 2–1 for Chicago, said the crowd was 5,000 and noted the weather was fine and warm. The *Chicago Tribune*, Oct. 6, 1876, p. 5: Referred to the game as an "exhibition," set the attendance at 4,000 and erroneously listed the score as 2–0 for Chicago.
8. *Clipper*, Oct. 14, 1876, p. 227.
9. Voigt, *American Baseball*, p. 93.
10. *Cincinnati Enquirer*, Oct. 7, 1876, p. 2.
11. Wills, "Safe At Home" in *Sports Illustrated*, June 12, 1989, p. 97.
12. *Hartford Courant*, Oct. 17, 1876, p. 1: Concluded that the struggle for second place was decided by Hartford defeating Cincinnati 7–4, 11–6 and 11–0 in the series. The *Courant* reporter argued that this left St. Louis third. Leaving out the Mutual and Athletic games already played by Hartford, St. Louis and Chicago, he noted, Chicago had a 38–12 record, Hartford was 32–16 and St. Louis, 31–18. The *Courant*, Oct. 23, 1876, p. 3: Reiterated Hartford's having finished second.
13. *Clipper*, Nov. 18, 1876, p. 266.
14. *Clipper*, Oct. 14, 1876, p. 229.
15. *Clipper*, Oct. 14, 1876, p. 229.
16. *Clipper*, Oct. 14, 1876, p. 229.
17. *Clipper*, Oct. 14, 1876, p. 229.
18. *Clipper*, Oct. 14, 1876, p. 229.
19. *Clipper*, Oct. 14, 1876, p. 229. Thorn & Palmer, *Total Baseball*, pp. 926–927: Addy played for Cincinnati in 1877 and, p. 1539, White played for Boston in 1877.
20. Gold & Ahrens, *Golden Era Cubs*, p. 8.
21. *Cincinnati Enquirer*, Oct. 16, 1876, p. 8.
22. *Chicago Tribune*, Oct. 10, 1876, p. 7.
23. Nemec, *Great Encyclopedia*, p. 89.
24. Reidenbaugh, *100 Years*, p. 7.
25. *Clipper*, Dec. 27, 1876, p. 307.
26. Author-calculated data from statistics in *Clipper*, Oct. 14, 1876, p. 229.
27. Thorn et al., *Hidden Game of Baseball*, p. 29.
28. Thorn et al., *Hidden Game of Baseball*, p. 27.

29. Dickey, *History of the National League*, p. 8.
30. *Baseball Century*, p. 59.
31. Dickey, *History of the National League*, p. 8.
32. Bartlett, *Baseball and Mr. Spalding*, p. 102.
33. Okrent & Lewine, *Ultimate Baseball Book*, p. 24.
34. *Baseball Century*, p. 59; Nemec, *Great Encyclopedia*, p. 89.
35. Smith, *Economic History of the United States*, p. 94.
36. *Cincinnati Enquirer*, Oct. 16, 1876, p. 8.
37. *Clipper*, Nov. 25, 1876, p. 274; Dec. 2, 1876, p. 282.
38. Danzig, *Oh How They Played the Game*, p. 13.

Chapter 23

1. *Chicago Tribune*, Dec. 10, 1876, p. 7; *Chicago Tribune*, Dec. 3, 1876, p. 7; *Louisville Courier-Journal*, Dec. 3, 1876, p. 7.
2. *Clipper*, Dec. 16, 1876, p. 299.
3. *Louisville Courier-Journal*, Dec. 14, 1876, p. 3.
4. *Louisville Courier-Journal*, Dec. 4, 1876, p. 3.
5. Jones, *Former Major League Teams*, p. 70.
6. Maher & Ivor-Campbell, "William Henry Cammeyer," in Ivor-Campbell et al., *Baseball's First Stars*, p. 21.
7. *Louisville Courier-Journal*, Dec. 14, 1876, p. 3.
8. *Louisville Courier-Journal*, Dec. 14, 1876, p. 3.
9. *Louisville Courier-Journal*, Dec. 14, 1876, p. 3.
10. *Louisville Courier-Journal*, Dec. 14, 1876, p. 3.
11. *Louisville Courier-Journal*, Dec. 14, 1876, p. 3.
12. *Chicago Tribune*, Dec. 10, 1876, p. 7.
13. *Clipper*, Dec. 27, 1876, p. 307.
14. *Louisville Courier-Journal*, Dec. 14, 1876, p. 3.
15. *Chicago Tribune*, Dec. 24, 1876, p. 3.
16. *Louisville Courier-Journal*, Dec. 14, 1876, p. 3.
17. *Chicago Tribune*, Dec. 7, 1876, p. 7.
18. *Hartford Courant*, Dec. 15, 1876, p. 1.
19. *Clipper*, Dec. 23, 1876, p. 307.
20. Melville, *Early Baseball*, p. 93.
21. *Chicago Tribune*, Dec. 10, 1876, p. 7.
22. *Clipper*, Dec. 23, 1876, p. 307.
23. *Chicago Tribune*, Dec. 10, 1876, p. 7.
24. *Cincinnati Enquirer*, Dec. 1, 1876, p. 8.
25. Thorn & Palmer, *Total Baseball*, pp. 2161–2162.
26. *Chicago Tribune*, Dec. 10, 1876, p. 7.
27. Bartlett, *Baseball and Mr. Spalding*, pp. 102–103.
28. *Louisville Courier-Journal*, Dec. 14, 1876, p. 3.
29. Bartlett, *Baseball and Mr. Spalding*, pp. 102–103.
30. *Louisville Courier-Journal*, Dec. 14, 1876, p. 3.
31. *Clipper*, Dec. 23, 1876, p. 307.
32. *Louisville Courier-Journal*, Dec. 14, 1876, p. 3.
33. Reidenbaugh, *100 Years*, p. 8.
34. *Louisville Courier-Journal*, Dec. 14, 1876, p. 3.
35. *Chicago Tribune*, Dec. 10, 1876, p. 7.
36. *Louisville Courier-Journal*, Dec. 14, 1876, p. 3.
37. *Louisville Courier-Journal*, Dec. 14, 1876, p. 3.
38. *Clipper*, Dec. 23, 1876, p. 307.
39. *Louisville Courier-Journal*, Dec. 14, 1876, p. 3.
40. Thomas R. Heitz, "Rules and Scoring," in Thorn & Palmer, *Total Baseball*, p. 2219.
41. *Louisville Courier-Journal*, Dec. 14, 1876, p. 3.
42. *Chicago Tribune*, Dec. 10, 1876, p. 7.
43. *Louisville Courier-Journal*, Dec. 14, 1876, p. 3.
44. *Chicago Tribune*, Dec. 10, 1876, p. 7.
45. *Louisville Courier-Journal*, Dec. 14, 1876, p. 3.
46. *Louisville Courier-Journal*, Dec. 14, 1876, p. 3.
47. Orem, *Baseball from the Newspaper Accounts*, p. 264.

Epilogue

1. Deane, Bill, "Awards and Honors" in Thorn & Palmer, *Total Baseball*, pp. 517, 518, 523, 524, 526.
2. *Bellingham Herald*, March 28, 1995, p. D3.
3. Gold & Ahrens, *Golden Era Cubs*, pp. 3–4.
4. Nemec, *Great Encyclopedia*, p. 113.
5. Twombly, *200 Years*, p. 74.
6. Wheeler & Baskin, *Cincinnati Game*, p. 94.
7. Ivor-Campbell, "Henry William Chadwick (Chad, Father of Base Ball)," in Ivor-Campbell et al., *Baseball's First Stars*, p. 27.
8. Joseph M. Overfield, "William Arthur Cummings (Candy)," in Ivor-Campbell et al., *Baseball's First Stars*, p. 44.
9. *Encyclopædia Britannica*, 1960, vol. 14, p. 52.

10. *Encyclopædia Britannica*, 1960, vol. 10, p. 912.
11. Nemec, *Great Encyclopedia*, p. 102: In 1877, "Collectively, the players on the top six IA clubs accrued more past or future seasons of major league baseball than the players on the six National League clubs."
12. Nemec, *Great Encyclopedia*, p. 101.
13. Nemec, *Great Encyclopedia*, p. 125.

Bibliography

Newspapers

The *Chicago Tribune, Cincinnati Enquirer, Hartford Courant, Louisville Courier-Journal, New York Clipper, New York Times,* and *Philadelphia Inquirer* were consulted for the period June 1875 to January 1877. The *Bellingham Herald*, March 28, 1995, p. D3 provided material on Hulbert's induction into the Hall of Fame.

Books

Adair, Robert Kemp. *The Physics of Baseball*. New York: Harper and Row, 1990.
Adelman, Melvin L. *A Sporting Time: New York City and the Rise of Modern Athletics, 1820–1870*. Urbana: University of Illinois Press, 1986.
Allen, Lee. *The Cincinnati Reds*. New York: G.P. Putnam's Sons, 1948.
_____. *Hot Stove League*. New York: A.S. Barnes, 1955.
Anson, Adrian C. *A Ball Player's Career*. Chicago: ERA Publ., 1900.
Appel, Martin, and Burt Goldblatt. *Baseball's Best: The Hall of Fame Gallery*. New York: McGraw-Hill, 1977.
Astor, Gerald. *The Baseball Hall of Fame 50th Anniversary Book*. New York: Prentice Hall, 1988.
Baker, William J. *Sports in the Western World*. Totowa, N.J.: Rowman and Littlefield, 1982.
Bartlett, Arthur. *Baseball and Mr. Spalding: The History and Romance of Baseball*. New York: Farrar, Straus & Young, 1951.
Bartlett, John. *Familiar Quotations*. 15th ed. Boston: Little, Brown, 1980.
A Baseball Century: The First 100 Years of the National League. New York: Macmillan, 1976.
Black, J. Anderson, and Madge Garland. *A History of Fashion*. New York: William Morrow, 1975.
Bowman, John, and Joel Zoss. *Diamonds in the Rough: The Untold History of Baseball*. New York: Macmillan, 1989.
Clark, Patrick. *Sports Firsts*. New York: Facts on File, 1981.
Collett, Ritter. *The Cincinnati Reds: A Pictorial History of Professional Baseball's Oldest Team*. Virginia Beach, Va.: Jordan-Powers Corp., 1976.
Collins, Robert. *The Age of Innocence 1870/1880*. Toronto: N. S. L. Natural Science of Canada Ltd., 1977.
Danzig, A. *Oh How They Played the Game: The Early Days of Football and the Heroes Who Made It Great*. New York: Macmillan, 1971.

Deutsch, Jordan A.; Richard N. Kohen; Roland T. Johnson, and David S. Neft. *The Scrapbook History of Baseball*. New York: Bobbs-Merrill, 1975.
Dickey, Glenn. *History of National League Baseball Since 1876*. New York: Stein and Day, 1979.
Dickson, Paul. *The Worth Book of Softball: A Celebration of America's True National Pastime*. New York: Facts on File Books, 1994.
_____, ed. *The Dickson Baseball Dictionary*. New York: Avon, 1989.
Dreifort, John E. *Baseball History from Outside the Lines*. Lincoln: University of Nebraska Press, 2001.
Emery, Edwin, and Michael Emery. *The Press and America: An Interpretive History of the Mass Media*. 5th ed. Englewood Cliffs, N.J.: Prentice-Hall, 1984.
Encyclopaedia Britannica, 1960, vols. 4, 10, 12, 14, 22.
Fox, Stephen. *Big Leagues: Professional Baseball, Football, and Basketball in National Memory*. New York: Morrow, 1994.
Furnas, J.C. *The Americans: A Social History of the United States: 1587–1914*. New York: G.P. Putnam's Sons, 1969.
Gershman, Michael. *Diamonds: The Evolution of the Ballpark*. Boston: Houghton Mifflin, 1993.
Gold, Eddie, and Art Ahrens. *The Golden Era Cubs: 1876–1940*. Chicago: Bonus Books, 1985.
Golenbock, Peter. *The Spirit of St. Louis: A History of the St. Louis Cardinals and Browns*. New York: Avon Books, 2000.
_____. *Wrigleyville: A Magical History Tour of the Chicago Cubs*. New York: St. Martin's Press, 1996.
Gray, Henry. *Gray's Anatomy (Anatomy, Descriptive and Surgical)*. New York: Bounty, 1977.
Guttman, Allen. *Sports Spectators*. New York: Columbia University Press, 1986.
Harper, William A. *How You Played the Game: The Life of Grantland Rice*. Columbia: University of Missouri Press, 1999.
Heitz, Thomas R. "Rules and Scoring." In John Thorn, and Pete Palmer, *Total Baseball* (New York: Warner Books, 1989), pp. 2217–2261.
Holtzman, Jerome, and George Vass. *The Chicago Cubs Encyclopedia*. Philadelphia: Temple University Press, 1997.
Ivor-Campbell, Frederick; Robert L. Tiemann, and Mark Rucker, ed. *Baseball's First Stars*. Cleveland: Society for American Baseball Research, 1996.
James, Bill. *The Bill James Historical Abstract*. New York: Villard, 1986.
Jones, Donald D. *Former Major League Teams: An Encyclopedia*. Jefferson, N.C.: McFarland, 1995.
Kaese, Harold. *The Boston Braves*. New York: G.P. Putnam's Sons, 1948.
Kirsch, George B. *The Creation of American Team Sports: Baseball and Cricket, 1838–72*. Urbana: University of Illinois Press, 1989.
Krieghbaum, Hillier. *Facts in Perspective: The Editorial Page and News Interpretation*. Englewood Cliffs, N.J.: Prentice-Hall, 1956.
Kross, Herman E. *American Economic Development*. 2nd ed. Englewood Cliffs, N.J.: Prentice-Hall, 1966.
Landers, Daniel M., and Robert W. Christina. *Psychology of Motor Behavior and Sport—1977*. Champaign, Ill.: Human Kinetics, 1978.
Levine, Peter. *A.G. Spalding and the Rise of Baseball: The Promise of American Sport*. New York: Oxford University Press, 1985.

Lowrey, Philip J. *Green Cathedrals.* Manhattan, Kan.: AG Press, 1986.
Lucas, John A., and Ronald A. Smith. *Saga of American Sport.* Philadelphia: Lea and Febiger, 1978.
McBride, Joseph. *High and Inside: An A-to-Z Guide to the Language of Baseball.* Chicago: Contemporary Publishing, 1980 (1997).
McCullough, Ron, ed. *From Cartwright to Shoeless Joe: The Warwick Compendium of Early Baseball.* Toronto: Warwick Publishing, 1998.
Melville, Tom. *Early Baseball and the Rise of the National League.* Jefferson, N.C.: McFarland, 2001.
Monteleone, John, and Mark Gola. *The Louisville Slugger Ultimate Book for Hitting.* New York: Henry Holt, 1997.
Morrill, John F., and T. O'Keefe. *Batting and Pitching, Illustrated.* Boston: Wright and Ditson, 1884.
Morse, Jacob. *Sphere and Ash.* (Original 1888). Columbia, S.C.: Camden House, reprint 1984.
Mott, Frank Luther. *American Journalism: A History, 1690–1960.* New York: Macmillan, 1962.
Nemec, David. *The Great American Baseball Team Book.* New York: Plume (Penguin), 1992.
_____. *The Great Encyclopedia of 19th Century Baseball.* New York: Donald I. Fine Books (Penguin), 1997.
_____. *The Rules of Baseball.* New York: Lyons & Burford, 1994.
Okrent, Daniel, and Harris Levine, ed. *The Ultimate Baseball Book.* Boston: Houghton Mifflin, 1979.
Orem, Preston D. *Baseball (1845–1881) from the Newspaper Accounts.* Altadena, Calif.: self-published, 1961.
Peterson, Harold. *The Man Who Invented Baseball.* New York: Scribner's, 1969.
Rader, Benjamin G. *American Sports: From the Age of Folk Games to the Age of Spectators.* 2nd ed. Englewood Cliffs, N.J.: Prentice-Hall, 1990.
_____. *Baseball: A History of America's Game.* Urbana: University of Illinois Press, 1992.
Reidenbaugh, Lowell. *100 Years of National League Baseball, 1876–1976.* St. Louis: Sporting News Publishing Co., 1976.
Rice, Damon. *Seasons Past.* New York: Praeger, 1976.
Riess, Steven A., *City Games.* Urbana: University of Illinois Press, 1989.
Rosenberg, John M. *They Gave Us Baseball: The 12 Extraordinary Men Who Shaped the Major Leagues.* Harrisburg, Pa.: Stackpole, 1989.
Ryczek, William J. *Blackguards and Red Stockings: A History of Baseball's National Association, 1871–1875.* Jefferson, N.C.: McFarland, 1992.
Schmidt, Richard A. *Motor Control and Learning: A Behavioral Emphasis.* Champaign, Ill.: Human Kinetics, 1982.
Seymour, Harold. *Baseball: The Early Years.* New York: Oxford University Press, 1960.
_____. *Baseball: The People's Game.* New York: Oxford University Press, 1990.
Shannon, Bill, and George Kalinsky. *The Ball Parks.* New York: Hawthorn, 1975.
Smith, H. R. *Economic History of the United States.* New York: Ronald, 1955.
Smith, Robert. *Illustrated History of Baseball.* New York: Grosset and Dunlap, 1973.
_____. *Pioneers of Baseball.* Boston: Little, Brown, 1978.
Somers, Dale. "The Rise of Sport in New Orleans, 1850–1900." Unpublished Ph.D. dissertation, Tulane University, 1966.

Spalding's Official Base Ball Guide 1876. Chicago: A.G. Spalding and Bros., 1876.
Spears, Betty, and Richard A. Swanson. *History of Sport and Physical Activity in the United States*. Dubuque, Iowa.: Wm. C. Brown, 1978.
Spink, Alfred H. *The National Game*. Carbondale: Southern Illinois University Press, 1910 (Reprint 2000).
Sullivan, Dean A., ed. *Early Innings: A Documentary History of Baseball, 1825–1908*. Lincoln: University of Nebraska Press, pp. 92–95.
Thorn, John, and Pete Palmer, eds. *Total Baseball*. New York: Warner Books, 1989.
Thorn, John et al. *The Hidden Game of Baseball*. New York: Doubleday, 1985.
Tiemann, Robert L., and Mark Rucker. *Nineteenth Century Stars*. Kansas City, Mo.: Society for American Baseball Research, 1989.
Twombly, Wells. *200 Years of Sport in America: A Pageant of a Nation at Play*. New York: McGraw-Hill, 1976.
Tygiel, Jules. *Past Time: Baseball as History*. New York: Oxford University Press, 2000.
Vincent, Ted. *Mudville's Revenge: The Rise and Fall of American Sport*. New York: Seaview Books, 1981.
Voigt, David Quentin. *American Baseball: From the Gentleman's Sport to the Commissioner System*. Vol. 1. University Park: The Pennsylvania State University Press, 1983.
Wallace, J. *The Baseball Anthology*. New York: Harry N. Abrams, 1994.
Ward, Geoffrey, and Ken Burns. *Baseball: An Illustrated History*. New York: Alfred A. Knopf, 1994.
Wheeler, Lonnie, and John Baskin. *The Cincinnati Game*. Wilmington, Ohio: Orange Frazer Press, 1988.

Articles

Ballard, Sarah. "Fabric of the Game." *Sports Illustrated*, April 5, 1989, pp. 108–118.
Berman, Bob. "Two Dog Night." *Discover*, January 1994, p. 23.
Burns, Ed. "The Chicago Cubs." *Sport*, September 1950, pp. 24–29, 79–84.
Wills, Bret. "Safe at Home." *Sports Illustrated*, June 12, 1989, pp. 89–99.

Baseball's First Stars, SABR, 1996

The following articles from Ivor-Campbell, Tiemann and Rucker's *Baseball's First Stars* were utilized:

Article Subject	Author
Adrian (Cap) Anson	William E. McMahon and Robert L. Tiemann
George Bradley	Jim Rygelski
Morgan Bulkeley	David Pietrusza
John Burdock	Mark S. Sternman
William Cammeyer	Ed Maher and Frederick Ivor-Campbell
Henry Chadwick	Frederick Ivor-Campbell
William Craver	Phil Brown
Candy Cummings	Joseph M. Overfield
David Eggler	Frank Phillips
Richard Higham	Larry R. Gerlach
Jack Manning	Jack Kavanagh and Frederick Ivor-Campbell
Dick McBride	Robert Tiemann

(Article Subject)	(Author)
Mike McGeary	Richard Puff
Ed Nolan	J.J. Miller
Jim O'Rourke	Bernard J. Crowley
Albert Spalding	William E. McMahon
James Wood	Robert Tiemann
Harry Wright	Mark Alvarez

Nineteenth Century Stars, SABR, 1989

The following articles from Tiemann and Rucker's *Nineteenth Century Stars* were utilized:

Subject	Author
Tommy Bond	Bob Richardson
Joseph Borden	Randy Linthurst
Robert Ferguson	Frank V. Phelps
West Fisler	Joseph M. Overfield
William (Dummy) Hoy	Joseph M. Overfield
William Hulbert	William E. Akin
Henry Lucas	Ralph Horton
Cal McVey	Frederick Ivor-Campbell
Deacon (James) White	Joseph M. Overfield

Letters

William Hulbert Collection (Chicago Historical Society)

Web

St. Louis Plan — Commission 1969. Website of St. Louis, Missouri. Organization/heritage/history

Index

Actives of Reading, Penn. 69
Addy, Bob 69, 79, 82, 91, 107, 206
Admissions 8, 47, 88–89, 124
Alcohol 2–3, 5–7, 23, 26, 33, 39, 49, 50, 73, 107, 128, 158–59
Allen, Lee 111
Allen, Tom 103, 186, 188
Allison, Art 91, 138, 198
Allison, Doug 76–77, 89, 147, 219
American Association 31, 219
Americus of Philadelphia 25
Andrus, Fred 73, 85, 182
Anson, Adrian (Cap) 19–20, 37–39, 45–46, 71, 73, 77, 82, 91, 94, 96, 127, 177–78, 202, 206, 209, 213–14, 219
Appolonio, N.T. 28, 43–44, 52, 57, 154, 212–13, 218
Atlantics, Brooklyn 9, 30, 48
Attendance 31, 116, 118, 164, 209–10
Avenue Grounds, Cincinnati 181

Baker, Johnny "Cannonball" 147
Baltimore Baseball Club 28, 31, 69
Barber, Steve 148
Barnes, Ross 14–15, 17–18, 74, 77, 82, 91, 96, 107–8, 117, 121, 153, 191, 202, 206–7, 208–9, 219
Battin, Joe 81, 108, 130, 151, 177, 213, 219
Beals, Tommy 95
Bechtel, George 6, 159, 164, 198
Belden, John G. 173
Belmont Park, N.Y. 124
Bielaski, Oscar 90–91, 127, 182, 208
The Big Four 18, 43
Bishop, Campbell Orrick 35, 39, 45
Blong, Joe 160, 198
Bond, Tommy 17, 76–77, 86, 112, 121, 127, 146, 149, 153, 165, 169, 177–79, 182–84, 186–87, 193, 203, 206, 209, 216, 219
Booth, Amos 104, 154, 207, 210, 219–20
Booth, Ed 77, 79, 134, 137–38, 196, 198
Borden, Joe 69, 74–75, 95, 99, 102, 111, 113, 119–20, 123, 152, 174, 176–77, 179, 199
Boston Globe 118

Boston Herald 113, 160
Boston Plan 78, 205
Boston Red Stockings 3–4, 10, 12–3, 17–19, 22, 25–6, 28, 30, 41, 43–4, 49, 52, 56, 68, 73–75, 92–102, 205, 212
Boyd, William "Bill" 77, 79, 88
Bradley, George "Foghorn" 180
Bradley, George "Grin" 76, 81, 105, 108, 117, 130, 141, 143–44, 147, 149, 150–54, 160, 165, 168, 176–77, 180, 182, 191, 206–7, 209, 213–14, 219
Brainard, Asa 49, 89, 179
Brooklyn 9
Brooklyn Argus 199
Brooklyn Atlantics 9, 25, 48, 80
Brooklyn Eagle 70
Brown, Lew 75
Brown, Mordecai 221
Brownell, Hardy 148
Buffalo Baseball Club 25, 28
Bulkeley, Morgan Gardner 28, 44–45, 52–3, 56–7, 90, 117, 120–1, 127, 158, 161, 172–74, 182–83, 193, 212–13, 219
Burdock, John "Black Jack" 76, 127, 144
Burke's Law 6
Burlington Baseball Club 25

Camdens of New Jersey 69
Cammeyer, William 5, 7–9, 11, 15–16, 30–31, 36, 46–48, 57, 61, 65, 77–78, 83, 84, 106, 110, 119, 121–24, 133, 141–42, 158–59, 186–88, 193–96, 201, 212–14, 220
Camp, Walter 211
Capitoline Grounds 7–8, 89
Carbine, John 91, 198
Carey, Tom (J.J. Norton) 76, 146
Cartwright, Alex 144
Casseday, Sam 188
Caylor, Oliver Perry "O.P." 111, 152, 165, 207
Centennial Exposition 194
Chadwick, Henry "Chad" 9–10, 16–17, 23, 36, 44, 46, 49, 51, 53, 61–64, 66, 69, 70, 74, 77–79, 81–83, 89, 118–19, 141, 153, 183, 193, 200, 203, 205–9, 218–20

251

Index

Chapman, John 80, 85, 91, 157, 166, 198
Chase, Charles 27, 33–34, 36, 39–41, 50, 57, 181, 188, 212–13, 218
Chicago Daily News 42
Chicago Times 18
Chicago Tribune 4, 21, 32–33, 35, 38, 42, 58–59, 63, 66–68, 85, 104, 117, 141, 151–52, 169, 175, 178, 185, 191–92, 195, 201
Chicago Union 66
Chicago White Stockings 1, 4, 6–7, 11–14, 17–19, 26, 29, 37, 56, 68, 73–74, 208–9, 212, 215
Cincinnati baseball 25
Cincinnati Enquirer 35, 104, 112, 118–20, 164, 180, 186–87, 203
Cincinnati playing grounds 87
Cincinnati Red Stockings 10, 12, 15, 25–26, 33–35, 39, 42, 56, 68, 73, 79–80, 212
Clack, Bobby 80, 107–8, 117, 210
Clapp, John 81, 151, 206
Cleveland Forest Citys 14, 25, 28
Collins, Dan 166
Columbus Buckeyes 202–3
Concannon, George 5, 11, 30, 45, 60, 65, 67, 69, 80, 157, 205, 207
Constitution, National League 35, 53
Coon (Coons), Bill 96, 98–100
Cooperstown 1
Corporative-cooperative teams 22–23, 31, 61, 63
Covington Stars 40
Craver, Bill 5, 69, 77–78, 133, 158, 164, 220
Cricket 7, 21, 124, 168
Cummings, Candy 75–77, 83, 113, 146, 149, 153, 178–79, 183, 186, 189, 203, 209, 219–20
Curve ball 17–18, 82, 113, 150, 179
Custer, George Armstrong 129
Cuthbert, Edgar "Ed, Ned" 45, 80–81, 151, 177

Daniels, Charles 129
Dean, Dory 165, 168, 189, 203–4
Decker, Reuben S. 7
Dehlman, Herman 81, 151–52
Delaware Baseball Club 69
Detroit Aetnas 28, 31, 183
Devinney, Dan 216
Devlin, Jim 5, 24, 80, 85, 117, 119, 128–99, 133, 135–39, 153, 164, 196–97, 209, 215–16, 220
DiMaggio, Joe 72
Doubleday myth 10
Doubleheader 188–90
DuPont, A.V. 188

Eggler 79, 94, 99, 101, 117, 161, 214

Father of Baseball 10
Father of Professional Baseball 10
Feller, Bob 149
Ferguson, Robert 9, 23, 77, 113, 127, 145–46, 165, 174, 179, 182–84, 186, 192–93, 212–13, 216, 218–19

Field, Sam 80
Finances, Club 9, 24, 26, 28–30, 40–41, 45, 48, 61, 63, 111–12, 118, 158, 161, 172–73, 180, 188, 192, 194–95, 202, 214, 216–17
Finzer, Nicholas 188
Fisher, Charley 154, 160
Fisher, William "Cherokee" 5, 69, 80, 90, 105, 154, 159–60, 164, 168, 174, 217, 220
Fisler, West 79, 96–99, 101–2, 129, 171, 206
Foley, Charles "Curry" 179
Foley, Tom 71
Foley, Will 165, 200, 207
Football 21, 66, 211
Force, Davy 45–46, 79, 94, 97, 100–1
Fort Wayne Kekiongas 26
Fouser, Bill 98, 101–1
Fowle, Charles 6, 26, 29, 33–36, 39, 53, 56–57, 567, 194, 212–13, 215, 218
Fowler, "Bud" (John W. Jackson) 70
Frisch, Frankie 148
Fulmer, Charles "Chick, Chuck" 80, 120, 133–34, 138, 160, 197–98, 206, 220

Gambling 2, 5, 6–7, 22, 30–31, 38, 48, 49–50, 103, 105–6, 121–23, 141–42, 158, 192–93, 198–99, 210
Gerhardt, Joe 80, 110, 120, 133–36, 139, 168, 198
Glenn, John 82, 90, 108, 206
Gonzales, Mike 6
Goss, Joe 103–4, 186, 188
Gould, Charlie 79, 86, 90, 105, 117, 119, 129, 157, 203, 206, 210
Graffen, S. Mason 178, 197
Grand Avenue Grounds, St. Louis 179

Hague, Will 91, 110, 135, 138, 198
Haldeman, Walter H. 27, 39, 40, 41, 53, 188
Hall, George 79, 94, 98–99, 105, 121, 130, 145, 153, 164, 196, 220
Hall of Fame players 37, 219
Hallinan, Jim 77–78, 133, 135–36, 138, 158, 196
Harbidge, Bill 76–77, 83, 117, 127, 146–47, 189, 219
Harrisburgs 183
Hartford Courant 112–13, 116, 152, 159, 179–80, 204
Hartford Dark Blues 17, 19, 25, 28, 36, 41, 43–44, 52, 56–57, 73–77, 204–5, 212, 215
Hartford Times 59, 161, 172–73, 193
Hastings, Scott 80, 133–34, 138, 155, 198
Hatfield, John 60
Hickok, Wild Bill 165
Hicks, Nate 60, 76–77, 79, 134–35, 137–38, 158
Higham, Dick 6–7, 30, 60, 67–68, 76–77, 120, 131, 132, 144–45, 209
Hines, Paul 37–38, 77, 82, 108, 127, 153, 206, 209

Index 253

Hippodroming 3, 7, 48–49, 65, 157, 160, 174, 220
Holbert, Bill 197
Holdsworth, Jim "Long Jim" 88, 128–29, 133–34, 137–38, 167
Horse racing 5, 70, 103, 110, 124, 201
Houtz, Charles 165–67
Hulbert, William vii, viii, 1–4, 6–7, 11–15, 17–26, 28–54, 56–57, 59–53, 65–68, 81–82, 93, 103, 105, 107, 110, 124, 141, 155, 160, 163–64, 175, 187–88, 193–95, 202, 205–8, 210, 212, 214, 216–19, 221

Indianapolis Baseball Club 28, 183
Indoor walking 21
Injuries, ailments 89–90, 106–9, 113, 115–17, 119, 131–32, 161, 164–65, 174, 203–4
International Association of Professional Base Ball Players 220

James, Jesse 188
Jefferson Street Grounds, Philadelphia 2, 58, 92
Jerome Park, N.Y. 201
Johnson, Walter 149
Johnstone, Charles W. 188, 212
Jones, Charley (Rippay, Benjamin Wesley) 80, 105, 107, 109–10, 121, 145, 153–54, 157, 165, 210, 219
Joyce, Joan 148
Joyce, John 34, 170

Keck, George 171, 173, 180, 207
Keck, Josiah "Si" 39, 41–42, 53, 87, 154, 159, 164, 168, 171, 176, 180, 202, 210, 212, 218
Keeler, Wee Willie 221
Keith, Josie 32
Kentucky Derby 70
Keokuk Westerns 25–26
Kessler, Harry 129, 210
Knight, Lon 79, 83, 86, 96, 98–101, 169–70

Lardner, Ring 118
Leonard, Andy 74–75, 77, 97–99
Lewis, Oliver 70
Live Oaks of Lynn, Mass. 180
Lord Baltimores 15
Louderbeck, D.H. 121–22
Louisville Courier-Journal 7, 27, 35, 41, 58, 73, 85–86, 90, 112, 118–19, 126, 130, 152, 157, 161–64, 168, 171, 178–79, 181–82, 185, 187, 189, 191, 196, 218
Louisville Grounds 87–88, 163, 166, 167
Louisville Grays 25–27, 33–35, 39–40, 56, 58, 68, 80, 212
Lucas, James H. 26,
Lucas, John B.L. 26, 53

Mace, Jem 103–4
Mack, Denny 81

Manning, John "Jack" 74, 95, 97–98, 100–1, 177
Mantle, Mickey 72
Maple Leaf Baseball Club 184
Massey, Bill 148
Mathews, Bobby 17–18, 76–78, 121–22, 133, 135–39, 158, 167, 192
Mays, Willie 72
McBride, Dick 112–13, 119
McGeary, Mike 5, 29, 69, 81, 108, 116, 118, 151–52, 156–57, 159–60, 177–78, 192
McGinley, Tim 74, 95, 97–100, 102
McGraw, John 221
McLean, William 96, 100
McMahon, William 39
McVey, Cal 14–15, 17–18, 74, 77, 81–82, 91, 106, 109–10, 116, 127, 131, 191, 202, 206, 209, 219–20
McVey, Lulu 106, 109, 115
Meacham, Lewis vii, 4, 12, 15, 21, 32–33, 35, 41, 63, 66, 67, 141, 178, 201
Melville, Thomas 6
Memphis Red Stockings 183
Meyerle, Levi 45, 69, 79, 94, 97, 99–100, 102, 130, 153
Millennium Plan 171
Miller, Bob 76,
Miller, Thomas 114–15
Mills, A.G. 212, 214
Mills, Everett 76, 79, 127, 146, 167
Mills, Frank 172
Milwaukee Baseball Club 28
Morrill, John 74–75, 90, 119,
Morris, John 133, 136, 167, 216
Morrissey, John 49
Murnane (Murnan), Tim 69, 74, 95, 99, 100–1, 117, 154

Naismith, Dr. James 21
National Association of Base-Ball Players 48–49
National Association of Professional Base-Ball Players 1–6, 8–10, 15, 17–19, 21–23, 25–27, 30–33, 37, 39–41, 43–45, 48–50, 52, 55–57, 61–63, 66–67, 69, 193
National League constitution 35, 53
National League of Professional Base Ball Clubs vii, 10, 14, 31, 39, 47, 52–56, 59, 63–64, 116, 140, 169, 205, 207, 212, 218, 220–21
New Castle Neshannocks 69, 183
New Haven Elm Citys 25, 28–29, 36, 40, 56, 60, 65, 67–70, 90, 173, 182–83, 186–87
New Haven Palladium 60–61
New Haven Register 60–61
New Haven Stars 69
New Haven Union 60
New York Chronicle 10
New York Clipper 7, 16, 46, 62–65, 69–70, 62, 79, 82–83, 113, 129, 185, 193, 203, 208, 215
New York Gothams 31
New York Metropolitans 31

New York Mutuals 4, 5, 7–9, 16, 25, 29–21, 35, 41, 43, 50, 52, 56, 61, 68, 73, 77, 79, 193–94, 212, 214
New York Times 57, 70, 169–70, 195–96
Nichols, Al 77–78, 134–35, 137–38, 164, 220
Nichols, Fred "Tricky" 179
Nolan, Edward "The Only" 171
Nops, Jeremiah 221
Northwestern University 66, 70
Norton, J.J. *see* Carey, Tom

O'Rourke, Jim 74–77, 95, 97–100, 206, 219

Palmeiro, Rafael 136
Parks, baseball 7–8, 15–16, 21, 31, 48, 58, 71–72, 83–85, 87–89, 91–92, 106, 109, 114, 124–25, 158–59, 163, 166–67
Parks, William 75, 95, 100–1, 123–24
Pearce, Dickey 79, 81, 151
Pearson, David (Pierson) 90, 106, 109, 207
Peters, John 82, 91, 108, 153, 206
Phelps, Cornelius "Neal" 169–70
Pike, Lip 81, 192, 219
Pittsburgh Alleghenys 14, 28, 31, 183
Philadelphia Athletic 5, 19–20, 25, 29–31, 37–38, 41, 43, 45–46, 52, 56, 61, 65, 69, 73, 79, 92–102, 169, 180, 193–94, 212, 214–15
Philadelphia Atlantics 69
Philadelphia Centennials 5, 25, 29, 46, 69
Philadelphia Inquirer 168, 188
Philadelphia Item 60, 119
Philadelphia Kleinz 46, 69
Philadelphia Quakers 31
Philadelphia Times 60
Philadelphia White Stockings (Pearls, Philadelphias) 4–5, 7, 9, 13, 25, 29–30, 45–46, 63–65, 67, 69, 75, 168, 173
Pike, Lipman "Lip" 15, 108, 117, 151, 156–57, 159, 192, 219
Polo Grounds, N.Y. 71
Press 19, 34, 36, 49–51, 53, 59–70, 77–78, 88, 111, 121–22, 142, 144, 175, 184, 197, 205, 207
Prizefighting 15, 21, 49, 103–4, 166, 185–86, 188
Prospect Park, New York 206
Providence Baseball Club 28

Quickstep of Wilmington, Delaware 69

Racism, 19, 20, 37–39, 56, 70, 109, 156–57, 159
Radcliffe, John 5
Raiding 28, 57, 140–1
Rankin, John 86
Rating teams 73–82
Reach, Al 52, 162
Reach ball 196, 210
Remsen, Jack 77, 127, 130, 143–45, 155–57, 167, 192, 219
Resolutes Baseball Club 186
Revolving 3, 49

Rice, Grantland 118
Richter, Francis C. 171
Rippay, Benjamin Wesley *see* Jones, Charley
Ritterson, Edward "Whitey" 169
Rose, Pete 148
Rules, baseball 49, 219
Runyan, Damon 118
Ruth, George "Babe" 147–48
Ryan, John Joseph "Johnnie" 80, 133, 135–36, 138–39, 155, 198
Ryan, Nolan 149

St. Louis Brown Stockings 25–26, 33, 35, 39–40, 56, 68, 73, 80, 204–5, 209, 212, 215
St. Louis Globe-Democrat 60–61, 183
St. Louis, Missouri 26
St. Louis Red Stockings (Reds) 25–26, 40, 69, 183
St. Louis Republican 86, 152, 157, 191
St. Louis Times 174, 178
Scandals 24, 29, 44, 49–50, 66, 107, 116, 121–23, 130, 141–2, 144, 157, 159, 164, 182–84, 186–88, 192–93, 197–98, 205–6, 220
Schafer, Harry 74, 95, 100–2
Scheduling 40, 49–50, 57, 180, 185
Science of Baseball 147–50, 209
Screwball 150
Seibert, Fred 121–23
Seward, George 192
Shanley, Jim 79
Sherley, Thomas 188
Smith, Charley 78–79
Smith, Thomas 45, 162
Snyder, Charley "Pop" 69, 80, 85, 107–8, 110, 133, 135–38, 197, 198
Snyder, Emanuel 107, 181
Somerville, Ed 68, 80, 133–35, 137–38
South End Grounds, Boston 21, 71, 106, 114
Spalding, Albert vii, 5, 10, 12–13, 17–26, 28, 30, 32–34, 36, 47, 65, 74, 76–78, 81–82, 90, 108–10, 112, 123, 131, 149, 153, 177–78, 183, 202, 206, 209–10, 212, 216–17, 219
Spalding, J. Walter 65
Spalding's Official Base-Ball Guide 1876 10, 90
Spectators (Cranks) 4, 23–24, 26, 46, 49, 63, 89, 92, 103–5, 107–9, 111–18, 120–21, 125–29, 131, 136, 140–41, 155–56, 162–64, 168, 171, 177, 181–82, 187–89, 192, 195, 199–200, 209–210, 215
Speed, George 188
Sperling, Charles 45, 172, 180
Sporting Life 210
Sporting News, Philadelphia 171
Spring Training 71, 73, 83–91
Stanky, Eddy 183
Start, Joe 77, 78, 79, 133, 137–38, 158, 167, 206
Stovey, George 20
Sunday baseball 23–24, 26, 33, 39, 44, 50
Sutton, Ezra 20, 39, 79, 94, 96, 99–100, 102, 130, 136–37, 153

Sweasy, Charlie 71, 80
Switch-hitter, first 219
Syracuse Baseball Club 28, 184

Territorial rights 46
Thayer, Fred 89
Thompson, G.W. 37–38, 52, 194, 196, 212–14
Tiemann, Robert 39
Treacey, Fred 5, 29, 133–35, 138–39
Troy Haymakers 28, 49
Twain, Mark 200
Tweed, Boss 8, 49
Twenty-Three Street Grounds, Chicago 91, 106, 109, 124–25, 199

Umpires 19, 40–41, 50, 129, 133, 136–37, 144–45, 164, 165–67, 177–78, 192, 197–98, 216
Union Grounds, N.Y. 7–8, 15–16, 31, 48, 71–72, 83–84, 88–89, 158–59, 182, 187, 195, 220
United States (Baseball) Championship 69

Waddell, Rube 221
Wages, Players 13, 20, 22, 24, 38, 46, 123, 140, 154–55, 169, 218
Wagner, Honus 221
Waitt, Charlie 89
Walker, Billy (Philip Koster) 166, 186
Walker, Moses Fleetwood 20
Walker, Will 177
Walsh, Mike (ump) 216

Ward, John Montgomery 20
Washington baseball club 25, 27–28, 31
Waterman, Fred 49
Weed, Hamilton 7
Western interests 4
Wheedon, Jimmy 166, 186
Wheeling Standards 184
White, James "Deacon" 14, 17–18, 74, 77–78, 82, 90, 108, 116, 127, 176–77, 206, 209, 219
Wilkes, George 70
Wilkes' Spirit of the Times 70
Williams, Dale 171, 173, 189
Williams, Ted 148
Wood, Jimmy 13, 91
Worcester Baseball Club 28
Wright, Al 45–46, 96, 162
Wright, George 18, 74–75, 77, 89, 95–96, 99, 120, 206, 219
Wright, Harry vii, 4–5, 10–12, 15, 18, 21, 28, 43–46, 52–53, 55, 68, 74, 78, 84–86, 95, 97, 104, 113–14, 119, 154, 180, 205, 212, 216, 218–19
Wright, Sam 68

Yale University 89
York, Tom 146, 206
Young, Nicholas 52, 57, 208, 212, 218

Zettlein, George 5, 7, 26, 69, 129, 197

www.ingramcontent.com/pod-product-compliance
Ingram Content Group UK Ltd.
Pitfield, Milton Keynes, MK11 3LW, UK
UKHW041935140426
5217IPUK00014B/492